BREEDING DEVILS IN CHAOS

Breeding Devils in Chaos

THE UNITED RITE

SVEN DAVISSON

ARABI MANOR
A REBEL SATORI IMPRINT
New Orleans & New York

Fonts: The title is set in Austen Pen and the main text is Diorite both by Three Islands Press (3ipfonts.com). The chapter titles and drop capitals are in fonts inspired by William Morris.

Cover & book design by Sven Davisson

Paperback ISBN: 978-1-60864-306-6

Library of Cogress Control Number: 2024938654

Published in the United States of America by
Arabi Manor
A Rebel Satori Imprint
www.rebelsatoripress.com

JUNGITUR EN VATI VATES

Contents

Acknowledgments

I want to express my heartfelt appreciation to everyone who contributed to the creation of this book. First and foremost, I raise my glass in honor of the ancestors—both those of my blood and the Mighty Dead of the Craft.

I am deeply grateful to the seekers, Outer Court students, and members of the New Orleans Grove of the Minoan Brotherhood, who kept me on my toes with insightful questions and in-depth discussions.

A special thank you to Joseph Campbell, Tom Cardamone, Peter Dubé, Eron Mazza, Leonidas, Lady Rhea, and Tunlathit "James" Sojisirikul for their valuable feedback and support throughout the writing process.

I have the deepest appreciation for the beta readers who dedicated their time and effort to provide insightful input. A special thank you to Lee Morgan, Dave Gaddy, and Kenny Garza for their dedication and constructive criticism.

A special thank you to Nicholas Andrews and Ryan Tyler for their ongoing feedback and encouragement. Their contributions have been invaluable in shaping this work.

Most of all, I am profoundly grateful to my husband, Nathaniel, for his unwavering support and patience during the long hours spent locked away with books and a computer. I would still be writing page ten if it were not for him. Of course, the fur babies provided support in their own way.

I extend my sincere thanks to all those who believed in this project. This book would not have been possible without you.

Rocks

BY RUTH MOORE

The rocks of the earth are its history.
Dinosaur tracks they hold,
They tell what's known of who got here first,
They say how old is old.

Fossil shells on mountain sides
Mark there the depth of seas
That rose and fell with the changing tides
Of numberless centuries.

Creatures came, but not to stay.
Diplodocus lies in his deep.
Time-tried and tossed away
The ammonides sleep.

But not the same are the fossils found
In the Age of Inquisitive Man,
For the tallest mountains wore down to the ground
Three times and are rising again.

Who can write on Time's dust
The secret ebb and flow
Of what roared over the earth's crust
Billions of years ago?

Fierce fires still rage on earth, and within

Rocks shift and fissures crack.
What difference now to who started in A
nd never did come back?

For the home of Man is already rock,
While his triumphs are shouted and sung,
Whatever volcano or earthquake shock
Tell him how young is young.

The rocks of the earth hold secrets,
Weathered, battered, brown.
Yet a pebble found in a wayside ditch
Might be cut for a king's crown;
And a certain beach-rock, tossed by the tides,
Holds a shimmer all its own.
It takes a polish of silent dark,
As if a black moon shone.

The lapidary who cuts a gem,
Slices his agates thin.
With professional care he handles them,
Finds out what lies within.
For the outside crust of an agate stone
Looks dingy - of little worth.
But inside, when shaped and polished, are some
Of the loveliest colors on earth.

Design is there - mathematical –
A scientist wouldn't be fooled
Over what happened inside a rock
When the gases stiffened and cooled.
But sometimes a difference creeps in,
As the lapidaries know,

When polish shows up a landscape of trees,
With a background of snow.

Or a perfect scene of a big white owl
Sitting poised on the limb of a tree.
What of scientific logic then?
For how could this happen to be?

Does some hidden consciousness live in rocks,
Who pokes fun at the human race,
And leaves a portrait for someone to find
Of the devil in hell with flames at his back
And a horrible monkey face?

The lapidary who found this scene
Is thinking, wondering, still.
But nobody has an answer to this,
And I don't think anyone will.

Introduction: Bona Fides

As I prepare to write this, I hold a small, polished piece of agate with swirls of red, orange, grays, and white. Rectangular. Little more than an inch at its longest dimension. Look closely, and a monkey-faced devil emerges from the chaos of color, flames at his back and a puff of smoke.

On weekends, we would visit my great aunt Ruth—Uppy to those in the family. My maternal grandmother's sister, Ruth Moore was a best-selling Maine author. After many years spent in New York City and California, selling her second novel to Twentieth Century Fox gave her and her partner Eleanor the means to return to their home state and build a compound together. One afternoon, sitting in her living room of the house they built, the early summer sun filtering through the trees and coming through the windows surrounding her on two sides, she read a poem she had been working on, "Rocks." After she finished, she extricated herself from the depths of her recliner and went to her bedroom with me following along behind. She opened a drawer in a small curio cabinet beside her bed and brought out a small polished stone. Handing it to me, *look closely*.

And I saw the image described in what she had just read,

a tiny devil figure, clear as a photograph, surrounded by flame and smoke. She taught me that a hidden consciousness lives in rocks, but more importantly, she taught me that life was a little bit more enjoyable with a touch of mystery.

My father bought me my first tarot deck when I was twelve. While staying with his mother in California, we visited a Kay-Bee Toys in the Eastridge Shopping Center in Santa Jose. It was the early eighties, and malls were the wondrous oversized centers of the retail universe. He asked the clerk to show us their small selection of decks. I selected the Morgan Greer, which I continue to use to this day. On those trips to visit his side of the family, we would also see the Rosicrucian Museum, at my grandmother's suggestion, with all its Egyptian wonders.

On one trip, we drove out to the Winchester Mystery House. I still remember the wonder of that place, which began even before the tour. While waiting in the gift shop, I was captivated by a vintage mechanical fortune-telling machine, Zelda. She had a crystal ball, and her animated arm moved a deck of Rider-Waite-Smith tarot cards. I was mesmerized and knew I had to have a similar set. The kitschy magic of Zelda combined with the sprawling physical manifestation of Sarah Winchester's obsessive mystical impulse made quite an impression. Returning from California with that first tarot deck marked a beginning.

When I was very young, I'd watch *H.R. Pufnstuf* (in reruns, I'm not quite that old!). I was captivated by the character Wilhemina W. Witchiepoo, played by Billie Hayes. Sure, she was the witch stereotype, complete with a pointy hat and crooked nose with its required wart. But I felt a connection and knew I wanted to be a witch, whatever that meant. I found a large wooden bowl and spoon. That was my caldron, and I would spend hours in the yard and woods of my grandmother's house collecting plants and herbs, making my witch's brews.

I had the ironic blessing of growing up in a household blissfully free from religion. I had nothing to leave, nothing to react against, and nothing to imbue me with scars and baggage. My mother is a respected scientist, and my father was a journalist and writer—if not a communist, at least communist adjacent. We would have long conversations about existentialist philosophy. In his view, organized religion was a dangerous palliative for the masses. When my parents moved to Bar Harbor, my father suggested the fastest way to get into the community was to join the Catholic church. He volunteered my mother, and she said no thanks. He never pushed, and that was the end of the matter.

In Chicago, my father had been a successful editor and critic for daily *Variety*, the entertainment trade paper. I have two publicity photos of him from this time: one, he sits at the center of a group of people who are surrounded by papers, all dressed like characters in *Mad Men*; the other, the consummate reporter pad and pencil in hand interviewing Kukla and Ollie from the popular television show. Not sure where Fran was that day.

He moved to Maine with his first wife in the 1950s. Watching the film *Good Night and Good Luck* about Edward R. Murrow years later, I realized McCarthyism had driven my father to drop out and write his novel. I don't think many fourteen-year-olds had as detailed a knowledge of Roy Cohn as I had from conversations with him. Before I understood my own queerness, I knew how the denial of the closet could create one's demons. I recalled my father summing up McCarthyism and the Hoover FBI as a conspiracy of alcoholics and homosexuals. The danger of denial, hypocracy, and self-loathing was something I learned to detect early.

My father held two books close and would return to them

often. One was Walt Whitman's *Leaves of Grass*, filled with notes and observations. The other was R. H. Blyth's *Games Zen Masters Play*. The latter is a collection of classic, translated Zen koans with commentary in English. This book was published in the late 1970s and wasn't more than a few feet from his typewriter until he passed. In the last few years of his life, the tenor of our conversations changed. He had moved from the potential nihilism of existentialism, the dark futility-of-understanding embodied by Camus, to the peaceful worldview of the Zen masters. As his mortality approached, he spent more and more time in the stillness of Zen, settling into a beautiful wonder of nature in the present moment. His final piece of writing was a few words scribbled on a news clipping—an image of ice dripping off red berries from the local paper: *thank you for this life.*

His copy of Whitman has his name and *Daily Collegian* written on the back of the front cover. That would mean he acquired the edition while he was a faculty advisor of the student newspaper at Penn State in the sixties. I recall the Blyth appeared in the house in the early eighties.

Whitman writes in the opening of "Song of Myself":

> For every atom belonging of me as good belongs to
> you

I can see a direct line from the nineteenth century poet's words to the Zen koan:

> One thing is all things; All things are one thing.

It would be years before my journey would bring me to the Zen my father had embraced in those last years. After a trip that took me through Rajneesh, Tibetan Buddhism, Hinduism, Ram Das, LSD, chaos magic, and some very dark years, eventually, I underwent the Jukai ceremony, taking the Buddhist precepts, in 2017.

As my mother's career progressed, she traveled more frequently for scientific conferences and meetings with colleagues. When I was fourteen, she took me along to the United Kingdom. We spent several summer weeks driving around England and Wales in a little Ford Fiesta with Baedeker's Great Britain travel guide in hand. We went through the Cotswolds in South West England, into Wales and down along the Cornwall coast, finally ending up with a crowning week in London. This was the first of several summers partially spent in the United Kingdom, where she would meet with colleagues, and I'd explore.

That first trip, we visited Glastonbury, Tintagel, and the Museum of Witchcraft and Magic in Boscastle; trekked through fields and navigated sheep gates to find Stone Age ruins, small megalithic tombs, and barrow mounds; and marveled at dozens of castles along the way. I found a copy of *The Witch's Way* by Stewart and Janet Farrar in Oxford. Between Cecil Williamson's museum and the Farrars's writing, my path was set, and a lifelong connection between my practice and Britain was formed. Old Horny, the life-sized goat-headed figure in the museum—at the time with a nude female initiate offering up a baby in a lurid tableau—made quite the impression. On subsequent trips, I discovered the historically significant Atlantis Bookshop on Museum Street, London, in the shadow of the British Museum—a location critical to the life stories of Aleister Crowley, Gerald Gardner, and many others. On each trip, I would return with a suitcase of books by Gardner, Crowley, Doreen Valiente, and other British writers of craft and magical practice. Perhaps it was my family's frequent trips to the United Kingdom or my penchant for British folk horror films such as *The Wicker Man,* but my magical practice has long had a strong British references.

Soon after returning from that initial trip, I began working with an Alexandrian-styled coven of eight to ten people. This cemented the influence of what we on this side of the pond term British Traditional Witchcraft. Lacking lineage, we were an island unto ourselves. We were blithely ignorant of American witchcraft stemming from the work of Scott Cunningham, Starhawk, and others. It wouldn't be until college, when I began practicing with a campus pagan group of witches from diverse backgrounds, that I first encountered the work of Starhawk and other American authors.

On those weekend visits, Uppy often called herself a witch—tongue firmly planted in cheek. She told how the women born on the offshore islands were considered witches, and that she and I were descended from those accused of witchcraft in the Salem trials of 1692. She described two instances where she used her 'powers.' The first was after an unfulfilling time as a screenwriter in Hollywood during the 1940s when she soon realized the role of female writers was to sharpen pencils for their male coworkers. On her final drive out, she told the city to go to hell, and a gas main promptly blew beneath the street behind her. Then, much later, after a gravel pit had opened near her Maine house, she got exasperated at the constant traffic of dump trucks. Again, she muttered where the noisy truck passing could go, and the transmission obligingly fell out onto the pavement. You could tell she took pleasure in taking credit for both. I relished these moments when she told her colorful stories. In addition to writing and books, we shared many mutual interests. We would trade copies of the pagan magazine *Circle Network News*, produced by Salena Fox and Circle Sanctuary, and, at the opposite end of the spectrum, *The Skeptical Inquirer*, published by the debunking-focused Committee for Skeptical Inquiry.

Building on my mother's research, I have spent long hours tracing my family tree as far back as possible. Uppy was indeed descended from several Salem "witches," including Ann Foster, who died in prison, her daughter Mary (Foster) Lacy, and granddaughter Mary (Foster) Kemp, as well as Elizabeth (Dane) Johnson and her daughter Abigail. On my mother's paternal side, we are descended from Rebecca Nurse (executed July 19, 1692), Samuel (executed June 1692), and Sarah Wardwell.

On the other side of the same coin, I am descended from multiple accusers who testified during the Salem witch trials: Hannah Bixby and George Lang. In 1658/9, William Osgood provided testimony that resulted in the death of Susanna Martin. Of course, charges of witchcraft were not limited to Salem or 1692. Midwife Goody Dutch, my tenth great-grandmother, was accused of witchcraft in Gloucester in 1653. My fifth great-grandmother Aunt Nabby Joab Gray, practiced witchcraft and, according to her neighbors, could craft charms and "put on curses."

My family reflects both sides of early New England settlers—those fleeing religious persecution and those sent across the Atlantic against their will. Our research has found that we count no less than fourteen Mayflower passengers among our ancestors, including both Myles Standish and John Alden. In addition, we have two Scottish prisoners of war captured by Oliver Cromwell's army during the War of the Three Kings (the English Civil War) and sent to the colonies as indentured servants, including my Davisson immigrant ancestor, Daniel Davison (likely an English mistranscription of Davidson).

Despite the more than three centuries that had passed,

my grandmother retained some faint ghosts of her heritage. It wasn't until I moved south that I realized that everyone else seemed to mean the white purple-topped root vegetable when they said "turnip." To my grandmother, a turnip was what everyone else called a rutabaga. Though I don't particularly care for fish, I still fondly recall her making finnan haddie, a lightly salted (slack-salted to old Mainers) smoked fish stew originating from Findon, Scotland, that remains popular in Down East Maine.

From 1989 to the mid-1990s, I worked with a small group of queer magickal explorers, The Brotherhood of SeTh. It was my first experience working with an all-male, all-queer group and though it was small, it was a potent time of magical experimentation. In the nineties, I operated a queer occult alternative store. Our group met in its labyrinthine basement, which we used as our temple. The principal framework of our explorations was the Egyptian god Seth (or Set) and his contentious relation to his brother Horus. In Egyptian mythology, the two were seen simultaneously as combatants and lovers. One represented chaos and the other stability, yet both were required for the pharaoh to rule. Images of the two gods often flank the ruler on his throne, and the king was said to rule by the Horus and the Set. Some of this material from this period is included in my book *The Star Set Matrix*.

Riffing on the words of inventor and philosopher Buckminster Fuller, Robert Anton Wilson observed:

> Don't believe totally in your own B.S. This means that, as Bucky Fuller said, 'The Universe consists of non-simultaneously apprehended events.' Non-

> simultaneously. The universe consists of non-simultaneously apprehended events. Which means any belief system or reality tunnel you've got right now is gonna have to be revised and updated as you continue to apprehend new events later in time. Not simultaneously.

Our history is not our identity. We arise out of our historicity but continually engage in a dance of recreating ourselves. Our "reality tunnel," as Wilson calls it, may seem constant and consistent, but looking back across large expanses of time, the *longue durée,* you now is not you then. Your body replaces your cells at a rate of about 330 billion a day. This means in eighty to one hundred days, you physically are not the same person you were three months prior. This is just as true of your mind and beliefs. One should always be moving, learning, growing, and dancing with the wind that blows through the pines.

In some respects, so much of this "past" is indeed bullshit. I learned my first lessons in witchcraft from a relative who called herself a witch but I do not consider myself a "hereditary witch." I'm not particularly a joiner. I have intersected with a few groups and belief systems during my travels. I received *sannyasa* initiation from Acharya Rajneesh long-distance while he was on his 'world tour' during months when no country would allow him admittance. I received apostolic succession in the Gnostic Church, though I do not style myself a bishop. I did a stint as Grand Master General in charge of the Traditional Axis of the UR-OTO, but do not now claim any degrees in The Ancient and Primitive Rite of Memphis-Misraïm or the axis's other currents. I received XI° initiation in the Ordo Temple Orientis Antiqua from a Dutch brother but have never joined an OTO body proper.

What isn't bullshit is that I have been blessed by intersections with teachers in the flesh on numerous occasions, some long-standing and some fleeting and ephemeral but no less profound. When I was nine, I happened into the bead shop my friend Gail owned just before our family moved to Bar Harbor. Whenever our paths intersected over the next two decades, we spent many hours discussing spirituality. She nicknamed the young me "Babaji" and told me amazing stories of her travel to India's Maha Kumba Mela, which she wrote about in an early issue of the *Ashé*. She spent her last years working with orphans with HIV and AIDS in Southeast Asia. Her inspiring book, *In A Rocket Made of Ice*, is a moving read.

Gail, in turn, introduced me to Syamasundara dasa, a Vaisnava who had come to adulthood traveling with A. C. Bhaktivedanta Swami Prabhupada, the individual primarily responsible for bringing Krishna Consciousness to the West. He told me a first-person recollections of the compassion of his Master. After a passing homophobic comment from a fellow devotee, Srila Prabhupada asked Syamasundara, "What is the difference if a person is held in this Material World by a gold chain or a silver chain?"

A college friend introduced me to Baba Raul Canizares. In the few years we knew each other before his untimely passing, he taught me a lot about Santeria and his blending with Hindu heart devotion, giving rise to his own Orisha Consciousness Movement.

I spent two evenings conversing with Allen Ginsberg following a reading and lecture on Wordsworth's "breath machine" at the University of Maine. That was followed by a short postcard, an aerial view of Nashville, with the comment: "Remind me when we meet again, whether it be Maine, Naropa, or somewhere on the moon." I still smile when I think of the bard lighting a cigarette directly beneath the auditorium's No Smoking sign. When asked *what is enlightenment*? Ginsberg replied, "Trungpa described it as stepping on the step that isn't there."

My path first crossed that of my initiator in the Brotherhood soon after Hurricane Katrina while he lived as an exile in Salem. It would be almost ten years before we both found ourselves living in New Orleans and were finally in a suitable space for him to bring me into the Minoan Brotherhood. He elevated me to the degree of Minos just as he was heading to begin the next phase of his life in Chicago, leaving the New Orleans Grove in my hands. This initiation has been the most profound journey experience thus far and was an inflection point in my work and practice. It was a culmination of my decades-long research on queer magic. It brought me in contact with a lineage tracing back to the Brotherhood's founder, Eddie Buczynski, and beyond that to the greater family.

This book developed out of a series of Outer Court lessons I developed for seekers of the New Orleans grove. It expands on a curriculum honed over years of interactions with students. Additionally, it draws on nearly four decades of my own, at times idiosyncratic, practice and research in queer magics. Before they embark on our Outer Court lessons, I advise seekers that some of the material may be familiar. Similarly, not all of what follows is likely to be new, but hopefully readers will find it at least novel in context and juxtaposition.

In Hinduism, there is a concept *seva,* compassionate service. In Buddhism, *dana,* giving or generosity, is the first of the ten virtues (*paramitas*). I approach this work as a gift and service to those who find in it some value. I have many who approach the grove who are not in the southern Louisiana region. This book is for the seekers near and far alike. The book format is capable of delving into more detail than the ten lesson format permits. As this work evolved, parts were shared with the grove's current seekers and initiates. Their feedback is deeply appreciated, and it is my hope that their input has helped create a work in which some will find kernals of value.

It is not about the Minoan Brotherhood, though it would likely be very much different if I had not been sojourning with the Brotherhood over these years. In some ways, I think of this book as a "requeering." It is not about turning something on its head or claiming a tradition for ourselves where one did not exist prior. Eddie already "queered" the traditions stemming from Gerald Gardner when he founded the Minoan Brotherhood and Sisterhood and established the Knossos Grove. He showed us that the crooked path could also be a little bit bent. In some respects, witchcraft was queer from the start, queer in the modern sense of sexual and gender nonconformance and its other meaning as something askew and at the edge of normative society. Much of this history was occluded in early modern Wicca by the homophobia and strong prejudicial views of its founders and early adherents. It's time we call bullshit on this and work a practice that is ours, rooted in deep analogs of history, and embracing that our queer place in the world is just that—a little queer. A little apart from the mundane. We exist in the space between the seen and unseen, and as our ancestors knew, we are predestined toward the magical.

To draw inspiration from the words of out singer Marc Almond, we are Fabulous Creatures Shining Brightly. We are ephemeral, otherworldly, fabulous.

ORTHODOXY VS ORTHOPRAXY

> When asked if he "believed" in God, one of my earliest teachers answered, "I don't believe in believing... Only fictions, not facts, have to be believed.[1]

Our method is one of orthopraxy, right action, rather than orthodoxy, blind faith. The United Rite is a continuum of practice where matters of belief are left up to the individual. The word ὀρθοπραξία is a modern Greek compound, formed from "orthos," meaning straight or erect, and "praxis," meaning action. Tradition is transmitted not through articles of faith but through uniformity of ritual, sacrificial offerings, ethical conduct, and an aligned experience of the universe.

A central concern of the later work of queer theorist Michel Foucault was the Greek concept of *askesis*—particularly *The Use of Pleasure,* the second volume in his series on the history of sexuality. *Askesis,* though the root of our modern word "ascetic," does not denote the same concept of self-denial and self-inflicted severity. Instead, in Hellenic Greece, it stood for a practice of living and exorcizing oneself, a focus on transformative self-mastery. It is the "living substance of philosophy," writes Foucault, "which should be understood as the assay or test by which, in the game of truth, one changes, and not as the simplistic appropriation of others."[2]

In his discussion of Foucault's philosophy, Palmer describes Foucault's asceticism as a process "not to decipher what we 'really' are, but to strive to cultivate what we might become."[3] Foucault himself argued that "the main interest in life and work is to become something else that you were not in the beginning."[4] For Foucault, the self should be "cultivated," tended, and shaped through a creative mechanism. Knowledge is the knowledge one presents to the world and discovers through creation, not the knowledge that one finds hidden in oneself. The mind, body, and spirit reach to grab at a great, limitless truth rather than delving internally for an essential atom of meaning.

Though one of us may carry the lantern, we walk the path together. I consider my work more that of caretaker than priest.

A NOTE ON GENDER & DESIRE

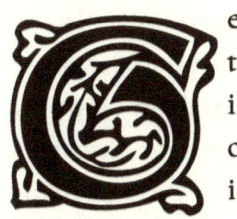

Gender and biology are two distinct concepts that have become increasingly dissociated in recent decades. While biology is based on physical characteristics at birth, gender is a mental state that may not always align with one's biological sex. The idea of gender is not new, but it has evolved, with some cultures recognizing a third gender or multiple gender roles. Furthermore, biology is not always a binary truth, with examples of intersex individuals and variations on the genetic X-Y binary. When I refer to males in this context, I mean anyone who identifies as male, whether cisgender or not.

The origins of queer theory can be traced back to two opposing views: essentialism and constructionism. Essentialists believe that LGBTQIA+ people have always existed, while constructionists view modern sexualities as a product of contemporary culture and a post-Freudian world. Queerness, as used here, represents a transhistorical and transcultural understanding that same-sex desire has existed throughout time. However, depending on the time and place, it has taken on different meanings. For example, same-sex relationships were present in ancient Greece. Still, they were not socially constructed as romantic relationships as they are today but rather as related to power, mentoring, and the state.

I believe in a continuity of desire that individuals who have sought intimate and emotional connections with their same-sex have always existed. As Eve Sedgewick proposed, the homosocial arc represents a shift from same-sex friendship and emotional connection to something outside of normative social boundaries. This shift occurred at different times and in different cultural contexts, with same-sex desire taking on different meanings. Interestingly, the word "homosexual" was coined in the late nineteenth century during the psychological mapping of difference, while "heterosexual" came years later.

Over time, concepts of gender and sexuality have evolved and changed. For instance, in the 1919 naval trials in Newport News, RI, undercover naval investigators were sent into bars where sailors and civilians were said to meet. Only the civilians were charged, and the sexuality of the sailors, presumably in the dominant sexual position, was never questioned. Though the term "homosexual" had already existed for decades, it was never mentioned during the trial, showing the lack of penetration of medical terminology into the prevalent mindset. Similarly, we see a connection between sexual position and perceived gender in other cultural contexts, such as prisons, and in the practice of witchcraft in the Iron Age Nordic context.

At some point over the past century-plus, there was a transition from individual actions to persisting identity. The notion of a homosexual identity had entered the popular mindset enough to be used as a recurring trope encoding criminality. This is exemplified by the use of encoded homosexuality as a shorthand for the criminal mindset in Hollywood-produced film noirs—think Joel Cairo (Peter Lorre) in John Huston's *Maltese Falcon*. Though we now live in a world with diverse identity options based on gender, sexuality, and their intersection, it is essential to recognize that identity has not always been perceived positively.

In this book, I use queer, same-sex desire, and male+male to discuss the universality of sexual interaction. While it is written for men who love men, it is meant to be a project of empowerment, not exclusion.

A NOTE ON TRADITION

I am a third-degree high priest in the Minoan Brotherhood—a member of the lineages created by Eddie Buczynski, Lord Gwydion. My experience with Lord Gwydion's 's teachings and legacy inform much of this work, but nothing within this work should be misconstrued as representative of the Minoan tradition or its practices.

Nothing that follows should be taken as a total negation of the legacy of Gerald Gardner or the Gardnerian system. One of the ways we can honor our ancestors is to acknowledge their shortcomings openly. I started as a fledgling witch working within a framework borrowed from Alexandrian witchcraft. I am initiated into a rich lineage that is a branch on the family tree descending from Gardner's work. What follows *is* my personal practice and grows from my experience within and outside these frameworks.

"British Traditional Witchcraft" (BTW) is an Americanism meant to differentiate the lineal traditions downline from Gardner, Sanders, and Raymond Buckland from the more homegrown varieties popularized by Mary Nesnick, Zsuzsanna Budapest, Scott Cunningham, Starhawk, and others. The term is perhaps a little like an accent— only distinguished when away from home. There is another, confusingly similar, term: traditional Craft, which has quite a bit of overlap, especially in contemporary practice. They have referred to different sets of practices, personalities, and, at times competing, historical claims to authenticity.

In recent years, there has been an increase in interest and quality writing on traditional Craft. This has been spearheaded by the books by Gemma Gary and those published by Troy Books, Limited.

BTW refers collectively to those (sub)traditions that hold a lineage ostensibly going back to Gerald B. Gardner, also known as Alex/Gard, while traditional witchcraft claims pre-Gardnerian roots. Significant early proponents included Robert Cochrane, the Clan of Tubal Cain, and later, Nigel Jackson and Andrew Chumbley (Sabbatic Craft). Today, the writings of Gary and Nigel Pearson present some of the most straightforward descriptions of the practices.

Interestingly, Gardnerian High Priestess Doreen Valiente bridged the gap between the two as she was an associate at different times with both Gardner and Cochrane. Otherwise, there was much animosity between the two camps in their early days. This has lessened greatly in the present day. The two collectives of practices and practitioners no longer stand at odds in the twenty-first century. We dialogue and learn from each other's works. Indeed, the same folkloric and historical antecedents that traditional Craft draws from can be powerful practices for the Gardnerian traditions.

THE TITLE

This colorful turn of phrase is emblematic of the heterocentrism that infected much of twentieth century occultism. The quote derived from British occultist Kenneth Grant's Typhonian Trilogies, specifically *Nightside of Eden* (1977). In discussing a line from Crowley's *Book of the Law* (I:37) referencing the "work of the wand" and the "work of the sword," Grant extols the dangers of practicing magic without the opposite sex. He describes "the blasphemy of the homosexual formula" being that, in his view, it denies Babalon, the female operative vehicle, and thus are acts "breeding devils in chaos."[5] This is ironic for a man who considered himself the true successor of a bisexual magician, Crowley, and who also self-identified as the successor head of his magical order the Ordo Templi Orientis, a group that elevated sodomy in its most secret grade. Grant appears to have been doggedly homophobic in his approach to sexual magic. In the next paragraph, he belies just how much he was in thrall of the prejudices of his age. He refers to homosexual magicians as "Black Brothers" and the forces they actuate "sterile stars born of the speechless or *lisping* Aeon." (Emphasis added.)

In apparent contradiction to these views, in *Cults of the Shadow*, Grant celebrates the work of Michael Bertiaux. Grant describes him as "undoubtedly one of the most colorful and creative contemporary occultists."[6] The Chicago-based Bertaiux was the leader of the Cult of La Couleuvre Noire and The Monastery of the Seven Rays, as well as being an adept of the Ordo Templi Orientis Antiqua, a Haitian order allegedly founded in 1921 by occultist and Vodoun priest Lucien-Francois Jean-Maine.

In addition, Bertiaux was the central figure of the Choronzon Club—a self-described magical cabal of gay men.[7]

Part One

Ploughing the Field

Chapter I
Beginnings

Every magical act has a definite starting point. It wouldn't make a good tale if it didn't. Indeed, a spell is much like a story with beginning, the arc of rising action to climax, followed by the denouement. When you pay attention, you might be able to pinpoint the moment precisely. Immediately, you sense that something has happened, something has changed, and a new mode has begun. It is not that there is no rising action, precedents, subtle hints moving you forward—but your perspective shifts in one singular moment, and you know you're not in Kansas anymore. If you are alert and open at this moment, you realize you are on your way.

On the other hand, you may shut your eyes and turn back. Rest assured, however, you'll be here again, and it may not be as easy to ignore next time. The universe knows exactly what you need and tends to give it to you a few moments before you think you're ready. Like a baby thrown into the deep end, the choice to sink or swim in a heartbeat is yours. Transformation works when it is instinctual. The universe knows this. When sanity and survival are at play, we tend to pay attention. At any other time, inertia and comfort are often too seductive.

This spell, this book whose weight you hold in your hand,

is rooted in such moments. The preparation took decades, but the impetus of the work came together in a few short days. Each question that had dogged the project, preventing me from beginning, was answered directly, without room for question. The universe, or my trajectory within it, had decided that, ready or not, it was time to go! The crooked path has one thing in common with its historicity, if nothing else: Don't argue with the universe; listen to it. It would still take years to gel into something approachable.

Like many a magical operation, this work began with a historically distant invocation... not a ceremonial fancy dress party, reenacting nineteenth-century mumbo jumbo, but the cooption of unsuspecting bodies. Evocation is the act of conjuring, adjuring an otherworldly entity to appear and be subjected to the operator's will. On the other hand, invocation means to draw spirit, the divine or a particle thereof, into oneself. The act of invocation rests on opening and inviting spirit in. It is an act of creation, not subjugation.

Looking back, this book began in that third space arising from the contact of two bodies: smooth chest presses against smooth chest, silky semi-hard cock against semi-hard cock, mouth against mouth. Tongues, the source of the word, tangle, intertwine, and work against each other. Breath transfers from one body to the other and back again. Spirit flows in a circle, melding and seeding portions of one in the other. Urban angels surround this talisman of flesh and unapologetic desire. Saints and Sinners. Dr. John, St. Theresa "the Little Flower," Marie LaVeau, Erzuli Dantor. Collected by the winds of Oya, the flesh lifts them, bearing them away on secret verses toward hidden places. These indistinguishable energies and shadows fill the room, pressing into the space, blanketing. Outside in the air, an interlude, walking the few blocks through the streets, the spirits dance about, reflecting in the light of a red cloud sky.

Afterward, the two cling together, spent. They hold to the night tightly, not wanting to cleave for the rising day.

Two enter in, a third is created, and none return unchanged. Connections are made that penetrate deeply. Clockwork gears are set in motion far below the surface. Neither is left unscathed. Both come back *remixed.*

Though you cannot put it into words, you cannot grab hold of it tightly; you know you have awakened in a different world. Everything is the same, yet different. Your perception is heightened. Like one on the sharp edge of pain, everything appears more evident, outlined, and sharply defined. But things are not the same. Something has shifted a perceptible touch. You've shifted. You are no longer what you were and are not yet what you are becoming. In this moment, you have moved into a fragile space with a vast opening of frightening possibilities. You have entered a new vista along the path you have chosen as your life. You are different, and different, they say, is not always easy. Fears you had twenty-four hours ago have dissolved to nothing, replaced by new concerns and apprehensions. A clear, discernible future has become one in which you are unsure and acutely aware.

In moments like these, coming back from that liminal space, it is hard to interpret the messages and symbols presented to you. Everything has changed color, making it difficult to pull out from the infinite images that cut into each of the ones that mean something to you now. You know the signs are all there, but you need to be careful not to force their interpretation and, inadvertently, corrupt the direction you are moving. This particular juncture is rife with irony. You are the only one capable of ferreting out the signs, yet you are also the most prejudiced regarding their import. You still carry your former self with you. It remains fresh in your mind, and you must keep vigilant lest you sink back to where you were. The trap of becoming dazzled by your wishful thinking is ever-present. Your old self is a siren calling you back toward the rocks of the mundane.

You've changed; you know it. You can feel the uncomfortable fit of your old self like yesterday's clothes. We build cold temples around ourselves, pulling in possessions, ties, and obligations. Our lives concrete us in. They stabilize us and keep us safe. And safety is the most dangerous place to be in terms of our evolution. Comfort plays to our inertia. That's why the universe likes to shake things up. If you don't do it for yourself, be prepared for a swift kick in the ass. Once you embark on this path, you get what you need—often with a smile and a mischievous twinkle in the cosmic eye. Being prepared really defeats the purpose.

Often, others can see you've changed. They sense it. It makes them nervous. Just like animals can smell fear and desire, they know something is unsettled—not quite right. You appear out of sorts. Certain things, no matter how much your rational mind would like them to, do not stay in Vegas. You wear them back like a new t-shirt, displaying the comedic slogan of your juxtaposition.

The spiritual path is simply learning to decode the messages and staying clear of the pitfalls. Waves of potentiality will carry you, but only if you are moving with them and not working against them. Every particle of the universe is magic if you have the eyes to see. Every rhythm sings with poetry if you have the ears to hear. Every possibility possesses the kernel of mystery if you open yourself to it.

This path leading to this work may have been long, but it begins in the heat of two bodies and a flash of cum across the night's dark.

Chapter II
The Mighty Dead

Neo-pagans and witches have diverse beliefs. This applies as much to what we believe happens after the moment of death as anywhere. Generally, Wiccans call the afterlife the Summerlands. Even within this concept, there are varying conceptions of what is being referred to. In *Wicca: A Guide to the Solitary Practitioner,* Scott Cunningham writes:

> This realm is neither in heaven nor the underworld. It simply is: a non-physical reality much less dense than ours. Some Wiccan traditions describe it as a land of eternal summer, with grassy fields and sweet flowing rivers, perhaps the Earth before the advent of humans. Others see it vaguely as a realm without forms, where energy swirls coexist with the greatest energies: the Goddess and God in their celestial identities.[1]

Like many concepts of modern Wicca that have a strong odor of deep antiquity, when looked at a little closer, that may not entirely be the case. The term first appears in the work of American spiritist Andrew Jackson Davis, also known as

"The Poughkeepsie Seer." In his encyclopedic work, The Great Harmonia, Davis describes the Summerlands as the highest sphere of human spiritual attainment in the afterlife.

The Theosophists, a late nineteenth-century spiritual movement based on the work of Madame Helena Blavatsky, also used a similar term, without the definite article, in their teachings. Summerland was an astral-like plane where souls hung out between physical incarnations.

Often, I have been asked for my views on the concept of an afterlife. My initial answer is: I do not know. But then, what difference does it ultimately make? If the level of one's rebirth or chances in the afterlife are based on how one lives one's current life, there is no difference between the two from the vantage point of how we live today. An authentic, honorable life covers your bases.

As a Buddhist, I should hold to an understanding of reincarnation. On the other hand, ancestral reverence is underpinned by an appreciation of an afterlife. This dichotomy of belief is common throughout modern Wicca. If one thinks of the concept of multiple souls discussed later, they may not be as antithetical as they first appear. Rajneesh taught that memory survives physical death. He meant this more literally than the dead simply being remembered. He suggested the memory component of consciousness was projected out into the world at death. Powerful individuals can project their memory toward a future birth. This may explain the phenomenon of the reincarnating spiritual leaders of Tibetan Buddhism. They are identified through proof that they hold the memories of the closest preceding incarnation. When we feed our ancestors, light a candle, or raise a glass in their names, we honor their memory however we conceive of the afterlife.

One of humans' earliest expressions of religious activity was the construction of passage tombs. We see these in Ireland's Boyne Valley at Newgrange and Knowth. The West Kennet Long Barrow, part of the Avebury sacred landscape, was built during Britain's Early Neolithic period around 3650 BCE. The site was only used to bury the dead for around thirty years. However, the area remained active for the next thousand years. Evidence shows individuals continued to enter the tomb and leave offerings of shells, carved bones, and sacrificed animals. These sites show that early humans maintained an active relationship with their ancestors. We continue this practice today. When we sit before our ancestral altars, we honor our ancestors and a traditional understanding of the interrelation between the living and the dead extending far back into our deep past.

The earliest evidence of human (Homo sapiens) burials yet found dates back about one hundred thousand years in the Middle East and Africa. Much earlier mortuary practices have recently been discovered in Rising Star Cave in South Africa. These are not our species, however. The remains are those of Homo naledi, a now-extinct branch of the hominid family tree, and were found in the far reaches of the cave in a chamber nearly impossible to access, dating from approximately 250,000 years ago. Not only did these early individuals carry the bodies of their ancestors deep beneath the earth, but they also buried some of them in pit graves. These actions demonstrate a conception of death and are the oldest examples of communal handling of the dead. A stone tool was also found in one of the burials in a child's hand. This shows these individuals not only had a particular relation to death but also had some concept of an afterlife. Grave goods are left with the dead so that they may use them. A valuable tool would not have been left with a corpse unless those leaving it understood that the deceased individual would need it. Perhaps dual concepts of the otherworld/underworld and an afterlife state are encoded in our DNA. Homo sapiens would not start exhibiting these practices, defined as behavioral modernity, until 100,000 to 200,000 years after Homo naledi had been doing them. It puts things in a new perspective to realize that mortuary practices predate the earliest humanity.

The Mighty Dead within our craft are the spirits of our witch ancestors, with particular emphasis on those of the Wiccan lineage and its forebears. We also honor the blessed dead of our families, both those of blood and choice. Some comprise the unnamed Ancient Dead, or spirit guides, who first looked up to the skies and entered caves to descend into the magical, dark realms of the underworld. I suspect that caves inspired our ancestors to construct the first passage tombs.

ANCESTORS AND ELDERS

In the Craft, it is essential to remember and celebrate those who have gone before, both living and those who have passed on to the other side. Ancestor veneration is very important to many traditions. All religions and cultures have honored their ancestors in some fashion. Quite simply, without our ancestors, we would not be here. We owe them our very lives in a literal sense. They are the historicity from which we come physically and spiritually. Our blood is the amalgamation of their blood. If we stand tall, it is because we stand on their shoulders. We are each the apex of a triangle stretching back into the deep darkness of history beyond memory. Ancestors are connected to us by blood, adoption, and initiation. Our ancestors are also those who have touched us deeply and now passed on.

It is critically important that we serve and lift up our

ancestors. When we do this and have their support, life is sweeter. Dedicate a space to honoring your ancestors. Remember the Mighty Dead when offering libations in circle. Visit their graveside.

Learning to listen to your spirits is a critical component of spiritual work. Find a place to establish a shrine to your ancestors, both blood relatives and chosen family.

This altar is for honoring, remembrance, and contemplation rather than working witchcraft. Start with a clean white cloth. Add photos of close ancestors and any physical artifacts that connect to them. I also added Day of the Dead and memorial items. Add at least one candle—white, purple, or black are the most traditional. My altar is draped with the Clan Davidson tartan in honor of my father's forebears.

I offer an alcoholic spirit of their liking and refresh it each week. One may use anisette or the alcohol of their choice. In my case, I use scotch or bourbon and water as that was the preferred beverage of many of my ancestors. I switch the offering to a drink of their choice on particular birthdays. I also burn incense such as myrrh.

Many of us have ancestors that we had issues with in life. While it is essential to come to personal terms with these ancestors, it is unnecessary to honor them on your shrine if doing so causes distress.

WALT WHITMAN

Walt Whitman, born on May 31, 1819 and passed away on March 26, 1892, is regarded as one of America's most exceptional poets. His self-published 1855 masterpiece, *Leaves of Grass*, is still considered a significant literary work today. Whitman, a deist, expressed an all-encompassing religious understanding in his writing, reminiscent of the Transcendentalists and Buddhism. Despite communicating with prominent gay rights advocates such as John Addington Symonds for two decades, Whitman never identified as a homosexual. Whitman's writing emerged just before the medicalization of sexual differences. *Leaves of Grass* celebrates a natural, earthy companionship, and the "Calamus" poems are a touching tribute to romantic male friendship. The original, unpublished manuscript of the series of twelve poems was titled *Live Oak, with Moss*. Whitman referred to them as "the manly love of comrades" and "the love of man for man." Calamus, or sweet flag, is a marsh grass whose pink roots resemble the phallus and are associated with male-to-male love in Greek and Roman mythology. They've also been used as a mild hallucinogen.

For much of his life, Whitman advocated for temperance and wrote about his distaste for alcohol. During the latter part of his life, his opinion softened, and he was known to imbibe wine and champagne occasionally. Something other than alcohol would be an appropriate offering, though locally sourced craft or sparkling wine would also be good. I would not offer any stronger spirit, however. Calamus root has long been used as incense, going back to the Egyptians who incorporated it into Kyphi incense. One can also find Tibetan sweet flag or calamus incense.

OSCAR WILDE

Oscar Wilde (October 16, 1854 – November 30, 1900), Saint Oscar, is our first modern queer martyr. Following his release from Reading Gaol in the spring of 1897, his health continued declining, and he was never the same vibrant person he had been. His reputation in tatters, he spent the last three years of his life in exile in France. He assumed the name Sabastian Melmoth after Saint Sebastian. He died of meningitis and is buried just outside Paris in the Cimetière de Bagneux. His likely apocryphal last words: *Either this wallpaper goes, or I do.*

Fitting offerings to honor St. Wilde are absinthe, the drink of choice of fin de siècle decadents, and strawberries, a symbol of the gay life of London referenced often in The Picture of Dorian Gray.

GERALD BROSSEAU GARDNER

Gerald B. Gardner (June 13, 1884 - February 12, 1964) is considered the father of modern Wicca. Those traditions stemming from him are collectively grouped under British Traditional Witchcraft. He was initiated by a New Forest Coven who, he claimed, carried on the "old ways." He was the first genuinely public figure who talked openly about the practice of witchcraft. His book *Witchcraft Today* brought the Craft into the open. Covens in lineal descent from those initiated by Gardner are known as Gardnerians. Like many ancestors, Gardner was not perfect. He held on to his generation's homophobia and anti-German sentiment. It is important to acknowledge, not gloss over, the shortcomings of problematic relatives. Ancestors can be complex. I honor Gardner as the founder of my lineage while also openly confronting the issues of his prejudices.

DOREEN VALIENTE

Doreen Valiente, born on January 4th, 1922 and passed away on September 1st, 1999, was a follower of Gerald Gardner and held the position of high priestess in his coven for a period of time.

She played a crucial role in the initial development of Wicca and was responsible for revising the *Book of Shadows*. Many of the liturgical texts that Gardnerians still use today were written by her. Valiente also wrote several significant publications on witchcraft, including the beautiful poem "Witches Rune."

MAXINE & ALEX SANDERS

Alex Sanders (June 6, 1926 – April 30, 1988) and Maxine Sanders (born December 30, 1946) were an English married couple who became very public witches. As the story goes, they were declined entrance into several Gardnerian covens, so they obtained a copy of the Gardnerian *Book of Shadows* and started their own group. The tradition stemming from their lineage is now known as Alexandrian. As this and Gardnerian are very similar, they are sometimes referred to collectively as Alex/Gard tradition. They were instrumental in the popular expansion of Wicca.

DR. LEO LOUIS MARTELLO

Dr. Leo Louis Martello (September 26, 1930 – June 29, 2000) was a Wiccan and gay rights activist. He publicly identified as a witch beginning in 1969, and after the Stonewall riots, he aligned himself with the Gay Liberation Front. Similarly, Martello founded the Witches Liberation Front and served as director of the Witches International Craft Association (WICA) and the Witches Anti-Defamation League. On Halloween 1970, he organized the first "Witch In" in New York's Central Park despite opposition from the city's Parks Department. Born into an Italian-American family in Dudley, Massachusetts,

Martello practiced a variant of Italian witchcraft called Strega and claimed initiation from New York City relatives into what they termed La Vecchia ("the Old Religion"). In 1973, he spent six months in England, where he associated with Patricia Crowther and her husband Arnold, who ran the Sheffield coven. Crowther initiated Martello and brought him through the three Gardnerian degrees before his return to the States. Martello was an outspoken advocate for homosexual inclusivity in the Craft. He authored several works on witchcraft, psychic defense, and the tarot. I still refer to his *Understanding the Tarot* often and recommend it as an excellent reference to start one's journey with the tarot.

I find the Italian herbal liqueur Strega a fitting offering. The name is Italian for witch. It is a strong liqueur (eighty proof) produced since 1860 by the S. A. Distilleria Liquore Strega in Benevento, Italy. It gets its distinctive yellow color from the inclusion of saffron.

> Mindless morons can't be a complement to our Mother Goddess [...] A happy person is always a powerful person and hated by those who aren't. A happy person is in many ways selfish: In the Craft we must protect our best interests and ensure that the power that comes from joy remains constant, knowing that none of us are immune to the vicissitudes of life, but that our Old Religion will help us handle any adversity — Leo Martello[2]

RAYMOND BUCKLAND

Raymond Buckland (August 31, 1934 – September 27, 2017) was among the first to bring British Traditional Witchcraft to the United States. He was a prolific author. His *Complete Book of Witchcraft*, affectionately known as the Big Blue Book, has introduced many to the Craft. Raymond and his wife Rosemary traveled to Scotland, where they were initiated by High Priestess Monique Wilson (Lady Olwen) in the presence of Gardner. Raymond took the Craft name Robat and Rosemary chose Rowan. After they returned to the States, they founded a coven on Long Island. Raymond and his wife divorced in 1973. Both left the coven at this time. In 1974, he established a branch of witchcraft called Seax-Wicca—a fusion of Gardnerian and Anglo-Saxon paganism. I still have my copy of the 1978 edition of The Tree, his book of *Seax-Wicca*, that I came across in my teens. Eddie and Herman were initiated by Theo and Thane, whom Robat and Rowan brought in. As I am downline from Eddie, though not in the Gardnerian tradition, Robat is a direct Craft ancestor.

HERMAN SLATER & EDDIE BUCZYNSKI

We've already touched on the history of Eddie Buczynski (January 28, 1947 – March 16, 1989) and Herman Slater (February 6, 1938 – July 9, 1992). I sit with each and offer them their preferred libation on their birthdays. When I asked Lady Rhea what was their go-to, she replied that Eddie drank wine when they were together, and Herman liked his gin.

> The Pagan Way has an interesting history that is a very important part of the Earth Religious Movement in North America and the entire continent. Unfortunately, as a whole, the Pagan "movement" is more akin to a "bowel movement" than a spiritual movement. And I have found that

> many so-called "pagans" are more of a threat to themselves, each other, and true spirituality, than even "born-again (were they ever really born?) christians". —Herman Slater[3]

JEFFREY WHITFIELD

Jeffrey Whitfield (died 1987) was a Minoan brother active in New York City and a practicing Buddhist. During the summer of 1982, his assistance was instrumental in helping Lady Rhea and Lady Miw Sekhmet (Carol Bulzone) get the Enchantments shop ready to open by the deadline stipulated in their lease. He then went to work at the shop and was responsible for crafting many of the oils and decorated candles they supplied. Rhea describes him as a sweetheart, scholar, and gifted medium. "He could make the Ouija talk like a magpie," she recalls. Several of the oils that Enchantments sold were his formulations—some recipes received directly from spirit via the board. He created a blend designed specifically for gay male love called Hyakintos discussed in the formulary. Jeffrey suffered from AIDS-related dementia at the end and was supported by the love of his New York pagan friends. He passed to the summer lands and was cremated on Samhain in 1987.[4]

HARRY HAY

Harry Hay (April 7, 1912 – October 24, 2002) co-founded the Radical Faeries movement and the Mattachine Society, one of the earliest gay rights organizations, established in 1950. Hay began the Faeries with Don Kilhefner in 1979. The first fairy gathering was held in Arizona that September. Hay became critical of mainstream gay rights organizations as they developed. His own libertine and Marxist beliefs generally placed him to their left. Later in life, he took controversial positions: He protested the exclusion of the North American Man-Boy Love Associations (NAMBLA) from pride parades. He spoke out against ACT UP's confrontational tactics, saying that they were too close to the machismo of straight men. In 1999, he was the grand marshal of the San Francisco Pride Parade. In 2002, he died of lung cancer. His ashes were mixed with those of his partner, John Burnside, when the latter died in 2008. They were scattered in Nomenus Faerie Sanctuary, Wolf Creek, Oregon.

SCOTT CUNNINGHAM

Scott Cunningham (June 27, 1956 – March 28, 1993) was a highly influential Wiccan author. His books introduced untold numbers to the Craft. Beginning in 1980, he trained with Raven Grimassi. While still a first degree, he broke off onto his own in 1982 and paved the way for many "solitary practitioners" to follow. His *Cunningham's Encyclopedia of Magical Herbs* and *Wicca: A Guide for the Solitary Practitioner* are classics. Cunningham fell unexpectedly ill while on a lecture tour in 1990. He was diagnosed with cryptococcal meningitis related to HIV infection. He died at age thirty-six.

EDUARDO GUTIERREZ

Eddy 'Hyperion' Gutiérrez founded The Unnamed Path in 2007. The Unnamed Path is a spiritual tradition received from the Ancestors of Men-Who-Love-Men. It integrates of Eddie's diverse spiritual background while discarding parts irrelevant to the energy current that gay/queer men naturally tap into. In 2009, he initiated his first three students in California. He passed away on January 14, 2014, and his spiritual legacy continues on through the support of his family and the Unnamed Path Tribe.

JAMES M. MARTIN

James M. Martin (March 23, 1943 - December 13, 2015), also known variously as Belarion Israfel EL SHADDAI, Frater Sodomiticus ac Impudicus, and Sahajananda, was the founder of two magical groups, the Thelemic Ordo Templi Baphometis (founded 1985) and the Nath tantric Servants of the Star and the Snake (founded 1995). He published the important homegrown journal *Abrasax* for many years and *The Trident* journal of his SSS. A self-described polysexual, Martin authored several important works on queer magick, ritual transvestitism, and the power of the phallus.

PAUL BEYERL

Paul Beyerl was an important Wiccan priest and herbalist. He and his partner Gerry Beyerl lived in Minnesota at Hermit's Grove. He authored several books on herbalism and Wicca, and he founded the Wiccan organization Rowan Tree Church, which continues his work and teachings.

RACHEL POLLACK

Rachel Pollack is an American author, teacher, and tarot expert. She was born on August 17, 1945, in Brooklyn, New York. Pollack is recognized as an influential figure in the world of tarot, having written several books on the subject and taught workshops and classes on tarot reading. Pollack's interest in tarot began in the 1960s when she discovered a deck of tarot cards in a New York City bookstore. She was immediately intrigued by the symbolism and imagery of the cards and began studying them in depth. Over the years, Pollack has developed her own unique approach to tarot reading, which emphasizes intuition and personal interpretation.

Her most famous book on tarot is *78 Degrees of Wisdom*, which is considered a classic in the field and has been translated into several languages. In addition to her work on the tarot, Pollack wrote several award-winning novels of magical realism and authored the Doom Patrol graphic novel series, taking over after the run of Grant Morrison in the 1990s. During her time scripting the famous DC Comics series, Pollack, a trans woman herself, introduced the first trans superhero in Kate "Coagula" Godwin. Pollack passed away on April 7, 2023.

THE UNNAMED DEAD

In addition to the ancestors in our lineage, many suffered persecution and were accused of witchcraft during the Burning Times and after. In Scotland, 4,000 to 6,000 people were tried for witchcraft in successive witch hunts between the passage of the Witchcraft Act of 1563 and the outbreak of the English Civil War in the 1650s.

The hysteria that swept Salem in 1692 is, of course, well known. Not so familiar are the numerous other people, mostly women, accused of practicing witchcraft and being in league with the devil throughout the early decades of the American colonies. On my mother's side, I am a descendent of several accused: Grace (Pratt) Dutch was accused and acquitted in 1653 Gloucester (her daughter would later fall under the same suspicion in the Salem witch trials); Rebecca Nurse (hanged), Ann Foster (died in jail), Samuel Wardwell (hanged), and Mercy Wardwell (acquitted) caught up in the Salem trials.

The root cause of the crisis in 1692 Salem remains hotly debated. Often, scholars remind us that the accused were not witches. This gives the false impression that the trials were not about witchcraft. Witchcraft was an ever-present concern in colonial America. The presence of hex signs in old New England homes demonstrates that the influences of witchcraft and evil forces in league with the Devil were a constant area of fear and concern. Early in the hysteria, Mary Sibley, neighbor to the Parris's, whose daughter was among the first girls affected, suggested baking a "witch's cake" to determine if the children were bewitched. The "cake" was a mix of flour and urine from a possibly bewitched person. Once baked, it was fed to a dog. If the animal exhibited any adverse symptoms, that was considered proof the individual was indeed suffering from the malicious powers of a witch. The fact that a resident of the Salem colony would know of such a folk recipe shows the early colonists not only lived in a world where witchcraft existed as a material fact but also possessed tools of positive magic to detect and combat it.

I honor these ancestors and the other victims of the witch hunts, known and those yet to be identified, among my Craft ancestors. Whether they were witches or considered themselves such, even if they did practice folk remedies and spells, is immaterial. Witchcraft was proof that the Devil was abroad in the land. All were victims of a war against witches. Some unidentifiable numbers were also victims of a fight against independent women and gender/sexual transgressors. I honor my ninth great-grandmother, Rebecca Nurse, as both my personal ancestor and her being emblematic of all those who perished after being accused of witchcraft.

For queer men, there is another important facet to the unnamed dead. We lost a generation of our elders during the height of the AIDS crisis. It is important that we also reqcognize the many gay men who left us too early. The loss to our culture and heritage is incalculable. It is imperative that their names, whether known to us or not, are remembered and honored.

Chapter III
Queer & Chaos

At the New York City Pride celebration of 1990, an anonymous queer collective distributed a broadside emblazoned with the headlines in pink: *Queers Read This!* and *I HATE STRAIGHTS*. It was a shot over the bow of the silent and assimilationist impulses of the time and a direct calling out of straight privilege.

In 1986, the Supreme Court decision *Bowers v. Hardwick* ratified the criminality of homosexual acts.[1] The court's majority based its opinion on homophobic judicial precedent on the "ancient roots" of prohibitions against homosexual acts going back into antiquity. The court made many of us outlaws. We were angry. We lived amid an unfolding holocaust. We watched as more of our brothers, lovers, and elders died daily. AIDS Coalition to Unleash Power (ACT UP) was founded in 1987 and Queer Nation in 1990. The broadside, coming just a few months later, intentionally provocative as it was, gave queer people license to own our rage, embrace it, to use it. The authors highlighted that for queer people the act of living was a defiance: "everyday you wake up alive, relatively happy, and a functioning human being, you are committing a rebellious act. You as an alive and functioning queer are a revolutionary."

The authors recognized the power and potential in the

liminality of queerness. "It's about being on the margins, defining ourselves; it's about gender-fuck and secrets, what's beneath the belt and deep inside the heart; it's about the night," they observed. This is the space traditionally occupied by the shaman, the conjuror, the witch at the margins of normative society. It is the healing woman's cottage at the edge of the village, the cave in the forest, the remote grove. It is catching the eye of a stranger and exchanging a smile.

Coming of age in the late eighties/early nineties was itself an interstitial moment of sorts. The sickness and death of the generation immediately before us was a dark pall that hung over us and could rarely be ignored. We self-righteously preached the tenets of safe sex while all too often still becoming infected. Many of us nihilistically assumed we wouldn't see the millennium. I do not doubt this weight contributed to the suicides of several close brothers and sisters. It was like we had just missed a hedonistic golden era. My first (thankfully) unpublished novel, written in the early nineties, was entitled *I Thought Andy Would Be Here*. For a gay teen in rural Maine who got most of his exposure to gay culture through the pages of *Vanity Fair*, the death of Andy Warhol in 1987 was like the close of a party that had already ended.

The movement to reclaim the word "queer" and, through it, our otherness gave us intentionality and agency. The anonymous authors of the Pride broadside observed, "QUEER can be a rough word, but it is also a sly and ironic weapon we can steal from the homophobe's hands and use against him." Around this time, a sticker was appearing everywhere. In stark black sans-serif font on pink, it read:

GAY BY NATURE | QUEER BY CHOICE

In one moment, the debate between essentialism (there have always been LGBT people) and constructionism ("homosexual" is a concept of modernity where individual acts bestow identity for the first time) was put to rest. Nature made us men who loved men; being QUEER was intentional, political, and empowering. Out of our desire, we have the potential to create something new and marvelous.

French theorist Michel Foucault held a "distrust" for the concept of "coming out," especially in terms of coming out to oneself. He did not view homosexuality as a process of interiority, of self-discovery, but as one of creation and fabrication (in the positivist sense of the word). "The problem is not to discover in oneself the truth of one's sex," he told the French gay magazine *Gai Pied*, "but, rather, to use one's sexuality henceforth to arrive at a multiplicity of relationships."[2]

> The mapping of sexual desire and the development of a modern "gay" identity The dividing up of all sexual acts—indeed all persons—under the "opposite" categories of "homo" and "hetero" is not a natural given but a historical process, still incomplete today and ultimately impossible but characterized by potent contradictions and explosive effects.[3]

In an interview with *The Advocate*, Foucault elaborated:

> Sexuality is a part of our behavior. It's a part of our world freedom. Sexuality is something that we ourselves create—it is our own creation, and much more than the discovery of a secret side of our desire. We have to understand that with our desires, through our desires, go new forms of relationships,

new forms of love, new forms of creation. Sex is not a fatality: it's a possibility for creative life."[4]

For Foucault, same-sex relations "short-circuit" encoded institutions and power structures by introducing "love where there's supposed to be only law, rule, or habit."[5]

Chaos magic is a contemporary form of magical practice that emerged in the late twentieth century and is characterized by its eclectic and pragmatic approach to magic. It emphasizes personal experience and individual belief systems over traditional rituals and dogmas. Generally, chaos magicians believe that belief *itself* is a powerful tool for magic. This allows the freedom of adopting and discarding beliefs as needed for specific magical workings. Taking on the original meaning of "memes" as articulated by Richard Dawkins, chaos magicians view belief as a tool rather than an absolute truth. This allows the magician the freedom to draw inspiration from various magical traditions, religions, and philosophies. Chaos magic has no fixed set of rituals or symbols. Flexibility is encouraged with a preference for what works. The intent here is also to dispel the cultural compulsion to hold on to a given belief construct. In this way, the magician frees themselves from the chains of tradition.

Chaos magic arose in the late 1970s, "emerging," in the words of comic writer Grant Morrison, "from the eerie lunar zones between the polar fires of punk rock and the Thatcher rave years, Chaos Magic has grown and multiplied and diversified, evolving out from the minds of its practitioners; it has no shape, it breeds like a fractal and mutates as it goes.."[6] At its best, it applied the impulses of postmodernism and scientific chaos theory to the practice of magic. It sought to remove the obfuscations that had adhered themselves to the practice of magic and operative occultism. At its loftiest aspirations, chaos magic sought to recognize belief as an operative tool that may be constructively harnessed to affect change.

Writing in 1993, Phil Hine framed chaos magic in the words of revolution involving "the recognition that the scientific world-view which has set the limitations of acknowledged human experience is crumbling, that new visions and models are required, as are new ways of being, and more importantly, new ways of *doing*."[7] One may wonder now if his vision wasn't a bit rose-tinted, but there can be little doubt that the work of its early proponents shook things up in important ways.

The philosophy of chaos magic was brought to a much broader audience in the late 1990s and early 2000s by Morrison's comic book series *The Invisibles*. The initial arc of DC Comics published series follows the travails of angry loner teen Dane McGowan. He crosses paths with a ragtag cell of a secret society, the Invisible College, calling themselves the Invisibles, headed by the chaos magician King Mob. Through his contact with various members of the Invisibles, sometimes unknowingly, Dane learns there is magic throughout the everyday world. With his comrades' help, King Mob employs chaos magical techniques in opposition to their nemesis, the Outer Church. While trying to survive on the streets of London, Dane meets a homeless man named Tom. Unbeknownst to him, Tom is a member of the Invisibles. He begins to teach him the magic in the city around them and the co-existent virus of modernity. "Your head's like mine, like all our heads, big enough to contain every god and devil there ever was. Big enough to hold the weight of oceans and the turning stars. Whole *universes* fit in there! But what do we choose to keep in the miraculous cabinet? Little broken things, sad trinkets that we play with over and over. The world turns our key and we play the same little tune again and again and we think that tune's all we are."[8]

Morrison, himself an outspoken proponent, sums up the magical ethos of chaos magic in his essay "Pop Magic!":

"All you need to begin the practice of magic is concentration, imagination, and the ability to laugh at yourself and learn from mistakes. Some people like to dress up as Egyptians or monks to get themselves in the mood; others wear animal masks or Barbarella costumes. The use of ritual paraphernalia functions as an aid to the imagination only.

"Anything you can imagine, anything you can symbolize, can be made to produce magical changes in your environment."[9]

Just as with Foucault's view of same-sex desire, chaos magic opened up new potentialities where before there had been blind faith and religious dogma. Like the philosophies they shade, queer theory and chaos magic arose in parallel. Applying similar analytic methods, queer theory did to gay studies what chaos magic did to modern occultism. Using Foucauldian critical theory notions of social construction, queer theory deconstructed gay history and the historicizing process itself. Chaos magic exposed the social and ahistorical nature of magic by stripping away ideological window dressings and cutting the underpinnings of historical dogma, often a modern fabrication. Queer theory revolutionized gay activism and philosophical practice by exposing the absence of inherent identity and the constructed nature of self. Both queer theory and chaos magic introduced postmodernism to their respective domains.

It is important to understand history as best we can, and what follows is my attempt at reconstructing past patterns of antiquities. While inclusive of many references to history and archeology, this work is also intentionally ahistorical. Weaving my research and experience with the philosophies of French theorist Michel Foucault and American author William S. Burroughs, among others, what follows is a field guide for a particular type of queer male praxis. There are diverse ways to approach queer spirit, this is but one of many.

Both Foucault and Burroughs saw us at a crossroads. Foucault saw that gay men had a unique opportunity to create something fabulous and new: love, where there had only been law, rule, and habit. Burroughs viewed the world as coming to the end of the human line and, as a species nears extinction, anything is possible. Like Foucault's historical studies of the classical world, the self must be created, not revealed. Aleister Crowley highlighted that all intentional acts are magical in nature. This is no less true for acts of revolution as those of libertation.

Queer theory freed us from the essentialist imperatives of gay studies. Chaos sought, perhaps quixotically, sought to liberate magic from the constraints of dogma. Wilde, Crowley, Burroughs, and Foucault, in their own unique ways, all taught that limits are self-imposed and that the magician's job is to push those limits. Wilde spoke eloquently of aesthetic antinomianism in the unexpurgated text of *De Profundis*. In the practice of his own life, Foucault sought the 'limit experience' lying just past the boundary of what the body could conceive. These all invoke the shamanic experience of going to the depths.

We should embrace the fact that we are outlaws and not try to flee toward the soft light of we're-just-like-you. Witches, like traditional shamans, have always been queer, existing as they do in that strange, queered, space between worlds. The mists surrounding the sacred isle shift, swirl, and finally part...

there's Eartha Kitt, the heavenly mother, waiting for us on the island's holy summit... "I'm still herrreeeeee-ah."

The road can be a dangerous one. The lands of shadow are filled with many gods and spirits. And we all know that faeries can be tricky.

Chapter IV
Antecedents I, Wildean Antinomianism

Antinomianism has diverse historical precedents and, one may suspect, reaches back to the beginning of moral codes and religious strictures. Structured taboos and religious edicts often give rise to counter-doctrines of transgression. This can be seen in certain Gnostic sects and the Tantrik practitioners of the *vama-marga,* or "Lefthand Path." The leader of a twentieth-century Ophite-Cainite Gnostic church speaks of Carpocrates's theory of "salvation by reincarnatory fulfillment" as a notion "that if one does not commit some immoral act in this lifetime, he or she will likely commit it in the next."[1] The adept's goal in these doctrines is to reach a point beyond good and evil, free of social conditioning. For the adept to attain this higher vantage point, they must experience the evil and the good, for one cannot leave behind what one does not know. One cannot truthfully reject what one has not experienced; rejection without experience is based on conditioning, not personal knowledge, and therefore can never be complete.

In *De Profundis,* written to his lover Lord Alfred Douglas while serving his sentence in Reading Gaol, Oscar Wilde rejects morality, saying, "I am a born antinomian."[2] In light of the subtle spiritual nature underlying much of his work, it is certainly arguable that Wilde means here more than just simple moral transgression. He appears to acknowledge a purpose underpinning his antinomian stance. In "The Soul of Man Under Socialism," Wilde writes, "Disobedience... is man's original virtue." In this 1891 piece, Wilde links disobedience with rebellion, but by the writing of *De Profundis,* he had given up rebellion as being too debilitating. In 1897, Wilde stated, "He who is in a state of rebellion cannot receive grace," for "rebellion closes up the channels of the soul, and shuts out the airs of heaven."[3] He sees antinomianism as more than just rebelling against social norms; he is attempting to utilize his suffering and degradation for spiritual purposes.

Early in *De Profundis,* Wilde states "that the fool in the eyes of the gods and the fool in the eyes of man are very different." He continues, "The real fool, such as the gods mock and mar, is he who does not know himself." Since the fool to the gods lacks self-knowledge, Wilde implies the one who seeks to know himself is likely to be a fool to man. Wilde carefully avoids entangling self-realization with a moral requirement for goodness. At the root of his literary device, the transgressive paradox resides a theory that one must know all sides of life to pass beyond their social definitions. He stresses the soul's ability to transform all that one does and experiences, even evil and suffering, into something right. "The supreme vice is shallowness. Everything that is realized is right."[4]

Wilde describes his friendship with Douglas as "an unintellectual friendship, a friendship whose primary aim was not the creation and contemplation of beautiful things" for his fall from Art.[5] He blames his fall from the graces of proper society on his turning to that society to protect him. "The one disgraceful, unpardonable, and to all time contemptible action of my life was my allowing myself to be forced into appealing to Society for help and protection against [the Marquess of Queensberry]."[6] What he most considered his actual fall, making his name, as he says, "a low byword among low people," Wilde construes differently.[7] Wilde used those acts hidden in the dark parts of London to stimulate his art and as a vantage point to look upon the Beautiful. He explains, "Tired of being on the heights I deliberately went to the depths in the search for new sensations. What the paradox was to me in the sphere of thought, perversity became to me in the sphere of passion." We can see in Wilde's notion of "the depths" what Foucault called "limit experience" and what the witch knows as the liminal—those spaces outside the safe avenues of society that hold the potential of profound experience and knowledge.

Later in the work, he writes:

> People thought it dreadful of me to have entertained at dinner the evil things of life, and to have found pleasure in their company. But they, from the point of view through which I, as an artist in life, approached them, were delightfully suggestive and stimulating. It was like feasting with panthers. The danger was half the charm... They were to me the brightest of gilded snakes. Their poison was part of their perfection.[8]

The darker side of life, constructed by society as sinful, seems to have grounded Wilde's exalted privileging of Art and Beauty. He states this explicitly in this description of Dorian Gray. "There were moments when he looked on evil simply as a mode through which he could realize his conception of the beautiful."[9] These three examples appear to hark toward a higher, more spiritual definition of antinomianism. It isn't just transgression for transgression's sake.

Wilde's theory of experiencing beauty through evil distinguishes Wilde from Lord Alfred's appetite-driven search for pleasure and Dorian's fall toward degradation: Wilde sees a path toward realization in it. Wilde places his faith not in a higher power but rather in the ability of the soul to transform actions. For Wilde, the soul is the ultimate spiritual alembic. In Wilde's opposition to denial, he argues that the soul "can transform into noble moods of thought, and passions of high import, what in itself is base, cruel, and degrading."[10] This reflects itself in the refrain of *De Profundis*, "The supreme vice is shallowness. Everything that is realized is right."[11] In Wildean morality, no pure evil exists; nothing one does nor undergoes can be *inherently* bad. One always stands in relation to one's actions and possesses the ability to shape and reshape one's reflexive meaning. Like his near contemporary, Friedrich Nietzsche, Wilde levels out the constructed difference between good and evil, envisioning a metaphysical space beyond their duality. In Wilde's cosmology, the soul's transformative capacity depends on one's self-defined relation to one's actions. In *De Profundis*'s refrain, "realized" is the keyword. "Everything realized is right."

Wilde does not emphasize what is traditionally considered good or what is oppositionally conceived as evil. In his eyes, the gods do not distinguish between the two. "The gods are strange," Wilde writes. "It is not of our vices only they make instruments to scourge us. They bring us to ruin through what in us is good, gentle, humane, loving."[12] This sentiment is echoed later in the same text with even more certitude, "I must accept the fact that one is punished for the good as well as for the evil that one does."[13] Wilde's acknowledgment that one is punished equally for all actions, regardless of their conventional definitions, does not lead him to a conclusion of nihilism in the face of a cruel society.

In contrast, it brings him toward a heightened, spiritually centered transcendence of the good/evil binary paradigm instead. For Wilde, the gods' indiscriminate punishment is not so strange after all. He possessed "no doubt that it is quite right one should be [for] it helps one, or should help one, to realize both, and not to be too conceited about either."[14] Here again, Wilde places importance on the act of "realizing." Through the act of realization, the soul becomes capable of transforming actions into deeper significances. In this level, all conditioning, such as good and evil social constructions, are removed or transfigured. For Wilde, "One only realizes one's soul by getting rid of all alien passions, all acquired culture, and all external possessions be they good or evil."[15] Wilde places this power of realization and the soul in a concept of subjectivity and the seemingly paradoxical requirement of repentance.

When describing his philosophical outlook, Wilde adopts a skeptic's philosophical stance toward the notion of subjectivity. "I said in Dorian Gray that the great sins of the world take place in the brain, but it is in the brain that everything takes place." As Wilde continues, he could easily be paraphrasing from the dialogues of Sextus Empiricus or one of his successors. He bases his subjectivity on Sextus's argument of the senses as he continues:

> We know not that we do not see with the eye or hear with the ear. They are merely channels for the transmission, adequate or inadequate, of sense-impressions. It is in the brain that the poppy is red, that the apple is odorous, that the skylark sings.[16]

He posits his quest after "realization" internally from his theory of subjectivity. He writes, "If I may not find its secret within myself, I shall never find it."[17] The relation between Wilde's subjective self and the soul's transformative capabilities is self-definitional. For Wilde, repenting or "realizing" one's actions is essential.

Though Wilde does not judge particular actions, he significantly differentiates between various modes of relating to one's actions. He argues "that there is nothing wrong in what one does," but "there is something wrong in what one becomes."[18] Wilde centers spiritual importance on a differentiation between one who remains in a singular realm of degradation, a thrall to his appetites and drives (such as Lord Alfred), and the person who repents to reflect, thereby recognizing or "realizing" his actions. This separation is the crux of Wildean morality. "Of course the sinner must repent," Wilde states in *De Profundis*, "simply because otherwise he would be unable to realize what he had done. The moment of repentance is the moment of initiation."[19] Wilde's trial taught him, in retrospect, that it is not essential to have one's actions recounted to one or to be forced to confess them. In Wilde's conception, these are all spiritually meaningless. It is not what is said that is important, but that one says it oneself. Wilde defines "man's highest moment" as "when he kneels in the dust, and beats his breast, and tells all the sins of his life."[20] This marries nicely to *De Profundis*'s signature couplet: shallow people are the fools of the gods, and it is the process of realization that distinguishes right from wrong.

When one looks at Wilde's analysis of his scandalous fall from society during and after his trials, one finds a developed cosmology based on antinomianism, transcendence, repentance, and realization. Wilde's antinomianism is constituted by a knowledge of "evil" and "sin" based on active exploration rather than passively accepting one's carnal desires. He feels that "there is not a single degradation of the body which I must not try and make into a spiritualizing of the soul."[21] For Wilde, amorality is both artistically and spiritually stimulating. Wilde relies on a subjective stance relative to good and evil, where antinomianism allows one to remove oneself from a position of moral conceit. Repentance is the fulcrum of Wilde's relativist morality. Through repentance, a contemplative recital, one realizes one's actions and can learn from them. Ultimately, Wilde's philosophy is one of action, not faith—" people whose desire is solely for self-realization never know where they are going."[22] Wilde's understanding of antinomianism is based on a requirement to experience all sides of life; just as Wilde accepts the importance of suffering and pleasure, one must learn equality from good and evil.

Chapter V
Antecedents II, The Bard United with the Bard

Aleister Crowley is the most famous, some argue infamous, magician of the twentieth century. He espoused a libertine philosophy under the motto, "Do what thou wilt shall be the whole of the law." Rather than a complete license to do whatever one likes, in Crowley's terms, this meant following the nature of one's True Will—the personal destiny one is thrown into from birth. He also was very open about his bisexuality—perhaps more aptly characterized as voracious omni-sexuality.

He met his first male lover, Charles Jerome Pollitt, in his final year at Trinity College, Cambridge. Crowley described the nature of their relationship in his *Confessions*: "The relation between us was the ideal intimacy which the Greeks considered the greatest glory of manhood and the most precious prize of life."[1] Their relationship was only a few years after Oscar Wilde's sentencing to Reading Gaol. The famous libel trial that ended with Wilde's two-year imprisonment occurred during Crowley's first year at Cambridge in 1895. Despite his iconoclastic attitude toward Christianity, Crowley was still deeply ashamed of his attraction to men.[2] In his *Confessions*, Crowley veiled his relationship with Pollitt by referencing the Greek ideal and describing it as "pure." In *The World's Tragedy*, Crowley described the relationship as "that ideal intimacy which the Greeks considered the greatest glory of manhood." In his own copy, Crowley added, "I lived with Pollitt as his wife for some six months and he made a poet out of me."[3] The two quarreled over Pollitt's lack of interest in Crowley's spiritual pursuits. In the heat of argument, Crowley announced that Pollitt did not fit his plans and broke it off.

While at Trinity, Pollitt gained a reputation as a Decadent—a *fin de siècle* literary and artistic movement. He made quite an impression on his fellow students when he performed as his female alter ego, Diane de Rouge, as an undergrad at the all-male Cambridge Footlights Sketch Club. Crowley sometimes adopted a female persona he named "Alice." This was especially the case when he took on his preferred passive role during sex.[4]

Pollitt left Trinity with a Master's degree in 1896. He moved to London and became a collector and patron of the arts. He was a close friend and possible lover of Aubrey Beardsley. Frederick Hollyer photographed him as de Rouge, and Whistler sketched him. Crowley regretted the end of their relationship for years. Soon after the breakup, he wrote Pollitt a letter of apology but never brought himself to send it. The two ran past each other on Bond Street, and Crowley claimed he did not notice as they passed each other. Pollitt interpreted the incident as an intentional snub and never spoke to Crowley again.[5]

Crowley did not as quickly dismiss his affection for Pollitt. In 1905, years after their relationship ended, he composed a collection of poetry in the style of Persian ghazals. *The Scented Garden of Abdulah, the Satirist of Shiraz (Bagh-i-Muattar)* glorifies male+male anal sex. The book was privately published in London in 1910, in a limited edition of 200 copies, under a pseudonym.

Unfortunately, British customs seized and destroyed most copies when being shipped back to England from Crowley's failed abbey on the Sicilian island of Cefalu. One can see Pollitt was on Crowley's mind as he composed the works. In poem 41, the first letter of every line forms an anagram of Pollitt's full name. In his *Confessions,* Crowley describes the book as "a complete treatise on mysticism, expressed in the symbolism." Echoing the philosophical sentiment of Wilde in *De Profundis,* Crowley characterizes the mystic's path underpinning *The Scented Garden*:

> His religion ceases to be real and becomes formal; he falls into sin and suffers the penalty thereof. God prepares the pathway of regeneration and brings him through shame and sorrow to repentance, thus preparing the mystical union which restores man to his original privileges, free will, immortality, the perception of truth and so on.[6]

Though rare in its original edition (Teitan Press did issue a facsimile edition in 1991), the book remains a testament to Crowley's embracing of the male+male mystical formula and the enduring hold his brief relationship with Pollitt had over him.

Crowley was less guarded when it came to his next significant male relationship. Mutual friend J.F.C. Fuller introduced Crowley to Victor Neuberg in 1906. Their sexual relationship likely began in 1908 while the two were on a walking tour of Spain.[7] Neuberg was a poet and wrote of his admiration and love for Crowley. He dedicates his love poem, "The Coming of Apollo" to Crowley:

But still, the old silent garden
remembers the golden flush.
When the heavens seemed to harden
For a moment, they came and fled
When the whole green grew red
in a breathless spell and a hush
And the world grew young in the garden,
and trembled, and passed, and fled.[8]

And in his "Ophelia" he writes of his occult mentor:

SWEET wizard, in whose footsteps I have trod
Unto the shrine of the most obscene god,
So steep the pathway is, I may not know,
Until I reach the summit, where I go.
My love is deathless as the springs of Truth,
My love is pure as is the dawn of youth,
But all my being throbs in rhythm with thine,
Who leadest on to the horizon-line.[9]

The two would go on to conduct two of the most important magical operations of the twentieth century—the desert Enochian evocations and the Paris Working. It may surprise some modern occultists, and still be uncomfortable to others, that these workings centered around male+male sex magick. Katon Shual observes, "My feeling is that many magicians would rather not face up to the fact that some of the most influential magical work of the twentieth century was actually homosexual sex-magick."[10]

SOJOURN IN THE SAHARA

Crowley and Neuberg departed London for a walking tour of Algeria on November 10, 1909. When they arrived, Crowley found among the papers he had brought his notes on the Enochian work by Dr. John Dee. He had first attempted to conduct workings based on the material in 1900 but had not gotten very far. In the intervening years, Crowley had received higher initiations and felt it might be an excellent opportunity to attempt to work the system again.

Dr. John Dee (1527-1608/9) was an Elizabethan scholar, mathematician, alchemist, astrologer, and occultist. He was renowned in his time. During the reign of Queen Mary, he ran afoul of both secular and ecclesiastical authorities who distrusted his astrological work. In 1555, he was arrested for doing the chart of Queen Mary. A charge of treason was leveled against him. He talked his way out of the charges, but lingering suspicion hung over him for the rest of Mary's reign. Dee fared better under her successor, Elizabeth I. He became a trusted political advisor and court astrologer. He may have also served her as a spy. Dee was renowned for his wide-ranging scholarship. His library at his house, Mortlake, south of London, ranked among the best private libraries in Britain.

Elizabeth's patronage waned in later life, and Dee's political influence dwindled. He withdrew more toward his scholarly pursuits with a particular emphasis on occult knowledge. In 1582, he met Edward Kelly, a rather unscrupulous person by all accounts. Kelley would serve as Dee's medium for his most important magical work. The two came into contact with spirits who transmitted an entirely novel system of magic to them. They connected the spirits to Enoch, and the system became known as Enochian. The process involved a wax seal supporting a shew-stone, a mirror of black obsidian used for scrying, similar to how one uses a crystal ball.

Through Kelley, the spirits communicated an extraordinarily detailed and highly complex system involving five tables, or magical squares—one for each of the four prime elements and one known as the Tablet of Union. The spirits provided a unique alphabet and language—also known as Enochian. They described a system of calling specific spiritual entities deduced from the four tables, or Watchtowers. Additionally, they outlined a series of spiritual realms known as Aethyrs. The magician could progress through these using a series of textual keys or calls. The journey through the successive layers forms an internally coherent initiatory process.

With the assistance of his student, Neuberg, Crowley determined to work through the calls using a large topaz he had with him as shew-stone. They set out from the capital, Algiers, and reached the village of Sour El-Ghozlane, about seventy miles south, on November 21. On November 23, the two walked into the Sahara, where Crowley started up where he had left off at the 28th Aethyr. (The Aethyrs count backward from 30.) Crowley and Neuberg's book *The Vision and the Voice* contains a detailed account of these workings. They continued moving through the initiatory levels through the end of the year and into the new. Following their first working, they headed deeper into the country. They reached Sidi Aïssa on the 24th and conducted a working calling the 27th Aethyr. From there, they made their way to Bou Saâda. They would spend most of their trip there and work through the remaining calls in the surrounding desert.

On the afternoon of December 3, they climbed Mount Da'leh Addin and attempted to call the vision of the 14th Aethyr. The

Angel spoke, "All that thou wast hath he eaten up, and all that thou art is his pasture until tomorrow. And all that thou shalt be is nothing."[11] The spirit spoke of a moment of stasis where the adept is no longer who he has been but not yet who he will be. Ultimately, the working was less than satisfactory. Crowley could not penetrate dark veils in his vision. Finally, the spirit told them to depart as he could only be invoked in darkness. After descending the mountain, Crowley received a message to gather rocks and form a circle around a stone altar dedicated to Pan.[12] He sensed that they needed to offer a sacrifice and decided on one of a sexual nature.

Crowley bent over the makeshift altar that night in the darkness and offered himself up to Neuberg. Their act was dedicated as an offering to the Greek god Pan, and this time, their evocation worked a vision of the 14th Aethyr opened before him. They were surrounded by a blackness darker than night. Crowley wrote that it was a darkness more black than ever he had seen. The spirit of the Aethyr began to speak to them. He announced he was standing in the sign of Apophis and Typhon—a magical posture. The Angel of the 14th Aethyr continued:

> I am the snake, that devoureth the spirit of man with lust of light. I am the sightless storm in the night that wrappeth the world about with desolation. Chaos is my name, and thick darkness. know thou art that the darkness of The Earth is ruddy, and the darkness of the air is gray, but the darkness of the soul is utter blackness.[13]

Apophis is the Greek variant of the Egyptian Apep, the devouring serpent, known as the "Lord of Chaos." He is also called the Evil Dragon. Apep is the enemy of Ra, the sun god, and the sun's death each day is seen as part of their battles. Not unimportantly, Apep is often represented as having been born from Ra's umbilical cord. Apep lives in darkness and is seen as an underworld deity. Typhon is the monstrous giant serpent within Greek mythology and may be seen as an analog to his Egyptian counterpart. The two are often grouped as a pair in occult references. The Greeks associated Typhon with Set, whom I will discuss later. We can sense echoes of this in Miðgarðsormr, the Midgard Serpent, whose tale will initiate the final world battle of Norse mythology, Ragnarök.

The Angel speaks of the "Pyramid of Initiation." In Greek, the pyramid is numerically linked to both the phallus and death. Crowley described the pyramid as "a Phallus which dies itself to communicate Life to others."[14] Crowley did not leave the ritual unchanged. He considered it his true initiation to the high grade of Magister Templi. It is also likely during this rite that Crowley finally shed his internal prejudices and fully embraced, at least for a time, the power of homosexuality as a magical formula. Katon Shual observes, "From then on an abyss had been crossed between personal and spiritual. The alienation of the sexual from the spiritual disappears. The old antagonism of Golden Dawn type occultism for the sensual is ditched along with Temperance."[15]

The pair arrived at the resort town of Biskra on December 16. Crowley dictated a long letter to Fuller. In it, he complains of Neuberg's attraction to the bottoms of Arabic boys. This is undoubtedly a joke between Crowley and Neuberg as the letter is being dictated to Neuberg.[16] Demonstrating that it was not all magical work and that real passion existed between the two men, Crowley penned a poem during their stay, "At Bordj-an-Nus":

Thereby the palms, the desert's edge, I drew thee to

my heart and held
Thy shy slim beauty for a splendid second; and fell moaning back,
Smitten by Love's forked flashing rod –as if the uprooted mandrake yelled!
As if I had seen God, and died! I thirst! I writhe upon the rack!
El Arabi! El Arabi!
It is not love! I am compelled
By some fierce fate, a vulture poised, heaven's single ominous speck of black.
El Arabi![17]

Despite his affection for Neuberg, Crowley remained cautious about the bisexual side of his sexual appetites, however. When the poem appeared in *The Equinox*, it did so under a female pseudonym to disguise its true nature.

THE PARIS WORKING

Crowley and Neuberg were in Paris for the New Year 1914. On the cusp of the year, they embarked on a series of twenty-four magical workings spanning over six weeks. This concatenation of magical rituals is known as "The Paris Working" and was never officially published by Crowley, though transcripts of the magical journals have circulated and now exist online; Lashatal Press issued a hardcover edition in 2014. The focus of the workings was the Roman gods Jupiter and Mercury, inspired by texts from antiquity.

The work commenced with the first working on New Year's Eve. At the outset of the ritual, Crowley writes that he received the sacrament from a priest. The individual referenced as the priest was Walter Duranty, the *New York Times* foreign correspondent.[18] There is little doubt that the sacramental substance was semen. Neuberg opened the working with a banishing ritual in the form of a dance inspired by the banishing ritual of the pentagram infused with an invocation written by Crowley. During the working, Crowley flogged Neuberg's buttocks. This technique has been employed to induce a trance. Gardner used ritual scourging in his Wiccan rituals.

As others in the Central European Time Zone were toasting the New Year and singing "Auld Lang Syne," the second phase of the ritual commenced. Crowley and Neuberg engaged in ritual sex, the former taking the passive role, the latter the active. During their intercourse, they recited a line:

Jungitur en vati vates: rex inclyte rabdon hermes tu

venius, verba nefanda ferens
(Mine: The bard united with the bard, O Famous King of the Divining Rod, Hermes, may you come bearing forbidden words; AC: Jointly, the bard in the bard, O famous king of the wand, Hermes, mayest thou come bearing unspeakable words)

Unfortunately, their intent was not realized when Mercury failed to fully manifest in Neuberg.

The third working commenced the night of January 3. This time, Mercury did show up and manifest within Neuberg. He lectured the participants on the power of semen and excoriated them about shame. It is evident that Crowley retained some of his negative thoughts on male+male sex that should have been expunged during the pair's desert Enochian workings. "Every drop of semen Hermes sheds in a world." Mercury then calls the participants "fools" and damns them for holding on to shame. "There is no shame about me, is there?" he asks. He then suggests Crowley must perform a public act to shed all remnants of shame within him. This would take the form of Crowley and Duranty having sex in front of the latter's girlfriend, Jane Chéron.

The ritual space consisted of a bed, an image of the god to the east, sacred words in the west, the priest in the south, and a censer with burning incense to the south. At the center was a square stone altar. For the first workings, the altar held the "Supreme, Vast, Forbidden, Ineffable, Most Holy God." What precisely this means has been lost to history. For the third and subsequent rituals, Crowley crafted a new-made Image of the God in the East, a terminal phallic figure in yellow wax, very beautiful" which they placed in the east.[19] This is reminiscent of the creation of wax poppets common in witchcraft.

The Paris Working has become an infamous part of the

popular mythology that is Crowley's legacy. I read stories of the working ending in either Crowley or Neuberg or both going insane. I've read entirely erroneous stories about it, resulting in the death of Crowley's son (an individual who did not exist). Much of this stems from the overwrought writings of Dennis Wheatley. He dined with Crowley several times as he prepared his book *A Devil Rides Out*. Wheatley included different retellings of his salacious version of The Paris Working in *The Devil and All His Works*, his introduction to one edition of Crowley's *Moonchild*, and his memoirs *The Times Had Come*. In one version, Crowley spent four months in a lunatic asylum. His other depictions are much of the same. He describes a Paris coven coming together for the workings in his memoirs. Wheatley's retelling of his version has contributed in no small part to the negative mythology of Aleister Crowley.[20]

Late in Crowley's life, while he was living at Netherwood in Hastings, the entertainer Arnold Crowther brought a visitor to his door. This was a man interested in magic and witchcraft named Gerald B. Gardner. Following their initial meeting, Gardner would visit the old wizard several more times. Given the degree Gardner claimed in Scottish Rite Masonry, Crowley acknowledged him as at the level of the Seventh Degree within the OTO. He provided Gardner with a charter to found an OTO camp or lodge and wrote to Karl Germer that he hoped a lodge would soon be established in London. The lodge charter in Gardner's calligraphy and signed by Crowley is now in the possession of the Atlanta OTO lodge. I had the opportunity to examine it while it was displayed at the 2023 Mystic South conference during Richard Kaczynski's lecture "From Thelema to Wicca." Gardner assumed the occult name Scire, under which he would later publish his first foray into becoming a public witch disguised as fiction in *High Magic's Aid*.

In addition to the charter, Crowley provided Gardner with the OTO rituals at least through the Sixth degree. In addition, Gardner possessed several works by Crowley within his library. A rumor has long circulated within witchcraft circles that Gardner paid Crowley to write the rituals for his new religion of witchcraft. Though debunked, this tale has not disappeared completely. It persists in many current publications and abounds on the internet. We know Gardner did not invent his religion from whole cloth but was initiated into a witchcraft coven in the New Forest. Whatever material he received from this group, there is little doubt it proved insufficient for Gardner's purposes. His initial Book of Shadows is a pastiche of material from various occult sources, including grimoires and the works of Crowley. Traditionally, a witch's Book of Shadows resembles a recipe book, so the cut-and-paste approach is unsurprising. One's recipe book is often a collection of recipes taken from various sources. In this first iteration, Gardner's BOS was as much as forty percent drawn from Crowley's writings or magical writings after him.[21]

After joining Gardner's Bricket Wood coven in 1953, Doreen Valiente began crafting what she felt would be a more fitting Book of Shadows. A central component of this effort was to erase the influence of Crowley within the revised text. In contrast, she retained the elements that Gardner had borrowed from Leland's study of Italian witchcraft, Aradia, Gospel of the Witches, because this material represented actual historical witchcraft. Gardnerians to this day invoke the idiosyncratic combination of the Italian Aradia coupled with the Celtic and Gallo-Roman Cernunnos as the central deities. Janet and Stewart Farrar worked to restore some of the Crowley material into the Book of Shadows, attempting to get closer to Gardner's original work. This they included in the Gardnerian/Alexandrian rites that comprise their *Witch's Bible.*

It is hard to calculate the impact these meetings had on Gardner and the early formation of the modern witch cult. Obviously, the initial encounter was profound enough for Gardner to return on several occasions. One wonders how different Gardner's public witchcraft would be if it weren't for these interactions. Given where Gardner was in his occult pursuits at the time, it is hard to imagine that the impact wasn't formative. Though we can now say with some definitiveness that Crowley did not author the initial rituals under contract, it is unlikely Gardnerian witchcraft would be the same—or perhaps exist at all—if it weren't for the influence of the Great Beast in retirement.

Chapter VI
Wicca's Beginnings

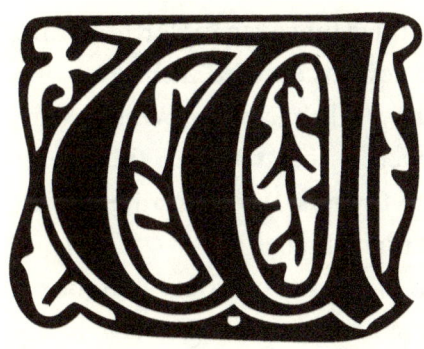

Wicca is now a relatively uncritical and ubiquitous term with the feel of something with deep historical roots. It has become an almost generic term nearly synonymous with 'witch' within popular culture, especially in the USA. It has the feel in many instances of denoting a New Age eclecticism of neo-pagan practice. The term entered modern English relatively recently in the second half of the last century. It has its roots in the Old English word *wicca,* denoting an Anglo-Saxon sorcerer, from which we get our modern English word 'witch.'

Gerald B. Gardner is considered the founder of modern Wicca. It is interesting to note that the word rarely occurs in his writing. He referred to his practice as the 'Craft of the Wise, 'the Witch Cult,' or simply 'witchcraft.' He did use 'the Wica' on occasion to describe the growing witch community. The use of the term grew in popularity in the early to mid-1960s and increasingly with the now more common spelling of two C's. During the early years of its adoption, the term was used exclusively to refer to those within British Traditional Witchcraft, those initiated by or downline from Gardner. By the late 70s and 80s, the term gained a more encompassing and universal meaning through the influence of a new generation of writers such as Scott Cunningham and Silver RavenWolf.

The 'Father of Witchcraft,' Gardner came into contact with a coven of traditional witches secretly operating in the New Forest, likely through his association with a Rosicrucian fellowship operating in the area. He was initiated into the coven in 1939. He believed this group to be a surviving pre-Christian pagan tradition.

In the late 1940s, Gardner founded his coven in Hertfordshire, known now as the Bricket Wood coven, centered at the Fiveacres Country Club, a nudist or "naturist" club Gardner owned. Many important figures in the Craft were associated with this group, including 'Dafo' Edith Woodford-Grimes, Doreen Valiente, Lois Bourne, and Gardner biographer Jack Bracelin.

In 1949, he published an account of these witchcraft practices disguised as fiction in a novel, *High Magic's Aid*, under the penname Scire. He followed this with two non-fiction books, *Witchcraft Today* (1954) and *The Meaning of Witchcraft* (1959). Through these, he became the first public witch and a de facto spokesperson for witchcraft.

He initiated Patricia Crowther, who then brought her husband in. They founded the Sheffield Coven in 1961. Eventually, those tracing their lineage back to Gardner became termed 'Gardnerians' and the tradition 'Gardnerian'—a term first coined as derogatory in the contemporary pagan press.

In 1963, American Raymond Buckland traveled to Scotland to meet Gardner. He was initiated by Gardner's high priestess, Monique Wilson (Lady Olwen). Upon his return to Long Island, Buckland initiated his wife Rosemary, and the following year, they formed the Long Island Coven—the first coven downline from Gardner to be established in North America. Buckland would later go on to found the Seax-Wica 'tradition' of Anglo-Saxon witchcraft.

THE OLD KENTUCKY LINE

The Bucklands's initiator, Lady Olwen, implemented a rule that only a third-degree High Priestess could cast a circle. This exists in no other branch of Gardnerian practice. Since the Bucklands were her downline, they inherited this rule. When Raymond split with his wife Rosemary, she retained control of the Long Island coven—and it became known as the 'Long Island Line' of Gardnerian. Two initiates, Theo and Thane, had received their first and second-degree initiations in a circle cast by Rosemary. When it came time for their third-degree elevation, the Bucklands had divorced, and Raymond cast the circle. This meant the rest of the US Gardnerians viewed those downline from the pair as illegitimate given Olwen's rule and that most American Gardnerians descended from her. This line became known as the Kentucky, now Old Kentucky, Line. I mention this as a little historical digression, as this is the line from which Eddie received his Gardnerian initiation. The Old Kentucky Line is pretty much extinct, as its initiates have been absorbed into the Long Island Line proper.

ALEXANDRIAN

Alex Sanders was another figure hanging around in the early 1960s. He had contact with the Crowthers seeking initiation to the Sheffield Coven and Gardner. Sanders claimed, somewhat dubiously, to have been initiated into the Craft by his Welsh grandmother and, alternatively, a Scottish witch who called herself Medea. He was likely initiated in Gardner's lineage by Pat Kopinski, an initiate from the Crowthers' coven. Sanders gained access to the Gardnerian Book of Shadows through this contact or elsewhere and ran a coven based in Manchester. In the early to mid-1960s, Sanders initiated hundreds of people into the Craft.

There was much controversy ostensibly surrounding Sander's lineage, and his downlines were held suspect by those legitimately downline from Gardner and his high priestesses. Alex Sanders was bisexual and ultimately split with Maxine over his relationship with a male witch. Undoubtedly, homophobia played a significant role in the Gardnerians' animosity toward him.

The lineage tracing itself back to Sanders is termed 'Alexandrian.' Much of the animosity between these two has lessened over the years, and the lines are often collectively referred to as 'Alex/Gard.'

GARDNER AND MODERN DRUIDRY (AN ASIDE)

Gardner's Wicca and modern Druidry draw inspiration from the early Celtic peoples of the Isles. It is not as widely known that Wicca and the largest Druid group in the world, the Order of Bards, Ovates, and Druids (OBOD), share more than an underlying inspirational folkloric framework. Gerald B. Gardner and OBOD founder Ross Nichols were colleagues and friends. They likely met through their interest in "naturism." They were in the circle that formed around the Atlantis Bookshop in London. Both were members of the Ancient Druid Order, a group similar to Freemasonry.

Gardner formulated his conception of modern Witchcraft while Nichols was launching OBOD. The two have many similarities as well as some substantial differences. They adopted the eightfold Celtic festival calendar of cross quarter days, equinoxes, and solstices. Their approaches also differed. While Gardner brought his strong interest in naturism into his ritual practice, Nichols kept his nudist philosophy to himself.

The two traditions that descend from these figures continue to speak to each other. One interesting area is Wicca's emphasis on the four elements, something Gardner borrowed from the Golden Dawn and Western esotericism, compared to Druidry's view of land, sea, and sky. Four vs. three may seem like a fundamental cosmological difference. But how do these seemingly divergent conceptions inform each other for a richer understanding?

First, we know that even in witchcraft, the four are five: air, fire, water, earth, and spirit. Spirit is the top point of the pentagram above the other four elements. As the center of the circle, it is ever present and everywhere.

Druidry, too, has the essentialized conceptions of fire and spirit. Fire is responsible for everything in creation—it creates and consumes. Additionally, there are the two Celtic fire festivals of Beltane and Samhain. There are four faces of the moon, not three: the waxing, full, waning, and hidden dark one. Spirit, too, is ever present in every living thing as the life force *nwyfre*.

If we think of our witchcraft and the faces of the goddess, Hestia, the fire mother is not represented in the wheel of the year. Instead, her altar is the home and hearth, and she is celebrated continuously throughout the year. Add this to the Druid triune cosmic iconography, and we have land, sea, sky, and hearth. This well-rounded and evocative conceptualization rests well in deepening our understanding of tradition.

Chapter VII
Homophobia in Early Modern Wicca

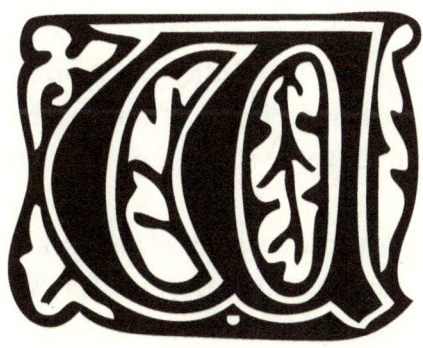

When I began practicing, heterosexism was still prevalent in Wiccan coven practice. My first coven had a High Priestess and High Priest; members were essentially broken into male-female working pairs. They practiced in the Alexandrian style, and initiations had to be by the opposite sex. Janet and Stewart Farrar's writing accepted homosexuals, noting same-sex covens existed, but to my mind, at least still implied homosexuals should work as heterosexuals in the circle. This mindset was still far better than the prevailing attitudes of many Wiccan covens in the three previous decades.

The concept of polarity was an important tenant of nineteenth-century occultism. Despite the notable exception of the divine androgyne depicted in the work of the Symbolists, this notion translated often into a binary symbolic relationship between male and female. In turn, this engendered an entrenched heterosexism and outright homophobia that continued well into the twentieth-century. Many occult theorists put homosexuals in the same category as drug users and child molesters. There is, of course, the example referenced in this book's title. In mid-twentieth-century Britain and America, these views were not out of step with those of the larger society.

Not surprisingly, for a man of his age and time, Gerald Gardner was virulently homophobic and held negative views about gay men and lesbians. He also borrowed generously from ceremonial magic, and their views on male/female polarity would have reinforced his own. He stated emphatically on several occasions that homosexuality was antithetical with witchcraft and that gay men or lesbians couldn't be witches. Upon learning that a man interested in joining his Brickett Wood Coven was gay, Gardner angrily declared: "There are no homosexual witches, and it is not possible to be a homosexual and a witch."[1]

For Gardner, homosexuality was "a disgusting perversion and a flagrant transgression of natural law, negating the life force and the fertility aspect represented by the God and Goddess." Valiente describes how she was told that homosexuality "was abhorrent to the Goddess, and her curse would fall upon people of the same sex who tried to work together."[2] She initially took this view herself, but eventually she concluded the Goddess would not exclude anyone from her love and worship.

Early adherents viewed Wicca as essentially a fertility cult and thus primarily heterosexual by definition. This echoed a general sentiment held by many occultists that only a male and female pairing could raise magical power during sexual workings. Regretedly, they adopted the prevailing occult view that power could only be raised through the interaction of male and female. The Great Rite was Wicca's heart, and heterosexuality was paramount.

Any attempt at working same sex magick was thus infertile and impotent. Tanya Luhrmann, in *Persuasions of the Witch's Craft,* cites an incedence that occured in the pages of the occult journal *Acquarian Arrow*. In 1978, a member of an occult group had mentioned at a gathering that she would consider working with homosexuals. The Arrow published a rejoinder from other members of the group stating unequivocally that no "genuinely contacted fraternity" could "coutenance working with secual deviants of any sorts." A member of the group in question told Luhrmann "... you can't work magic with a homosexual. Homosexuals just can't create a current."[3] This attitude has also persisted within Wicca for far too long.

Things were a little different on the other side of the pond. American practice had a more, though certainly not universal, progressive bent. Feminists brought their own perspective in contrast to the chauvinism of Gardner's practice. During the early days, women were told they "could not be a witch alone."[4] In other words, a male witch was always necessary—an ironic position for a religion that elevated the goddess. By the late 60s and early 70s, influenced by American witches, a growing progressive environmentalist philosophy took root in the Craft. Many Wiccans were also involved in the nuclear disarmament movement. Despite these influences of progressive politics, most Wiccans, especially in England, remained opposed to homosexuality and, in many cases, abortion and inter-racial practice.

John Scone, editor of the pagan periodical *The Wiccan*, was particularly persistent in his attacks on homosexuality (among other things). He espoused the view that single men should be required to prove their "heterosexual attainment" before being accepted into a coven. He gave Martello the derogatory nickname "Marshmallow."[5]

Eddie Buczynski sought initiation amidst this environment where many Wiccans felt homosexuals could not be real witches. At least one coven denied him initiation due to his homosexuality. And his refusal of Lady Gwen Thompson's sexual advances likely led to his expulsion from her New Haven Celtic Coven. This environment speaks to just how radical Eddie's founding of the Minoan tradition was.

In 1978, Arthur Evans published *Witchcraft and the Gay Counterculture,* which strongly impacted the development of the Radical Fairies, a movement of queer eclectic, expressive neo-pagan spirituality. Scott Cunningham often wrote of feeling excluded from traditional practice and initiatory Wiccan lineages due to his sexuality. This led him to develop a primarily solitary practice. His 1988 book *Wicca: A Guide for the Solitary Practitioner* was a watershed moment in American practice. When feminist witch Starhawk published her revised edition of *A Spiral Dance* in 1989, it was still radical for her to assert that thinking of the universal energy represented by the God and Goddess as purely male/female was inappropriate.

I wish I could write that these attitudes within Gardnerian practice are a thing of the past. Unfortunately, even as recently as a few years ago, the tension between rigid gender polarity encoded in practice and twenty-first-century attitudes clashed again. In 2022, forty-seven Gardnerian elders anonymously issued "A Declaration of the Traditional Gardnerian Wica." In this document, they made their position very clear:

> It is...necessary to practice biological female to biological male and vice versa, within a Traditional Gardnerian circle. We acknowledge that anything other than this is not Traditional Gardnerian practice, and will lead to different currents of power and different mysteries.[6]

Though this is certainly not the attitude of *all* Gardnerian and Alexandrian elders, or perhaps even a majority of them, it demonstrates dramatically that the issue persists.

ANTI-GERMAN SENTIMENT

Due to the first and second world wars, most Britains had a strong prejudice against anything German through at least the Fifties. King George V founded the House of Windsor in 1917, changing the family's surname from the Germanic Saxe-Coburg-Gotha. Anti-German sentiment during WWI also meant that the German Shepherd breed became Alsatian in Britain. Despite founding a controversial new spiritual tradition, Gerald Gardner was very much a person of his times. His anti-German sentiment ran deep and cast a shadow over his formation of Wicca. He seems to have ignored anything Anglo-Saxon, with its German roots. Like James Fraser before him, he went to great lengths to cast everything with a gloss of British Celtic inspiration.

One could ask why Gardner chose the Theban magical alphabet for his witch's runes rather than the Anglo-Saxon runes in his own backyard. Theban derives from Heinrich Cornelius Agrippa's *De Occulta Philosophia*, published in 1533. Central to Wiccan worship, his two principal deities are a strange amalgam. Cernunnos is a Celtic horned deity, while Aradia comes from Italian Strega no doubt lifted from of Charles Godfrey Leland's famous book *Aradia, Or the Gospel of the Witches.*

Gardner's most famous high priestess Doreen Valiente observes:

> It seems a pity that Hitler and his thugs should be able to prevent the study and appreciation of runic lore, which, after all, is part of our heritage as descendants of the Anglo-Saxon race.[7]

This could be correctly said of much of Wicca's intentional blindness to all things Anglo-Saxon.

Modern practitioners of Asatru, Norse heathenism, must be vigilant against its cooption of their faith by racists and neo-Nazis. Wiccans also need to recognize where the personages we honor display uncomfortable tendencies toward similar philosophies. An example is Valilente's troubling connections to British neo-fascist organizations.

After reading a pamphlet, she joined the National Front in 1973. She even designed the organization's flag. She also displayed interest in the Northern League and the Nazi-rooted Thule Society. Valiente appears to have mixed views on race. She espoused a belief that all races were important in their own right. However, she also feared the mixing of races could lead to a diminution of each race's uniqueness. It is interesting to note that in her letter parting ways with the National Front, she highlighted the exception to the NF's chairman's, John Hutchyns Tyndall. His positions espoused in the *Spearhead* were opposed to women's rights, sex education, and homosexual liberation. In his writings and speeches, Tyndall railed against the "gay plague," the mixing of races, and the "Jewish conspiracy." These views did not come later in his life. In 1960, when the National Labour Party merged with the White Defense League to form the British National Party, Tyndall was one of the new group's founding members.[8]

Though these views would have been readily apparent in the early 70s when Valiente joined the NF. Despite this, her resignation makes no mention of these abhorrent views, instead noting she had "every respect" for Tyndall's "sincerity and integrity."[9] Instead, her letter suggests her bridge too far were Tyndell's stances against contraception and abortion rights, but not against white supremacy. Given the mythology that has developed around British witches raising a cone of power against a Nazi invasion, it's inconceivable that such a prominent figure as Valiente would associate herself, even briefly, with outspoken neo-fascists.

WARLOCK, WHAT'S IN A NAME?

Though the vast majority of individuals accused of witchcraft were female, the term witch is unisex and has historically denoted both women and men. This was true throughout Europe, England, and the American colonies. The only place that differed was Scotland, where "warlock," or "wizard" in the case of the social elite, was frequently used to denote male witches. In the decades post-Gardner, a pejorative meaning has become widespread within the Wiccan and witchcraft communities that the word denotes one who breaks their oath to the coven. Thus, the word has a negative connotation among many modern pagans. In fact, "warlock" refers to one who had broken their covenant with the church in favor of a more abiding covenant. Thus, the warlock denied the church in favor of his allegiance with the Devil for sixteenth and seventeenth-century Scottish witch prosecutors. This negative, historically unfounded meaning of the word as an oath breaker and traitor to one's coven continues to permeate modern witchcraft communities.

Warlock appears frequently in Scottish literature, often referring to a male witch or wizard. This is especially true of the poems of Robert Burns, who frequently references the word. Sir Walter Scott references a "Warlock hoar," meaning old warlock, in his retelling of the tale of Thomas the Rhymer. It is an odd word whose origins are somewhat mysterious and debated. The most common etymology in the *Oxford English Dictionary* is that the word derives from the Old English wærloga, meaning "oath breaker." Scots witch persecutors then adopted it as denoting a male witch who had made a pact with Auld Hornie, Clootie, e.g., the Devil. In Old English religious poetry the term commonly referred to "one who has broken faith with God" in favor of an alternate allegiance with the Devil.

The term may have come to Scotland from Scandinavia, where the Norse were themselves influenced through interactions with other cultures during the Viking Era. Indeed, the Nordic influence on Scottish culture and magic is strong. Witchcraft historian Michael Howard provides an alternate etymological reference that links warlock to the Old Norse *varð-lokkur*, "one who calls spirits," Icelandic *varolak*, or as Howard defines it, "one that enclosed something and locks it in."[10] There is a Scottish word, "warlocke," meaning to secure a horse, and the English expression "warricking and warlocking" relating to binding either physically or magically. Both these would seem to support the derivation of warlock as connected to the notion of binding.

The negative notion that a warlock is a person who has broken their oath with the coven is still tightly clung to by many in the witchcraft communities. The topic has caused many a flame war in online forums. I use the term warlock often when describing myself. In no small part, this is a reflection of my connection to my family's Scottish heritage. A few recently have also chosen to, at times, employ the term relative to themselves and their practice. Storm Faerywolf has talked about reclaiming the word as a positive alternative to refer to male witches.[11] The counterargument has often been to question why one would want to use such a traditionally negative term. Well, it wasn't too long ago that the word "witch" was universally negative. The 80s and early 90s saw the powerful, political reclamation of the adjective "queer."

Chapter VIII
In Search of... British Origins

Historian Ronald Hutton calls Wicca the only "truly British religion."[1] Wicca, as we know it today, arose in the 1940s. Its early proponents claimed that it built on the folk survival of pre-Christian religious practices of the British Isles. Before one embarks on a discussion of modern witchcraft, it is prudent to have an understanding of who the ancient Britains actually were.

Near where I'm writing, I have a copy of Oxford University's *Illustrated History of Great Britain*, first published in 1984 and considered by many to be the definitive single stop for British history. The first chapter starts out with the Claudius-led Roman invasion of 43AD. A few sentences do allude to pre-Roman British history, but only in relation to what the Roman legions encountered upon arrival. The 'original' peoples of the British Isles exist only as Pictish shadows of the pre-Roman period... and even then, only really through Queen Boudica and her ruthless barbarian resistance.[2]

For centuries, historians have perpetuated a particular narrative of British history. Everything that is British begins with the Roman conquest—the invaders and colonizers bringing Hellenic civilization to the far backwater of Europe. In no small part, this view of the Roman Empire helped to shore up the predestined righteousness of its modern equivalent, the British Empire, with its civilizing paternal colonialism. This version of history ignores something like ninety-eight percent of the history of the Isles. History may be prologue, but our understanding of history is always, to some degree, a contemporary fiction.

In this longstanding mythology of Britain, the full historical arc begins with the earliest peoples who were pushed aside by the western migration of the Celts. Then came the Romans, and when they pulled out their military support in the early fifth century, they turned the lights out on their way off the islands, and BOOM, the Dark Ages descended. Then came along some German tribesmen from the continent invading what is now eastern England—historians called them Anglo-Saxon. The Celts, failing to push out the new aggressors, were themselves pushed farther to the west to Wales and Ireland. Then came along the Viking raiders, the Danelaw, and finally, the definitive conquest by the Normans in 1066.

The only problem is that very little of this long-standing narrative is accurate. Historians have had a strong tendency to view cultural shifts from the prism with which they are most familiar, from their own immediate historical period of aggression, invasion, conquest, colonization, genocide, and replacement. The problem is with the advent of genetics and other more precise methods of scientific analysis, we realize much of this long-held narrative is simply not consistent with the evidence now at hand. Archeologist Francis Pryor points out that "the archeological record can provide no convincing evidence for mass migration into Britain prior to the Roman conquest."[3]

As the ice of the last Ice Age receded northward, humans moved into new territory. They moved into Britain as long ago as 12,600 BCE while the Scottish Highlands were still covered in glaciers.[4] The oldest intact human skeleton found in Britain was discovered in 1903 in Somerset. "Cheddar Man," as he is now known, was a Mesolithic hunter-gatherer. Modern genetic markers show he was likely dark-skinned and blue-eyed. The mitochondrial DNA handed down the maternal line of the British (and British expats) is the same as that of the earliest permanent settlers of the Isles during the Cro-Magnon period. These first peoples were quickly cut off from Europe by the final severing of the land bridge and the triumph of the North Sea in about 5,900 BCE. The British coastline today remains remarkably similar to that of six thousand years ago. After Britain was cut off from the continent, farming developed very independently of the rest of Europe. While much of Europe was agrarian, evidence at Flag Fen and the Dartmoor Reaves shows the field systems of early Britain were primarily focused on containment and movement of livestock.[5]

Much evidence of stone structures survives from the Neolithic. Long barrows began to be constructed around 3500 BCE. The Stones of Stennes on Orkney are the oldest stone circle in Northern Europe, built around 5400 BCE. In Ireland, the passage tombs of Newgrange and Knowth were first built around five thousand years ago. The chambered cairn Maes Howe also on Orkney, was constructed around 2800 BCE; the Orkney village of Skara Brae was built between 3180 to 2000 BCE; the Ring of Brodgar 2,500-2000 BCE. The area in Salisbury, now occupied by Stonehenge, began to be used at least seven thousand years ago. Archeologists believe the ditch was constructed in 3100 BCE. The smaller blue stone circle was erected in 2600 BCE. The sarsens of iconic Stonehenge today were erected around 2000 BCE.

The Celts were not a band of migrant travelers from Central Europe that slowly spread across the continent in a drive westward until they finally made it to Britain and Ireland. Instead, archeologists are now drawing a picture of a spread of art and expression, of culture and style that did finally cross the channel and take hold in Britain. The "Celts" occupied the same areas and often the same houses as those they allegedly replaced.[6] The insular peoples of the islands then put their own spin on the style, making it distinctly British. It's as if historians found it difficult to give credit to the "original" peoples with any advances in technology. Farming, they argued, came in with migrants from the more advanced continent. The complex agrarian divisions discovered at Flag Fen over the last several decades have demonstrated that island dwellers developed their own unique approach to mixed crop and livestock farming quite distinct from elsewhere in Europe.[7]

Then, as the story continues, came the Romans to civilize the barbarians. The landscape they found was one of small, orderly farms and livestock divisions. Society seems to have been organized around the family and then, likely secondarily, larger tribal units started to form with a learned or spiritual class of Druids.

In his biography of his uncle Gnaeus Julius Agricola who served as governor of Britain 77–83 CE, Tacitus writes of the attraction of Roman amenities:

> Step by step they were led to things which dispose to vice, the lounge, the bath, the elegant banquet. All this in their ignorance, they called civilization,

when it was but a part of their servitude.[8]

When the Roman legions left less than four centuries later, they did not take all these "civilizing" structures and institutions with them. Instead, there remained an indigenous elite that styled themselves after their Roman counterparts. The Romans left spoken or vernacular Latin as a common language across the previous Roman occupied territories. The early Christian Church still had footholds. The Dark Ages really weren't all that dark.

In the wake of the Roman departure, we've been taught that the Anglo-Saxons, in mass or as a small cohort of powerful warrior elites, invaded during the early medieval period, exploiting the vacuum left behind. From the Arthurian tales, we know that he heroically attempted to fight off this new incursion. The venerable Bede calls this the *advents Saxonum* and places it in 450 CE. Bernard Cornwell writes of these adventures evocatively in his trilogy of Arthurian novels, and it is certainly powerful reading. Unfortunately, we find little contemporary archeological evidence for such violent and chaotic disruption.

What we know of those who would later be labeled Anglo-Saxon was deduced from grave goods, burial customs, and material culture characterized by particular styles of pottery and adornment. Burials with material culture that historians classed as Saxon were, therefore, those of Saxon interlopers. Part of this was based on the very limited historical textual material, most written long after the period which they discussed, their authors plagued with problematic agendas. What this interpretation ignored was that these "new" peoples who allegedly wiped out the previous peoples occupied the same spaces and continued much the same way of life as those before them. This is not at all characteristic of genocide and replacement. Francis Pryor sums it up:

> It is probably fair to say that serious scholars who believe in large-scale Anglo-Saxon mass migrations are now in the minority. Most people, myself included, accept that there was a certain amount of movement in and out of Britain, just as there was in the Iron Age and the Roman period. We might well discover one day that certain Anglo-Saxon cemeteries in, say, East Yorkshire, contain the bodies of immigrant populations. I do not believe, however, that such discoveries will invalidate the consensus that the changes attributed to the arrival of Anglo-Saxon were usually caused by people changing their minds, rather than their places of residence.[9]

With modern genetics and dental isotope analysis, we now know that though the Isles always had visitors and continental immigrants, there is simply no evidence for either mass replacement theory. Instead, there appears to have been a general movement of individuals over a long period of time. A recent genetic and archeological study published in *Nature* looked at the impact of Anglo-Saxon migration on the English gene pool. The authors found little to no evidence of either a distinct mass migration event as described by Bede or the takeover by a small group of powerful elites. In contrast to the previous hypothesis, they concluded that the evidence supported "a complex, regionally contingent migration with partial integration that was probably dependent on specific families and their individual members."[10]

Research on the graves contained in a cemetery at Oakington from the Anglo-Saxon period shows clusters of culturally Anglo-Saxon individuals who are genetically mixed. This is strong evidence for intermingling and intermarriage between immigrants and the existing population. It is interesting to note the wealthiest individual whose grave was examined was found to be of genetically British ancestry.[11] Analysis of teeth in another Anglian cemetery in West Heslerton showed only four individuals with Scandinavian backgrounds. Surprisingly, all were female, one being a child, and none were "high status" burials.[12] Classing a dead person's culture or ethnicity simply based on the context of objects is extremely reductive and proves problematic. Think of a future archeologist analyzing a twenty-first century Chinese grave where the person was buried in Levis, and the surrounding archeological strata contained glass Coke bottles. The logic that has given us a preponderance of Anglo-Saxon invaders would interpret the grave occupant as an American invader. One can quickly see the circular nature and fallibility of this approach.

The invasion and replacement hypothesis is not supported by the archeological investigations of the land. We know from history that invasion and genocide leave their distinct imprints, but we see no such evidence in Britain. What we do see, however, is a continuity of farming practices and land boundaries. The two remain unchanged. In an April 2023 paper published in *PLOS Genetics*, the authors found "regional continuity between the Late Iron Age and the early medieval periods, but likely with complex patterns of migration."[13] Overall, their analysis found fine-scale relatedness between the Scottish of the Iron Age and the modern dwellers of the United Kingdom. This is not what would be expected with an invasion, even with a small group of elites taking control.

The continuance of land boundaries across generations speaks to a transference through generational inheritance. The easiest explanation is usually the best. The consistency of traditional boundaries and agricultural styles over time most likely means that it was the same peoples maintaining the land

and doing the farming/livestock management. As Pryor argues, what we see in the transition of material culture from the Celtic to the Anglo-Saxon in the east of the British Isles reflects a process of "acculturation not migration."[14] The eastern areas of the British Isles that show a shift in material culture toward the Anglo-Saxon were also those areas that had heavy trade connections across the North Sea with the Teutonic regions of Northern Europe. The widespread adoption of Anglo-Saxon goods may very likely reflect availability rather than dominance.

Then, of course, in 793, Viking raiders showed up at the monastery on Lindisfarne and quickly realized what easy pickings were to be found on the British coast. This led to an injection of Norse DNA into the mix with longer-term settlements and the temporary rule of the Dane law.

Even the defining Norman conquest of 1066 was less conquest and more military solution to a highly politicized dispute over succession—most of it of the previous King Edward's own making, promising the crown to multiple parties.

The historic boundaries of the three kingdoms—England, Wales, and Scotland—are really about power and land. It reflects intracountry mistreatment between regions. The notion of distinct "peoples" within the British Isles is a modern concept with its roots firmly planted in Victorian notions of racial purity rather than actual historical divisions.[15] These "peoples" were not distinct, and the boundaries between them blurred. There would have been much crossover between the Anglo-Saxon, Celtic, and Pictish peoples of the Isles through nearness, trade, and intermarriage. We have but to look at the language. For a long period, the peoples of Britain were multilingual to varying degrees, speaking Britain Celtic, late-spoken Latin, and Old English.[16] While modern English reflects its Anglo-Saxon roots, the sentence structure is quite distinct from modern German. What we see in today's English is a preponderance of Anglo-Saxon words with a sentence structure from Celtic Gaelic. If we look at modern English, seventy percent of the words come from Latin, half via Roman Latin and half from France. The other thirty percent derive from German and Scandinavian languages the roots of Old English. Interestingly, though, Old English accounts for the vast majority of words used in the daily spoken English of today.

So, how does it aid in our understanding of Wicca? What does this quick recap of twelve-plus-thousand years of British history have to do with witchcraft and our practice in particular? Well, Gardner's view of B, in British Traditional Witchcraft, was not particularly well-rounded. The now-debunked history would have formed the basis of his understanding. Additionally, and to me critically, like most practitioners of his day, he had a strong prejudice against all things German. Due to this, in his development of Wicca, he ignored all Anglo-Saxon (read Germanic) influences in favor of an at times strained reliance on Celtic references. These editorial impulses can be seen in Gardner's choice of the Theban alphabet, instead of the Northumbrian or "Anglo-Saxon" runes.

The other babies thrown out with that bathwater include the Norse/Scandinavian influence, which is particularly pronounced in Shetland, Orkney, and the Western Isles. This compounds Gardner's ignoring all things Saxon, which in turn brings their own Germanic influence to complement other Scandinavian reference points. Importantly, this intentional myopathy completely ignores the potent queerness of Scandinavian *seiðr*!

Chapter VIII
The Occult Empire

Following the European "rediscovery" of the Americas in 1492, the English showed little interest in the new territories. This allowed the Spanish, Portuguese, and French to get a head start. The Dutch soon followed them. During the late sixteenth-century English-Spanish religious wars, English-authorized privateers harried Spanish vessels in the Caribbean. Despite this, Queen Elizabeth showed comparatively little interest in the new territories. This changed when the queen's advisor, John Dee, strongly encouraged her to move beyond exploration and establish colonies in English-claimed North America.

John Dee was more than a trusted royal advisor. He was also a spy, astrologer, and free-thinking occultist. He had the view to establish an occult empire in the new lands. Of course, this is problematic because it ignores the indigenous people who already occupied the land. The queen turned to another trusted advisor, Walter Raleigh, and tasked him with establishing a permanent British presence in the New World. Raleigh also had his personal objectives, not the least of which was making himself richer. He had heard tales of large quantities of gold being brought back by the Spanish and had a mind to find the fabled El Dorado.

Under Raleigh's direction, the first British settlement was established in 1584 on Roanoke Island in what is today Virginia. The colony was not well supported and did not fare well. The colonists had vanished by the time an expedition finally returned to Roanoke in 1590. They left a single word carved into a tree, CROATAN. The missing colonists have come to be known as the lost colony. They had previously made an emergency plan that if they had to abandon the colony, they would leave behind a message about where they went. Croatan was a local Native American group friendly to the settlers. It makes sense they would decamp to their neighbor's support when their situation became dire. They were not so much lost as relocated.

Raleigh launched several missions to find the lost colonists. These were either delayed due to weather or distraction or diverted to support Raleigh's other interests in gold and sassafras. It also was in Raleigh's interest if the colonists remained lost and not found dead. The possibility of a British presence in North America bolstered their territorial claims. The colonists most probably found a safe harbor among one of the friendly tribes in the area. After several years, they would have been unlikely to return with their rescuers. As with many Europeans who had remained with indigenous communities for some time, they likely would have resisted attempts at "rescue," choosing to stay with their new society.

Raleigh and Dee fell out of favor with the ascension of James I to the English throne upon the death of Elizabeth. Raleigh was ultimately executed as a traitor, and Dee died in poverty. Their occult empire was not to be. That does not mean that occultism and witchcraft were not present in the colonies from an early time. In the early eighteenth century, Masons could be found in the colonies before the establishment of the Grant Lodge in London. Many of these early Masons were associated with lodges chartered by the Grand Lodge of Ireland and not Britain. Many of the founding fathers were Masons—Washington being the most famous. However, early colonial Masonry was stratified into two distinct groups. English Masonry connected to the Grand Lodge of London was the purview of the wealthy elite, while "irregular" lodges were home to free-thinkers and the common folk.

Puritans seeking a new Eden and adventurers searching for the fabled City of Gold were not the only immigrants to this new Western land. Among their number were also free-thinkers, English dissenters such as the Levellers and Ranters, as well as those not coming by choice—indentured servants and the enslaved. Many came to this new land with dreams of paradise. Some even came to escape Europe and disappear into the wilderness. While the new settlers were attempting to build a utopia in small patches of Englishness—villages with their timber-frame houses—they were surrounded by the wild. They saw the woods and forests of North America as the terrifying domain of the Devil. Most indigenous peoples were aligned with the French in the numerous wars that marked the first century and a half of occupation. The constant threat of attack on the frontiers of their territory did not help matters.

The occupiers brought witchcraft with them as well. Like much of Europe at the time, England and Scotland under James I/VI were obsessed with witchcraft and finding witches. The Witchcraft Act of 1604 transferred jurisdiction over witchcraft trials from the church to civil courts. The new law eventually made its way to the English colonies. Alise Young was tried, convicted, and executed for witchcraft on 26 May 1647 in Hartford, Connecticut. Between then and 1663, fifteen individuals were executed in New England, most of which were in Connecticut. The Massachusetts legislature, which served as the ultimate appellate court, was resistant to witch trial convictions before 1692. This all changed in January of that year when Rev. Paris's daughter became afflicted by inexplicable symptoms. Several other Salem children were similarly taken ill. By the end of February, the first warrants were issued. A well-known witch panic ensued, resulting in nineteen executions, one death by pressing, and four dying in jail. The last death associated with the hysteria came in March 1693 when Lydia Dustin died in jail, having been unable to come up with her jail fees.

The consensus is that the Salem witch trials had nothing to do with actual witchcraft. Instead, diverse causes and motivations have been proposed over the years: greed, land disputes, and revenge. The episode has become isolated as an aberration resulting from mass hysteria, ergot poisoning, or mass panic. Fear of witchcraft was commonplace throughout the British colonies. Concern over witches' dark influence had peaked under James I, and that social and judicial concern was soon brought to the colonies. Witches and the power of the Devil could be anywhere—danger surrounded on all fronts. Far from being a new Eden, the dark forests were the home of the Devil and his servants. A fear of the indigenous peoples comingled with terror of the supernatural.

The practice of magic was also commonplace in the form of countermeasures against witches and their evil influences. We can see this in an early episode of the Salem hysteria of 1692. After Reverend Paris's daughter first became afflicted with symptoms, Mary Sibley knew how to determine if witchcraft was indeed the cause. She suggested the creation of a 'witch cake.' This particular confection was a mixture of rye flour and some of the afflicted girl's urine. This then was fed to the family dog. The dog dying or becoming ill, was a certain indication witchcraft was present. The result proved inconclusive. The fact that she knew the recipe for such a cake shows that folklore of countermagic was pervasive. Further evidence of the commonness of such protective measures may be found in apotropaic warding marks found in old houses throughout Britain and its colonies. These so-called 'witch marks,' commonly daisy wheels and crosses, were meant to keep witches and their malign influence away from the home.

The English colonies were an uneasy place for many reasons. The Puritans attempted to create a theocratic utopia in the Massachusetts Bay Colony. After the first wave of the Great Puritan Migration, others began to make the crossing in search of freedom to practice their beliefs. These did not always fit well with the Puritan's religious views. The Protestant Reformation hit England hard. The Pope's denial of Henry VIII's divorce from Catherine of Aragon precipitated a permanent break with Rome. Decades of upheaval and religious fighting followed. The dissolution of the monasteries and establishment of the Church of England was a tumultuous time for the religious life of the Isles. The religious conflict between Catholics and Protestants became even bloodier under his successors, Edward and Mary.

Just as things began to settle under Elizabeth, the last Tudor monarch, and the early Stuarts, the War of the Three Kingdoms broke out in 1639. More uncertainty followed with the conclusion of the Second Civil War in 1648 and the execution of Charles I in early 1649. The establishment of the Commonwealth of England would have also destabilized the English colonies. Regicide of a king is no small matter, especially when many still held the belief, emphasized by Henry VIII, that the will of God crowned the king.

By the seventeenth century, the British Isles were rife with alternative religious views. In addition to the Puritans and Quakers, small groups of dissenters or separatists abounded. These included the Diggers, Fifth Monarchists, Grindletonians,

Levellers, Mugggletonians, and Ranters. Many who traveled across the Atlantic held beliefs heretical to the Puritan ideal. The situation was made worse in 1650 when Parliament passed an act of toleration toward Protestants. Several of these groups had fringe ideologies even by today's standards. The Ranters believed in absolute predestination; one's salvation was set long before they were born, and nothing could change that. Given that, they lived lives of drinking, swearing, and sexual freedom. The Fifth Monarchists believed that the death of Charles I presaged the immediate return of the Holy King, the Messiah.

The Antinomian, or Free Grace controversy erupted in Boston in 1636. This unrest between two political and religious factions lasted two years. The debate pitted religious leaders against each other and centered on two alternate views of divine grace. Puritan preacher John Cotton and his followers Anne Hutchinson, her brother-in-law Reverand John Wainwright, and Henry Vane the Younger, son of a former privy councilor to Charles I, disrupted the Puritan theocracy.

The controversy ended in a series of civil and religious trials. All the major players were disenfranchised and banished. In the long run, the sentences only seriously impacted the outspoken Hutchinson. She and a group of followers made their way on foot to Quaker, Rhode Island. Eventually, she settled in the more tolerant Dutch colony of New Netherland. Unfortunately, she was killed in an Indian attack in 1643. Wainwright's banishment was removed in 1644, and he was vindicated in 1654. He returned to England in 1655 and later crossed back in 1662 to become pastor of the church in Salisbury, Massachusetts, until his death. Cotton continued as a minister in Boston until his death in 1652. Vane returned to England and was Treasurer of the Royal Navy within two years.

Quakerism was on the rise in the second half of the

seventeenth century. This was the root of much anxiety across New England, but particularly on the coast of New Hampshire where the Old Planters (Anglicans) were being outnumbered by Puritans moving north from Boston. The religious movement was looked on with distrust from multiple directions. Known today for their pacifism, at the time beliefs led to quite contrary actions. Many Quakers joined with the Fifth Monarchists and Baptists in an attempted revolt following the restoration of Charles II in 1661. The leaders of the Massachusetts Bay Colony resisted the Act of 1650. They saw the Quakers's way of worship as a direct threat to their authority and the stability of their City on a Hill. In addition, many believed that Quakers practiced sorcery and witchcraft based on their strange trances, which gave them their name, and their ability to attract numerous followers. Despite the English law of toleration, the Massachusetts General Court ordered the death penalty for any banished Quaker who returned to the colony. Four were executed under this decree between 1656 and 1661 when it was softened to the Cart and Whip Act.[1]

This civil and social unrest would have only been compounded by two shiploads of Scottish POWs sent over in the early 1650s after the Battle of Dunbar and the Battle of Worcester. They were sold into indentured servitude, many to the iron works at Saugus and the rest to individuals. Two of my ancestors were among them: Duncan Stewart, arriving in 1650 on the *Unity*, and Daniel Davison, likely coming in 1652 on the *John & Sarah*. These Scottish Covenanters certainly did not hold to the Puritan religious beliefs and were not inclined to fit with the strict social structures. Numbers vary, but as many as 400 Scottish prisoners were transported. This was the most significant immigration of Scots until the nineteenth century. This influx must have proved very disruptive to the fledgling colonies.

In his detailed examination of witchcraft and supernatural disruption in early New England, *The Devil of Great Island*, Emerson Baker discusses another change that would have compounded the above. We can see the influence of the *wetiko*, a Native American concept of a selfishness virus which I will discuss in more detail later on, in the European drive for colonization and collateral genocide of indigenous peoples. During this time, there was also a drastic shift in the social compact that had persisted in small English villages for millennia.

Small groups of subsistence farmers had long cared for neighbors who had fallen on hard times. Neighbor looked after neighbor. In the seventeenth century, this had begun to change; neighbors were not always in a position to lend aid to those in need. This transformation would have been more pronounced in New England, where commodities were scarce. Shortage and other cofactors were producing a shift toward individualism and the beginnings of modern capitalism. Baker notes these changes likely also produced feelings of anger on the part of the one asking and guilt for the person not being able to assist. The *wetiko* virus was mutating and warping the longstanding social compact that bound small village life.[2]

Those who perished in 1692 may have been the last to be legally executed in North America. However, they were not the last to die due to fear of witches. Owen Davies has found that more people died accused of witchcraft after 1692 than before.[3] The Catholic missionaries harshly challenged indigenous practices in Spanish-controlled territories. They all too often saw indigenous practices as Satanic and diabolic. The forced importation of enslaved individuals brought a variety of African cultures and spiritual practices to North America. Later, German and Eastern European immigrants brought their own folk beliefs and traditional practices.

By the second half of the eighteenth century, the United States was a gumbo of spiritual and folk traditions, the particular recipe varying by region. So-called "doctors" and spiritual healers abounded. The practitioners cut across race, ethnicity, and cultural background. In the 1880 census, sixteen men listed their profession as "root doctor." Of these, ten identified as white and six as Black. Among them were a Prussian and a Norwegian.[4]

There was much cross-dialogue among traditions. Often, individuals needing magical assistance would seek help from those of other races. There was often a perception that another culture's folk wisdom was more potent. Magical practitioners, faith healers, and fortune tellers reflected a diverse cultural makeup. A study covering 1644 to 1850 showed that almost half were African American, Native American, or of mixed background.[5] The alternative spiritual landscape of nineteenth-century America was nothing if not diverse.

Historian Owen Davies sums it up like this:

> There seems to have been a considerable degree of interethnic consultation with African Americans consulting European hex doctors, and whites seeking out black root and conjure doctors. Irish and British visited German practitioners and vice versa. In fact, witch doctors played a crucial role in transmitting magical ideas and practices from one cultural group to another.[6]

By the dawn of the twentieth century, America was a rich tapestry of folk practices, spiritual traditions, and magical techniques.

Fear of witchcraft also persisted, especially in recently-arrived immigrant communities. In a place now called Hex Hollow, Pennsylvania, a sensational murder took place. In 1928, one man, John Blymire, and two young men visited the house of locally renowned hex doctor Nelson Rehmeyer. Blymire was convinced by another local magical practitioner, Nellie Nap, aka Emma Knopp, that Rehmeyer had placed a curse on one of them. Their mission was to find his magic book, *The Long Lost Friend*, and cut a lock of his hair to break the curse. Instead, they ended up perpetrating a gruesome murder that made national headlines. They struck and bound the pow-wow doctor and then attempted to cover their actions by setting fire to his house. Ultimately, neither the house nor Rehmeyer burned. The three assailants were convicted of murder and sentenced to life.

Fast forward a few decades, and British expatriate Raymond Buckland returns in 1963 to the land of his birth and is initiated into Wicca by Gardner's High Priestess Monique Wilson. He and his wife, Rosemary, introduce the Gardnerian lineage of the Craft to North America. He establishes a coven on Long Island, and we're off to the races. Witchcraft and other non-traditional spiritualities soon became part of the burgeoning countercultural landscape. Astrology and the tarot soon became commonplace. Witchcraft began to intersect with feminism and ecological activism. American writers emerged in Barbara Walker, Marion Weinstein, Selena Fox, and Starhawk. Leo Louis Martello blended his gay and witchcraft activism. In 1972, Herman and Eddie founded the Warlocke Shoppe in Brooklyn followed by the Magical Childe in Chelsea. Perhaps here, after the dawning of the twenty-first century, Dee's vision has borne its fruit.

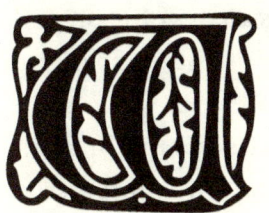

What does practicing a quintessentially British religion mean in post-colonial, post-modern America? Many residents in the United States are of British origin, and just as many are not. In many ways, however difficult it may seem at times, given some winds in our political climate, we live in unique and interesting times. From the outset, North America has been a mix of British, French, and Spanish control in, more often than not, contentious relationships with the indigenous peoples whose land they occupied. We have the wisdom and culture of those brought to these shores in chains and sold into slavery. Layer over these origins successive generations of immigrants, and we have this imperfect yet promising new world founded on the idealistic aspirations of the Enlightenment.

Today, we have access to an unprecedented amount of information. Often, it is not easy to discern where particular practices originate. It is always good practice to seek out the source and understand the cultural context from which a given practice, technique, or recipe originates. Give credit as credit is due. I feel strongly from my experience that it is important to immerse oneself in a singular practice or tradition when one approaches one's practice. It is not that one ignores others, but rather works to gain a deep respect for their own. One should learn from other practices, traditions, and cultural sources. Such knowledge can deepen one's own practice while acknowledging and respecting their source.

It is critical for us as practitioners of British traditional witchcraft to seek beyond its imperialist origins. This is why I have written at length on pre-Roman Britain. It is critical that we resist the parasitic influence in our own work. When I was at Hampshire College, there was a course developed by Jill Lewis called "Unruling Britania." We, too, must dismantle any residual colonialism in our practice. This is an ongoing process of awareness and acknowledgment. Our tradition's origins have gifted us a rich tapestry of evocative potential, while at the same time, their modern incarnation is also rooted in some dark prejudices. While we celebrate the latter, it is imperative we acknowledge the former.

Chapter IX
The Edwardian Tradition

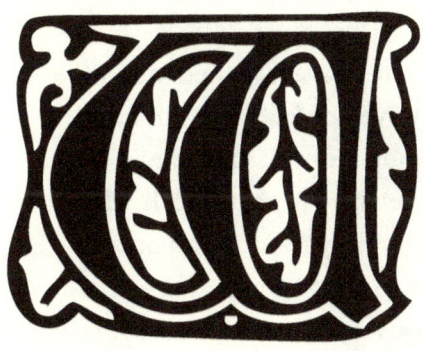

When I was a teenager, two New York shops formed a veritable spiritual lifeline: The Magickal Childe and Enchantments. I recall the first time I walked into the Childe. Herman Slater, known (likely of his own making) as "Horrible Herman," may have been intimidating from his perch at the shop entrance, but his influence was immense. The two catalogs were our coven's source for all things witchy. It would be only later that I would learn of the queerness of all involved.

Herman Slater opened his first store in Brooklyn, the Warlock Shop, with his partner Eddie Buczynski. The shop moved to Chelsea in the 70s under the now-infamous name Magickal Childe. Lady Rhea, mother of the Minoan Sisterhood, and Carol Bulzone worked at the Childe and ventured out to open Enchantments in 1982. Except for what I picked up during UK trips, all my books and magical supplies during those first few years of exploration came from the Childe or Enchantments' catalogs. One of our two coven swords we use today came from the Childe during that time. I loved the oils I purchased from Enchantments. I wore Hykintos Lovers Oil often, and typing this evokes its evocative scent. Later, I would learn that these oils were blended by—and Hykintos invented by—Jeffrey Whitfield. I'm glad my life has come full circle, and Lady Rhea is now a friend.

Herman and Eddie created a space that was the epicenter of occultism during the 70s and 80s. The backroom of the Childe served as a space for Wiccan rituals and the New York OTO of the time. The two published the *Earth Religion News*. In his memoir, James Wasserman gives a good description of Slater:

> Herman himself seemed to have stepped out of the pages of an occult novel or a Hammer Film production. Bright as they come, Herman was the ultimate social butterfly. He had built the Magickal Childe into a legendary Manhattan occult emporium. He had contacts throughout the world in small publishing houses and among purveyors of esoteric goods, who support his efforts, despite the fact that he was never overly concerned with the rigors of financial management. His charm and sincerity of purpose won over the hearts of all who knew him, dating back to the store's origins in Brooklyn, when it was known as the Warlock Shop. Herman was a true believer, a practitioner of the magical arts as well as a shopkeeper. The Magickal Childe's motto was "Hard Core New Age" and Herman wasn't kidding.[1]

They both had a strong interest in witchcraft. Eddie founded several related witchcraft traditions during his work. These may be collectively called the Edwardian Tradition. Lady Rhea recalls how Eddie joked, "Imagine if one day they call my (Craft) children Edwardian?"[2]

Lady Gwen Thompson first initiated Eddie into a system

called Traditionalist Witchcraft or Traditionalist Initiatory Witchcraft, which later evolved into today's New England Covenant of Traditionalist Witches (NECTW). He parted company with Lady Gwen and, around 1972, founded his tradition known as New York Welsh Traditionalist Gwyddonaid (NYWTG), New York Welsh, Brooklyn Welsh, Welsh Tradition.

Eddie met Lady Gwen Thompson, leader of the NECTW and High Priestess of a Welsh coven in Connecticut. Lady Gwen initiated Eddie, and he eventually became the High Priest of her coven. Eddie gave dates for his initiations in the late 1960s, with his taking the role of High Priest in 1970. There are inconsistencies with his stated dates and some controversy about whether he received the third degree from Thompson. The two eventually split over Eddie's denials of Thompson's sexual advances.

In 1971, Eddie sought out Leo Louis Martello, an author of metaphysical books and gay activist. Leo had begun to be publicly recognized as a witch starting in 1969. He practiced a version of Italian-inspired witchcraft he termed the Strega Tradition. I count Leo among my early teachers. To this day, I am grateful for the time he took to exchange correspondence with a teenage queer witch reaching out from an island off the Maine coast. He introduced the young Eddie to several other witches and occultists, including Herman Slater. Eddie and Herman hit it off, and they soon became lovers, moving in together in Brooklyn Heights.

After his disappointment of falling out with his first High Priestess and losing a coven connection, Eddie began to seek out another coven that might admit him. He reached out to two covens within the Kentucky Line of Gardnerian Witchcraft. One turned him away because of the distance between New York and Louisville; the other denied him because he was homosexual.

WELSH TRADITIONALIST - 1972

Following his expulsion from Thompson's New Haven coven, around 1972, Eddie established the first of his three witch traditions: alternatively called New York Welsh Traditionalist Gwyddonaid (NYWTG), New York Welsh, Brooklyn Welsh, or simply the Welsh Tradition.

NY WICA - 1974

Eventually, Eddie was initiated into the Old Kentucky Line by HPS Lady Hela. He quickly became disillusioned by the heterosexism and homophobia of Gardnerian practice at that time. This led him to found his own progressive and egalitarian Coven of Witches, combining what he had learned from the Welsh and Gardnerian traditions in late 1973 or early 1974. This lineage is known today as NY Wica.

> Finally, sick of all the shit flying back and forth from coven to coven, along with threats, death curses, and slander, I decided that in order to find fulfillment in my religious beliefs, I must find a pagan cult which would welcome me as I am - a proud gay man. I began to research ancient religions involving the worship of the Mother Goddess ... All I needed now was to find a place in which I could function openly and freely as myself. Most of the pagan Mother Goddess cults of antiquity were overtly tolerant of homosexuals; most had a homosexual priesthood. —Eddie Buczynski

MINOAN BROTHERHOOD - 1977

The Minoan Brotherhood was officially founded on January 1, 1977, establishing the Knossos Grove in New York City. The Sisterhood, headed by Lady Rhea, soon followed. The two practiced their particular workings separately and came together for the sabbat celebrations.

Eddie, known by the Craft name Lord Gwydion, began formal studies in the eighties, first at the City University of New York and then graduate studies at Bryn Mawr College in Pennsylvania. Eddie started to become ill in the early spring of 1986. In November 1987, he was hospitalized with pneumonia. While there, he was diagnosed with AIDS/HIV. That Christmas, he and his then-boyfriend, Gene Muto, traveled to Crete. He was awarded his Master's degree in May of the following year. His condition deteriorated as he battled toxoplasmosis infection. He moved to Atlanta so Muto could care for him. He passed to the summerlands on March 16, 1989. Herman lost his battle with AIDS on July 9, 1992, at age fifty-four. Eddie and Herman left enduring legacies. Eddie's children are growing in number, and the various lineages within the Edwardian Tradition continue to thrive.

Herman and Ed will always live on as the founding fathers of the Craft in New York City. Through all of our efforts as a community it is to keep the future generations of the Craft to come to know this, that these two great men will never be forgotten and will always be recognized. As it was upon the shoulders of these two men that many of our covens and New York's Pagan community were founded. I will always honor my Fathers.

So Mote It Be!
Many Blessings,
Lady Rhea[3]

Chapter x
The Wild Boys Take No Prisoners

During my college days and the years just following, I worked with a small collective of queer magickal experimenters, The Brotherhood Of Seth (TBOS). Much of our exploration focused on extrapolating a magickal system out of the later writings of William S Burroughs. I first encountered Burroughs's writing when exploring the work of the Beat movement. When I read *The Wild Boys* and its companion, *Port of Saints*, with their queer sex magickal rites, I was hooked. The work of Burroughs and his collaborator Brion Gysin are foundational to my practice.

Burroughs's fascination with the occult was kindled at an early age when his Irish nanny taught him the secret of calling toads and a simple curse to cause the target to fall down a flight of stairs. The latter would reoccur in his works all the way through his monumental final Cities of the Red Night trilogy. At age four, he describes how he saw a tiny green reindeer he would later identify as a totem animal while walking in a park. Gysin's interest in magic began upon finding a cursed object hidden in the nightclub he operated in Tangiers. The written spell accompanying the object was sealed with the Arabic word mektoub, "it is written." For both men, writing itself was a magical act. They both wrote books of the dead, travel journals of the road to the afterlife akin to the Egyptian and Tibetan Books of the Dead: Burroughs The Wild Boys, subtitled "A Book of the Dead" and The Western Lands, the culmination of the Red Nights trilogy; and Gysin's The Last Museum, an underground journey through the bardo.

Both Burroughs and Gysin were practicing magicians. They viewed their art as magical acts. They also conducted numerous magical operations. Similarly, to the textual cut-up method, Burroughs used a tape recorder to capture and remix reality for a magical effect. He was highly influential on early chaos magicians, and they, in turn, were influential on him. Later in life, he received initiation into the chaos magical order founded by Peter Carroll, Illuminates of Thanateros.[1] He contributed artwork to the cover of Peter Hine's *Prime Chaos* and was buried wearing his ring bearing the eight-arrowed chaos symbol.

Burroughs and Gysin were highly influential in the work of Genesis P-Orridge (later Lady) and Alex Fergusson, founders of the experimental bands Throbbing Gristle and the overtly magical Psychic TV. Subsequently, his influence was widespread in the particular space where British avant-garde music intersected with metaphysical—bands such as Coil and Current 93. The Temple of Psychic Youth (TOPY), a variant of the chaos magic scene, grew out of Psychic TV and P-Orridge. TOPY is a loosely federated network of magical experimenters whose work centers on ceremonial and sex magic with a particular emphasis on sigil magic derived from the writings of Austin Osman Spare.

THE ONE GOD UNIVERSE

> Mais qui fut celui qui inventa cet art? ce fut le premier fripon qui rencontra un imbécile. Voltaire[Œuvres complètes de Voltaire, volume 11 often colloquially translated as “Religion was invented when the first con man met the first fool.”)

A critical analysis of control and control structures rests at the core of William S. Burroughs’s writing, from *Naked Lunch* to the channeled voice of the cut-up experiments to the wondering thoughts captured in his final journal, *Last Words*. Burroughs associates Control (the capital his) with imprinting objectives onto an unsuspecting general population. Burroughs’s writing artfully illustrates how culture and the media are utilized to produce a crisis of contradiction in the viewer, reinforcing a position of safety—personified in middle-class comforts.

Within his work, Burroughs outlines the objectives he perceived underlying Control’s plan and exposes how Control reinforces the concept of the One God Universe (OGU) as a reality of contradiction that negates the dreaming subject. Burroughs argues that under the guise of the OGU, secular Control attempts to eradicate free thought by producing a monotheistic, nonmagical world that lacks both dreams and multiple gods. Burroughs theorizes that a universe predicated on a concept of multiple gods is necessary for one to dream. What is at stake in Control’s attempts at maintaining a static OGU is a monopoly on Space or immortality. Burroughs asserts humanity is moving toward its destruction due to the implementation of the OGU and the problems inherent in humanity as a species. Since Burroughs views the human condition as a biological dead end, the only choice humans have is to mutate or become extinct. We are "here to go."[2]

Burroughs argues Control masks itself behind the façade of the OGU since, as he says, "all control systems claim to reflect the immutable laws of the universe."[3] The universe of the One God is a world of absolute control and "rationality." The OGU is created in opposition to what Burroughs views as a magical universe consisting of many gods and a privileging of the dream space. Burroughs proposes the objectives of the OGU are the destruction of the magical universe through the annihilation of humans as dreaming subjects. Burroughs writes that the OGU "is controlled, predictable, dead."[4] For Burroughs, the OGU is a world of absolutes, where no one is allowed to be free to think for him/her/themself. Such a universe ensures its power through the destruction of critical communities, achieved by the processes of constructed contradiction and determined "safety." In a system such as this, free or critical thinking substantially threatens the stability of the Control systems. Burroughs writes in *The Western Lands*:

> So the One God, backed by secular power, is forced on the masses in the name of Islam, Christianity, the state, for all secular leaders want to be the One. To be intelligent or observant under such a blanket of oppression is to be 'subversive.'[5]

The motivation behind the OGU, then, must be the eradication of intelligence and free thought. The immediate objectives of Control, as manifested under the guise of the OGU, are, for Burroughs, the destruction of magic, as characterized in a mythic component to human existence, and the cutting off of dream space. Through these conjoined objectives, Control seeks to ensure its primary goal of maintaining a monopoly over Space, variously characterized in Burroughs's work as immortality and evolution.

Burroughs describes the impossible contradiction of monotheism:

> Consider the impasse of a one God universe. He is all-knowing and all-powerful. He can't go anywhere since He is already everywhere. He can't do anything since the act of doing presupposes opposition. His universe is irrevocably thermodynamic having no friction by definition. So, he has to create friction: War, Fear, Sickness, Death, to keep his dying show on the road.[6]

In contrast, the world Burroughs presents in his writing is filled with myth, magic, and dream experience. The mythic components of Burroughs's writing can be read as an expansion of his cosmology of a subversive magical universe within a world under the control of the One God. He states, "The most basic concept of my writing is a belief in the magical universe, a universe of many gods, often in conflict. The paradox of an all-powerful, all-seeing God who nonetheless allows suffering, evil and death, does not arise."(Burroughs 1991, 266) Burroughs here is not merely resurrecting archaic forms of human religion—myths such as utopian matriarchies or primal androgyny. Instead, he is positing a cosmology where mutation is a necessary corollary to an existence that directly opposes the OGU and the objectives of Control. If Control's manipulative power rests on a world of contradiction, then the OGU is the only acceptable cosmology. A magical universe, as

Burroughs discusses, is a world without contradictions since all seemingly inherent contradictions can be ascribed to the contendings of diverse gods, each with their objectives and agendas. Burroughs perceives safety as an artificial construction of Control that cannot exist in a universe without a Supreme Being.

Burroughs, like his character Joe the Dead in *The Western Lands*, is engaged in a "desperate struggle" to alter the outcome of Control's deployments. His fiction attempts to track down "the Venusian agents of a conspiracy with very definite M.O. and objectives," i.e., Control. Joe understands these objectives to be the propagation of an "antimagical, authoritarian, dogmatic" universe. Control, therefore, is the "deadly enemy of those who are committed to the magical universe..."[7]

Burroughs views dreams as one of the most essential components of human existence. Free thought cannot exist without them; therefore, Control attempts to destroy the dreaming self by imposing the OGU. Burroughs describes dreams as a "biologic necessity."[8] Dreams are the only things humans possess outside of the sphere of Control's influence. Being spontaneous and unpredictable, they are contrary to their dogmatic objectives. When one is free to dream, Control's power cannot be absolute:

> These magical visions are totally devoid of ordinary human emotion and experience. There is no friendship, love, hostility, fear or hate. There are no rules, no series of steps by which one can see. Consequently such visions are the enemy of any dogmatic system.[9]

Dreams remove one from the conscious assumption of the forces that seek to define and confine one. Existing outside of

Control's direct conditioning, dreams can produce random constructions that have the potential to work to undermine Control's influence over the reactive mind. Dogmatic paradigms must, therefore, alienate people's connection to their dreams since, as Burroughs argues:

> Any dogma must postulate the way, certain steps that will lead to the salvation, which the dogma promises. The Christian Heaven or pearly gates and singing angels, the Muslim paradise of eternal whores and plenty of water, the Communists' heaven of the worker state. Otherwise there is no place for the hierarchical structure that mediates between dogma and man, that dictates the way.[10]

Dreams provide a space where random options and alternatives can arise, and this possibility represents a threatening field of uncertainty for Control. In Burroughs's fiction, Control's survival is based on its ability to establish and re-present the way. Thus, in a world with multiple forms of seeing, Control cannot long retain power.

The importance of the mythic, magical universe, as manifested in dreams and multiple deities, is central to Burroughs's work. As cited above, Burroughs regularly casts this as a basic premise underlying his theories. For Burroughs, humanity, dreams, and the magical multi-god universe are fundamentally connected. In *The Western Lands,* he writes, "You need your dreams, they are a biologic necessity and your lifeline to space, that is, to the state of God. To be one of the Shining Ones. The inference is that Gods are a biologic necessity. They are an integral part of Man."[11] Control prevails when dreams are policed since dreams allow one to project a future intrinsically different from one's present condition.

Burroughs argues that the lack of dreams, or the alienation of the dreaming subject, works to contain one in a mode of stasis where future projection and creative thought are impossible. Control's ultimate objective, produced through the elimination of dreams, is the continuation of its monopoly on power.

Dreams, at their deepest levels, are projections of our past into our future. Burroughs argues that "the function of dreams is to train the being for future conditions." Burroughs sees this "future condition" as a future in space. "The human artifact is biologically designed for space travel," he writes.[12] Throughout Burroughs's work, he quotes Gysin's mantra, "We are here to go," along with his corollary phrase, "Over the hills and far away." These maxims establish their opinion that a movement into space, other worlds, is necessary for human survival. Burroughs writes in the introduction to *The Place of Dead Roads*:

> The only thing that could unite the planet is a unified space program [...] the earth becomes a space station and war is simply out, irrelevant, flatly insane in context of research centers, spaceports, and the exhilaration of working with people you like and respect toward an agreed-upon objective, an objective from which all workers will gain. Happiness is a byproduct of function. The planetary space station will give all participants an opportunity to function.[13]

Burroughs sees that the fundamental human drive is for immortality and proposes that space is the means of obtaining immortality. Burroughs began the writing he termed his mythology of the Space Age with the material that became *The Wild Boys* and *The Port of Saints*. In a 1972 interview with Robert Palmer in *Rolling Stone*, Burroughs stated, "The future of writing is to see how close you can come to making it happen."[14] Like his namesake William Seward Hall in *The Western Lands*, Burroughs is attempting in his fiction "to write his way out of death."[15] This process attempts to create a modern mythology suited for humanity at the brink of the mutational breaking point. Burroughs holds the theory that the process of writing creates something real. This is expressed in his use of the Arabic work *mektoub*, "it is written," a word traditionally used to seal magical spells to ensure their success. This word embodies Burroughs's belief that writing has the power to create, alter, or transform actual events.

Burroughs's texts, then, work at two levels. As signified by the word *mektoub* as a magical seal, his work reflects his understanding of the writing process where the act is an evocation of future events. On another level, his texts are a frontal assault on present conditions. His words are as potent a weapon as those wielded by the wild boy tribes. The work of creating a mythology for the space age represents, for Burroughs, the actual attempt at creating a new reality. In this manner, Burroughs opposes the forces of Control that seek to keep a careful check on any possible movement into space. Burroughs argues that Control does this through its program of dream destruction, as presented in the OCU film. Control is, therefore, an absolute enemy that stands in the way of the realization of free people. Burroughs writes, "You will know your enemies by those who attempt to block your path. Vampiric monopolists would keep you in time like their cattle."[16] Control is a force that acts contrary to human evolution, blocking the means of moving beyond present human conditions.

For Burroughs, however, this movement toward extinction is not simply a product of Control. It is also a situation that has been the logical outcome of factors endemic to the human condition since its inception. "Thoughtful citizens are asking themselves if the whole human race wasn't a mistake from the starting gate," Burroughs wonders.[17] Burroughs asserts that the causes of our extinction as a race have been with us since the beginning. He argues that the virus of our destruction has always been an endemic element of being human— "we are all tainted with viral origins." In *Cities of the Red Night*, the virologist Dr. Peterson maintains that "the whole quality of human consciousness, as expressed in male and female, is basically a viral mechanism."[18] Burroughs often writes that we carry our death with us; Dr. Peterson further suggests that humans, as a species, have their extinction with them. This extinction is based on a world of humans trapped in a binary existence. Burroughs wonders if "the separation of the sexes" isn't "an arbitrary device to perpetuate an unworkable arrangement."[19] Burroughs theorist Robin Lydenberg writes that Burroughs sees "the only possible relationship between two sexes defined in binary opposition to each other is one of conflict."(Lydenberg 1987, 162) For Burroughs, this arena of perpetual conflict, enacted through and on the zone of the body, is one of the most significant elements between humanity and the potential to mutate into something with even half a chance of survival.

In *The Place of Dead Roads*, Burroughs's alter ego, Kim Carsons, points out that the body's weight is inappropriate for space travel.[20] In his interview with Jorgen Ploog, Burroughs refers to studies showing that a body in a weightless environment quickly loses its skeletal structure. He faults modern immortality experiments and space exploration procedures for attempting to continue the body beyond its usefulness. Current research meant to prolong life centers on replacing body parts, which Burroughs sees as creating a divided world of tenuous immortality for the rich and rotting death for the poor. Those who can afford parts receive a new heart in a week, while "the poor wait in part lines for diseased genitals, cancerous lungs, a cirrhotic liver."[21] For Burroughs, immortality experiments along these lines are guaranteed to fail since they don't address the problem of death itself. Instead, they treat the symptoms of death as expressed in atrophy, cell death, and decay. Death is a condition of having a body, as Gysin observes in *The Last Museum*, "When we are born, we start to die."[22]

Despite the pessimism above, Burroughs's position is not nihilistic. In *The Western Lands*, he writes, "The human condition is hopeless once you submit to it by being born... almost. There is one chance in a million and that is still good biologic odds."[23] This "almost" is a very important almost for Burroughs since it contains his hope that the present state of human affairs can be transcended or moved beyond. For Burroughs, the chance may be slim by human standards. Still, these standards, most notably characterized by the relational construct of time, become entirely relative when discussing issues in biological/evolutionary terms. Again, in *The Western Lands*, he speaks of the death camp, that is, planet Earth, as "the last game."[24] (Thus, Burroughs argues that humanity may be in the last stages of its destruction, but he does not see this process as inevitable.

Burroughs's texts are his attempts to create a new magical mythology to assist humanity in thinking in the terms required for its continuation. His writing is, in a sense, both a glimmer of hope and an austere warning of impending destruction. In *The Western Lands*, he describes a picture "of a balloon suddenly and unexpectedly soaring and some people still holding the ropes." Most of these people, he writes, "didn't have the survival IQ to let go in time." Seconds later, it's too late—the distance to the ground has become too great. Burroughs points out that they did not heed the "basic survival lesson" of letting go "when your Guardian tells you to let go." Where you hear the voice of your guardian spirit, you must heed the call, or it is lost. He continues by posing a question to the reader:

> Suppose you were holding one of those ropes? Would you have let go in time, which is, of course, at the first upward yank? I'll tell you something interesting. You would have a much better chance to let go in time now that you have read his paragraph than if you hadn't read it. Writing, if it is anything, is a word of warning... LET GO![25]

The above demonstrates that Burroughs does hold out some hope for humanity. His fiction is an artful word of warning. His message: "Let Go!" Throughout his work, Burroughs tells his readers to let go of the outmoded forms of human existence that traps them, characterized by modern control systems such as monotheism, and move into the unknown.

The mutational escape Burroughs proposes is intrinsically connected to sex. "This is the space age," he writes in *The Wild Boys*, "And sex movies must express the longing to escape from flesh through sex. The way out is the way through."[26] In a similar way to Foucault, though articulated quite differently, for Burroughs, sex and male+male sex in particular, becomes the means of beginning the break with Control. While engaged in sexual acts, one of the wild boys envisions himself as a celestial body. "I see myself streaking across the sky line a star to leave the earth forever. What holds me back? It is the bargain by which I am here at all. The bargain is this body that holds me here."[27] Magickal evolution is again depicted as requiring a move away from the body, a vision that begins in sexual machinations.

In Burroughs's work, the moment of homosexual union represents the beginnings of a new imagining. In *The Place of*

Dead Roads, he writes, "Sex forms the matrix of a dualistic and therefore solid and real universe. It is possible to resolve the dualistic conflict in a sex act, where dualism need not exist."[28] Like Foucault, to Burroughs, male same-sex desire represents the means of reaching a state beyond binary existence, a space beyond the reach of Control—a condition where biological mutation is conceivable. It directly opposes the sexual and cultural imperatives enforced by Control. Simply put, it is an ill-defined territory.

The sex in Burroughs's fiction, especially as exhibited in *The Wild Boys* and *Port of Saints*, is the sex of young males who are beginning sexual identity construction. When he speaks of the desire to "escape from flesh through sex" and the shift in "sex movies" that this entails, he follows with an example. Johnny and Mark are wild boy agents who "become astronauts playing the part of American married idiots," i.e., the traditional middle-American, heterosexual, married couple. They remain thus until months after take-off, at which point they disconnect radio contact with Earth. As Burroughs called his fictional sequences, this routine shatters with the images of their sexual memories lifted from their 1920s childhoods. "Lawn sprinklers," "classrooms," "frogs in 1920 roads," and "a naked boy hugging his knees sunlight in pubic hairs" are all resurrected in an explosion of space sexuality. Burroughs appears to view the personal sexual mnemonic landscape as a film written in early adolescence. This "sex film" becomes a catalog of individual metaphors in space and his texts—a self-referential, potent, and symbolic magical landscape. Within his work, sex becomes the present-time invocation of these personal sexual encodings of history and memory.

This scene suddenly shifts from these loosely connected, isolated images to "a suburban room afternoon light bleakly clear."[29] Mark says he heard that Johnny "got laid," Johnny replies that it was a prostitute "down on Westminster Place." He admits that since that encounter, his crotch has itched. Mark orders Johnny to drop his pants and begins inspecting his genitals. During the process, Johnny gets an erection: "Christ it is happening he can't stop it." The focus then shifts to fragments of solitary sexual conditions with "sad muscle magazines over the florist shop pants down green snakes under rusty iron in the vacant lot the old family soap opera look of yellow hair stirs in September."[30] The story shifts with brief glimpses of past sexual relations and fantasies. "The film stops..." and turns again—moves to Mexico City, London, and St. Louis—until "the film stops in his eyes" at the point of orgasm:

> A shooting star silence floats down on falling leaves and blood spit the smell of decay shredded to dust and memories pieces of legs and cocks and assholes drifting fragments in sunlight ass hairs spread on the bed dust of young hand fading flickering thighs and buttocks smell of young nights.[31]

Sex is a catharsis formed by "drifting fragments" of image and memory; each act is the product of all that has gone before. Burroughs presents homosexual intercourse as particulate matter in the light projection of Control's film, the OGU. In the case of Johnny and Mark, "the sex scenes of their adolescence are seen as image dust in space through which they pass."[32] Think of the dust in the light stream of a movie projector. As dust in the light, it both obscures and refuses the image on the screen, thus breaking down Control's monopoly on space.

In Burroughs's novels, queer sex begins the space exploration process, but in his theories, humans cannot envision the full scope of the movement into space. In his essay "Immortality," Burroughs suggests, "Mutation involves changes that are literally unimaginable from the perspective of the future mutant."[33] Elsewhere, Burroughs compares the evolutionary step he projects for humans with the step made by fish onto land. Certain fish developed rudimentary lungs as the great seas, which once covered much of the Earth, began to recede. These they used to move over land from one body of water to another. At some point, they lost the use of their gills and were forced to remain on land. In this way, in their search for water, they found land. Burroughs suggests that the human jump may be made in the same way. "The astronaut is not looking for space; he is looking for more time—that is equating space with time... Like the walking fish, looking for more time we may find space instead, and then find there is no way back." (Burroughs 1985, 126) "Evolution," Burroughs points out, "would seem to be a one-way street."[34]

THE MAGICAL UNIVERSE

From early childhood, Burroughs held an unwavering belief in a magical universe. To him, the world was filled with gods, spirits, and occult forces:

> Like The Great Gatsby, Kim believes in the green light the orgiastic future. He believes in a magical universe, unpredictable, spontaneous, alive. A universe where anything is possible. A universe of many gods often in conflict. So the paradox of an all-knowing all-powerful god, who, nonetheless,

permits suffering, evil and death, does not arise.[35]

The wild boys, fugitive survivors, escape to a magical place set apart from the world known as the Blue Desert of Silence. As news of their existence spreads, more boys rush to join them. Eventually, they begin to evoke new members of the tribe through ritual sex magic. These new magical creatures are termed Zimbus.

The boys formed a circle in a natural amphitheater that sloped down to a platform of sand. They spread a round blue rug about eight feet in diameter on this platform. The four directions were indicated on this rug by arrows, and its position was checked against a compass. The rug looked like a map crisscrossed with white lines and shaded in striations of blue from the lightest egg blue to blue-black.[36]

One of the wild boys enters the circle. He stands naked and tilts his head back to look at the sky. The phallic Elder Gods of antiquity surround them. He raises his hands slowly and draws a blue mist from the rug. The mist coalesces near his crotch. He molds it, and it begins to take shape. "A red being was now visible in front of the boy's body lying on his back knees up transparent thighs on either side of his flanks." The wild boy penetrates the Zimbu. The other wild boys around the circle can see his penis through translucent flesh. He then fucks him into corporeal existence. "The boy leaned forward and fastened his lips to the other mouth spurting sperm inside and suddenly the red boy was solid..."[37]

In *Cities of the Red Night*, the book's protagonist, a hard-boiled detective named Clem Snide, is hired to find Jerry, the missing son of a millionaire. During their investigation, Snide, with the aid of his assistant Jim Brady, calls upon the "Shining

Ones" by way of a magical rite of invocation. (Evocation is when one summons an external entity to appearance, such as demons in old grimoires, while invocation is the summoning of a god form to enter one's body during a ritual.) The cardinal points are marked: red candle for fire in the south; a sigil on parchment representing air to the west; a container of earth to the north; and a bowl of water to the east. The altar is a square of marble. On it are two bowls, one with milk, the other with water, burning rose incense, and a mint sprig. They enter sky-clad and begin their rite at sunset. They "pay homage" to the cardinal points by dipping the mint into the bowls and sprinkling water and milk in each direction. They then commence invoking the Egyptian god Set. The god takes possession of Jim. "My phallus is that of Amsu," he exclaims. Now begins the *heiro gamos,* the climactic act of ritual sexual union. As Jim enters Clem, "pictures and tapes begin to swirl" in his brain, and then:

> Shadowy figures ruse beyond the candlelight: the goddess Ix Tab, patroness of those who hang themselves ... a vista of gallows and burning cities from Bosch ... Set ... Osiris ... a smell of the sea ...[38]

Their rite complete; they send the Shining Ones back to their realms and go to bed.

This ritual is inspired by one in Richard Cavendish's *Occult Primer.* Burroughs and Cavendish knew each other to some extent, though the latter has demurred from discussing the length or depth of their acquaintance.

Gysin's writings are also occult treatises. *The Process* is an initiatory journey, a pilgrim's progress, through the desert, Daath on the Qabalistic Tree of Life. Gysin described it as "a fiction based on prophecy of future fact."[39] *The Last Museum* is a journey after death through a postmodern bardo, the post death realms described in *The Tibetan Book of the Dead*. "A Book of the Dead must be horrific," Burroughs writes in his introduction to Gysin's *Last Museum*. "In the Land of the Dead all pretense is swept aside. Attics yield up their dirty secrets. All hidden places and beings stand revealed, the caves and catacombs of human history, the 'foul rag and bone heaps of the heart.'"[40]

Gysin was inspired by the Master Musicians of Joujouka from a village in the Rif Mountains of northern Morocco and helped introduce them to the other Beats and Brian Jones, the original leader of The Rolling Stones. In the Beat Hotel in Paris, he spent hours mirror-gazing, a magical technique to bring on a trance state where visions come through the mirror akin to scrying. He was very captivated by the ubiquitous occult practices in Morocco:

> Magic, practiced more assiduously than hygiene in Morocco, through ecstatic dancing to the music of the secret brotherhoods, is, there, a form of psychic hygiene. You know your music when you hear it, one day. You fall into line and dance until you pay the piper.[41]

He invented the flicker machine, also known as the dream machine, which consisted of a lampshade-like cylinder cut with carefully spaced holes, mounted on a turntable, and lit from within. As it spun, the flicker of the lights through the holes would induce an altered state of consciousness. "The Dream Machine may bring about a change of consciousness since it throws back the limits of the visible world and may, indeed, prove that there are no limits."[42]

NOTHING HERE BUT THE RECORDINGS

In the introduction to h/er interviews with Brion Gysin, P-Orridge provides a well-constructed summation of Gysin's view of the universe, the self, and the role of magic. He conceptualized his concept of the Self and the potency of operative magic. At the outset, s/he points out that mythologies are "edited highlights (and lowlights) from another person's perspective." If the universe is prerecorded, as Burroughs and Gysin argued, then the Self also starts as a prerecorded track. P-Orridge observes:

> All the information we have at our immediate disposal as self-consciousness develops is from someone else. Everything about us is true. Everything about us is false. Everything about us is both. It is by omission that we are described exactly, creating an unfolding program not of our own choosing. We are edited bloodlines seeking an identity with only partial data and unknown motivation and expectation.[43]

For Gysin and P-Orridge, magic empowers the operator to craft an identity that is new and distinct from our original self—and is distinctly our own. Magic is a tool of evolution for ourselves and, through our change, the entire species. "As no two people see the same view along the Way, all trips from here to there are imaginary: all truth is a tale I am telling myself," Gysin wrote in *The Process*.

Magic and ritual provide glimpses into other worlds, other realities coexistent with our own but outside the operative sphere of Control. Our behavior, perception of the world, and character are recognized as "malleable matter equal to all other forms of matter." We have the potential to be both interdependent, the nature of this reality, and unique simultaneously. "If there is any right, any birthright," P-Orridge states, "it might well be the right to create one's Self."[44]

P-Orridge put this concept into practice using h/er own body as the ground of h/er experimentation. Through radical physical transformation via plastic surgery, he and his partner, Lady Jaye Breyer P-Orridge, strove to become a pan-androgynous single entity. S/he submitted a manifesto of sorts to issue 2.3 of *Ashé Journal*:

> This is the final war, a jigsaw
> A war to re-possess your SELF.
> There is NO gender anymore
> Only P-Androgeny is divine.
> Sexuality is a force of nature that cannot
> Be contained. Get up.[45]

P-Orridge recalls Burroughs pointing out that if the universe was prerecorded, one could edit those recordings. "This is magick."[46] This is precisely what Burroughs attempted to do in his cut-up experiments. With random textual manipulations, he received mediumistic messages from unknown entities. He was working magic to alter reality via his street recordings, subsequent editing, and playback.[47]

Gysin explained to P-Orridge that "magick is passed on by the touching of hands." Transmission of the Craft is more than words on paper. It must be transmitted in the flesh, IRL as it were, person to person, teacher to seeker. The text is only half there until it is brought to life by the physical transference beyond words and worldly explanation. This is the nature of and the reason for the survival of initiation. The mechanisms that control people, culturally, nationally, and globally exist because people have surrendered, however unwittingly, to a closed system. The transference of magical knowledge between two people is what wisdom means. It is a subversive act that is actualized outside the realms of enslavement and control. Crowley argued that every act is a magickal act—every *transgressive* act certainly is.

A theme that weaves throughout Burroughs's writings is the concept of communal groups or tribes set against evil forces: the wild boys vs. the militarized forces of Control; the Johnson family of honorable outlaws set against the righteous, virus-occupied Shits. In *Cities*, the Iguana girl prophecizes the creation of a grand coven set in opposition to the One God Universe:

> All religions are magical systems competing with other systems. The Church has driven magic into covens where practitioners are bound to each other by common fear. We can unite the Americas into a vast coven of those who live under the Articles, united against the Christian Church, Catholic and Protestant. It is our policy to encourage the practice of magic and to introduce alternative religious

> beliefs to treat the Christian monopoly. We will set up an alternative calendar with non-Christian holidays.[48]

Burroughs often denounced the concept of "coincidence." The universe unfolds as it will. Things often arise in series. A pleasant clerk wishes you good morning, followed by a concatenation of friendly people throughout the day. A rude attendant begets a surly afternoon. We can think of these linked occurrences as synchronicities. Coincidence is the rational mind making the universe a little less interesting. Life is not a disassociated series of random events, as the dismissive concept of coincidence implies. Everything happens for a reason. However, this is not meant to say that everything happens with a purpose or portend. It is an excellent stance to passively observe the world and understand the connections as the past progresses to the future. Listen. See. Understand the patterns. It's never a good idea to double down when one is losing. Knowing when to cash in when one's ahead is also smart.

THE RECLAMATION OF JOAN VOLLMER

Even if one has read none of Burroughs's writing, they often know of one incident if they are unfamiliar with anything else about his biography. In September 1951, while living in Mexico City, he accidentally shot his wife, Joan Vollmer. Both had their ongoing struggles with addiction—Burroughs's heroin and Vollmer's alcohol. On the day of the fatal incident, Burroughs returned home from town to find a party in progress. A drunk Vollmer put a glass of gin on her head and told her husband it was time for their William Tell act. Some witnesses suggest she goaded him, but that is now legend. At the time, Burroughs claimed the gun accidentally discharged. It is more likely that he went along with her "game" and tragically missed.

In 2022, when Rebel Satori published *Fever Spores: The Queer Reclamation of William S. Burroughs,* many a Facebook troll jumped in to say that he should not be reclaimed, citing his "murder" of his wife. Sam Desmond contributed a powerful essay on Vollmer to the *Fever Spores* anthology. She strongly points out that characterizing this unfortunate accident as spousal abuse strips agency away from Vollmer by giving her only the victim role. She was a powerful creative force in her own right, serving as both a muse and an autonomous artist within the Beat movement. This general narrative underlying the comments, compartmentalizes her and strips all else away from her identity apart from the instance of her death. Viewing it in this way leaves Joan a mere footnote.

This mischaracterization also ignores the critical role of spirit possession in the episode. Burroughs writes in his 1985 introduction to *Queer* that earlier that day, he was overcome by a "feeling of loss and sadness." Rereading and thus reliving the manuscript from that period, "a smog of menace and evil rises from the pages." Later, Gysin would receive a mediumistic message: "The ugly spirit shot Joan..." Burroughs had a firm belief in possession, not the psychological form, but the true Medieval sense of an outside force entering however covertly one's body. Burroughs describes it as "a dead hand waiting to slip over his like a glove."[49] Like Crowley's demon Choronzon, the specter of the ugly spirit would haunt Burroughs for the rest of his life.

Chapter XI
Parasitic Possession: From Witch Hunts to Cannibal Corporations

Burroughs's philosophy was essentially Manichean— a world divided between good and evil forces continually in conflict. He saw the process of evil as a viral mechanism. He identified this possessing force as the "Right Virus" and labeled the infected as "Shits."[1] "'A wise old black faggot said to me years ago: 'Some people are shits, darling.' I was never able to forget it."[2] You know the type. They are all too prevalent these days. They think of themselves as on the right side of everything because they ARE RIGHT. Dunning Kruger effect—a cognitive bias where the more ignorant one is, the less one realizes it—is in full effect with devastating impact.

The Shits are everywhere, and their attempts at control are multi-level: evangelists, the modern money-changes in the temples; the police and the disproportionate use of deadly force that appears more pandemic than systemic with each passing day; the military leaders itching to use their weapons in a world littered with proxy-wars... Burroughs writes:

> God-loving, epicenter, the vile groveling worshipers of the Slave Gods. When a disease agent moves from one host species to another, with no natural immunity to that strain, the agent can become incomparably more efficient.[3]

If history is to prove anything, it is that we have been a superb host. Importantly, Burroughs perceived this as a parasitic alien virus, not one endemic to the homosapien species. Though it's been with us so long, it can be hard to tell.

What we see in the world is not a simple power-from-above situation. Power is a force that emanates from everywhere and moves along multitudinous lines. Some of these pathways are the avenues of viral occupation and parasitic replication. Foucault spent much of his career engaged in a deep analysis of power. He did this through histories of select power conduits such as knowledge, medicine, discipline, and how society has directed or constrained sexuality. In *Disciple and Punish*, Foucault observed:

> Power is not an institution and not a structure; neither is it a specific strength we are endowed with; it is the name that one attributes to a complex strategical situation in a particular society.[4]

Power is everywhere. The universe is based on interdependence. We live in a complex web of power relationships. Understanding the subtleties of these power relationships is critical for the magical practitioner.

Synchronously echoing Burroughs's viral theories, Native American thinker Jack Forbes also sees a viral pandemic at the very heart of civilization. First published in 1978, his *Columbus and Other Cannibals* is, according to the back cover, one of the founding texts of the "anti-civilization" movement. Forbes came "to the conclusion that *imperialism and exploitation are forms of cannibalism and, in fact, are precisely those forms of cannibalism which are most diabolical and evil.*"[5] He calls this cannibalistic drive the "Wétiko disease." The word is a Cree term synonymous with the Wendigo among other Algonquin-speaking First Nations peoples. It denotes an evil supernatural creature that terrorizes the forests of North America. They are cannibals and possess an unquenchable bloodthirst. Many legends hold that the Wendigo were once human but were transformed by greed and lust for power. For Forbes, the Wétiko is woven into "the very fabric of European evolution."[6]

Uppy was fascinated by folklore. She would retell stories of fantastical creatures that lurked in the Maine woods. Many of these were used to scare new arrivals to Maine logging camps. Among these was the frightening Wendigo. These she incorporated in her poem "The Hang Downs":

> There's a hill on Bartletts Island
> So steep and high and round,
> Where the Wendigo on his big flat feet
> Makes tracks all over the ground.
> —Ruth Moore, "The Hang Downs"

Thus, when I first encountered Forbes's work, his imagery was not unfamiliar to me.

The cannibal is not a cryptozoological specter lurking

out there. They are all too often us. The elite power brokers of society are not the only ones susceptible to this contagion. Forbes emphasizes that the Wétiko disease:

> *is not limited to the brutes and goons who handle the gun, the lash or the instruments of torture.* Nice people in the offices, the typists, the lab technicians, the clerks and, of course, the owners, directors, stockholders, senators, generals, and presidents who use, profit from, and feed on human exploitation are also cannibals to one degree or another.[7]

Just as with Burroughs, the threat comes from all sides. The small-town clerk refusing a marriage license is just as immediate a threat as the conservative senator. Modernity has brought with it significant innovations, while at the same time, it has allowed for the institutional inflection of unspeakable horrors. The *Citizens United* Supreme Court decision only compounds the situation, extending as it does the rights of the people to corporations.

Forbes sees this process extending back at least two thousand years. Is it just a coincidence that this overlaps nicely with the coming of the Messiah? If not entirely concurrent with the advent of Christianity, the destructive cannibalistic impulse within civilization's fabric found an all-too-welcoming host in institutional Christianity. Forbes sees this transformation not just in political or productive power. He also views it as a spiritual cooption:

> The conversion of Europeans to Christianity was apparently accompanied by a transformation of the pre-Christian spirit realm from a generally positive world into a negative, "devilish" influence. That is,

> pre-Christian spirits continued, as it were, to haunt the forests, the moors, and the darkness of night, but instead of being benign, they became an evil threat to the good Christian's Salvation.[8]

The spirits of the pre-Christian world became the devils of the new. This transformation realized some of its bloodiest expressions during the Burning Times, the persecution of witches and warlocks of the early modern period.

In his groundbreaking work *Witchcraft and the Gay Counterculture,* Arthur Evans argues that the witch hysteria was not just a war against women but was also a persecution of sexual deviance. In the fourteenth century, Pope Innocent issued a papal bull railed against attacks of incubi and succubi, sexual demons, luring people of both sexes away from Christian salvation. The issuance of this papal decree marked the beginning of the witch trials. The evocation of demonic forces attracting people away from the Christian faith through sex was not limited to Innocent. Church fathers' condemnation of the worship of sexual organs, transvestitism, and sexual transgression show that the vestiges of pagan worship were inextricably linked in their minds to the dark sexual crossroads of the old nature spirits. During his research of contemporary confessions and trial records, Evans observes that in the sixteenth and seventeenth centuries, those who were "sexually unorthodox" were often accused of witchcraft *and* heresy.[9] He further notes that some historians may be confused about this connection due to the *Malleus Malleficarum,* the first witch-hunters' guide to obtain the papal blessing. The *Malleus* considers homosexuality so beyond the pale that even demons would not sink that low! It held that those practicing such acts after age thirty-three were so beyond redemption that it required a special intercession of the Redeemer for their soul to be saved.[10]

Homosexuality and witchcraft became so interlinked during this period that they often appeared together in popular anti-heresy tracts. Concurrent with a trial at Arras, France, a fifteenth-century pamphlet read:

> Sometimes indeed indescribable outrages are perpetrated in exchanging women, by order of the presiding devil, by passing on a woman to other women and a man to other men, an abuse against the nature of women by both parties and similarly against the nature of men, or by a woman with a man outside the regular orifice and in another orifice.[11]

A French pamphlet appeared in 1589, accusing King Henry III of France of being both a witch and having sex with men.[12] The Orleans legal code of 1260 prescribed mutilation for the first and second offenses and burning for the third for anyone convicted of gay or lesbian sexual acts. The proliferation of secular laws against sodomy was concurrent with the rise of the Inquisition. At times, this caused consternation among authorities regarding which crime took precedence. During the Lisbon trials of 1612, local authorities were confused about whether the convicted should be executed under secular criminal law for being sodomites or under church protocols for being witches.[13] Under torture, many accused confessed or admitted that homosexual acts were common to the witches' Sabbat.[14] In Scotland in 1670, an elderly bachelor, Thomas Weir, without the compulsion of torture, confessed to witchcraft, infernal fornication, and sodomy.[15]

While in college, I attended a lecture by Joan Nestle, writer, activist, and cofounder of the Lesbian Herstory Archives. In the speech, she described queer individuals as being a colonized people. Her words have stayed with me as the discourse around colonization has progressed and deepened in the last three decades. Do I think her use of the term is problematic in hindsight? I do not. A friend recently observed that "excluded" peoples are not in a competition of pain. In Nestle's "A Letter to My Community: A Sturdy Yes of a People," she draws on the perspective of Frederick Douglass. Her choice of wording was intentional and important. Queer people have been excluded. We have suffered numerous privations amid an aggressive, dominant culture and, just in the context of the last century, excluded from places of power, from our livelihoods, from keeping our children, and from our sanity. Our queerness, our particular "deviance" barred us from employment opportunities and government positions. Children could be removed from loving households simply by the choice of one's partner. Our families could commit us to the asylum or conversion "therapy."

For much of that time, dominant society has given us one choice: SILENCE. For too many of us, the reality is that not speaking has not been complicity but survival. Ironically, this silence, the threat of exposure, also meant we were viewed as a threat to national security. We, gay men, were locked in a closet of our making, correctly perceived as potential targets of blackmail. The catch-22 of our own silence prevented us from obtaining security clearances in the US government. This policy wasn't reversed until 1995. Exposure was an ever-present existential threat. And not one with little or no consequence. We have but to look to the damage done by J. Edgar Hoover as he wielded a truly weaponized FBI to attack leftists from perceived Communists to the Black Panther Party. All the time, he spent his off hours and Christmas holidays in Florida with FBI Associate Director Clyde Tolson, his special friend. Roy Cohn, the virulent architect of McCarthyism, denied his homosexuality until his last breath from AIDS. Communists and homosexuals were indelibly linked in the common vernacular.

Around that same time I heard Nestle, I had the powerful experience of hearing Larry Kramer lecture at Amherst College. He described the HIV/AIDS epidemic as a modern holocaust. He noted that it was not just "modern" but a product of the very mechanisms of modernity. Drawing from the writings of Zygmunt Bauman, Kramer pointed out that the Nazi Holocaust was not, as it was often characterized, an aberrant throwback to barbarism, but, instead, could not have occurred but for the innovations of modernity.[16] It could not have happened without utilizing the tools of the modern era, multi-level bureaucracies. Purges and genocides had occurred in the past. Still, nothing on the unprecedented scale would have been possible without the innovations of the assembly line, the modern bureaucratic state, and mass production.

Queer theorist Eve Sedgewick noted that Western culture is "fractured by a chronic, now endemic crisis of homo/heterosexual definition, indicatively male, dating from the end of the nineteenth century."[17] The creation of "the other" has long been a tool used by those in power to move the masses in opposition against an external, and oftentimes societally internal, group. In each instance, it is less about the threat posed by the other than it is a means of controlling and directing the masses. We see this in the Nazi's villainizing of the Jews, Romani, homosexuals, and communists; the internment of the Japanese by the US Government during World War II; the inner-city gangster during the war on drugs; Arabs during the war on terror; and, most recently, attacks on Asian individuals. Homosexuals have long been one of the defining "others" within Western society. The recent global reaction to the COVID pandemic starkly contrasts responses during the early darkest years of HIV/AIDS. Death was easy to ignore as long as it happened to us and not them. In the early emblematic slogan of Act Up, our silence did indeed translate all too often to death.

Ignorance is not a lack of knowledge. It is, instead, a particular form of knowing. Ignorance is not the innate state of humanity devoid of any learning. It is taught and transmitted; Control uses it for a particular purpose. Sedgewick observes, "Ignorance and opacity collude or compete with knowledge in mobilizing the flows of energy, desire, goods, meanings, persons."[18] Ignorance is always used with a purpose. Young males are taught not to observe the indications of lack of consent. The notion of the other prevents one from seeing and understanding others. In these cases, it is a dangerous way of knowing that strips away humanity and blocks otherwise humanizing impulses.

In this analysis, ignorance is a particular knowledge taught by culture, environment, and secular/ecclesiastical authorities. Take the laws and juridical practice around rape that has privileged the accused over the accuser. At trial, the defendant's ignorance or claim of not knowing all too often what the accuser has perceived. Sedgewick writes, "The rape machinery is organized by this epistemological privilege of unknowing, in turn, keeps disproportionately under discipline, of course, woman's larger ambitions to take more control over the terms of our own circulation."[19] In 1986, the Justice Department ruled employers could dismiss a person living with AIDS if the employer claimed ignorance of the medical fact that the employee posed no threat to fellow employees. Ignorance here gives license to discriminate. In his dissent from the 1984

Supreme Court decision in *Bowers v. Hardwick* upholding states' right to enact anti-sodomy legislation, Justice Blackburn called the majority opinion "the most willful blindness."[20]

Silence and ignorance conspire to devastating effect. Over the past several decades, queer people have claimed our voices. Despite the attempt to wipe out a generation of gay men, we now have our history. We must speak our truth while at the same time preserving the voices of those who have gone before. Not remaining safe in our silence is a choice we are asked to make daily. At that moment when a person at a work event asks what your wife does, we have a choice without knowing the immediate consequence. The transformation of our desire into speech is an intentional magical act.

"Desire begins as a personal voice," Nestle observes, "but when we as a people assemble in the name of desire, we are a political community forcing a new understanding of the complexities of human choice."[21]

The rise of far-right extremism is a leading indicator of freedom. Burroughs observed, "Hell hath no more vociferous fury than an endangered parasite."[22] The more the possessed are backed into a corner, the greater the death throes of the host's occupying force. The machinations of the Ugly Spirit are all too apparent in today's world.

The preceding may seem a bleak take, but human society's final movement is not yet written. There is hope that everything will turn out all right. But—and it's a big but—nothing is guaranteed. We must not forget the militarized crushing force of the Third Reich followed the liberal and sexual freedom of the Weimar Republic. The good news is that history is not circular but cyclical. History does repeat, but we have the advantage of previous experience at each repetition. As Forbes sees it, "The process of genesis is also evolutionary, a gradual unfolding of stages of creation."[23] The arc of history is a spiral.

The truth is the hard-core Shits are few in number. Burroughs estimates these "incorrigible troublemakers" at no more than ten percent.[24] They know this, as demonstrated in the lengths they will go to maintain their grip on the levers of power. We can see this in the craven actions of current conservatives within the Republican party. The push for anti-LGBTQIA+ legislation represents attempts to force us back into silence. It's not about drag queens and children's books, but about our voicing our existence and living our truth. The many moves to curtail voting rights and access to the ballot are all mobilized to contain the political voice of the historically marginalized. These actions have a long history in the United States and remain a present danger.

One imagines a permanent solution to the crisis, Burroughs describes Shit hunting squads spreading out across the land. Snipers sit on roofs in small towns and take out the local good-ole-boy lawmen. The right wing politician is gunned down while delivering his stump speech about the threat of brown people, characterized as rapists and drug smugglers streaming across the southern border. The wall may be a con, but the villainization of the other is a longer one.

In actuality, even Burroughs realized that this solution was not tenable. He argued the Shits would be ignored into extinction through widespread indifference to their position. The right to privacy here is a critical component—the right to mind one's own business. The Supreme Court's overturning of *Roe v. Wade* was more than just an attack on a woman's right to choose. It was intended explicitly as a torpedo to the judicial precedent of a constitutional right to privacy. They understand that the right to do what one chooses provided it harms no one, threatens extinction to their very existence. The concept of victimless crime, the acts we enact within the domain of our bodies, is "the lifeline of the right virus," just as oxygen is to a tumor. The understanding of inalienable rights to our bodies and voices is akin to modern anti-cancer drugs. "Cutting off this airline would have the same action as interferon," Burroughs writes, "which blocks the oxygen from certain virus strains."[25]

Towards the end of *Witchcraft and the Gay Counterculture,* Evans proposes: "Magic is one of our most powerful allies in the struggle against patriarchal industrialism."[26]

Chapter XII
As Brothers Fight Ye!

In the summer after my first year in college, I tagged along with my mother to Oxford for the Third Annual International Mouse Genetics Conference. Our accommodations were in The Queen's College, a constituent college of Oxford University originally founded in 1341. Our rooms were off the back quad near the library, which houses a fantastic collection of medieval manuscripts. The college was mainly rebuilt in the seventeenth and eighteenth centuries, replacing the original medieval structures with a more cohesive architecture. It's likely the oldest structure where I've laid my head down. There was a small cellar pub off the quad in which I spent several evenings. One night, the jukebox was permanently stuck on the recently released Erasure track "Stop!" and I spent much of that evening chatting up a particularly handsome postdoc at the bar while Andy Bell's voice was on insanity-inducing repeat in the background of the close-quartered cellar.

During the conference, I had my days pretty much to myself to wander around and explore Oxford. One day, I walked out through the Porter's lodge and set off down the High Street with no purpose or thought to a map. I took a right out of the gate—err, I mean left; I'm always wrong with those two. I remember crossing a small stone bridge or two. Eventually, I happened on a tiny bookshop and ventured in. I was pleasantly surprised the shop had a decent occult section with locally published titles and zines. There, I purchased a small book by Katon Shual entitled *Sexual Magick*. The cover had an evocative image of a nude man with a kundalini serpent drawn up his back.

The book was groundbreaking and proved seminal (pun intended) for my magickal praxis for a long while after first contact. Shual summed up his desired outcome and central premise:

> We want to change the traditional roles and power relationships forced on Magical groups by previous generations. Central to this is the desire for a complete balance and equality between the various partners, whatever the gender.[1]

At the time of his writing—the book came out in 1989—gender inequality and structurally encoded gender binaries were still common within magickal practice. Gender polarity within Gardnerian and Alexandrian traditions was only one manifestation. Crowley often approached his female working partners as tools or vessels. Unfortunately, this magickal mistreatment did not die with him, continuing in subtle and less subtle ways in a male-dominated magick. Shual takes it further and explicates an inspiration myth for male+male magickal practice.

He points to a single line in *The Book of the Law*: "As brothers fight ye!"[2] The book is the originating "holy book" of Crowley's religious system of Thelema. It was a received text dictated to him by a preterhuman intelligence over three days in April 1904. The three chapters are each aligned with a particular

Egyptian conceptual deity. The first is the voice of Nuit, the goddess whose arched body forms the night sky. The second is the voice of Hadit, the winged sphere. Nuit is limitless potential; Hadit is the individuating point at the center of the universe. The circumference is arbitrary, and the central point is everywhere. Ra-Hoor-Khuit, an aspect of the god Horus, takes the lead in the third and final chapter. As the god ascendent in the aeon, or age, to come, within Crowley's system, he speaks of the disruption as the Aeon of Osiris, the dying god, is superseded by the conquering child Horus. Warlike imagery is not uncommon in chapter three, so the line Shual points to is usually interpreted as a give-no-quarter or fight-honorably sort of sentiment.

In his analysis, Shual takes it in a different direction indeed. He first points us to the Lovers card in the tarot (VI in the major arcana). In *The Book of Thoth*, Crowley gives an alternate title for this card: the Brothers.[3] We see two small children before the bride and groom figures. Crowley links them to Cain and Abel. The card is ascribed to the zodiac sign of Gemini, reinforcing the twin brothers concept. It is related to the Hebrew letter Zain, or the sword, which alludes to the fact that identical, or monozygotic, twins are created from dividing a single egg into two, which then are fertilized. This division and reconstitution resembles the magickal formula *Solve et Coagula* written on the arms of fin de siècle depictions of Baphomet. Crowley notes that the card reflects the world's creation, but here the operants "were concerned, create a new universe of their own."[4]

Going back to *The Book of the Law*, the personage represented by the third chapter is Horus. He has a famous relationship with his brother (and sometimes uncle) Set or Seth. The latter often gets a bad rap. Early Egyptologists viewed him as a sort of destroyer or evil deity. He was the god connected to the South of Egypt with its heat, fire, and foreigners. He is the prototypical

SOLVE
COAGULA
ELIPHAS
LEVI DEL.

other. Even his animal visage is unfamiliar with its squared-off ears and split tail. It has confounded Egyptologists as no analogous living creature has yet been identified. Importantly, Set is critical to the Egyptian's conception of an ordered universe. The pharaoh is said to rule by the Horus and the Set. The pharaoh's throne is often flanked by depictions of the two on either side. In Egyptian cosmology, Horus represents the order when the king is on the throne. Set is that interstitial space between one ruler's death and their successor's ascension. Both are necessary aspects of the divinity of kingship at the pinnacle of Egyptian civilization.

The two are linked in intrinsic oppositional combat, the fighting brothers. Indeed, they are sometimes represented by a single, two-headed hieroglyph, Heru-fi. Their conflict is a central myth. As the story goes, Set makes sexual advances toward Horus. Isis warns her son about taking a submissive or passive role. Horus gives in to Set's overtures, and the two have sex either anally or via *coitus interfemoris*, the insertion of Set's penis between Horus's thighs.

When Set climaxes, Horus loses his power, and his famous eye—which symbolizes the anus—is said to close or go dark. The myth tells how, at this point, Horus grabs Set's balls and regains his strength. This is often interpreted as a symbol of castration, but it is much more likely, given the next part of the myth, that Horus takes Set's semen into his hand, thus using the product of their union to reopen his blinded eye. Horus then sprinkles the cum onto the sacred lettuce of Set. The latter then eats the salad with cum dressing. From this ingestion, the god Thoth is born. It is important to note that no aspersions are cast upon Thoth for the queer nature of his origin.

The disorder is critical for order. Primordial chaos precedes law and stability. In the traditional Qabalah, the levels of Nothingness come before the first emanation on the Tree of Life in the sephirot Kether, which is so sublime it is unknowable. In *The Vision and the Voice*, Crowley observes that the second sphere, Chokmah, represents Chaos, "the unformed potential that precedes the formulations of Saturn in Binah."[5] It is first in the disordered that Nothingness coalesces into form. It then moves on to its initial ordered state in the third sphere, Binah, thus completing the supernal triad of the Tree. I am reminded here of the Buddhist *Heart Sutra*, which states that emptiness is form and form emptiness.

Set is mentioned in another Thelemic received text, *Liber A'ash vel Capricorni Pneumatici*. There, he is described as Horus's "holy covenant, that he shall display in the great day of M.A.A.T."[6] Internally, the text interprets M.A.A.T. as the Master of the Temple grade of Crowley's Golden Dawn-styled occult order, the Argenteum Astrum. We've discussed the Magister Templi grade previously. Maat is the Egyptian goddess who presides over the moment of judgment in *The Book of the Dead*, where the deceased's heart is weighed against her feather. She is the embodiment of order, harmony, and truth. A covenant is a promise—here, a promise against something. Set is the force that stands against the eruption of undirected chaos. Again, we are reminded of the Lord of Misrule, the element of disruption in the Yule time festivities whose existence channels disorder and prevents it from appearing the rest of the year.

Shual's book was an inspiration to me. Later that year, it led to my cofounding a magickal order, The Brotherhood of SeTh (TBOS). We drew a small body of queer experimenters who worked on fleshing out the magickal current embodied in the myth of Horus and Set mixed with the magical writings of William S. Burroughs. TBOS was active from 1989 to around 1995 and produced the occult zine *mektoub*. It may have been a small group, but we were attracting some important contemporary figures to our fun, including Frater Belarion, the editor of the journal *Abrasax*. In 1992, we established a physical lodge, Heru-fi, that operated in the labyrinthine basement beneath the occult store Ananael, which I owned in Portland, Maine. You may find more on TBOS's work in the group's collected papers, *The Star Set Matrix*. Additionally, I will be writing in more detail about the magical system practiced by TBOS in a future book.

DESTRUCTION OF THE HOUSE OF GOD

We shall return to the tarot to explore this current a little further. We discussed The Lovers, or The Brothers, card earlier. We will now turn to four Major Arcana cards, beginning with XIII through XVI. The Major Arcana is a name given to the twenty-two trump cards of the tarot, Atu Zero through Atu XXI. Each card corresponds to a particular path on the traditional occult Tree of Life. They may be viewed as representative of the initiate's journey from the Fool (0) to the World (21). We will examine in some detail a sub-sequence in this initiatory formula, incorporating four cards in Aleister Crowley's Thoth deck, drawn by Lady Frieda Harris.

We shall begin with card XIII, Death. In the Crowley/Harris deck, we find death, scythe in hand, reaping souls and sending them spiraling into the afterlife. One can see the individuals represented as ghostly figures becoming less distinct in form as they move up a geometric ladder of spheres. We will see this echoed in a couple of cards when we get to the Devil. The card represents the cleaving of the souls, whether one or many, from the corpus or physical remains. It is also symbolic of a splitting apart of the self. We go back to the first half of the alchemical formula of Baphomet—*Solve* to dissolve. This is the first step of this subroutine. We must be dissolved before we may be built up again.

The next card (XIV) in the Thoth deck is called Art. The dissolution process continues here. This card depicts the most crucial moment in the alchemical formula of transubstantiation. The card centers on an androgynous figure with two faces pouring materials into a crucible. Looking back to The Lovers, you may realize that the two faces of the figure represent the combination of the bride and groom into one person. Here, things are reversed in their union. The dark face wears the white crown, while the lighter face face wears the gold. The arms are countermatched with the colors of the faces.

In the Lovers card, A red lion and white eagle are in the lower two corners. These are alchemical sex magickal symbols. The lion represents the male, and the eagle is the female. The red lion is the male essence, semen, while the white eagle is the menstruum, or "magical solvent of the female organ."[7] The latter may represent mucous membranes, most notably the vulva, mouth, and anus. We also find these figures in the art card, but again, like the bride and groom, they are switched up. The lion is now white and the eagle red. It is as if we've entered the mirror universe in *Star Trek*. I can't help but think of the nature of this card being very gender-fluid. Sex identifiers are switching it up all over the place.

The figure pours white liquid from the chalice formerly held by the bride and dissolves the groom's wand into the molten material in their crucible—an alchemical melting pot used in the purification process. This is a process of removing contaminants, analogous to the purification of the soul. The Latin that forms an arc around the figure (Visita Interiora Terrae Rectificando Invenies Occultum Lapiiderm) translates to:

"Visit the interior parts of the Earth; by rectification thou shalt find the hidden stone."[8] This process is not easy or singular. Rectification is a process of purification through repeated distillations. We must repeat the cycle of life from death to afterlife to birth over and over each time, coming through a little differently than the time before. The initials of the Latin spell out VITRIOL, the Universal Solvent. Thus, the formula continues.

The crucible is linked to death through Harris's incorporation of the *caput mortuum* symbol, the raven atop a skull, on the crucible. The seed element represented by the orphic egg between the brothers on the Lovers card is the entirety of the Art card. The soul has gone through the putrefaction process in Death and is now undergoing purification of repeated distillation. The card is aligned with the zodiac sign Sagittarius, which Crowley links to Diana the Huntress.[9] She is the Great Mother of Fertility. Crowley remarks that Art is the "culmination of the Royal Marriage" depicted in the Lovers card.

Now, we move on to the Devil (XV). Here, we complete the formula begun in the Death card with *coagula*, coagulation, and combining elements following the dissolution and distillation/purification processes. The orphic egg in the Lovers card is now two globes. The souls dissolved after being cleaved by the grim reaper's scythe have coalesced as white figures in the Devil's balls. They are potentially waiting to erupt back into the world. The Goat God, crowned by a wreath of flowers, looks out at us through his three eyes. Indeed, the Hebrew letter associated with the card is Ayin, meaning the Eye. His horns echo the receptivity of spread legs. His enormous cock presses its tip through a halo, the vagina or anus. Crowley defines this card as "creative energy in its most material form."

The card is linked to Capricorn, "the goat leaping with

lust upon the summits of the earth."[10] In the previous card, our journey took us to the depths of the earth; here, we are reaching, as raw potential, towards its highest peaks. The Devil here is the pre-Christian horned god, Pan Pangenetor, the all-begetter. We are reminded of Eliphas Levi's depiction of Baphomet, an androgynous, goat-headed god depicting the two sexes combined. On their arms are written the formula *Solve et Coagula*. Between his horns is the flame of occult illumination. This image is reminiscent of the Bucca, which we discuss in more detail later. Older images on this card often show two individuals chained to the Devil's throne. Rather than constraint or constriction, the symbolism is one of fomenting potential.

Echoing the phallic central image of the Devil card is the Tower Atu XVI, alternatively called The Destruction of the House of God. The stone tower bends in post-coital tumescence as it shoots forth individuals. These black geometric figures are the white figures that swirled within the orbs of the preceding card. The Tower card is attributed to the Hebrew letter Pe, meaning mouth. This is represented in the creature in the lower right whose open jaws spew fire. The mouth is a sexually charged element, igniting the conflagration that causes the tower's demise, replacing the lightning of more traditional examples of this trump. The serpent or dragon hinted at by this fire-breathing creature we only get a glimpse of may be linked to the kundalini serpent, whose fiery energy moved up through the chakras during sexual arousal.

Above the structure, Crowley has added an eye or moon. Crowley describes this as the Eye of Horus, or Sivas eye, through the opening of which the Universe is destroyed. Crowley adds an interesting note regarding the hidden meaning of this card:

> Besides this, there is a special technical magical meaning, which is explained openly only to initiates of the Eleventh degree of the O.T.O.; a grade so secret that it is not even listed in the official documents. It is not even to be understood by study of the Eye in Atu XV. Perhaps it is lawful to mention that the Arab sages and the Persian poets have written, not always guardedly, on the subject.[11]

By alluding to the secret formula of the OTO's XI°, Crowley is linking the Tower card to anal sex—the order's worst kept "secret." His allusion to "Arab sages" and "Persian poets" reinforces that he is alluding to male homosexual activities. We recall how he masked himself as an Arab poet when publishing his collection of explicit homosexual verse, *The Scented Garden*. Interestingly, the eye of the Tower card is placed in a similar position in the composition to the ring through which the Devil's cock is inserted on Atu XV. Perhaps the first is the initial insertion of the phallus, while the Tower is the resulting climax. As we saw in the myth of the contending of Horus and Set, the Eye of Horus is also a euphemism for his anus. In many respects, the Tower is an iconographic depiction of the magical formula in the myth. At times, the eye above the tower is also described as a moon. I doubt it is a coincidence that the moon has been English slang for the buttocks since at least 1743.

So here, in this subroutine within the Fool's journey, a process of transmutation is demonstrated where the putrefying corpse is transformed into unbridled lusty potential. This culminates in a secret formula where the brothers are united in the magical union—*Jungitur en vati vates*. The Bard joined with the Bard; the world is disrupted. This is the Devil's plantation, the uncultivated field as an exhibition of unbridled natural potential.

ALIM: THE FORMULA OF WITCHCRAFT

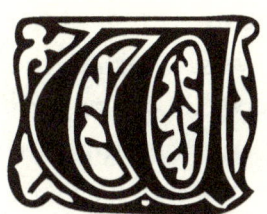

We will pause momentarily to consider a cryptic footnote in Crowley's *Magick in Theory and Practice,* the third part of his tetralogy, *Liber ABA: Book Four.* In Chapter IV, Crowley elucidates two magical formulas: ALHIM and ALIM. The former he describes as an operation of consecration; the latter he links to witchcraft. ALIM is a formula that lacks the female element, the Hebrew letter Hey. One thinks of the ritual operation of the Wild Boys, where life is created without the involvement of the female principal. He describes ALIM as a formula "of a very special kind."[12] Through gematria, a form of analysis through the addition of the numerical values of the Hebrew alphabet, the formula has the value of 81, which is the same as the moon. Here, we think of the eye or moon above the Tower. Crowley links this with witchcraft under the dominion of Hecate.

He describes the practices of witchcraft contained within the word as "illusory" and states seemingly unequivocally that "no true Magical operation can be performed by the formula."[13] Beneath the text proper, he includes an intriguing and detailed footnote. In it, he notes that initiates of the Eleventh Degree may know an alternate interpretation of the formula. Instead of the moon as a celestial body, Crowley suggests that the numeric value 81 may relate to the sephirot Yesod, the foundation of the Tree of Life. He points to this being the hidden nature of the formula. Yesod corresponds to the sacral, or genital, chakra and its relation to sexual energy.

Here, we have an operation without the feminine

component, where the force arisen is employed for purely deliberate purposes and thus "is entirely absorbed in its own sphere." He describes the operation as "holy" and expounds how "its effect is to consecrate the Magicians [male and plural] who perform it in a very special way."[14] Continuing with gematria, we can combine 8+1 to come up with 9, which Crowley links to Leo, the alchemical lion we saw earlier, the male principal, and the Serpent, which may be related to both the male generative force of the phallus and the kundalini serpent energy that moves from the sacral to the crown chakra.

In the footnote, Crowley alludes obliquely to "the well-known poem of Catullus." The official OTO version of *Magick*, the Weiser edition edited by OTO Caliph Hymaneus Beta and sometimes referred to as "the Blue Brick," points us to Catallus's poem number 74.[15] I find this suggestion challenging to sustain. The poem involves screwing one's uncle's wife, doing as one wishes, and forcing said uncle to suck him off. I'm unsure; I see no readily apparent connection to what Uncle Al discusses. I think this may be what is known in the magical tradition as a blind or intentional textual deceit to set one down the wrong direction. A red herring, if you will. There is a much more notorious poem by Catullus so scandalous it was not officially translated until comparatively recently. Stephen Skinner, in his edition of *Magick*, I think correctly, points us to poem 16, which begins, "*Pedicabo ego vos et irrumabo...*" In English translation:

> I will sodomize you and face-fuck you,
> bottom Aurelius and catamite Furius,
> you who think, because my poems
> are sensitive, that I have no shame.
> For it's proper for a devoted poet to be moral
> himself, [but] in no way is it necessary for his

poems.
In point of fact, these have wit and charm,
if they are sensitive and a little shameless,
and can arouse an itch,
and I don't mean in boys, but in those hairy old men
Who can't get it up.
Because you've read my countless kisses,
you think less of me as a man?
I will sodomize you and face-fuck you.[16]

Micaela Wakil Janan provides a modernized translation in her work *When the Lamp is Shattered: Desire and Narrative in Catullus*:

> Fuck you, boys, up the butt and in the mouth, you queer Aurelius and you fag Furius! You size me up, on the basis of my poems, because they're a little sexy, as not really decent. A poet has to live clean – but not his poems. They only have spice and charm, if somewhat sexy and really not for children – if, in fact, they cause body talk (I'm not talking in teenagers, but in hairy old men who can barely move their stiff bums). But you, because you happen to read about "many thousands of kisses," you think I'm not a man? Fuck you, boys, up the butt and in the mouth![17]

Thus, there can be little debate about the true nature of the witches' formula Crowley alludes to. While ALHIM is a formula for consecrating one's magical implements, ALIM is an operation that involves two or more male magicians and consecrates *them* in a very special way under the dark night sky at the crossroads of Hecate.

Crowley continues:

> The great merits of this formula are that it avoids contact with the inferior planes, that it is self-sufficient, that it involves no responsibilities, and that it leaves its masters not only stronger in themselves, but wholly free to fulfill their essential Natures.[18]

It is holy in and of itself—self-contained and self-sufficient. The myth of binary existence is disrupted. "The Western Lands," Burroughs writes, "are reached by the contact of two males, the myth of duality is exploded and the initiates can realize their natural state."[19]

In the same work as our title derives, Grant attacks any homosexual interpretation of the ALIM formula despite Crowley's pretty clear references in his footnote. He employs rather stretched references to the qabalah to argue that this method of sexual magick includes the female through reference. He flatly states, "This form of occultism is sometimes confused with homosexual techniques that are in no way cognate."[20] Decidedly, he misses the point, and the joke, of Crowley's text. The moon is not universally viewed as female. When two men come together sky clad beneath the moon, the contact of flesh is just as fertile with possibility. Camile Paglia calls this intersection "the uncanny crossroads of Hecate." This "point of contact between man and nature", she writes, is where "morality and good intentions fall to primitive urges."[21]

ALIM was a particular formula experimented with by the brothers of TBOS.

Chapter XIII
Friendship As a Way of Life

You never change things by fighting the existing reality. To change something, build a new model that makes the existing model obsolete. —R Buckminster Fuller

Michel Foucault perceived LGBTQIA+ individuals as residing in a privileged space based on potentiality relative to the transformation of personal relationships. He viewed alternative sexualities as "an occasion to re-open effective and relational virtualities" since it has the potential to "introduce love where there's supposed to be only law, rule or habit."[1] He discussed this redelineation of desire as a reconfiguration of "friendship." In an interview just months before his death in 1984, he proposed that "the disappearance of friendship as a social relation and the declaration of homosexuality as a social/political/medical problem, are the same process."[2]

In the modern world, there exists very little to structure friendship. After the breakdown of the 'cult of friendship' in the nineteenth century, as outlined in Carroll Smith-

Rosenberg's "The female world of love and ritual," friendship has become ambiguous and ill-defined. Social media and its digital-age "friends" have not filled this constitutional void. Under the rubric of "friendship," Foucault begins positioning his notion of male+male askesis, or ascetic practice. Foucault's use of the Greco-Roman concept of askesis is very precise. By it, he points to a process of creating or inventing what it means to be homosexual rather than *discovering* an essentialized homosexual "identity." He states:

> The world [regards] sexuality as the secret of the creative world; it is rather a process of our having to create a new cultural life underneath the ground of our sexual choices.[3]

For Foucault, sexuality becomes meaningful through a dynamic exploration, expansion, and creation process. This is in contrast to the early modern notion of a static realm of private revelation and confession. He asked gay men to begin to understand what can be established through new ways of coming together. He said, "We have to understand that with our desires, through our desires, go new forms of relationships, new forms of love, new forms of creation."[4]

In the era after the sexual revolution, the gay liberation movement, gay assimilation, and the rise of Queer politics, new possibilities for relationships exist. As interpersonal relations begin entering a realm relatively free from legal and social restraints, gay men need to refigure their relationships outside of the realms of "law, rule or habit." Through his discussion of homosexual askesis, Foucault argued that gay men should seek to establish an art of living based on creating the domain of personal sexuality. "Sex," he wrote, "is not a fatality; it's a possibility for creative life."[5]

Michel Foucault

In many ways, modern sexualities remain undefined territory. The definitions that the medical and scientific movements developed in the late nineteenth century never fully encompassed significant portions of our subcultures. One cannot live long under the assumption of sin; critical attitudes must evolve in response to adverse conditions. The history of same-sex desire in the modern West can, thus, be viewed as a search for meaning. The process can be observed strongly in the work of Walt Whitman, my father's favorite poet, with his attempts at creating a mythic system based around the Calamus symbol. It can also be seen in the work of early homosexual rights advocates, such as John Addington Symonds, Edward Carpenter, Karl Ulrichs, and, to some extent, Aleister Crowley.

This formative process of homosexual definition is most

poignantly manifested in the life and style of Oscar Wilde. Indeed, to a large extent, Foucault's discourse can be seen as having been begun by Wilde. He always spoke of his life as a work of art—a work of creative presentation. He asserted, "I have put only my genius into my work; my art I have put into my life." Wilde seemed to feel that the act of living, especially as a gay man, was a work of artifice. "The first duty in life is to be as artificial as possible," he wrote.[6] Like Foucault, Wilde felt that, in a world lacking appropriate modes of being, the only choice a homosexual has is to begin a creative process of experimental practice and presentation.

Surrounded by the medical movement to define difference that characterized same-sex desire in the nineteenth century, Wilde attempted to transpose his desire into a style of living. He seems to have recognized a particular element of social construction a century before Foucault's work. He argued that "most people are other people. Their thoughts are someone else's opinions, their life mimicry, their passions a quotation."[7] In the quips and maxims that characterize Wildean dialogues, he reveals his methods for dealing with a desire that was at once both dangerous *and* improbable. I must pause here to say I do not wish to be accused of hero worship. He did not always make wise choices. He certainly problematized his social creativity, as can be easily observed in the arrogant banter that characterized his courtroom testimony during the three trials he endured. I want to point toward the relatively long history of the connection between the modern expression of same-sex desire and the exploration of designing an art of living. What Foucault talks of in his later interviews on homosexual askesis does echo Wilde's cultural philosophy in several fundamental ways.

In his work on Wilde, *Who Was That Man*, gay novelist and actor Neil Bartlett argues that homosexual life must be intentional forgery (self-creation). He writes:

> There is no intrinsic value to homosexuality. There is no "real" us, we can only ever have an unnatural identity, which is why we are all forgers. We create life, not out of lies, but out of more or less conscious choices; adaptations, imitations and plain theft of styles, names, social and sexual roles, bodies.[8]

As Foucault frequently argues, there is no "essential" innerness of being "gay." Any internal search for such a nature must result in a discursive dead end. More often than not, this cul-de-sac of personal interrogation results in a reliance on the ideological assumptions that lie at the heart of the crisis of identity politics. The definitions that gay men have been given—by religion, medicine, and law—provide little basis for living life. They do not speak, nor have they ever genuinely spoken to, the ways we must see to survive. Dominant culture provides few imperatives to which gay men can subscribe, therefore we must always pose as something. After one rejects the definitions of deviance and unnaturalness, what is left? We do have several choices in the modern cultural arena. However, the central choice still lies in the division between attempting to shape one's life around the heterosexual imperatives that permeate every level of society or removing oneself into a zone of identity presented by our own subculture(s).

The history of "homosexuality" has been broken along these lines since the word was first coined. Gay men have chosen between the marriage-based family unit and the liberalizing agendas of gay politics, others remaining marginalized on the sidelines of both. Gay and bisexual men have attempted to find their own comfort within the marital ideal through an attempt at de-heterosexualizing the family. In the 1990s, I recall gay couples on *Oprah, Donahue,* and *Sally Jesse Raphael* dressed up as young preppy boys/girls just out of college. Could anything be more natural than two young people attempting to find a life together after graduation? One of them always says, "We are not here to destroy the family; we just want the definition to include us." This choice implies a position of isolated homosexuality, where "the choice of love" is only a minor character difference from the American ideal.

On the other hand, some choose to define themselves relative to their love of other men completely. They place themselves in one of several political/fetishistic camps that have shaped and reshaped both before and after the mythic awakening of the Stonewall riots. For these men, same-sex desire is fused with an extensive portion of their lives. Both these positions may prove tenuous or transitorily satisfying, however. A redefinition of the American family could destroy it since it has never been more than a myth existing in a given temporal locus. The sexual revolution shatters the American family of the 1950s. Homosexuality continues to be a powerful defining other in conservatives' political and religious mythologies. Gay men are the antithesis of everything those few who still rely on the familial myth hold dear. We queers will never be welcome at their tables or reunions. Identity based on political positioning presents an alternative that isn't any more stable. Political ideologies and social pressures are continually shifting, aspects moving on and off the cultural center stage, while personal political stances remain all too often static. The political activist of today quickly becomes the dated stalwart of tomorrow.

In many countries where men engage in same-sex intercourse, such activity is criminal. We are indeed forgers, conscious or not, who routinely pose as law-abiding citizens. Gay men have power when they refuse their criminality, as illustrated in the fiction of William S. Burroughs, Jean Genet, and Dennis Cooper. Burroughs describes his character Joe the Dead as a "Natural Outlaw" who breaks the laws of nature.[9] More often than not, however, gay men ignore the implications of their criminality, carefully constructing a separation between the bar and the bank. Later in the same work quoted above, Bartlett discusses how criminality and personal homosexual interpretation play out their relation within gay male life. He writes of a weekend night at the bar:

> It is our commonest experience that after breaking the law we become law-abiding citizens. . . . We regularly watch ourselves turn into the most improbable creatures, transform back again, then set off to the office or the dole office just like anybody else. . . . Morning does not disrupt the night any more than the glamour, the ferocity and wickedness of the night challenges or abolishes the day.[10]

He continues:

> After the moments of harsh intimacy with ourselves or with others we like the world to fall back into place again. We acknowledge, with extraordinary calmness, given how much this all costs us, that there is no radical impulse beneath our radical acts.[11]

Bartlett argues that gay men's intimate actions move them momentarily "up or down" but never "forward."[12] Gay men lack a unifying system, a mythic structure of interpretive stories, to critically engage with their "radical acts." No matter how much ecstasy we experience Saturday night—even if we stretch it long into Sunday—morning comes. Experience of such heights moves us up and down but rarely forward.

My college friend Chris Cutrone observes: "The idealist construction of the subject founders on its falsely taking subject to be objective in the sense of something existing in-itself, precisely what it is not: measured against the standard of entities, the subject is condemned to nothingness."[13] If we're not gazing deep within looking for a Queer "self" where are we going with all this? Despite how his philosophy has been characterized, Foucault did not hold that the individual was a social construction—a semi-homogenous amalgam of history, culture, and environment. In a 1982 interview, Foucault articulated his position in a lighter tone, "I don't feel that it is necessary to know exactly what I am. The main interest in life and work is to become something else that you were not in the beginning."[14]

On the high-tops once more gathering he will celebrate with naked dances the glory of the human form and the great processions of the stars, or greet the bright horn of the young moon which now after a hundred centuries comes back laden with such wondrous associations — all the yearnings and the dreams and the wonderment of the generations of mankind — the worship of Astarte and of Diana, of Isis or the Virgin Mary; once more in sacred groves will he reunite the passion and the delight of human love with his deepest feelings of the sanctity and beauty of Nature; or in the open, standing uncovered to the Sun, will adore the emblem of the everlasting splendor which shines within. The same sense of vital perfection and exaltation which can be traced in the early and pre-civilization peoples — only a thousand times intensified, defined, illustrated and purified — will return to irradiate the redeemed and delivered Man. —Nineteenth century queer activist Edward Carpenter, *Civilization: Its Cause and Cure* (1889)

Chapter XIV
Brilliant Creatures

As we've discussed, gender and sexual variance have had a long connection with the practice of magic, stretching back into the time before history and flickering across cultures. Unfortunately, this linkage had been lost as Western society approached the modern era.

The cave engravings found in caves at Addaura, near Palermo, Sicily, date between the late Epigravettian (late Upper Paleolithic) and the Mesolithic eras. One of the carvings depicts a circle of men, some with erections, wearing bird masks or headpieces. At the center are two prone figures with lines between them. The traditional interpretation is that the image depicts human sacrifice. It is, however, quite possible this stems from the chauvinistic and hetero-centric lens of modern male anthropologists.

In *Blossom and Bone,* Randy P. Conner offers an alternate interpretation where he sees the two central figures as engaged in a ritual act of homoeroticism.[1] It is not difficult for gay men to see it this way—two men, one on top with an erection facing at the butt of the bottom on all fours facing away. Here are the predecessors of Burroughs's Wild Boys in their fabulous zoomorphic guises. It is interesting to note that some bystanders appear to have bird masks. The wild boys gather in the Blue Desert of Silence and form a magical circle around the ritual operant as the Zimbu takes form. "Zimbu Xolotl Time is the wild boy festival where the different tribes gather to meet, exchange fighting techniques, and indulge in communal orgies whereby zimbus are created," Phil Hine writes. "The festival has no fixed date or place – the boys converge there instinctively."[2]

Arthur Evans, author of *Witchcraft and the Gay Counterculture*, links the modern derogatory term "faggot" with the fuel used to burn witches and heretics. Evans was highly influenced by Margaret Murray's now generally discredited theories, so this etymology has to be taken with at least a few grains of salt. On the other hand, Conner does propose a similar connection through a more circuitous yet probable linguistic route. Whether the relationship exists or not, by the time of the anti-witch hysteria that swept Europe, sexual and gender variants were grouped with witches, prostitutes, sorcerers, and other heretical criminals. One only needs to look at Joan of Arc.

Like witches, sexual and gender variants walk in the on the outside of society, culture, criminality, and transgression. Writer and magician William S. Burroughs described his protagonist in *The Western Lands* thus:

> Joe the Dead belongs to a select breed of outlaws known as the NOs, natural outlaws dedicated to breaking so-called natural laws of the universe foisted upon us by physicists, biologists and, above all, the monumental fraud of cause and effect, to be replaced by the more pregnant concept of synchronicity.[3]

As noted in our previous discussion of the Devil, ordinary outlaws break artificial laws. Laws against theft and murder are broken every second. You only break a natural law once. To the common criminal, breaking the law is a means to an end: obtaining money or removing a source of danger or annoyance. To the NO, breaking a natural law is an end in itself: the end of that law. Coincidence is replaced with the Jungian concept of synchronicity.

In conversation, my friend Trebor Healey observed that gay men are naturally shamans. Our domain has long been the interstitial space between worlds, between culture and the subversive, between seemingly mundane surface materiality and the co-existing dimensions of spirit. We trod a path that stretches far behind us—with origins in prehistory—accompanied by the echoing footsteps of those who have walked before: the galli, hierodule servants of Cybele; the crossdressing priests of Isis dancing to call the Nile to rise; the *seiðrmen* of the Norse sagas; the Taoist immortal Lan Zai He; the two spirits of the native peoples; the visionary artists of the Renaissance, Romantics, and fin de siècle Symbolists. Within our brotherhood's jewel box, we are gifted a postmodern framework of myth and magickal praxis to individuate new possibilities out of our rich historicity.

There is no time like the present to reclaim your birthright...

Part Two
Sowing the Seeds

The most merciful thing in the world, I think, is the inability of the human mind to correlate all its contents. We live on a placid island of ignorance in the midst of black seas of infinity, and it was not meant that we should voyage far. The sciences, each straining in its own direction, have hitherto harmed us little; but some day the piecing together of dissociated knowledge will open up such terrifying vistas of reality, and of our frightful position therein, that we shall either go mad from the revelation or flee from the deadly light into the peace and safety of a new dark age. —HP Lovecraft, "The Call of Cthulhu"

Here There Be Monsters

Proceed with a certain degree of caution. Following initiation, or dedication, you move into territory at the very edge of the map. Some mysteries are hidden because they are meant to be. As you contemplate proceeding, you are on the verge of embarking on a journey for which the course is uncertain. Your guidebook may tell you not to panic, but any master is simply a friend holding a lamp ahead of you on the path. Your progress follows not a charted way but advances through the experiential. As Alan Watts famously said, "The map is not the territory."

> The elder sorceries of the warlock and the witch-wife now exfoliate into lush growth and the forbidden sciences and mystic arts hold sway over men's minds—deeper secrets yet will be uncovered and the sons and daughters of men will once again learn the shadowed arcanae from the Gramarye if the Old Faith. —Nigel Jackson *Masks of Misrule*

Chapter XV
Vikings Were Bottom Shamers

Viking magical practice was divided into two forms: runic magic and *seiðr*. The former was considered the realm of men, while the latter was women's domain. *Seiðr* practices were likely similar to those known in Old English or Anglo-Saxon as wiccecræft, from which we derive our modern word Wicca. In a culture that prioritized strength and virility, male individuals who practiced Norse witchcraft, *seiðr*, were considered less than manly. The term *ergi* was a derogatory word for men who took on women's traditional roles or appearance. It likely also denoted those that took the passive position during anal sex. Yes, in the words of Amy Jefford Franks, the Vikings were bottom shamers.[1]

Much of what we know about Norse culture and magical practice comes from the Icelandic sagas written down at least a century after the height of the Viking Age (793-1100CE). These tales are our earliest written records of Viking practices and attitudes. It should not be ignored that the authors of these tales were themselves Christians with their own particular biases. Each, to a greater or lesser degree, brought their own Christian beliefs to bear on the histories they recorded. In these instances, however, the impact of the author's own religious beliefs may have had less of a pejorative agenda than the ecclesiastical authors who provide us with the earliest records of Anglo-Saxon belief. The Icelandic author Snorri was driven by a desire to preserve Icelandic culture, not principally to set paganism against "superior" Christian beliefs, as with English writers.

Like much of the pre-Christian West, magic was ever present in the Viking world. We know magical practices and practitioners were essential in Viking culture. We know less, however, about the belief system underlying these practices. Vikings may have held less to an articulated religious system and more to a uniformity of practice—much as we follow a system of orthopraxy as opposed to orthodoxy. We must be careful in thinking the Vikings were so far removed from the present day to be something out there and back then. Archeological historian Price encourages us to consider the Vikings as "unfamiliar" but *not* "other" as we approach them.[2]

From the sagas, we know that males who practiced *seiðr* were often called *ergi*, a term denoting those who crossed, or more accurately blurred, gender and sexual boundaries.[3] While this term is often used derogatorily, it is hard to tell how much of that was true in the early Viking Age and how much was the influence of the early Christianization of Iceland. While it is entirely possible Viking culture held a negative opinion of homosexuality, there may also be far more nuances. We can discern that *seiðr* was considered the domain of the feminine, the gift of the goddesses, and those males who practiced it were considered something different from those who didn't. Indeed the term *seidberendr*, sorcerer or male witch, may have also meant male anal sex. It seems the practice breaks gender roles and makes the practitioner something else, but I wouldn't go as far as to suggest the development of a "third gender" as observed in some shamanic cultures. Price argues this is less about *another* gender as much as a "blurring" of normative gender roles.[4]

All we need do is look at Óðin, the uber-manly warrior-father of the Aesir gods. He is known as the magician who brought the runes to humankind. On the other hand, he is also known as the king of the *seiðr* practitioners. Tales tell of Óðin practicing *seiðr* and even refer to him as *ergi* as a result.

In *Lokasenna,* Loki appears at a feast and famously taunts the other gods and goddesses. He accuses Óðin of practicing "womanly magic," "living as a witch among the humans" and thus being a "pervert."[5] In *Harbartholjoth's* "Graybeards Song," Óðin disguises himself as a ferryman and denies Thor passage. The two get into a match of insults, in which Thor calls Graybeard "you sissy."[6] The *Ynglinga saga* discussed Óðin's practice of *seiðr* and concludes, "And this magic, when it was practiced, comes with such great queerness that it was shameful for a man to practice it, and the skill was taught to the goddesses."[7] Furthermore, in the *Prose Edda,* Óðin is referred to as a "gelding," which may have a direct link to his feminization due to his practice of witchcraft.

It is important to note that *ergi* is not just about what a person does—how he performs during sex with another male. We may observe by studying records from the early American colonies one's actions are not always interpreted as connected to a discrete identity. One could be caught buggering behind the barn, confess one's sin in front of the congregation, and be elevated to an Elder of the Church shortly after. In a context where everyone was capable of sin, being caught in the act, as it were, did not mean one was something different. This does not appear to have been the case among the Iron Age Norse. From the various contexts in which we have the word used, *ergi* seems to have been not just the performing of a particular sexual act but had more the sense of a quality or tendency of the individual.[8] Here, *queerness* is not simply what was internally, an essential nature but is a particular relation in resistance to normative power structures and social/cultural boundaries.

In the enigmatic *Gisli Saga*, one may find a complex reification of normative gender roles in Norse society through subtle codings of the character's deviance from them. Early in the tale, the titular character is accused of being *ergi*. Later, Gisli sends all the men out haymaking except his brother Porkell. The home interior is generally considered a women's domain in Norse attitudes. Porkell remains behind here, which sets him apart from the other men in the story. He is close to the partition dividing the women's area of the dwelling and can hear them gossiping. The word used here has a particular connection to female chatter, and its use further links Porkell to their domain. Elsewhere in the tale, their sister is chased by an unwanted suitor. Their father remarks if his youngest son were present, he would deal with the unwelcome guest. Gisli takes affront at this aspersion on his manly ability to handle the situation and promptly kills the suitor. Here, we have a dramatic overreaction to his father's negative comment.[9]

We can again observe this harsh reaction to those men who practice witchcraft, and thus, through association, are considered unmanly in *King Harold's Saga*. In the story, Harold Fairhair, from whence the tale gets its name, has a son, Rognvald Rettilhbeini. His name translates to "straight limbed" and may be a not-so-subtle reference to erection. Thus, the sexual undercurrent is there from the outset. Harold learns that his son is practicing women's magic. He sends his other son to deal with the situation. And deal with it, he does. Rognvald's brother sets fire to the house where his brother is staying, killing him and eighteen other men. Thus, Rognvald is murdered for practicing *seiðr* and warping gender roles. He was found only in the company of other men, and his brother felt the need to kill them all. One wonders what the straight-limbed Rognvald and his companions were doing when his brother interrupted them.[10]

In these tales, the male magical practitioner is transformed into the "Other" through his adoption of the traditionally feminine contact with the supernatural. As Dan Laurin argues, this creates a hybrid, I would say outsdier, masculinity.[11] Through his actions, the sorcerer moves by choice to the fringe of the dominant hypermasculine heroic culture. He becomes a social outlaw through his practice of witchcraft and is subjected to ridicule or worse. There is also the not-insignificant tinge of colonialism in Rognvald's story. The text makes clear his mother is of the Sami people. Indeed, it is perhaps from her that he learned of the rites that would lead to his condemnation. The Sami were a particular defining Other within Old Norse society. They were the ever-present element of primitiveness, the supernatural, and the strange to which the colonizing Norse could contrast themselves. Through his practice of magic and possibly Sami shamanism, Rogvald is queering normative social rules of gender and sexuality, setting himself apart as the Other.

In his study, *Man as Witch,* Rolf Schulte finds a similar attitude to men who practice witchcraft prevalent in other parts of Europe. Through trial records, he finds that male witches accused "were often ascribed female tasks, space, and roles." These trial records seem to echo a similar view of male practitioners to those of the Norse. Schulte's analysis found that on the continent, about a third (thirty percent) of those accused of witchcraft were male.[12] In Scotland, across all court types, thirteen percent (242) of those charged were recorded as male. Women comprised seventy-nine percent, while the sex of the remainder was not recorded.[13] Unlike the Continent, between 1554 and 1720 in Iceland, only nine out of 125, seven percent, accused were men.

One of the most detailed studies of *seiðr* is that of Brit Solli. She was the first to find explicit associations between *seiðr* and archeological evidence. In her work, she argues for "clear evidence for a discrete gender of queer shamans, whose deviant activities were crucial for the definition of normative in Viking society."[14] The term "shaman" can be a loaded one, and much debate surrounds its application outside of the context of the circumpolar peoples. Some question its use in any context outside of Siberia.

The term is often overused and popularized in both sociological and, even more so, New Age contexts. Its use here may be much less problematic. The Scandinavian people had a distinct relationship to the nearby Sami peoples of the circumpolar region. It is not as if a distinct line across the Scandinavian peninsula separated the two. No doubt, their domains overlapped in geography, trade, and, likely, intermarriage. Much like Britain's Celtic and Anglo-Saxon peoples, these connections would have led to a degree of cultural transference. Some aspects, if not the majority, of *seiðr* practices may have derived from the Sami shamanic traditions.

Importantly, if not an explicit third gender, the Norse of the late Iron Age did seem to have a notion of a 'type' of man who was sexually and gender fluid. Interestingly, unlike the shamanic third-gender individuals, transvestitism was not necessarily one of the "defining characteristics."[15] What we can observe is closer to the modern concept of queer. Unlike seventeenth-century colonial America, where no abiding nature was connected to discrete acts that transgressed the normative, we can detect the notion of an identity that is more than just the summation of a collection of "sinful" actions. Here among the Viking raiders and their gods, we can see individuals closer to our modern concepts of gay or, more aptly, queer. These were not just men who sinned but, rather, transgressed against the very laws of "nature." Through this otherness, this betweenness, the men who practice witchcraft found their power. In his examination, Price points out that: "Above all, in Queerness that Stolli resolves, I think convincingly, the apparent contradictions in Óðin's role as the masculine god of elites and simultaneous the master of the deviant cults of magic"[16]

After recently attending a lecture by Ocean Keltoi at the Mystic South Conference, I realized I would be remiss if I didn't include a discussion of Loki and the controversy surrounding his worship in modern Heathenry in this chapter. Beginning in the 1990s, many looked upon the veneration of Loki negatively. One of the most inclusive heathen organizations, The Troth, banned honoring Loki during their blots. This ban was lifted in 2019, and the prohibition against honoring Loki's sons Fenrir, the wolf, and Jormungandr, the Midgard serpent, was not reversed until 2023. The debate over the worship or inclusion of Loki has developed into two distinct camps: Lokean and, aptly named, Nokean. There is a sense among many—not least of which the early Christian compilers of the Norse myths that have come down to us—that Loki is a Norse Satan figure. Whether discussing medieval Christians or modern Nokeans, one does not have to lift the veil very high before realizing that their negative views of Loki stem from prejudicial views of pagans, outsiders, or queer people.

Brad Waggoner points to the three primary arguments used to discredit or warn against Loki worship: "Loki is evil; Loki contributes to moral decay; and Loki was never worshipped in history."[17] As Keltoi notes, "these arguments are far more intertwined than separate."[18] The first two would appear to be a circular argument. Loki is evil because he inspires moral transgression; Loki causes his followers to transgress normative societal boundaries and is, therefore, evil. The third argument is somewhat ironic, as many of the deities honored in modern Heathenry do not have much evidence of their worship in history. Some have argued that even Óðin himself is a Christian literary composite and did not have a historical cultus (see the Óðin trilogy by Shani Oates, for example). In Ragnorak, which Loki is blamed for instigating, we see little more than a grafting of the Christian end-times narrative in the biblical Book of Revelations onto Norse myth.

From what we can glean, Loki was one of the gang of Norse gods. He was a brother, or blood-brother, of Óðin and a traveling companion to Thor. At the same time, he was somewhat an outsider and possessed the nature of trickster deities in general. He liked to play jokes on his fellows and, often, buttressed his jokes with a particularly legal mind. If an agreement had a loophole, Loki would find and exploit it in continuance of his jape. In the end, though, his joking often ends to the benefit of his divine friends: Óðin's horse, the walls of Asgard, Thor's hammer, Sif's hair, Óðin's spear, Freyr's golden boar, etc. So maybe he isn't that bad after all.

One of the contributors to *Our Troth* suggests that hailing Loki during a *blot*, a ceremonial toast or ritual offering, often results in minor accidents.[19] If the lore shows us anything, it is what happens when he is not invited to the party. Indeed, several of his pranks begin from his being left out. It appears better to have him as an invited guest than not. After all, what kind of a host would one be if they welcomed Thor through the door but left his traveling companion to stand outside?

As we've seen earlier, the world does well with a bit of chaos in it: the Egyptian Seth as the promise against catastrophic discord and lawlessness; the Lord of Misrule, or Scottish Abbot of Unreason, presiding over the Feast of Fools during medieval Christmastide. It would seem that controlled disruption is healthy for the maintenance of order. These personalities represent the eruption of the unexpected.

Divine personages may bring an element of chaos, and the unexpected is a common motif within many mythologies. We find the spider character Anansi in Western African and African American folklore. In Navajo tradition, we have the mischievous acts of Coyote. We find *Sakra* in some branches of Buddhism. In North American legend, we have the tales of Br'er Rabbit (Brother Rabbit) that originated in African stories of the hare. In Greek mythology, Prometheus steals fire from the gods and gifts it to humankind.

Interestingly, several of these have a connection to fire. Mongolian Buddhism's version of *Sakra* is viewed as the creator of fire. The debate continues as to whether Loki was a god of fire. Richard Wagner popularized this connection in his Ring Cycle. In Snorri's *Prose Edda* is the story of Thor and Loki visiting the giant king Útgarða-Loki. In the tale, Loki battles Logi, literally the personification of fire, his name meaning "flame" in Old Norse. Logi is also married to Glöð, the fire giantess. Confusion arising from the similarities in the names Loki and Logi may have resulted in some of the crossover in attributes. Contemporary Lokean Dagulf Loptson has suggested the contest between Loki and Logi as a metaphor for the battle between sacred and destructive fire.[20] Certainly, Saxo, who is responsible for the story's survival, did little, if anything, to hide his agenda of contrasting silly old pagan folk beliefs against the far superior religion of Christianity.

One of the few archeological artifacts attest to Loki's role in Norse society is a hearthstone discovered in Denmark known

as the Snapton Stone. The fact that it is a hearthstone may be a solid indicator of Loki's connection to fire.[21] A hearthstone, which was likely used in a forge from the hole where the bellows would have been inserted, connects Loki to the magic of blacksmiths.

Loki was also a gender bender. In the lore, he is, at various times, a mother and a father. In one of the earliest tales, the building of the walls around Asgard, a giant is promised the hand of Freya in marriage if he can complete the walls within one winter season and with only the assistance of his stallion. Freya is unhappy at this forced betrothal. As the end of winter approaches, it appears that the giant will complete his task. Seeing this, Loki transforms into a mare and lures away the giant's stallion, thus slowing down progress enough that he doesn't finish. When Loki returns to Asgard, he brings a foal, the product of the romantic liaison. He gifts the eight-legged steed to Óðin; we know him to this day as Sleipnir.

With the giantess Angrboda, Loki fathers the Midgard serpent Jörmungandr, the wolf Fenrir, and his daughter Hel.

Loki does not have long to rest in proud fatherhood for Óðin, fearing the prediction of a prophetess, casts Jörmungandr into the ocean to encircle Midgard, and binds Fenrir so the wolf can't eat him. Then, he exiles Hel to the underworld to rule over the restless dead. With the goddess Sigyn, Loki fathers two sons, Váli and Narfi. In the *Lokasenna*, when Loki crashes a party of the Aesir and trash talks everyone; as punishment, Váli is made to kill Narfi and use his entrails to bind their father to a rock. Over this is suspended a venomous snake. If my offspring were exiled, bound, and killed, I think I would be pissed, and my comrades would have more to worry about than a few pranks.

In the theft story of Thor's beloved hammer, Mjolnir, the giant Thrym makes off with the weapon. Loki negotiates for its return. He offers Freya's hand in marriage—it seems his go-to. She is not particularly thrilled, so Loki disguises Thor as Freya. Loki also shape-shifts into a maiden to accompany his friend to his forthcoming nuptials. Interestingly, in the retellings, Thor is always referred to with the masculine gender, while Loki is referred to as feminine while in female form. Here, Loki's gender is fluid, while Thor is always just a tough guy in a dress.

So, why is Loki considered the Norse Satan and ostracized by many modern Heathens? Some reasons pointed to include: He births monsters. He injures goats and sometimes ties his ballsack to their beard for a monumental game of tug-of-war. He is responsible for the death of Baldr, though he is at best a behind-the-scenes conspirator whispering in the ear of the murderer Haldr. And then he does that little thing where he instigates Ragnorak and brings about the destruction of the world. This last bit, which most likely casts him as a satanic figure, may have been more of a grafting of Christian authors' Biblical end times on the Norse sagas.

When we look again at the three arguments against Loki summarized by Waggoner, in the second charge of moral decay, we see an accusation that has been leveled against queer people from antiquity to the present day. LGBTQIA people have been long accused of contributing to the moral decay of society. This was true in 1895 when Oscar Wilde was carted off to Reading Gaol, in the 1950s when families sentenced their loved ones to the insane asylum, and today when children are sent off to conversion therapy camps. In the eyes of our accusers, the process is not passive. And this is a trope with a long historical arc as well. Harvey Milk played off this longstanding myth; he opened his "Hope Speech" with the words: "My name is Harvey Milk, and I'm here to recruit you." We groom children and lurk in dark alleyways to convert impressionable youth. Drag queens employ the weaponry of kids' books to corrupt the next generation.

Normative societies, especially the conservative, don't like differences. The reactionary need something to be reacting to; they need the other. We can see this in the resistant stances if we look at the hardline proponents of the Nokean camp. There is a distinct overlap between the Nokeans and groups that espouse racist and anti-Semitic ideologies: the Asatru Folk Assembly, the Circle of Ostara, Theodism, and the folkish Norroena Society. Indeed, many queer Heathens are drawn to the worship of Loki. Is this the crux of the resistance to honoring this gender-ambiguous deity? Keltoi, I think rightly, observes, "The moral decay in question seems to be the fact that there are LGBTQ Heathens who exist at all."[22]

Loki is described as slender or slight in many of the tales. He is not the image of hypermasculinity so prevalent in the Viking Age. His power draws on cunning and not brute strength or skill as a warrior. He may be a little off—I challenge anyone to retain all their wits after their offspring have been so mistreated. The anti-Loki camp clearly sees him as a little odd... a little queer.

Chapter XVI
The Otherworldly

In a time deep before history—before myth and legend—peoples spread outward from the east. They spread across Europe into what is now Germany, northwest into the Nordic peninsula, along the Mediterranean coast, and upward across the land bridge to what would become the British Isles. The goddesses and gods had not yet been born. Rich mythologies were yet to be divined. They took with them little as humankind went forth as hunter-gatherers.

What they did bring with them was a shared sense of the otherworldly and an animistic view of the environment. The earliest art, cave drawings, are a testament to their communal understanding of the world and their connection to it. They reflected the essential elements of their lives—the hunt and a ritual connection to the spirits of the land.

They had a sense of the otherworld, a territory contiguous with humanity but distinct and mysterious. The dark underworld lay below the earth and the sky above with its sun, moon, and stars. The tree was the logical connector of these three realms. The great oak's trunk grew through the land of the living, its branches reaching toward heaven and its roots deep in the underworld. Caves and water were seen as natural entrances into this otherworld. We can see this in the many instances where offerings were ceremoniously thrown into streams and lakes.

Eventually, these peoples developed the technology of farming and domestication of animals for food and support. The people settled and created tribes and sedentary communities. They built great tombs which survive to the present age. The dead were a part of the present. The first passage tombs were constructed caves. Unlike today, the dead were not simply sealed up and forgotten about. They remained physically present for their communities. Archeological evidence shows that these early tombs were active places where the living often visited and communed with the great ancestors that had gone before. The land of the dead and that of the living were closely aligned. The otherworldly was always close by.

These people gathered around the communal fire, and the ritual of custom arose. Eventually, these rings solidified in the sacred stone circles we see throughout Europe and Britain. We find these holy sites in northernmost Orkney with the Stones of Stennes and the Ring of Brodgar. We find these megalithic reminders at Avebury and, of course, immortal Stonehenge. They formed a place to gather and may have served as a calendrical system to time those great gatherings. These ritual landscapes were not static and evolved over time. When we join together inside a cast circle, we enact a mystery encoded in our deepest memory.

They viewed the world around them as imbued by spirit. Trees, rocks, waters, and animals each had a spirit force within them. Rivers were held sacred and were places of sacrifice. Natural springs provided essential fresh water and were honored. Throughout Britain today, springs and wells are still revered for their connection to the mother. To this day, the folk custom of tying bits of cloth around them as a symbolic offering continues.

Over time, legends became myths, and heroes became divine. Some of the spirits of the land may have been exalted in popular conception to the level of gods and goddesses. But what of the unrecorded, interstitial time between the primordial and the rich mythologies that survive today?

Chapter XVII
The All-Mother

In 1908, a small sculpture of a female was discovered at Willendorf, Austria. She was carved in limestone and colored with red ochre. Now known by the name of the site where she was discovered, the "Venus of Willendorf" is the most famous of several dozen similar figures uncovered throughout Europe. Her creators lived in the Upper Paleolithic period 28,000—25,000 BCE. A majority, though not all, of these figures are female. Many were only found as fragments, and their sex is not always identifiable. Anthropologists often discuss her as a fertility totem, but nothing is known about her meaning or use. One possible location for the limestone from which she is carved is a site in present-day Ukraine—similar human figures have been found in that region. If this is the case, she traveled over a thousand miles to make it to the site where she would rest for thirty millennia. Her palm-sized stature, at just under four-and-a-half inches, does make her ideally portable.

The oldest depiction of the human form yet found in Britain is the Dagenham Idol. It was discovered on the north bank of the Thames in 1922. It is a standing figure carved from a single piece of Scots pine and is about eighteen inches tall. It carbon dates to the late Neolithic period, approximately 4,500 years ago. There has been much debate about whether the idol is meant to depict a male or a female. There is a circular hole in the pelvic region. Some have suggested this may been used to affix a carved wooden phallus, but no such phallus was found in the area surrounding the initial discovery. In addition, the opening enlarges on the inside, making it less than suitable for securely holding an inserted cylinder of wood. A similar figure was discovered at Ralaghan, County Cavan, Ireland. Again, no phallus was found either with the idol or nearby. The Dagenham idol has broad, rounded hips, suggesting the female form. Lacking concrete evidence to the contrary, it is safe to assume that these figures represent the female spirits.

Given this archeological evidence, the first emanation of the divine was predominantly thought of as female. Women represent the great mystery of childbirth—though I resist the reductive characterization of these female totems as purely indicative of reproduction. From the advent of the domestication of livestock, the earliest herders must have understood the mechanics of reproduction. The primordial goddess certainly had a pivotal role in the fertility and productivity of the land. But this was certainly not all. Her reach would have been far more significant. She was not just the protector of the land but the land itself. Her influence was all-encompassing, extending from the heavens to the earth and the underworld.

Among the earliest recorded deities that survive are Inanna and Anu in ancient Sumer, around five thousand years ago. She paired with Anu, and both are likely of equal antiquity, though Inanna may reflect an early goddess cult that predates the invention of writing. Inanna features prominently in the ancient *Epic of Gilgamesh*, whose source material originated in Sumeria. One of the oldest poems ever written tells the story of Inanna's descent from the heavens to the underworld. Interestingly, she was viewed as both a goddess of fertility and war, belying the notion that the earliest goddesses exclusively derived their power from motherhood.

In short, the divine Mother in witchcraft is the mother of all. She is the first clue that the uncanny forces of the otherworld could be personified in a form resembling our own. The earliest goddesses were likely *genius loci* spirits of the land, springs, lakes, and rivers.

There is a particular Buddhist teaching which may be informative here. In a world with near-infinite rebirth across many ages and worlds, every person and creature has been a mother at some point. The math is simple. If the cycle of births and rebirths is so numerous, then every living creature today has been your mother at some point in the past, as you have been theirs. Buddhist teachers extoll us to consider this in how we interact with the world around us. Every sentient being we encounter has, at some point, been our mother and our child. Though we may or may not believe in reincarnation, this cognitive exercise may still serve as an aid to experience the universality of the mother.

For me, one of the most evocative images of the goddess is the Sheel-na-Gig. A small version hangs over my primary altar. The icon depicts a female form, often with an oversized head and hands spreading wide her vulva. They are at once grotesque, fascinating, and charming. Common in carvings from the mid-twelfth to fifteenth centuries, she represents an eruption of the All-Mother held over in folk beliefs into the medieval world. Sheel-na-gig images are familiar throughout England, Wales, Scotland, and Ireland. They are carved in churches, manor houses, and cemeteries. Though the largest number have been found in Ireland, they likely originated in Norman England, and were brought to Ireland by Anglo-Norman stone masons after the invasion of

Sheela-na-Gig carving on an exterior corbel at the 12th century Church of St Mary and St David, Kilpeck, Herefordshire, England

1171.

The Sheela images may be an echo in stone of the prehistoric wooden idols discussed earlier. Another figure found near Glencoe in Scotland in 1881 depicts a life-sized female, five feet tall, with her hands at her lower abdomen. Starr Goode, the author of a comprehensive study of the Sheela-na-Gig, suggests that the Ballachulish figure is a precursor to later Sheela imagery.[1] A notion that the many Sheelas were novel creations of their time does not pass the commonsense test. The inexplicable explosion of such representations following a century after the Norman conquest belies their pre-existence in the beliefs of common folk. It is unlikely that they arose fully formed in the minds of medieval masons in the twelfth century.

The image is often found over dooryards, near thresholds, or around window openings. She is thus an image of the space between—watching over spaces of transition from one space to another. Her open vulva may be seen as a threshold between the world and the otherworld.[2] Folk customs often hold a connection between particular Sheela carvings and fertility or luck. To this day, many a Sheela are touched by women hoping for assistance in conceiving a child.

In popular reference, however, she is not just an image of natal productivity. She is often referred to as the "hag of the castle." In this, she is symbolic of the mother, while at the same time, the venerable wisdom that comes with age. The image of the hag has longstanding historical connections with witchcraft and surviving folk belief in the power of a pre-Christian goddess. She is the All-Mother giving birth to the Universe.

The horseshoe is sometimes referred to as the mare's vagina. Here, then, we have an emblem of the Sheela in iron. This connection may relate to the horseshoe's link to luck.

Interestingly, this single item is thought of as being able to represent the female or male sexual organ (see the hood lamp, discussed below).

In practice, the divine Mother may be seen in the image of the pentagram and the five elements it represents. Each point, or triangle, may be viewed as one node of the goddess: the air or sky mother; the fire mother; the water mother of rivers, lakes, and sacred wells; the earth Mother; and the ephemeral mother of spirit. In this, I am not suggesting that all goddesses are one in varied forms—a belief held by many Wiccans and popularized by Janet Farrar. Instead, these are facets, as in a jewel, of the personality of the All-Mother. They represent, in essential form, the aspects of her dominion.

We can similarly think of these as we do elements on the periodic table. Just as the elements make up everything in the world, these primal elements also exist in all things to a greater or lesser degree. This is how we connect plants, rocks, etc., to the four elements. And the celestial realm is broken down in this manner through the twelve signs of the zodiac.

Chapter XVIII
The More the Merrier

Sometime in history, pantheons of goddesses and gods arose. From Gardner forward, modern Wicca reduces these complex mythologies into a single divine couple, the Lord and Lady. This simply replaces the last two thousand years of Western monotheism with duotheism. It's not an impressive trade if you ask me. Technically, Wiccans are primarily "soft pantheists," meaning they worship two divine personages. All other gods and goddesses are but aspects, or faces, of these two.

We discussed the problems with these listed theisms described by Burroughs. Compound that with the seemingly incongruous choice of pairing an Italian goddess, Aradia lifted from the writings of Charles Godfrey Leland, and the Celtic and Gallo-Roman Cernunnos. This may be appropriate in a universalist duotheistic system where all goddesses are considered one and all gods one, but not in a pantheistic one. Interestingly, in his visioning of Saxon witchcraft, Seax Wicca, Raymond Buckland retains the Wiccan soft pantheistic approach, switching the names to Woden and Freya. This modern approach heterosexualizes the divine. Within the Wiccan fertility cult context, they become the normative heterosexual couple rigid in the dyad of their gendered sexual roles. This view occludes the complexities of sex, attraction, and romance among the gods. It makes for a very droll and humdrum state of affairs. Each pantheon has their fascinating tales of sexual peccadillos. Distilling everything down to an archetypal Lord and Lady, or even Mother and Son, silences sexual difference, intrigue, and adventure. There is no room for Zeus and his Ganymede, the contendings of Seth and Horus, or even Diana and her earthly princesses. I much prefer a rich pageant of divine personalities, colorful in their interactions and unique in their countenances.

I've observed a tendency in modern witchcraft practice to treat deities in a somewhat utilitarian fashion. In this, gods and goddesses are viewed as corresponding to particular domains of influence such as love, wealth, or witchcraft. One picks a deity that *corresponds* to that which one wants to accomplish and incorporates them into a spell or offering. I find this very reductive and bordering on disrespect. It may have its roots in if all gods are one, the witch simply chooses an aspect to propitiate. This is very much the way Christians have approached saints—each with their own sphere of influence. To me, this reduces the highest spiritual entities into an ala carte menu of servitors.

From my experience, it is critical to develop a relationship with a deity. Our path is devotional, and the gods are not simply tools we use as a need arises. They are not hammers with our objectives as the nail. We offer to them like good friends, and they provide for us. Think back to interactions with people in your own life. If you call someone in an emergency in the middle of the night, your close friend is much more likely than a stranger to come to your aid. If you are seeking wealth and none of your personal spirits seem appropriate, as Lady Rhea put it, go to their neighborhood, the neighborhood of the wealthy deities and see who approaches you.[1]

I also resist the conception of the triple goddess—Maid, Mother, and Crone. Of couse, there were triune goddesses in history, such as the Gaulle-Roman Matres or Matronae, whose worship was widespread in Northern Europe from the first to fifth century CE. We also recall the Norns and the three witches in *Macbeth*. However, the Triple Goddess in neo-paganism stems from the writings of Jane Harrison (nineteenth century) and Robert Graves. Though triune goddesses may have antecedents, this precise configuration is not well supported. In recent years, the concept has gone out of favor among anthropologists, not as much based on new evidence as on the realization that the evidence at hand was open to other interpretations. Within modern paganism, it has also come under recent criticism by feminists. They point out that confining the goddess based on her relationship to childbirth and nothing else is highly problematic. Unlike the Danish and Icelandic sagas, no complex tales survive to inform us of their exploits.

We will now deeply dive into one pantheon of particular relevance to the work at hand—that of the Osgeard worshipped by the Anglo-Saxons. Understanding these deities is tricky as little information survives compared to the Greek, Roman, or Norse pantheons. This has proved a challenge for modern Anglo-Saxon attempts to reconstruct their religion. We can look to their Norse analogs, but this can only be informative. Not conclusive. They may stem from the same Germanic roots, but each developed in different contexts and may have had limited cross-pollination during their formative years. The connections may have been strengthened with the arrival of Viking settlers on British shores as a later component of the age of Viking marauders.

The Anglo-Saxon period of British history is relatively brief. It stretches from the departure of the Romans in the fifth century to the Norman conquest of 1066. This would have given their gods and goddesses less time to evolve away from their origins. This is, of course, compounded by Christianization beginning in the seventh century. Much of the limited source material derives from writings of early Christians, and, as with the sagas, the authors' agenda can highly influence this material.

We can surmise that the gods became linked with earlier spirits connected previously to sacred sites in the land. Shani Oates notes:

> In England, Woden, Dunor, and Tiw were celebrated as the spirits of place, close to strong elemental activity such as waterfalls, rivers, mounds, caves, and forests. Liminal borderlands imbued with unusual phenomenal activity were ultimately demonised by the non-Christian place names later attached to them, contrasting sharply with the very Christian place names attributed to hamlets, villages, and towns.[2]

Thus, we have a group of divine personalities worshipped for a brief historical time yet whose influences may be felt today. Indeed, the English monarchs still trace their mythological lineage back to the Anglo-Saxon kings lists that each had Woden as their starting point.

WODEN

First in the pantheon, and probably the most familiar, is Woden. His origins are in the same proto-Germanic Wodanaz from which Óðin derives. From him, we derive the name of our day of the week Wednesday through the Old English *Wodnesdæg*, or Woden's Day. Like Óðin, Woden is also both a warrior god

and the bringer of wisdom. The English Furthoc are his gift to humankind. He is often depicted as a gray-bearded man carrying a spear and wearing a cloak and broad-brimmed hat. He is accompanied by two wolves reminiscent of Geri and Freki that tag along with Óðin. There is some debate whether he had one eye or not. Evidence supporting this similarity to Óðin may be found in the famous Sutton-Hoo helmet, which appears to have a damaged eye.

Woden was known by many names, including Wise-one, One-Eyed One, Lord of the Undead, the Wanderer, and Grim. His appearance is similar to Tolkein's Gandalf, whom he had a large part in inspiring. Envisioning Sir Ian McKellen's portrayal would not be far off the mark. We can see similarities in some of the many names by which Óðin was variously known, including *Grimnir*. Early Christians, not surprisingly, connected Woden to the Devil. Another name by which he was referred was Herian, which has come down to us as Herne, the god of the hunt. As we discuss later, in Britain, he is seen as the leader of the Wild Hunt of the Dead that rides abroad in the longer nights of winter.

Did Woden also have two ravens as companions like Muninn and Huginn? Artifacts that predate the Viking Age depict a figure assumed to be Wodanaz accompanied by two birds. Bracelets from the Migration Period show a figure on a horse, carrying a spear and flanked by two birds. Anglo-Saxon scabbard decorations have been found that show a seated figure with birds to either side. The famous Sutton-Hoo helmet has pressed images depicting warriors with curved decorations resembling horns coming off their helmets and ending in bird terminals.

The world is not replete with images of Woden, not surprisingly. I use a beautiful carving of Óðin to represent him on my altar.

FRIGE

Frige is Woden's wife and a significant divine in her own right. She gives her name to Friday. She is the personification of the All-Mother and was propitiated for many things. She was the goddess of the home and domestic life, motherhood, and child-rearing. Offerings were made to her for the protection of crops and to ensure a bountiful harvest. She was also the goddess of necessary crafts such as weaving and dyeing. The plants utilized for coloring fabric all fall under her purview. Her sacred sites are places of flowing waters, rivers, and springs.

THUNOR

Thunor is analogous to the Norse Thor. It should not be a surprise that he lends his name to Thursday. He is the son of Woden and Frige. Like Thor, he is a god of thunder and lightning. He also carried a hammer—many examples of which have been found in Anglo-Saxon grave goods—and rode in a chariot pulled by two goats. While Thunor is the god of the weather and storms, he is also viewed as a powerful protector of humankind. His hammer was likely worn as a symbol of his protection, just as it continues to be by modern Heathens. He is connected to the forge and blacksmiths and, through this, the magical transformation of elemental metals into valuable tools. He also shares with Frige power over the productivity of harvest.

Crystals are seen as symbolic of his lightning. Sun-stones, Iceland spar, used as a tool in Viking navigation, are particularly well suited as an emblem of Thor's assistance. I keep one on my altar to guide me through the unfolding world's weather, storms, and calm alike.

TIW

Woden may be the god of warriors, but Tiw is the consummate god of war. More importantly, Tiw is the god of justice. Before Woden took up the role, it was to Tiw that oaths were sworn. He can be seen in the modern context as the god covering legal agreements. It would be wise to make an offering to him for the just outcome of matters involving courts and the legal system. Word of warning: do not invoke his name if you are guilty or know that the result should rightly be other than what you desire. His concern is justice and not manipulation of the legal system. Tiw represents what is right. He is the order of law and honor that prevents chaos in the world.

Tiw gives us our modern Tuesday.

HRETHE

Hrethe is the hearth goddess. The Anglo-Saxon month, similar to our March, is named in her honor. Though a little early, we celebrate her on Oimelc. She is similar to the Roman Hestia. She represents the sacred fire within the home. Her power provides warmth in winter and the ability to cook throughout the year. Historically, when families and friends gathered around the warming fire, this goddess brought them together. Otherwise, little is known of Hrethe. Her inclusion in the Bede's *Holy Tides* is the only reference that attests to her existence. Personal gnosis should guide those who choose to explore her worship.

EOSTRE

Eostre is the goddess of the spring, the coming sun, and fertility.

She is a goddess of beauty and youth. We celebrate her during and immediately following the spring equinox. Like Hrethe, Eostre lent her name to an Anglo-Saxon month, the one following corresponding roughly to our April. Her existence in Anglo-Saxon Britain is only attested to in the writings of Bede. Her name is linguistically similar to the High German Ostara—it would appear that they both derive from the same proto-Germanic source word.

Eostre and Ostara are both goddesses of the rising sun. She is the sun returning in the spring. We make offerings to her to coax the seed in the dark earth to germinate and poke his head out. This may run counter to some people's conception of the Sun and Moon, but the Anglo-Saxons considered the Sun female and the Moon male. Many think of the Sun as a symbol of virility and strength and, thus, male by definition. The Romans knew the Sun as Sol Invictus, the Unconquered Sun. In the later Roman period, the Sun became intrinsically linked to the Emperor and the source of his divine authority. In Roman myth, the Moon was personified in Luna sometimes a goddess in her own right and at others an aspect of other divine females most commonly Diana. Much of how we conceive the world today is a legacy of the Romans. The Germanic peoples held different belief structures that held the reverse view. A remnant of this may come down to us today in the popular image of the Man in the Moon.

As Bede provides the only extant near contemporary source for her existence, we owe much to him for her survival. Additionally, historians and linguists have pointed to the possible survival of Eostre in certain place names. For example, in 704 CE, the king of Northumbria is recorded as convening a council at a site then called Eostrefeld. In recent decades, there has been much unverified personal gnosis (UPG) from modern heathens that support her continuing influence within Middle

Earth.

Eostre and the month that bore her name are the etymology of the word Easter, given to the Christian Paschal holiday, which Bede notes replaced her worship some time before his chronicle. The connection to resurrection seems fitting as her month marks the sun's return, as days become longer than nights beginning at the equinox.

LOKI AND SIGYN

Did the Anglo-Saxons worship a cognate god to Loki? There is no written evidence of his existence. Bede makes no mention of him. At first glance, Loki is a later development within the eastern branch of Germanic beliefs, not present in the western. However, two pieces of archeological evidence point to Loki's existence in Britain. One is a tenth-century cross in Gosforth, Cumbria. The carved stone contains scenes identified as from the *Prose Edda*. Some of these include Loki. A second, perhaps earlier, stone in the Kirkby Stephen Parish Church has a single carving of a horned man bound in ropes. From its style, the Kirkby stone is identified as Viking. Considering the story of his binding, it would then follow the image is of Loki.

Interestingly, here, Loki has horns. This has led some to connect the image to Woden, the horns similarly representative of ravens to the helmed warriors depicted in relief on the Sutton-Hoo helmet. Both stones date from the ninth or tenth century and were probably products of the Viking occupation of parts of England. Therefore, they do not necessarily prove a god similar to Loki was articulated within the Osgeard of the Anglo-Saxons.

Of course, the absence of evidence differs significantly from proof that the Anglo-Saxons did not recognize him.

There is scant physical evidence in Scandinavia, Denmark, and Germany that attests to his existence, but that is often used in the Nokean argument that no worship of Loki, a cultus, did not exist in antiquity. As this remains an open question, whether we work with Loki or not is based on what is known as Unsubstantiated Personal Gnosis (UPG). Nothing is wrong with that as long as we acknowledge it for what it is and do not pass it off as historical fact. Indeed, UPG plays a not insignificant part in modern pagan practice.

Loki is inextricably connected to his wife, Sigyn. The two were a loving pair, with Sigyn known for coming to her husband's aid and mitigating his suffering. When the other gods punish Loki, binding him and suspending over him a serpent so that its poison drips into his eyes, Sigyn holds a bowl to catch the poison. This is depicted on Gosforth Cross in Cumbria.

Chapter XIX
The Witch Father

You may have been warned about meeting a dark stranger at a crossroads at night. Such is the stuff of legend on both sides of the pond. You've likely heard of the legendary blues musician Robert Johnson. It's said that he sold his soul to the Devil at the crossroads in exchange for his incredible guitar skills. Whether or not you believe the legend, there's no denying Johnson's impact on the blues genre. His haunting vocals and intricate guitar melodies continue to inspire musicians today. Meeting the Man in Black at the intersection could change one's life.

In traditional lore, the Dark Man comes to us unexpectedly. We meet him in the night. Even if we are unaware that we are ready, he knows. He is our guide to usher us along the ways of the witch, the crooked path. He is our contact point with the other. He is our touch with the unworldly. We come upon him at points of intersection and liminal spaces. His domain is that of the threshold. He is the Upright Man, honorable among thieves.

There is a truism that the gods of the old religion are the devils of the new. This could not be more true of the Christianization of the West. The pagan and heathen deities were transformed through the writings and rhetoric of

Christian monks in the Devil and his demonic hoards. This way, Woden and the Horned God were distilled into a single medieval personage. Conjure up an image of the Devil in your head. What does he look like? I bet he has horns... Nowhere in the Bible is he depicted in this way. In our popular media, Satan is a mosaic, a pastiche of pagan idolatry.

Many Wiccans will tell you that the Devil is a Christian concept with no place in modern pagan practice. In truth, the Devil rides rampant throughout centuries of folklore. We need but look to the many place names in Britain and North America that bear his name to substantiate his place. Often, these locations are on the boundaries, spaces between, and areas of transition. We find Devil's Dyke in Cambridgeshire that runs between the woodlands and marshy fens. In the United States, we have the Devil's Cauldron in Nevada and Devil's Punchbowl in Oregon, plus such colorful names as the Devil's Bathtub, Devil's Fork, and the evocatively descriptive Devil's Hop Yard. Of course, there is also the infamous Hell's Kitchen in New York City.

Under various guises, the Devil features prominently in many of the witch confessions. Of course, these statements were often elicited under duress and not infrequently torture. However, most accused were just as Christian as their accusers. They may very well have interpreted the appearance of the Old God as that of the Devil. In this way, the pre-Christian iconographies blended during the late Iron Age, medieval, and into the early modern period. The Old Ones became the syncretic Devil of modernity. A singular personage arises out of this dark history. He is not an artificial archetype that erases difference. He is instead an organically arising divine personality in his own right. He is Witch Father, the proto-Horned God, and the great seducer all in one. Doreen Valiente provides an apt description, speaking of him as "the secret, which allured while defying one to find it out."[1] The Man in Black is the whisper in the night. He lures us toward him and entices us out of our comfort zone. He represents the wild and untamed. There is a tradition to leave a section of the field unfurrowed. The patch was known as the Devil's Plantation or the Goodman's Croft.

As we evolve as a species, our deities evolve as well. The two processes are not disassociated. Woden and the horned hunter Herne coexisted in Britain for centuries. They are not synonymous with the Witch's Devil but are not altogether distinct either. To the hunters and ecclesiastical thinkers, their worship and associated practices were the work of devildom. They all existed on earth to attract people away from the one true faith. Valiente notes that Nik was a name for Woden and survives in "Old Nick," one of the names of the Devil.[2]

In addition to Old Nick, the Devil is known by many names across the British Isles. These names reflect the local and regional variations in how people perceived the Devil. It is not lost on one that these names are often closer to nicknames than honorifics. They hark to the familiar and often have more than a hint of humor about them. In Scottish folklore, he is Old Hornie; in parts of England, he is known as Scratch, which could be a reference to the Devil's supposed habit of making marks or symbols. He is the Black Goat, Aker to the Basque people, who presided over the witch's Sabbath. In the Highlands, he was known as Black Donald, *Domhnall Dubh*, whose cloven hooves betrayed his true nature.

He is the convenor, the cunning trickster. He is devilish but is not inherently malicious. As some of his names hint, he may first appear as an animal, often black. Mephistopheles appears first to Faustus as a small black dog. Though most commonly appearing as a dog or goat, there are also tales of his presenting himself in the form of cats, horses, cows, foals, magpies, and jackdaws.

In his 1584 *Discovery of Witchcraft*, Reginald Scott describes his appearance as "an ugly devil having horns in his head fire in his mouth and a tail and his breech eyes like a bison and fangs like a dog claws like a bear" and dark complexion. In contrast to this frightening image, in Scottish confessions, he is most commonly described as a comely man wearing either black or dark green clothing. He is handsome, beguiling, and bedeviling.

Far from being a frightening specter, the Devil is often depicted as a more commonplace personage. There is often a certain comfortable familiarity between witch and devil. In 1596 in Aberdeenshire, a group of witch trials were held following an incidence of disturbing the peace. A group had gathered in the market's center at a marker known as the Fish Cross, denoting the space for fishmongers. There, they danced to the Devil's music played by him on the pipes. One of the revelers didn't like his playing, so she took the pipes and hit him in the face with it. She then went on to play her own tune. This incident is often interpreted as signifying that the Devil was a man in costume.[3] An alternative interpretation is that the dancing witches had a familiar relationship with Old Scratch. Perhaps he was less evil spirit and more favored compatriot. We know that the devil is a trickster. However, in folklore, it seems just as often the intended victim outwits him in his own trickery. Robert Johnson may have sold his soul at the crossroads, but the Dark One did not fare well when he went down to Georgia.

As the handsome man in a dark green coat, he represents nature. This also shows the two sides of his heart. He is the Man in the Wood—the vestigial echo of Herne the Horned Hunter. Of course, the hunter wears green to camouflage himself. Thus, he represents the comely beauty of the natural world on the surface. But beneath that surface, there also lurks danger. The natural world has the potential for both breathtaking beauty and breath-catching destruction.

He is known by many names: Man in Black, the Dark One, the Black Rogue, the King of Elphame, Hob who Keeps the Lantern, Robin Goodfellow, Old Scratch, Auld Nick, The Black'un, Tubal Caine, Lucifer, the Star in the East, and simply the Elder. He is the Witch Father. He calls us to the Craft and presides over our revels. When we sign his black book, he becomes our guide and ally. The Magister of the Coven represents him when we come together. He is often a man in an animal mask or with a horned headdress. In the confessions and accounts of witches, the Devil is often a teacher imparting knowledge of specific occult skills and unique talents. We see this in the story of Robert Johnson, but numerous accounts survive where the Dark One teaches a witch specific witchcraft techniques, such as crafting poppets or wax effigies.

The twenty-two cards that make up the major arcana of the tarot are often interpreted as a mystical journey undertaken by the Fool. The sequence is frequently broken into two sets. However, the noted tarot scholar Rachel Pollack suggests setting the Fool aside and distinguishing the cards into three rows of seven. This way, the transformative process is separated into the conscious, unconscious, and superconscious.[4] Card fifteen, the Devil, begins the third row. Here, the Devil represents a gateway beyond the worldly conscious and unconscious minds. He is a porter ushering us into the realms of mystery. The road is not always easy. Burroughs notes that the road to the Western Lands is dangerous; however, he also notes that safety poses an even more significant threat. Initiation is followed by disruption; the Tower follows the Devil. Enlightenment comes in a flash, not as the anticipated result of a progressive process.

As noted, another name for the Tower is Destruction of the House of God. Here, we can see an allusion to the historical accounts of a witch's dedication to the Dark One. In historical accounts from Scotland and the New World, the witch often renounces their Christian baptism as part of the process. We are entering new realms, and all we knew before must be willfully left behind. The peaceful serenity of the Star follows the cataclysmic disruption of the lightning strike. Renunciation is followed by revelation. A new wisdom comes to us, symbolized by the Ibis, and the star guides our way. Compare this card to Temperance (or Art): the robed figure pours water between two vessels in card fourteen. The balance of realization gained during the second row remains within the unconscious.

In contrast, freed from past acculturation, the naked figure pours her waters freely. The star signifies the realization that the knowledge gained is unlimited. It is a card of overflowing abundance. The water flows from two pitchers—one into a pool, the other onto land. Here, we find a state that exists both in the material world and the other world. Like Temperance, she has a foot on the ground and a foot on the pool of water. But, unlike the former card, her foot does not penetrate the water's surface in most traditional depictions. Temperance remains confined to the unconscious, while the Star reflects one who has gained understanding but remains apart, untrapped, by both the physical and magical plains.

Card seventeen may be the guide star, but the card depicts no distinct way forward. That comes in the next trump, the Moon. Here, a path originates from the water's edge and winds off into the distance under the light of the full moon. On either side, two towers form a gate. They represent the rebuilt structure seemingly obliterated in the Tower. They also echo the pillars of the temple from the High Priestess. While the black and white columns in the second trump are a mere worldly representation of the mystical, here we are on the inside looking out. The crawfish rising half out of the water reflects the uncanny nature of the other world. The black and white dogs reflect the Devil's guise as an animal, but in a larger context, they are the black dog of folklore appearing as a portend—a mysterious other-worldly messenger.

The initiation process only begins with the meeting of the Dark Man at the crossroads. That encounter sets the process in motion. Eventually, the night path does lead back to the World, the final trump card and the ultimate card in this row. As we progress along, the moon sets and the sun rises. A new day is born, and we rise triumphantly from the tomb of initiation. Tantalizingly, the crossroads are reflected here as the cross—on the banner in the Rider-Waite-Smith deck or center of the trumpet in the Morgan-Greer. The Judgement card reflects a choice before us. As we re-enter the world, we carry our contact with the uncanny back with us. It is up to us whether we return to our old ways, a view of the material world, or return from our strange trip with a transformed vision. The crossroads or bifurcated path always represents a choice. It is the point of reckoning where we encounter the Dark Friend or the dark crossroads of the infernal Mother.

We may remain a fool, but now we are a Divine Fool reveling in the exciting mystery of all we don't know. We may have begun as the robed magician with our tools laid out before us and a wand raised in the power of command. Now we dance skyclad with a wand in each hand, cloaked only in the purple cloth representing the true sight of Justice. The victor's wreath surrounds us. Our working tools—pentacle, wand, cup, and sword—were mere representations of the primal elements. Now earth, water, air, and fire stand before us in their tangible and physical manifestations as shown in the beats the border the card at the four corners.

Historically, to be a witch meant to transgress the notions of "natural law" and pass beyond the boundaries of so-called normal society. Not only do we work in a space betwixt and between, but we also operate at the edges. We cohabitate with the spirits in the hidden places of the world. The handsome Man In Black is our guide. Nigel Pearson observes:

> In a magical context, i.e. in the view of the witches and folk magicians, he was seen as a being that was against the accepted norms of society. He was firmly linked to ideas of mayhem, civil disobedience, lack of good citizenship and ruthlessness. He was cunning in executing his will and desires and in achieving his ends. He was a being characterised by his lust for pleasure and the good things in life and, significantly, for his knowledge of arcane secrets and power over the things of this world - his magical knowledge and ability were things that normal society, and in particular the Church, deemed dangerous, forbidden and not to be indulged in.[5]

As Burroughs puts it, we are natural outlaws operating on the periphery, defying society's laws and bending nature's purported laws.

To know him is not something to be approached lightly. His power in the world is something to be respected. He holds the potential of the wild within his arms. Nigel Jackson elaborates on this:

> The Dark Man or Man in Black is the human vehicle and priest of the Horned Master, Gwynn/ Woden and mediates his presence; a wild, harsh power of the darkness and cold. This is the sombre and terrifying Spirit Hunter who bestows death, ecstasy and initiation upon his followers; Opener

> of the Way to the shadowy Underworld for the disembodied soul.[6]

He awaits us when we're ready. The Great Mother is the potency of earth and sky, while he is the assertive, fertile power of the wild there at the edges. He is the potency of the green. His is the continuity of life and movement in the natural world. He is action within the world. The Mother is a noun; the Horned One is a verb. In Egypt, there was Horus (heavenly sky) and Seth (the Cthonic realms); *xeper* was the activating force that mediated between them. It is through this nature that he is accessible to us. The Great Mother is all-pervasive and ultimately ineffable. She is the earth upon which we walk and the sky that crowns us. She rules the dark underworld realm and the starry kingdom above. Her light nourishes us each day and gives glow to the moon during the night. The Horned One runs beside us across Middle Earth. He is a guide and companion on our heroic quest. He is directly accessible through the nature that surrounds us. His joy is our joy; our sorrow is his sorrow.

He is the ruler of the time between times. He is both primordial and outside the cycles of time. The worship of Ol' Horny goes back to humanity's earliest days. Man Found in the Cave of the Trois-Frères, Ariège, France, a drawing known as *The Sorcerer* depicts a man wearing antlers and animal skins. Dating back fifteen thousand years, it reminds us that the power of the Horned One has been with us from the beginning. The prevalence of horned creatures in prehistoric art speaks to the magical importance in which our earliest ancestors held them. Drawings at the Chauvet-Pont-d'Arc Cave in southern France, Altamira in Spain, and Asphendou on Crete are other examples from the Upper Paleolithic era.

The rise of the slave god of the OGU pushed the Elder Gods farther into the shadows. But they have remained at the edges, waiting, like the gods in a Neil Gaiman novel. Their time has come again. When the priest dons the horned crown, he enacts a rite transcendent of space and time. The Dark Man is the Horned God's interlocutor. The High Priest is his embodiment in the circle. He again walks openly through the forest and rides with his fellow hunters through the wintery nights.

> For now the Old One is returned to liberate, illuminate and protect his people, the bearers of the Great Blood of Witchdom—the shadow of his horns is cast across the earth and his nocturnal summons reverberates through the empyrean.[7]

He is the god with two faces, similar to the Roman Janus. From the Feast of Flowers (Beltaine) to All Hallows, he is the Green God, the wild god of nature in its active, procreative potential. In the dark half of the year, he is the Dark God, the Man in Black. During this time, he is the Hunter riding with his spectral hoard through the clear, dark nights of the winter months. In the Caldragh Cemetery on Boa Island, County Fermanagh, Northern Ireland, there is an enigmatic stone figure with two faces dating from 400-800 CE. Woden, in his gray cloak and hat, unites these twin faces—the lord of nature and animals, as evidenced by his companions, and the god who knows death, sacrificing himself to bring secret knowledge to humanity. The Magister and the brothers of the Craft embody this dual nature within themselves. They know the mysteries of both the spring frolic and the somber, introspective dormancy of winter. His vernal aspect is the Green Man with his foliate mask; his autumnal aspect is symbolized by the skull and crossed bones at the center of the altar.

As the Lord of the Oak, he is a fellow traveler enticing the shadowing mysteries of the Green Wood. In his darker nature, he is the tomb, the hallow hill, of initiatory death and rebirth. Our flesh is leaf and flower, our blood the sap, and our bones the white skeleton of the undying.

While the mother surrounds us in her expansiveness, the Dark Lord is there beside us. He is our direct interlocutor with the other world. Queer men may have experienced more moments of profound aloneness. Too often, we experience judgement from conservative elements, distance from our family, and even hurt inflicted by our own brethren. Any one of these can prove isolating; in combination, the impact can be profound. Once we establish a relationship with our Witch Father, we are never truly alone. It is the pact he makes with us.

The Man in Black is a salve easing our hurt and helping us to put our past pain in perspective. He asks a lot of us, because we are capable of a lot. He stands with us in our power.

Chapter XX
The Smithy & the Infernal Forge

The blacksmith also holds a prominent place in folklore. He embodies practical skill, craftsmanship, and elements of the supernatural. Going back to the advent of metalworking, the smithy has been the custodian carrying the secrets of the forge through the generations. He is both a master craftsman and a magical practitioner. The forge and anvil are a locus of transformation to which he holds the keys.

Iron has particular connections to magic. In Scandinavia, sorceresses were often buried with an iron staff thought by anthropologists to have been closely connected with their Craft abilities. The blacksmith was said to be able to imbue objects with magical properties. His command of the fire is analogous to the wizard's command over spirits. Iron was thought to ward off the Faery Folk; thus, the blacksmith was linked to protective powers.

In Roman and Greek mythology, Vulcan (Roman) and Hephaestus (Greek) are the gods of the forge and blacksmithing. They are often depicted as deities associated with craftsmanship, fire, and the creation of divine weapons. In Norse mythology,

Wayland (also known as Volundr) was a legendary smith known for his exceptional skills. He was associated with the creation of magical and powerful weapons.

After breaking with Gardner during the early years of Wicca, Robert Cochrane founded a tradition called the Clan of Tubal Cain. The titular spirit was a descendant of the Biblical Cain and is considered the first blacksmith. For Cochrane, Tubal Cain was also a name for the witch God. Some refer to witches as the Children of Cain. The Mark of Cain has often been linked to the witch's mark. The stang is a significant element of Cochrane's Craft, essentially a forked staff used as a mobile altar. In his book, *The Roebuck in the Thicket*, Evan John Jones elaborates on procuring and decorating a stang meant for coven use.

The blacksmith often serves as an archetypal figure representing the power to shape one's destiny through hard work, skill, and determination. He is force and fire. He represents strength in defense as well as a sharp-edged offense. He is both an artisan and a sorcerer. This archetype endures. He forges the iron nail we employ to anchor the center of the universe. The smithy's craft is reflected in the hood lamp's horseshoe, the stang's iron horns, and the forged nail with which it is shod.

Near Ashbury in Oxfordshire, southcentral England, is a superb example of a Neolithic long barrow. Nearby is the chalk drawing known as the Uffington Horse. Today, the barrow is known as Weyland's Smithy, a name that likely derives from the Anglo-Saxon period. Stories of the blacksmith Weyland are common in pan-Germanic mythology and were well-known throughout early England. Weyland is a divine hero or god. He is a blacksmith who is unjustly imprisoned by the bad king Nithad. In an image reminiscent of Loki's punishment, Weyland is chained to his forge and forced to craft for the king. He manages to trick the king and gain some mark of revenge. In some versions, he kills the king's sons making offering goblets of their skulls and jewels of their eyes. He then impregnates the king's daughter. The Ashbury barrow's connection to the hero blacksmith long survived the Christianization of England. It is said that leaving a broken metal tool or an unshod horse at the barrow along with a six-pence overnight will find the tool repaired or horse shod in the morning. Weyland shares his feast day, November 23, with St. Clement, who seems to have transferred some of his craft, for Clement has long been viewed as the patron of metalworkers and blacksmiths.

Chapter XXI
Souls

In Christianity, we see the notion of a singular soul. For the past millennia, this concept has been a near constant. However, in other cultures, especially those antecedent to the rise of the One God, the understanding of multiple souls that can operate independently of each other has existed. They coexist, for a time, in a state of mutually aligned self-interest while the physical body is animated in the world.

Burroughs points us to the Egyptian conception of seven souls. The highest soul is known as Ren. It means one's secret name and corresponds to the life story. Ren is your destiny, the summation of what your life is all about. This topmost soul is the first to depart at the moment of death. Second is Sekem, which relates to light, power, and animating force. It is the next in line to board the lifeboats. Third is Khu, one's guardian angel. Khu is most closely tied to the individual and thus has a vested interest in the person making the right decision. His voice is the call of conscience described by Heidegger in *Being and Time*. These first three souls are eternal. Though they may be injured, particularly Khu, they always survive.

The following four souls have to make their way with the individual as they make their trek across the desert toward the eternity of the Western Lands. The first of this next set is Ba, the heart. This soul is a small, fist-sized hawk with the individual's face. The heart is weighed against the feather of Meat at the time of judgment in *The Book of the Dead*. Burroughs warns us that the Ba can be "treacherous. "Many a hero," he observes, "has brought down, like Sampson, by a perfidious Ba.[1]

The fifth soul is Ka. They are your double or spiritual doppelgänger. The Ka reaches adolescence at the time of physical death and is one's guide through the desert, the Duat, between life and eternity. The penultimate soul is Khaibit. This is your memory and represents all your past conditioning. Finally, we have Sekhu, the corpse or physical remains. In the Egyptian conception of the afterlife, the survival of the other three mortal souls depends on the remains' physical existence. The mummy is critical for the future immortality in the afterlife. Grave robbers thus constantly threatened one's survival, hence the lengths the rich went to protect their mortal remains. In this immortality model, an archeologist is the soul's best friend.

Burroughs uses the analogy of a film set to illustrate this multi-soul construct. Ren is the director. Sekem is the technician responsible for lights, cameras, and action. Khu is akin to a leech who adds little but can take much. Ba is linked to the sex drive and can be a dangerous distraction. Ka is the most trustworthy as their existence depends on the individual's. They are a reliable guide, but their call may be difficult to discern.[2]

Closer in geography and time, the Anglo-Saxons likely had a concept of nine souls, or parts of the self. Though it is hard to determine historically the details of Anglo-Saxon belief, we can discern some of their thinking from ancient sources and draw from Norse descriptions. What follows is admittedly drawn from modern reconstructions of this multi-soul construct.

THE FETCH

The Fetch is the Guardian Spirit, similar to the Khu. The Fetch may travel outside the physical body and go out into the world, usually in the form of an animal. We see this often in descriptions of historical witches going abroad in the astral form of their familiar, often a cat, dog, or toad. The Fetch remains connected to the seemingly asleep body of the witch through a thread of life force or breath, the Ealdor (Æþm). Cutting this connection was thought to result in the witch's death.

THE HAMA

Closely aligned with the Fetch is the Hama or astral body. This is a skin of spiritual protection, sometimes seen as the aura. The Hama forms an energy shield that defends against intrusion and possession.

THE MYNE

The Myne is the self that is the total of your memories. In this sense, it is similar to Khaibit. Our memory has a particular connection to our emotions because our first reactions are based on the totality of our past.

THE MÆGEN

The Mægen is similar to the Sekem. It is power or spiritually derived strength. Some Mægen is utilized when we work a magical act. In a sense, it is similar to the popular conception of karma. When we perform positive, honorable actions, our spiritual energy is replenished like the life force in a video game.

THE MÓD

Next, we have our conception of self-identity. This aspect is called the Mód, or the Ferþ, and is the source of our modern English word mood. This is our self-awareness, our visceral understanding of who we are. This self is closely aligned with and influenced by the Myne as memory forms so much of our conception of self.

THE WILLA & THE WÓD

Next, we have two aspects of the self that work together. First, we have the Willa, which relates to our willpower. This is the force of our desire and the root of determination. Closely linked to this is the Wód or inspiration. This is the power that underlies poetry and passion as well as anger transformed into rage.

THE HYGE & LIC

Now, we come to the two souls connected most with our daily existence. The Hyge is our conscious thought. This is the decision-making mind, the seat of judgment. Here, we have the concept of free or rational will that can sometimes be at odds with our will or destiny. Lastly, we have the Lic corresponding to the physical body, or Sekhu.

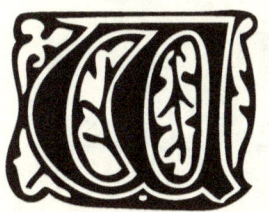

What is critical for our purposes is understanding that we are not singular. Instead, we comprise constituent parts, some not always entirely within our rational control. Our memories, emotions, and conscious and subconscious minds form the basis of our thoughts, actions, and perceptions of the world. Add to these the critical interplay of determination and inspiration. Apart from these "mental" aspects of our internal world, the witch should recognize the voice that speaks to us. Whether instinctual or just outside ourselves, heeding its call is critical to our success. We also have a shield of force that forms an outer invisible skin surrounding our physical epidermis. In the trance state, we may walk abroad in the form of our Fetch, the analog of our animal self.

Chapter XXII
The Weave of the Wyrd

The wyrd is a related concept that is not one of the constituent parts of the Self but is very connected to them. Generally described as "fate" or "destiny," it is the operative field in which the self operates. From this Old English word, we get our modern "weird," though the meaning has changed quite a lot. The concept is very similar to the Norse *urðr,* which is both fate and the name of one of the three norns, along with Verðandi and Skuld. Indeed, they gather around the well known as that nourishes the world tree Yggdrasill. Urðr and Verðandi derive their names from the Old Norse verb *verða,* meaning "to become." The former comes from the past tense, and the latter the present tense. Skuld comes from the Old Norse *Skuldu,* which means "shall be." Hence, we have three temporal states of past, present, and future—that which has happened (memory), that which is happening at the moment, and that which is to come.

Often described as a web, as in Web of the Wyrd, the image is one of woven fabric rather than a spider's web. Spinning has had a long historical connection with witchcraft. The norns are often depicted as spinning each individual's life thread. We may see echoes of Greco-Roman influence from the goddesses Moirai and Parcae, who were thought to spin fate. Fiber craft was historically considered "women's work," so here again, we have a connection between magic, witchcraft, and women's domestic realm. In this fabric, we have the interweaving of the individual self and the rest of the universe. The warp represents time and events; the weft is our placement in time and relation to others. The already woven fabric is the web of history, past actions, and memory. Our past actions define us. Our particular relation to space and time through our actions leaves their present pattern on the fabric. Ahead, there is only the warp, long strings of spun wool waiting to be taken up by the weft. The point where the shuttle is passed through them is the present moment unfolding, where past and present meet to complete the weave.

Like a tapestry, all things—people and events—are interconnected or interdependent in Buddhist terms. For success in magic, one must understand one's particular placement in relation to other forces in the world. The most important is closely tied to that which one desires to accomplish. We understand these interrelationships more deeply through meditation (calm abiding), listening, and divination. Here, the tarot spread known as the Celtic Cross is an ideal tool for analyzing a given situation and one's placement within the fabric of past, present, and possible future, seen and unseen influences, and what crosses our path in opposition as well as the thoughts of others and one's desires.

The shed defines the pattern of the weaving, the openings in the warp through which the shuttle passes. This is what is likely to happen. As the shuttle moves through the gaps, potential is solidified as history. One should strive to understand the relations of as many of the strings of the warp as possible. Often, magic involves changing the shed, where the foot is lifted from one treadle to another, shifting the warp's interrelation.

In the summer of 1916, Crowley spent several months at a home owned by American professional medium Evangeline Adams. The house was located in the tiny hamlet of Hebron in the White Mountains region of central New Hampshire on the banks of Lake Pasquaney, also called Newfound. The somewhat secluded cottage proved the ideal location for Crowley's magical retirement. While there, he engaged in occult and meditation practices. During one of these, he received a vision of the universe he would return to throughout his life, even calling it the "radix" of his philosophical outlook. This profound experience, Crowley described in his *Confessions* with the Sanskrit term Samadhi, is a point of meditative practice where one experiences instantaneously the enlightened state of consciousness. The realization came to be known as "Star Sponge Vision."

> I lost consciousness of everything but a universal space in which were innumerable bright points, and I realized this as a physical representation of the universe, in what I may call its essential structure. I exclaimed, "Nothingness with twinkles!" I concentrated upon this vision, with the result that the void space which had been the principal element of it diminished in importance; space appeared to be ablaze, yet the radiant points were not confused, and I thereupon completed my sentence with the exclamation, "but what twinkles!"

Crowley then continued to the second part of his vision, in which he perceived:

> that each star was connected by a ray of light with

> each other star. In the world of ideas each thought possessed a necessary relation with each other thought; each such relation is of course a thought in itself; each such ray is itself a star. It is here that the logical difficulty first presents itself. The seer has a direct perception of infinite series. Logically, therefore, it would appear as if the entire space must be filled up with a homogeneous blaze of light. This however is not the case. The space is completely full and yet the monads which fill it are perfectly distinct.[1]

This vision surprised Crowley. He had always imagined the state would be characterized by a bath of pure white light encompassing everything in a singularity. Instead, he was presented with a lattice, or web, of stars. The realization that everything is distinct yet simultaneously interrelated and interdependent is fundamental to the practice of witchcraft.

Crowley's vision was akin to seeing the tapestry of the wyrd. An important component of successful magic is that one understands one's position within the web of interconnectedness. Perspective is relative to position. There is a quote from Charles Addams, "Normal is an illusion. What is normal for the spider is chaos for the fly." The spider uses her position relative to the fly, the chaos created by the web, to its advantage. In Norse and Germanic mythologies, including Anglo-Saxon, this is called the Web of the Wyrd. This matrix of fate is woven by the mistresses of the web.

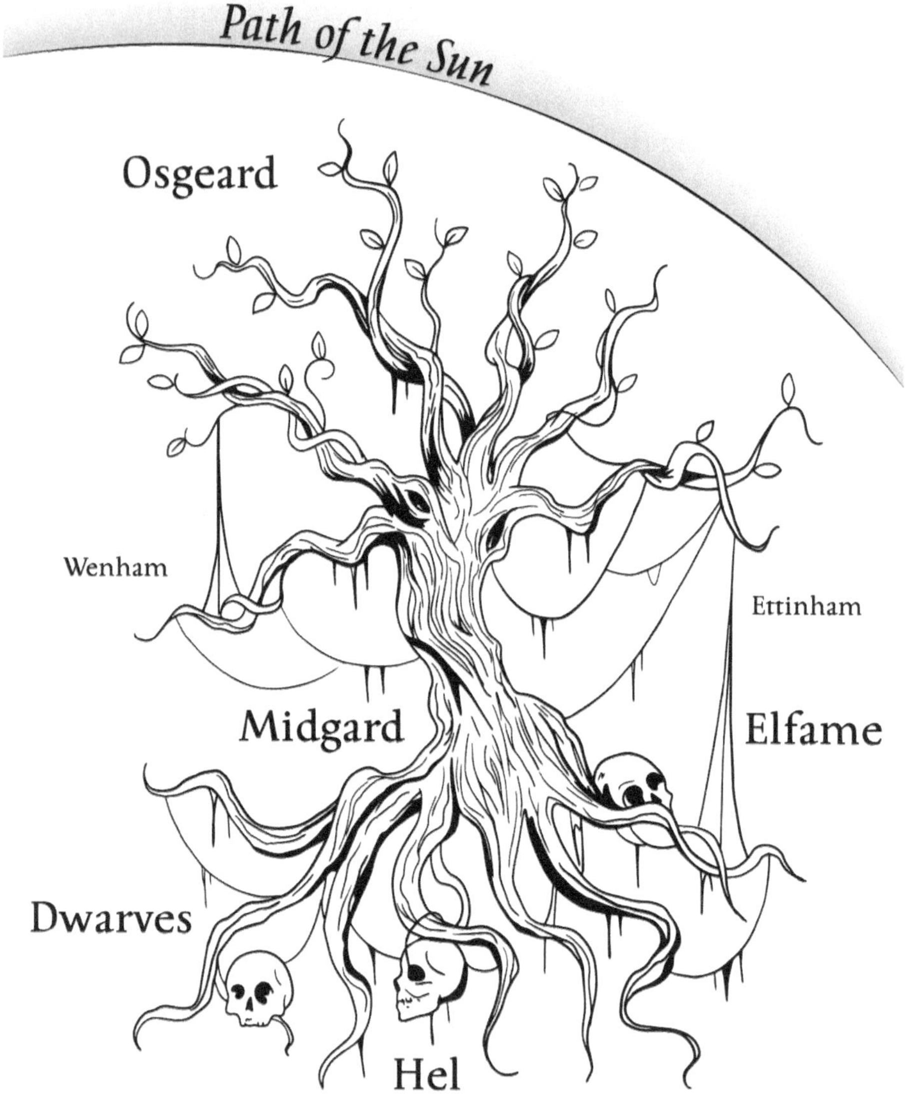
Path of the Sun
Osgeard
Wenham
Ettinham
Midgard
Elfame
Dwarves
Hel

Chapter XXIII
Old English Worlds

Norse mythology has the concept of nine mythological realms or worlds. Much less is known about how the Anglo-Saxons viewed the multiple worlds around them. The Nine Herb Charms references that fills and fennel were sent from the seven worlds. So, they believed in at least seven. Through the scant records and the work of reconstructionists, we can discern these seven worlds and their inhabitants: Osgeard, Middungeard (Midgard or Middle Earth), Wenham, Ettinham, Elfame, Dwarves, and Hel. The World Tree (Yggdrasil in the Norse) forms the structure that connects the worlds. At its base is the Well of the Wyrd.

OSGEARD

Osgeard is the home of the Ese, the deities of the Old English pantheon. It is analogous to the Norse Asgard, home of the Asir. The tremendous feasting halls of the gods and goddesses are in this world. Entrance to the world is guarded by the god Hama, and humans can't venture there. This is why we invite the divines into our world to attend our feasts.

MIDGARD

Our realm is known as Midgard, or Middle Earth. The name is likely familiar to you from the works of Tolkien. This is not a coincidence as much of his writing was inspired by Anglo-Saxon lore with which he was fascinated. Middle Earth is the world that we are most familiar with. It is the domain of humans, flora, and fauna. We also share this space with spirits of the land, *genius loci*. Elves, fairies, and dwarves living in worlds closest to ours often cross into our realm. When we cast a circle, it opens a portal or space between that transects our world and theirs. We then ask the gods and goddesses to descend from Osgeard and join us as our honored guests.

ELFAME & THE REALM OF DWARVES

Two realms coexist with Middle Earth and are the closest to us. They are home to fantastical creatures that should be pretty familiar. Stories of their interaction with humanity are common in folklore. The first is Elfame (Norse

Álfheimr), home to the light Elves. This space is sometimes seen as just above ours, intersecting at the top of hills and barrow mounds. It is more than just immediately adjacent to ours—a slight shift in space and time. Elfame is common in British stories and known as the home of the Fae or Faeries.

Elves were common throughout the Germanic pre-Christian worldview. Many references occur in early English (Old English ælf). Over time, the name elf appears to have been replaced by the now quite common fairy borrowed from the French *faerie.* For several centuries, we find the terms used interchangeably. Chaucer's *Canterbury Tales* contains several fourteenth-century examples. Sir Thopas takes a quest for the "elf-queen" who reigns in the "countree of the Faerie." The introduction to the Wife of Bath's tale talks of the land of faeries ruled over by the Elf-Queen and bemoans that there are no longer faeries in the land of men as the ecclesiastics have driven out all the elves.

Further examples abound during the Elizabethan period when references to faeries seem to have been quite popular in literature. Shakespeare's *Romeo and Juliet* describes tangled hair as an "elf-lock" created by the "midwife of fairies" Queen Mab. It appears it was during this time that the fae made their transition in popular conception to beings of a diminutive stature. Edmund Spencer's *Faerie Queene* treats them as human-sized in 1590, while Shakespeare's famous depiction in *A Midsummer Night's Dream* of 1595 gives a strong impression of little people, especially in the mischievous Puck.

The fae are the spirits of the green, the wyld wood. They are spirits of ecstasy—fecund and sexual. They are similar in energy to the Greek satyr and the Roman faun. In ancient England, they are Woodwose/Wodewose/Woodhouse from the Old English *wude-wasa.* The first part of the word may relate to wood.

But, despite their similarity, the compound may derive

from the Old English *wode*, meaning "wild" or "ecstatic" and not "wood." He is the great man of the woodlands characterized by the very nature of his wildness. The word has a Latin cognate in *vates*, "prophet," "seer," or "mouthpiece of the divine." The etymology of the Latin descends from the Proto-Indo-European *wéht-i-s* ("seer"), which itself incorporated the prefix *wéht-* ("to be excited"). The word is also linguistically connected to the Celtic *watis*, either through borrowing or having the same original common root, which gives us the modern English word ovate, a synonym of "Bard." Recall the use of the Latin in the invocation used by Crowley and Neuberg in the Paris Working.

Nigel Jackson speaks of our "Faery Ancestors," "the divinized spirits of the dead who have undergone metamorphosis" in the land of faery.[1] They are the spirits of the ancient wyld forests always present to the brothers of the Craft. The Green Man is the God of the Witches, whose phallus is the regenerative power within nature, evoking new greenery each spring. When garbed in green, the Magister of the Grove embodies this primordial nature within the circle. In France, the Magister was known as *Verdelet* wearing green as he presided over the witches' conventicle, the Sabbat.

The second is the realm of the dwarves (Old English *dweorg*), known as Nidavellir in Norse mythology. The dwarves reside in great halls beneath the earth. One may descend into their realms via caves and mines. All things of the world, such as metals, come under their purview. The blacksmith owes much to the dwellers beneath the earth as they gift the raw materials required for their craft. British tales of Brown Men or Bogles, such as those associated with the Simoside Hills in northern England, are connected to dwarves operating in the world of humans. This realm is related to dark elves, Norse *Dökkálfar* or *Svartálfar*. In some tellers' perceptions, the Brown Man was a solitary fairy. The dark elves and dwarves appear to be one and the same. Nigel Jackson makes this connection.[2] A reading that appears to be borne out by several references in the *Prose Edda* where dwarves and elves are linguistically associated.[3]

In Scottish folklore, there are considered to be two groupings of faeries known as the Seelie and Unseelie Courts. The former is a court of fairies generally perceived as benign and helpful to humans. The latter are typically considered wicked and often act with malicious disregard for humans. They are also called the Seely Wights, which may show a clue in the tales of fairies as particular spirits of the land.

Fairyland, the land of Elfame, is intrinsically linked to our own. It sits beside our world, perhaps just a shift to the left in perception. Nigel Jackson notes that the interconnectedness goes farther than mere proximity. He describes two realms conjoined by life, death, afterlife, and rebirth:

> The 'human' and the 'faery' are the two poles of our being between which we oscillate through our transmigrational cycles of rebirths, our countless discarnations and incarnations. In other words, the Sidhe are ourselves awaiting birth in middle-earth and we ourselves are the Sidhe awaiting our return to Elfhame.[4]

The witch moves back and forth between the world of humans and the shadowy, effervescent world of the fae.

HEL

Hel is the underworld and one of the places the dead may go after passing from Middle Earth. It is ruled over by a goddess of the same name, the daughter of Woden, who gave her dominion over the underworld realm. This is not the Christian Hell that has been used to scare people for centuries. Instead, this is a land where the dead slumber. Their dreams may indeed be visions of a land bathed in the soft warmth of the summer sun.

ETTINHAM AND WANHEM

Two additional worlds exist. Far to the east is Ettinham, home of the Ettin, or giants. Even farther from us to the west, Wanhem, home of the older Wan gods, is similar to the Vanir in Norse cosmology. The inhabitants of these realms have little to no interest in the affairs of humans. They are far removed from Middle Earth and do not intersect with its doings. They are ancient and exist in a timeframe greater than the geologic.

FIRE AND ICE

Norse lore preserves two additional worlds: Muspelheim (fire) and Niflheim (ice). These two worlds are the first to exist in the Norse creation myth. The land of Ice is to the north, and the land of Fire is to the south. This appears to be an ancestral memory of the preceding Ice Age. The other seven were created in the meeting of these two primordial worlds.

Chapter XXIV
Spirits of Place

As discussed previously, the earliest people had a concept of an otherworld and were animists, meaning they saw the world around them as imbued with spirit. Before what we know now as deities arrived on the scene, religious expression focused on the spirits of the land, or *genius loci,* and reverence for ancestors. The concept of gods and goddesses came relatively late. We can group these land spirits under the Old English term land wights (Old Norse *Landvættir*). These would have been localized spirits connected with particular features in the environment. These spirits would become the tutelary protectors of their tribes. They were agents of the otherworldly. Over time, some spirits were closed into diverse groupings of supernatural entities with various names in different cultures. There are fairies, elves, dwarves, gnomes, pixies, piskies, and many more.

Specific regional spirits are associated with particular places and elements of the natural environment. These may be the spirits honored by local custom or connected to specific geographic areas such as trees, groves, meadows, caves, springs, or wells. It is crucial to communicate with and honor these local spirits in the area in which you live. Spirits arise naturally out of the landscape. This is why particular spectral spirits are not universal and appear only in specific locals. Take the Black Shuck, for example. The apparition is a large, shaggy, black dog with flaming red eyes, encountered plodding along the roads and pathways of East Anglia.

The Scottish *daoine sith* (*Aos sí* in Ireland), the people of the mounds, are another prime example of this. Said to be the descendants of the Tuatha Dé Danann, Children of the Goddess Danu, in Irish folklore, they are commonly known to us as fairies or the fae, "wee folk" or simply the "good neighbors." These spirits exist in an interstitial space between the realms of gods, and men play a prominent role in Gaelic folklore.

Many local deities have been propitiated throughout the world. They are sprinkled across Roman Britain, where the Empire absorbed local traditions into their venerations. In her book *Lid Off the Cauldron*, Patricia Crowther provides the example of Verbeia, a Celtic goddess associated with the river Wharfe. She is known to us through a single stone altar and an associated image in Ilkley. She is depicted as a female figure with an overlarge head, reminiscent of Sheela-na-gig, holding a snake in each hand—very reminiscent of the Cretan Snake Goddess although specific to that locale.

Anthropologists and folklorists often state fairies do not seem to have crossed the Atlantic from the British Isles, unlike other supernatural creatures. One exception, they note, is Newfoundland, where a common belief in fairies persists. This assumption is not entirely accurate. British conceptions of the little people may not have been widely imported. Still, the concept of otherworldly creatures co-occupying the natural world with humans is common within Native American folklore.

Additionally, we can intuitively perceive spirits in the natural world around us. North America may not have fairies, per se, simply because the anchors in the land are different.

Fairies were often associated with the Old World burrow mounds and neolithic sacred structures. The British burrow mound simply does not exist in North America. This means spirits here will be different, but it does not mean they are absent.

As a child, my family often visited Gotts Island, the offshore island my ancestors settled in the late eighteenth century. One of my favorite spots there was a small section of woods. There, generations of children had carried on a tradition of building fairy houses amongst the trees. These fanciful tiny constructions were magical, tucked in amongst the pine and spruce's moss-covered roots. My cousins and I added our own during those summer visits. I hope the tradition continues.

Growing up, one of my favorite books was *Gnome* by Wil Huygen. I pored over my grandmother's copy often. Gnomes make their first appearance in Renaissance magic as the Latin *gnomus* in the writings of Paracelsus. A similar entity exists in Nordic folklore called *nisse* in Norwegian and *tomte* in Sweden. These tiny creatures existed in several forms, but the most commonly known is that of the household or spirits. My mother and I have welcomed in a *nisse* to our homes here in New Orleans. During the Yule season, we leave him an offering of porridge and a coin.

MARIE LAVEAU

New Orleans is a city filled with spirits. Paramount among them is the original Voodoo Queen, Marie LaVeau. Her image is ubiquitous among the tourist shops occupying much of the French Quarter. The city, at times, feels like it's been photocopied too many times like it is an attenuated version of an original. Gentrification has spread into new neighborhoods, while non-owner-occupied AirBNBs have eroded their soul. The Big Easy is a survivor. Look past the t-shirt purveyors on Decatur and the bars of Bourbon Street, and one can see the spirits are still resident.

Marie was born a Creole, free woman of color in 1801. She married a Haitian refugee, Jacques Paris, in 1819. He died the following year, and she gained one of the names by which she continues to be known today: "the Widow Paris." She attained renown as a hairdresser. She remains famous as a healer, charmer, and rootworker. She was a religious leader in the community, aiding the sick and visiting condemned prisoners. Marie died in 1881, and it is widely accepted that her daughter Marie carried on her work.

Today, one may visit the site of her cottage at 1020 St. Ann Street, where a plaque marks the location. Her tomb in St. Louis Cemetery No. 1 was open to the public until it was vandalized in 2013, painted Pepto Bismol pink. Since 2015, access is only possible through a tour group approved by the Archdiocese.

We maintain a shrine to Marie at our covenstead. It is decorated with her image and throws from the Zulu Social Aid & Pleasure Club parade, the city's oldest and largest predominantly African American Carnival crew.

SAINT EXPEDITÉ

St. Expedité is one of the local spirits venerated here in New Orleans. Requests and offerings often surround his statue at the Chapel of Guadalupe on Basin Street. He is the one to petition when you need a quick fix. As the story goes, a Roman centurion statue was separated from a crucifixion scene. When he arrived in New Orleans, the nuns were confused about what saint he was. Reading the label on the outside of the crate, "Expedité," he became St. Expedité. I've heard this same story told of other European locations, making it an urban legend not unique to New Orleans.

His iconography is interesting. He holds a cross with the word 'Hodie," Latin for today. His right foot is atop a crow, making the crow sound "Cras." In Latin, Cras is also the word for tomorrow. So, don't put off to tomorrow what you should do today. One makes a request of him, usually a written petition, and awaits his quick intercession. Once the request is granted, one repays his effort on your behalf with offerings—traditionally pound cake and red roses. It is also important to publicly thank him for his assistance.

He has a place in the foyer of our home. We regularly offer flowers and burn a red, cinnamon-scented candle.

LA MADAMA

One of the spirits I work with was taught to me by Baba Raul. La Madama is a Black woman, sometimes called a medium or fortune teller in botanicas. Sometimes confused by the casual observer as a racist stereotype of the "mammy," Madama is in actualilty a powerful image of a Black mother. She is the archetypal Black Madonna. Above her shrine in my home hangs an icon of Our Lady of Czestochowa, an image of the Virgin in the Jasna Góra Monastery in Czestochowa, Poland.

La Madama is a protector of the home and family. Her statue depicts a standing Black mother with a broom in one hand and sometimes a basket on her head as if heading to the market. Her icons come in several colors—red, blue, yellow, and green. Some hold that the different colors relate to different types of workings. Her statue is placed in a *potjie*, a three-legged cast iron cooking pot similar to a cauldron and available in various sizes. With her in the pot, I keep a few Mardi Gras doubloons and a deck of playing cards.

As a mother, she is a fierce protector of the home and family and those who do her honor. With her broom, she sweeps away malignant forces and negative energies from the house. I clean her statue with sweet waters and perfume her with dedicated oils. Before making an offering, I always sweep the area around her shrine. As offerings, I give her a white candle dressed with her special oil blend, a glass of water, black coffee, and, sometimes, a lit cigar. If I do other workings in sight of her space, I cover her with a red silk scarf.

These days, there is much discussion online about closed traditions. Much of this gatekeeping is counterproductive and too often serves to occlude meaningful debate of cultural appropriation within spiritual practices. Since the heady 60s, many spiritual traditions have been lifted from their cultural contexts without their sources being acknowledged. New Age philosophies are likely the worst offenders but are certainly not the only ones. The now ubiquitous practice of smudging is one of the best examples. It is rare to find a New Age, spiritual, or occult shop that doesn't stock a selection of smudge bundles. Their use has gained a universality that obstructs and obscures the practice's deep roots within indigenous spiritual practice.

While my practice is seated firmly in witchcraft, it is not exclusive of other cultural influences. My respect for La Madama would be but one example. There is a place for closed practices but in the sense of initiation-based lineage. It helps ensure continuity of practice and, one would hope, some protection for seekers as the teacher can't just set up shop. I am not naive enough to think that this is always the case, but it does afford a fraction of insurance that one is conversing with an individual empowered to speak with the authority bestowed on them by those who have come before. A lineage community can be self-protecting, and I know of rare instances where an individual's vouch has been publicly revoked for transgressing and causing harm.

When one incorporates an element from another culture or tradition, one *must* recognize and honor its source and consider its appropriateness! This is unequivocal. One shouldn't simply buy a smudge stick without an understanding of whence the practice comes—not to mention the ecological impact of its creation. The poaching of White Sage (*Salvia Apiana*) has become such a problem in California that it is nearing an environmental disaster decimating the native plant. It is vital that we approach any practice out of respect, not simply because it is trendy. Given the current state of things, it is hard, if not impossible, to separate the utilization of smudging from European colonialism and the forced assimilation of indigenous peoples. As discussed later, I choose to use juniper or pine bundles, a Scottish practice known as *saining*, in my practice as it is aligned with the heritage of my ancestors.

Chapter XXV
Sacred Space

The magical universe can be just as frightening and unpredictable as the physical world, if not more so. To begin this path, it is advisable to establish the boundaries of one's personal magical space. Much like the wolf marks his home territory by establishing boundaries within which he may exert his hegemony. Reflecting the birth of the Platonic, divided universe, this sets up a natural opposition between the inside working area and the outside. From this vantage, the shaman may safely watch, listen, and perceive.

Over time, this magical safety zone will be wherever you are. It will be carried with you like an auric coat of many colors or a cloak of invisibility, depending on the situation. At this point, you will establish your home base and remain in their den, where they return to rest psychically, if not physically.

Safety in the mundane world is generally not safe at all. The false perception of safety can be dangerous and more threatening than any demon from Lovecraft's dreams. Instead, this space is set aside for a purpose. For queer peoples, the threats are often more pronounced and the sanctuary offered by safe spaces harder to find.

The surrounding space should be clutter-free and straightforward to limit visual distractions. All elements within your perception become part of the experiment and must be considered. The working area forms a black box stage upon which you can enact an orchestrated symphony for the sensorium.

Having an area of your living space set aside for your witchcraft is essential. This may be as small as a shelf with meaningful but seemingly unremarkable items or a room set aside for your practice. Setting up a sacred space is a deeply personal practice that is uniquely yours. It's a space to engage in meditation, spellwork, divination, and other magical work.

Select a quiet and private area where you won't be disturbed. This could be a corner of a room, a unique altar, or a small room dedicated entirely to your practice. It is essential first to clean the physical space. Dust, vacuum, and declutter the area. Then, spiritually cleanse the space by burning incense, sprinkling salt, or using bells or chimes.

Next, choose a surface, like a table or a shelf, to serve as your altar. You can use a special cloth to define the space if you don't have a specific altar. You'll place your statues, tools, magical symbols, and offerings here. Over time, you will gather items that have meaning to you and your path. As you collect these items, you may add them to your altar or sacred space as you are drawn to.

Lighting is an important element to heighten the atmosphere of the space. Candles are typical, and I have at least one on almost all my altars and shrines. Remember always to use candle holders or fire-safe containers. Be mindful that candles are beautiful and evocative but pose a potential hazard.

This will be your primary working space and focal point of your practice. In addition to my main altar, I have numerous shrines throughout our home. Each represents a particular deity with whom one or both of us have a relationship. Certain items on my main altar are static and remain throughout the year; others, I will cycle by the season. For sabbats, esbats, and other circle workings, a temporary altar is set up within the working space particular to the festival or working at hand.

Keeping your working area clean and free of outside clutter is important. Regularly cleanse and refresh your sacred space. Remove offerings before they pass. I often leave food offerings such as fruit overnight and dispose of them. Flowers I keep watered as long as they are fresh in appearance.

Your intuition will be your guide. Do what feels right to you and not what you perceive others to think of as correct. This is your space, not anyone else's—unless you share with a partner, then some compromise may of necessity creep in.

SIMPLE CLEANSING

Before starting, ground yourself. Take five even breaths and gently clear your mind. Take a glass or bowl of water. If you have a cologne or perfume you usually wear or which may be generally associated with you, place several drops into the water. To this, add a few drops of your urine. As with the wolf, this "scent" is a clear and immediately perceivable signal that this is your space. You don't have to lift your leg on the new ottoman, but the principle is analogous. It becomes a ward against unexpected and uninvited interlopers—with its subtle counterpart/reflection in other directions. Pay particular attention to openings (marking windowsills and doorways) and potential gateways (corners and angles).

My own main altar (Old English *wéofod*) has a statue (Old English *wéoh*) depicting Woden/Óðin on it. Here he is a reflection in wood of both Anglo-Saxon and Norse gods, but he is also the Witch Father in his appearance as the Man in Black, with his dark cloak and wide-brimmed hat. He is the bringer of wisdom and the archetypal practitioner of transgressive witchcraft. On the wall behind hangs a Sheela-na-gig, her hands spreading wide her cavernous vagina. She represents the prototypical mother birthing the universe as well the embodiment of dark mysteries.

The altar itself is an antique buffet with a marble top. For an altar cloth, I currently have a goat hide. Inside the cabinet, I keep many of the items I use in circle, such as some of my working tools, altar pentacle, incense, seasonal altar cloths, and the like. Other items one is likely to find on the altar include an Anglo-Saxon rune set made from antler, iron or oak wands, my athame, and a collection of small mementoes with personal connection to my practice.

One of the advantages we've found living in New Orleans is that one can have religious statuary and icons just about anywhere around the house, and people don't think twice about it. It fits right in with the rest of the decor. The numerous shrines we have throughout our home are very different from my working altar. Each is dedicated to a particular spirit and honored in their own way. These are not spaces for workings but instead showing devotion, leaving offerings, and communicating with their presence.

St. Expedité greets visitors in our foyer. Marie Leveau presides over our New Orleans-decorated guest room with its Jack Cooley paintings and Krewe of Rex commemorative posters. The ancestral altar discussed previously is somewhat similar, though particular in meaning.

Chapter XXVI
The Blasted Oak

The sixteenth card of the tarot's Major Arcana, the Tower, was present in the oldest decks that survive today. Some of the earliest illustrations on them, however, did not depict a stone tower or similar structure. Several French and Belgian decks of the seventeenth century were illustrated with a tall tree struck by lightning and were labeled "La Foudre" or "the Lightning." The card's meaning is generally interpreted as sudden change through unexpected catastrophe. A traumatic experience causes us to shed unwanted parts of ourselves, symbolically represented by the bodies falling from the tower. As we know, change is not always negative, even when the cause is unwelcome in the immediate.

The tree is a symbol of age, strength, and health. That is undoubtedly the case of the Tree card in the traditional Lenormand. The lightning bolt represents the sudden and unpredictable power of nature that seems to come from nowhere. The sky has been linked to mysteries of the divine since time immemorial. Lightning has long been considered a consequence of the wrath of the gods. Zeus's thunderbolt is his signature power. It represents the Christian god's punishment. In Zechariah 9:14, his arrow is likened to a bolt of lightning.

We undoubtedly see an element of that understanding here—the wrath of god striking the tree of life. Of course, Thor is the ultimate god of thunder, lightning, and storms, and the oak is sacred to him.

Lightning-struck trees have had a long connection to witchcraft as well. Wood scorched by lightning is a prized element of magical work. The wood becomes imbued with the power of the divine, a powerful force that may be employed for protection. A wand crafted from such wood is potent. I have one such given to me by a close friend. Interestingly, Matthews resurrects the tree struck by lightning in his depiction of the sixteenth Atu in his Wildwood Tarot deck.

Trees, in general, all possess magical properties in and of themselves. The oak is supreme among them. It is the majestic king of the forest. Early Europeans were said by their contemporaries to worship among the oaks. Pliny, writing in the first century CE, described the residents of Gaul as worshipping in oak groves. It is a symbol of steadfastness, strength, and longevity. Modern Druidry logically assumes this was also the case with the Druids of the British Isles. St. Columba presumably founded churches at oak groves because these had previous associations with Druid practices he wished to supplant. The New Forest, the site of Gardner's initiation into the Craft, is an area that has remained unchanged for many centuries. It is one of Southern England's most extensive areas of pasture land, heathland, and forest covering southwest Hampshire and southeast Wiltshire. It boasts the highest concentration of ancient trees of any place in Western Europe.

Oak was also sacred to the Anglo-Saxons. Among their runes is Ác, which translates to "oak." In the associated rune poem, the oak is described as a gift to the children of men and is linked to the raising of livestock, specifically pigs. Acorns are often used as fodder. Oak trees are quite literally a gift from the gods.

Oak was long used to construct many dwellings throughout Europe. It is one of the best materials for shipbuilding. The poem also notes this, saying how the oak "often traverses the gannet's bath." The gannet is a large sea bird, and the gannet's bath is an Anglo-Saxon reference to the sea or ocean.

It is through its strength in keeping out the ocean water that the oak "proves" its honor. Oak tannins were important for tanning animal hide. Oak logs provided necessary fuel. After the transition from clay pots to wooden barrels, oak became an essential component in the fermentation of grain alcohol, beer, and wine, imparting its tannins to the liquid during the maturation period. Equal-armed oaken crosses tied with red thread are potent wards. A small piece of oak may be carried to bring luck. Acorns were placed on window sills or meeting rails to protect against lightning strikes.

Irminsûl is Old Saxon for "great pillar." Oak trees and groves were important sacred sites for the pagan Germanic and Anglo-Saxon peoples, and the tree pillar was central to the Saxons. Some have inferred a god called Irmin from its name. These god-poles were likely first dedicated to the Saxon god Tyr and then later to Woden or Óðin during the migration period. Like most period information, we know of their existence from non-Saxons' writing. During the Saxon Wars of the late eighth century, Charlemagne is said to have ordered the destruction of an Irminsul sacred to the Saxons in his pursuit to Christianize the heathens. A Benedictine monk, Rudolf of Fulda, relates how the Irminsul was the focus of worship in the open under the sky.

The most common modern image of the Irminsul is a twentieth-century creation. It is depicted as a pole split at the top into two horizontal branches reminiscent of a mustache or, as some have noted, a palm tree not precisely native to old Germany of Saxony. It is, in fact, a 1929 "reconstruction" by the German archeologist Wilhelm Teudt based on a Christian rock relief created circa 1000 CE. Teudt was a member of the Ahnenerbe, a "scientific" research branch of Himmler's *Schutzstaffel* (SS). His drawing of the Irminsul has proliferated. So here we have an easily accessible pagan image, employed from tattoos to beer mugs, whose origins are rooted in Nazi-era occultism.

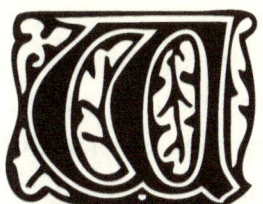

What did Charlemagne destroy? There is some question whether it was wood or stone. Either way, it was representative of the World Tree, Yggdrasil. We may infer that the erection of god-poles was a common, if not central, element of Heathen practice. For a better understanding of the importance of the sacred world tree, we will go back a few thousand years to the Neolithic period in Britain.

In 1998, a walker along the shore at Holme-next-to-the-sea in Norfolk, England, came across a bronze axe head. Soon after, he noticed wooden stumps sticking out of the sand between the tides. He had discovered a Neolithic wooden circle preserved by the wet environment. Beginning in 1999, Seahenge, as it had come to be known, was excavated by Francis Pryor and Maise Taylor, an expert on prehistoric wood. The site dates from the early Bronze Age. All the wood used to construct the ring was felled at the same time in the spring of 2049 BCE, while a central stump had been cut the year before. The surrounding area was salt marshes at the time it was built. Oak trees would not have grown in the area immediately surrounding the site, so they would have had to be brought from some way away. The structure was formed of a ring of fifty-five split oak logs, with a V-shaped log forming an entrance. The split sides faced outward, so those inside would have looked at the tree's bark.

Another post was placed outside the entrance to obstruct the view through the V-shaped log's opening. At the center of the ring was a large oak stump inverted to form an altar.

Just as with the older blue stones at Stonehenge, we can infer the importance those who constructed the monuments placed on these materials they brought over great distances. The material in and of itself had to have held powerful meaning for those who made these ritual monuments and those they were meant to impress. For me, the layout of Seahenge shows that it was primarily a sacred space to be used, not just a showpiece. The fact that only a small group could fit inside, and their actions would not be visible to anyone standing outside the wooden circumference speaks to the sacredness of the activity within.

Pryor notes that Seahenge isn't exactly like a woodhenge or a timber circle, and excavations do not show sufficient earth movement for a barrow mound. He suggests it may have been about the central tree itself. He describes his thoughts on its purpose:

> By inverting the tree in the ground, those life forces are being returned to the earth, the source of all life. Removing the bark was the purification process needed before the tree could release its energies back into the ground. But these powerful forces required constraint. They were dangerous and mysterious. A living thing must contain life, so the purified tree, perhaps with its human cargo, contrasted with a far more enormous symbolic tree, represented by the solid circular wall of posts.[1]

I agree with Pryor that it is about the tree. My sense, however, is that it is *all* about the tree. I do not see that it necessarily had to have carried a "human cargo" into the otherworld. The central oak, 167 years old when it was felled, could have had significance for a group of people for some time before the monument's construction. Passage tombs were active sites where the living regularly interacted with the dead and thus their otherworld. I think Seahenge was a similar sacred enclosure where a priestly class interacted with the underworld.

Oak is one of three trees commonly associated with the World Tree—the other two being Ash and Yew. Its branches grow to the sky, while its roots extend deep into the underworld. Here, this equation is inverted. In this place of worship, what lies beneath is above and facing skyward. In this mirror-mirror reality, corralled within a sacred circle, what was below is now above. This is an intentionally constructed liminal space, just as modern witches construct a circular space between worlds every time they cast a circle.

As crucial as oak trees were to Indo-Europeans, particularly those on the British Isles, North America possesses far more variety of oaks than the old world. About ninety different species of oak grow natively in North America.[2] Again proving their place as king of the forest, oaks support more forms of life—birds, insects, fungi, animals—than any other tree.[3] A handful of oaks are most common in our part of the northern hemisphere. These are separated broadly into white and red oaks based on the wood color when cut. They include the black, bur, laurel, live, pin, and water oaks. The northern red oak, including, ironically, the black oak, is the most common species in the Maine of my youth. Louisiana is, of course, famous for its majestic Southern live oaks. Examples of some of the states' oldest include the Seven Sisters Oak in Mandeville and the Etienne de Boré Oak in New Orleans's Audubon Park. One of the most famous oaks in the state, though not nearly as old an example as many, is the Evangeline Oak on the edge of

Bayou Teche. Local legend holds that it was beneath this tree that the Cajun lovers Emmeline and Louis reunited. Their story was immortalized in fiction by Henry Wadsworth Longfellow (a Maine native) as Evangeline and Gabriel.

The upstanding oak is the world tree, *Axis Mundi,* and the erect phallus. One of the central elements of my prime altar is a carving of a stylized oak flanked by stags representing the sacred tree. It symbolizes balance growing as it does, with its roots deep in the underworld and its upper branches reaching toward the sky. My wand of lightning struck is always close at hand, and I regularly empower the god-pole with its energy. My festival altars always include some acknowledgment of the sacred oak in the form of the godpole, a carved wooden phallus, oak leaves, and acorns, or some combination depending on the intent of the ritual and the season.

Also located on the primary altar, my offering vessel is made from copper and another sacred tree, the Holly. The Dancing Goats Folk Ways Studio at Oak Knoll Farm created this exceptional piece. The wood was from an old-growth tree whose trunk was thirty-six inches across and felled naturally during a violent storm. The crafter passed high-voltage electricity through the wood to create what are known as Lichtenberg Figures. This is a definite instance of a do-not-attempt-this-at-home project. The process creates lightning-like fractals running across the surface of the wood. For the vessel, these were then filled in with copper. Two painted ravens, Huginn and Muninn, fly amongst the lightning.

Chapter XXVII
The Compass Round

The Circle is one of modern Wicca's most familiar and emblematic images. It can be a noun and a verb, with "casting a circle" being a common practice. The Circle creates a sacred space separate from the ordinary world and contains the power raised within it. It also serves as a protective barrier against external forces and forms a secure space between different realms.

Going back to the Neolithic, circles have been used for thousands of years to create sacred spaces, with Stonehenge being one of the most well-known, but not oldest, examples. The standing stones of Stenness on Orkney, Scotland, predate Stonehenge by 500 years and are likely the oldest stone circle in northern Europe. Also forming part of the ceremonial landscape of Orkney is the Ring of Brodgar, with the Ness of Brodgar in between the two. Similarly, Newgrange in Ireland, which predates Stonehenge and the pyramids of Egypt, is a circular structure that symbolically mirrors the birth process in reverse.

The Circle is closely connected to the year's cycle, with the dark period giving birth to the young god in spring, leading to his peak in summer and, ultimately, his sacrifice in the fall. Similarly, the daily revolution of the sun mirrors this cycle. The

Circle represents both the cycle of life and light and serves as a space outside of time and the mundane. The dark turns to dawn, then to the high power of the sun at noon, moving on through its arc to dusk and the return of the seclusion and solitude of night. The seed grows in the dark earth, reaches toward the air, moves into the fiery heat of fertility, and then withers to the western waters of death (and initiation), returning to earth once again. The cycle continues—a continuous circle of life and light.

The circle demarcates an interstitial space between the world of man and the realms of the gods, spirits, and the dead. It is a space outside of time and the mundane. It is a marking out of sacred space. The Circle, or Compass Round, is a rampart to defend the work within it. When we draw a circle, we are delineating a small patch of known territory. It is a willful act of creation, defining a space for brothers to join with each other. It is a defense against the threats from outside, while being a gathering point within. When a coven gathers, it does so in perfect love and perfect trust. This is our spiritual oath we each make to our brothers. The sacred circle is its embodiment.

The Circle concentrates the energy raised by the coven and serves as a focal point for rituals and festivals. Through ritual dancing and chanting, the coven builds a cone of power that is contained and concentrated within the Circle. This is similar to how a pot constrains and focuses heat energy, bringing water to a boil.

A cast circle is a focal point in the ritual landscape of the coven or grove, just as the stone circles of old were the heart of their ceremonial landscapes. The Circle can be cast anywhere, with only the circumference and center being necessary. It is an intentional limit that creates a sacred space and serves as a balustrade to protect the work within it. All festivals take place inside a Circle.

The Minoan civilization of ancient Crete demarcated specific sacred spaces, set apart from the profane world. These areas were originally open spaces around a sacred tree, spring, or other natural focal point. Eventually, they were marked out by stones, walls, or a grove of trees. They were zones dedicated to the gods and were exclusively reserved for religious or spiritual practices. In ancient Greece, *temenos* (τέμενος) described a sacred precinct or enclosure that surrounded an altar or shrine. Eventually, temples were erected but in ancient times these sacred circles were in the open.

Carl Jung relates the temenos to the magician's circle. He characterized it as a space set aside. He describes it as a mental "square space" where one can encounter the unconscious. For Jung, the sacred circle represents a zone of safety where one can encounter one's shadow and higher spirit.[1]

The sacred circle is at the heart of our practice. Honoring the goddesses and gods in their space is what it's all about. Our simple act is what matters. When we enter the sacred space, stripped of all our clothes and material possessions, we are both humbled before ancient spirits and elevated, through our actions, to the threshold of our own liberation.

In the earliest times, the procession toward the sacred space appears to have been just as important as the actions that occurred within. We can see this in the bent avenue that connects the river Avon to Stonehenge. Lady Rhea recalls reading a book on ancient Crete culture by Authur Evans in 1972. She gleaned that the ancient Minoans worshipped their gods via the processional with offerings of pork, fruit, and minted wine. She and Eddie were inspired to conduct a ritual where they processed up the stairs at the Warlock Shop to the second story where they had set up an altar. They carried fruit sausage and wine with dried mint added (a drink she does not recommend). This was the first Minoan circle.[2]

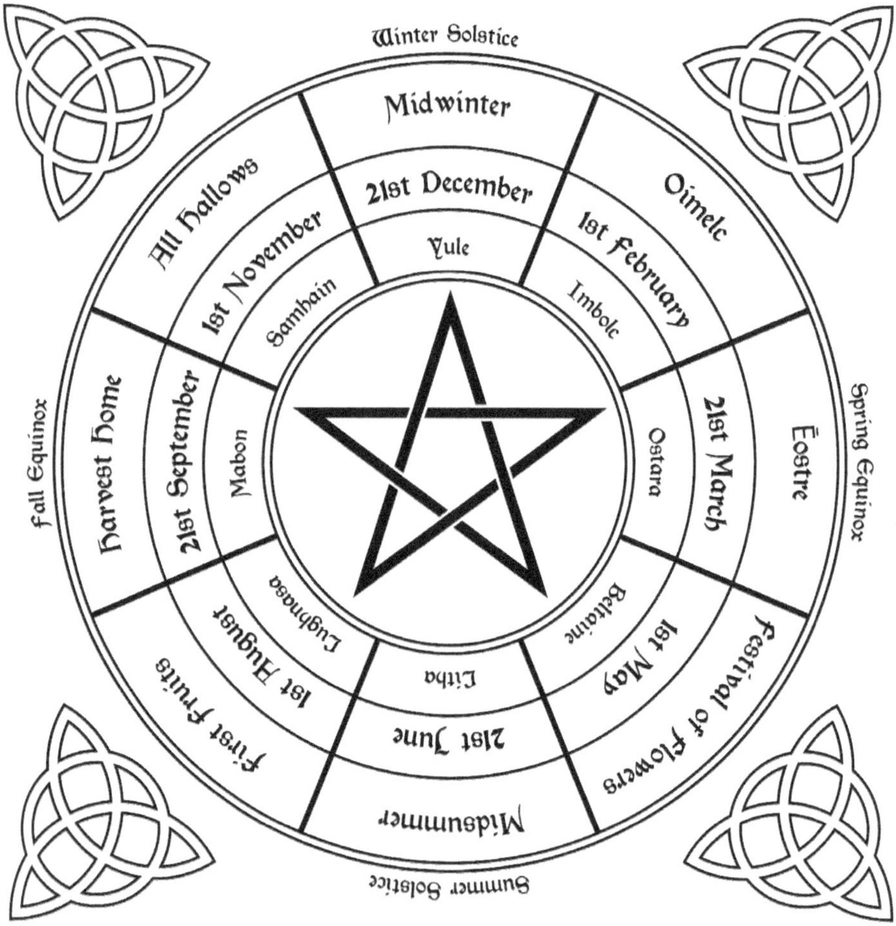

Winter Solstice
Midwinter
21st December
Yule
Oimelc
1st February
Imbolc
Spring Equinox
Eostre
21st March
Ostara
Festival of Flowers
1st May
Beltaine
Summer Solstice
Midsummer
21st June
Litha
First Fruits
1st August
Lughnasa
Fall Equinox
Harvest Home
21st September
Mabon
All Hallows
1st November
Samhain

Chapter XXVIII
The Wheel of the Year

One of Gardner's most important contributions to the Craft was outlining the Wheel of the Year and its eight festivals for his version of witchcraft. His colleague Ross Nichols adopted a similar eight-fold annual cycle for his Order of Bards, Ovates, and Druids (OBOD). There is a story that the two men developed the calendar together while on a nudist retreat. Nichols advocated for the four traditional Celtic holidays, and Gardner suggested one based on the equinoxes and solstices. They combined their suggestions, hence why Wiccans and Druids share a similar festival calendar. This may be an apocryphal tale, of course. Gardner in *Witchcraft Today* only writes of the four Celtic-derived festivals: May eve, August eve, November eve (Hallowe'en), and February eve.[1] Eventually, he added the four solar holidays so that modern Wicca now observes the Gaelic holidays of Beltane (May 1), Lughnasa (August 1), Samhain (October 31), and Imbolc (February 1 or 2), known collectively as the Cross Quarter Days; as well as the Summer and Winter solstices, and Spring and Autumn equinoxes.

In *De Temporum Ratione*, Bede provides a listing of the "holy tides" observed by Anglo-Saxon pagans. On the eve of the winter solstice was Mothers Night (Modraniht), a festival highly likely to have been held to honor mothers among the ancestors. It may have connected to the Germanic cult of the Matrons and, by extension, the concept of mother goddesses in general. This nighttime celebration kicked off the Yule season. Geol, as it is called in Old English, is the time surrounding the longest night of the year at the winter solstice. The twelve-day Yule festival marks the Midwinter, cognate to the Midsomer festival in June. On or following the spring equinox, Bede describes the festival Easter. Next is a festival of flowers known as Blostmfreols that has echoes in our modern May Day celebrations. The summer solstice was celebrated as Midsummer (or Midsumor in Bede's words). At the beginning of August, they honored the first fruits of the harvest with Hærfest. This feast survives today in the Anglican liturgical calendar as "Loaf-Mass." Finally, we celebrate the fall equinox or, more accurately, the first full moon following, Winterfylleð. The following Wheel of the Year maintains the structure Gardner and Nichols developed while adding to it what we can glean from Bede and more modern sources of Heathenry.

Further studies attest to four High Holy Days. Eosturdæg, where the modern world derives its name for Easter, fell on the full moon of Eosturmonaþ and likely honored a goddess bearing that name. They observed a midsummer festival around the time of the summer solstice like other Teutonic cultures. Winterfylleþ was observed at the end of October and beginning of November to mark the onset of winter. Geola is the winter solstice and marks the nadir of the year, the solar mother, and the promise of an end to the long, cold nights. The fact that Mother's Night is observed at this time may be due to the divine feminine nature of the Sun.

Numerous examples support the importance of Midsummer and Midwinter solstices to Stone Age Britains. There is also archeological evidence for a strong lunar influence on early timekeeping. Newgrange, a prehistoric passage tomb in Ireland overlooking the River Boyne constructed around 3200BCE, is generally thought to be aligned with the sunrise on the winter solstice day. The rising sun's rays shine through an opening above the entrance and onto a tall stone at the far end of the passage. There is debate about whether this was intended by the original Neolithic builders or resulted from twentieth-century reconstruction. The sun enters the tomb several days before and after the solstice.

Turning to the neighboring tomb of Knowth, we find western and eastern passages. These are almost aligned on an east-west access, but not quite. They are just a little bit off. Scholars have searched for a solar alignment and, at times, contorted the evidence substantially to make one fit. Charles Scribner, a Connecticut doctor, proposed a simple solution. The alignment makes sense if the builders reckoned time by the moon rather than the sun. A group of scholars have recently argued through analysis of cave drawings that Paleolithic, Ice Age hunter-gatherers throughout Europe reckoned the passage of time and the seasons through observance of the lunar cycles.[2] It seems common sense that the moon's cycles would be the most accessible means of reckoning time available to pre-agricultural peoples.[3] The twenty-eight-day lunar cycle is more present and observable than the more subtle change of position of the rising/setting sun at the horizons. The distinctive spiraling patterns found in rock carvings at both Newgrange and Knowth may be symbolic representations of the lunar cycle.

An archeological discovery (or more aptly, "decoding") of a Stone Age site in Aberdeenshire, Scotland, reported in 2013, may be the oldest example of a formal system of calendrical reckoning. The site has been dated to the Mesolithic period, between the Paleolithic and Neolithic, and thus the Middle

Stone Age. The site consists of twelve pits aligned to the southeast horizon at a point associated with sunrise at midwinter. The research team argues that the structure was created to track lunar months with the ability to resync to the asynchronous transitions of the sun to maintain calibration between the two. They write, "The evidence suggests that hunter-gatherer societies in Scotland had both the need and ability to track time across the year, and also perhaps within the month, and that this occurred at a period nearly five thousand years before the first formal calendars were created in Mesopotamia."[4]

Stonehenge has long been interpreted as a giant solar calendar. Archaeoastronomers have long noted that it appears to have an alignment to sunrise at the summer solstice and sunset at the winter solstice. Modern-day Druids gather at the site to observe the rising sun at the summer solstice. Others have interpreted the enigmatic stones as predicting eclipses, while still others have suggested a myriad of other solar and lunar alignments. It may be that, as Magli and Belmonte recently suggested, any attempt to interpret Stonehenge in calendrical terms is "purely a modern construct whose archaeoastronomical and calendrical bases are flawed."[5] Elsewhere in the Salisbury ritual landscape are two causewayed enclosures, Robin Hood's Ball and Larkhill. The older of the two, Larkhill, was only discovered and excavated recently. Built seven hundred years before the famous stones that neighbor it to the south, Larkhill hints that the focus of the religious shaping of the landscape was to the north of where we perceive it today. The famous cursus and Durrington Walls' entrance point toward the Larkhill enclosure. Intriguingly, its entrance points toward the rising sun at midsummer.

So where does all this leave us? Well, with a little mystery, which is not a bad thing. We can deduce that the moon and the sun were essential to homo sapiens, likely since the first person looked up. This should be no surprise, as they are both pretty apparent objects in our daily world. From the above examples, we can discern that Stone Age residents of the British Isles paid attention to the sky and the things within it. Numerous historians suggest that the need for tracking the periods of the year is related to the rise of farming and the raising of livestock. No experienced farmer, then or now, needs anything but his crops to let him know when it's time for harvest. They certainly would not have required a monumental feat of prehistoric engineering. Instead, I suggest that these monuments were about the timing of group gatherings rather than agriculture management. Any need to keep track of the year was more about knowing when to come together for the harvest festival and less about the harvest.

From what we can tell, the Anglo-Saxon calendar was lunar based, while they distinguished the time of the year by the sun. This makes sense, as the moon cycle could be observed every twenty-eight days, and the sun's changes could be seen across the seasons. Thus, they had a calendar of thirteen months and broke the year into two seasons—summer and winter.

The Norse had the same two-season system. In Gaelic cultures, Ireland, Scotland, and the Isle of Man, we have two supernatural entities, the Cailleach and Brigid. The former, recognized as an elderly woman or "hag," emerges around All Hallows and rules the year's winter months. In Scotland, she is seen as having created many of the country's lochs and rivers. She is thought to have a connection to mountains and standing stones. Her counterpart in summer, Brigid, makes her appearance at Beltane. Now known best as a famous Irish saint, she undoubtedly had her antecedent in a preexisting pre-Christian goddess. A similar motif is seen in modern Wicca, splitting the year between the rule of the Oak King in summer and the Holly King in winter. Though popularized in neopaganism, it is doubtful this heroic pairing predates its appearance in Robert Graves's imaginative, yet suspect, collection of folklore, *The White Goddess.*

There are two methods of reckoning days and months based on the moon. Synodic months are based on observance of its cycles, while sidereal months are based on its path. Which system the Norse and Anglo-Saxons based their calendars on is subject to much debate. There are clues, however. Bede compares the Anglo-Saxon system to the Hebraic calendar, which was synodic. For our purposes, we will reconstruct the Old English calendar, where each month begins at the new moon. The first month thus starts at the new moon following the winter solstice. This is supported by the name of the first month, Æfterra Geola, literally translated as after (or second) Yule. The year's final month is Ærra Geola, before (or first) Yule. Between the two are: Solmonaþ (cakes month), Hreðmonaþ (month of Hreða), Eostremonaþ (month of Eostre), Þrimilcemonaþ (three-milkings month), Ærra Liða (first gentle month), Æfterra Liða (second Litha), Weodmonaþ, Haligmonaþ (holy month), Wintermonaþ ("winter moon" akin to Norse 'Winter Nights'), and Blotmonaþ (blood month). To these was added Þriliða (literary third Litha) during a leap year to recalibrate the calendar.[6]

Here, we see people who lived off the land through agriculture and livestock raising. Blood Month would have been when the livestock were slaughtered for winter. Modern farmers and gardeners still pay close attention to the moon. My family taught me that we did not plant in Maine before the last full moon of May, as that clear night would likely be the last frost of winter. Harvest had to be completed by the first full moon following the fall equinox, as that would likely be the first frost. The timing of festivals depends on the local seasons of the area in which we live. My initiator taught that it was appropriate to hold celebrations on the actual date or until the full moon following. This echoes the lunar system where festivals were likely held corresponding to the full moon at the center of the month they fell. Most importantly, we should consider all festivals movable feasts and celebrate them in the times most appropriate to the local climate. In the Southern Hemisphere, we see the opposite timing as summer and winter follow the opposite times of the modern solar-based calendar.

We will use an updated version of the eight-fold year for our work. However, the precise date when each is celebrated may be adjusted to fit with one's location and sense of the timing of the year's transitions. As discussed in more detail below, the year begins with the festival corresponding to the winter solstice. It ends at the beginning of winter at All Hallows—the time between being an increasingly dark period in between.

Midwinter — Winter Solstice, Yuletide season
Oimelc — The full moon of February, Solmonaþ
Eostre — Spring Equinox or the first full moon following
Festival of Flowers — May 1 or the last full moon following
Midsummer or Litha — The Summer Solstice
The Feast of First Fruits — The first full moon of August
Harvest Home — The Autumnal Equinox or the first full moon after
All Hallows / Winter Nights — Traditionally, October 31/ November 1; in practice, the full moon of October or November or anytime in between is appropriate, depending on climate.

Gardner and those that followed have described Gardnerian witchcraft as a fertility cult. This focus on agrarian and livestock productivity is more often than not seen as connecting to the goddess. The fertility in question is seen as the intersection of the goddess and her consort, the god. We've previously discussed the duotheism of modern Wicca and our concerns with this binary theology. There are some traditions, ones that oftentimes keep their secrets close, that provide an alternate view. Rather than an essentialized divine couple, they understand the natural world's cycles as the unfolding of the Mother and her children—in our case, the divine son.

As we have seen, the mother is the first personification of the primordial otherworldly. She is everywhere and ever present. She is the first divine manifestation, and from her springs all life. She gifts her spirit, an element of herself, to all her children—from plants, trees, and animals, to humans. Biological entities, deriving their life force from the land, are her offspring. In this way, the fruits of the land, the annual cycles of agriculture, and animal husbandry are reflected in her child. We've dispensed with the need for divine kings ruling the seasons. Instead, we see in the year cycle the growth of the god, son of the mother.

Folklore, folk customs, and folk songs often contain the remnants of ancient wisdom. One traditional English folksong, popularized by Traffic, is that of John Barleycorn. The lyrics have the story of the male agricultural deity devolving into a semi-comical personage. Historic version preserved by the English Folk Socitey, Lancaster University:[7]

JOHN BARLEYCORN

There were three men come out of the West
Their fortunes for to try
And these three men made a solemn vow
John Barleycorn must die.
They ploughed, they sowed, they harrowed him in
Threw clods all on his head
And these three men made a solemn vow
John Barleycorn was dead.

They let him lie for a very long time
Till the rains from heaven did fall
Then little Sir John sprung up his head
And so amazed them all
They let him lie till Midsummer
Till he looked both pale and wan
Then little Sir John he grew a long beard
And so become a man.

They hired men with their scythes so sharp
To cut him off at the knee.
They've bound him and tied him around the waist
Served him most barb'rously.
They hired men with their sharp pitch-forks
To prick him to the heart
But the drover he served him worse than that
For he's bound him to a cart.

They've rolled him around and around the field
Till they came unto a barn

And there they made a solemn mow
Of poor John Barleycorn
They've hired men with their crab-tree sticks
To strip him skin from bone
But the miller, he served him worse than that,
For he's ground him between two stones.

Here's Little sir John in the nut-brown bowl
And brandy in the glass
But Little Sir John in the nut-brown bowl's
The strongest man at last
For the huntsman he can't hunt the fox
Nor so loudly blow his horn
And the tinker, he can't mend kettles or pots
Without a little Barleycorn.

Interestingly, the men originate in the West. This direction is often used to represent the coming of wisdom and otherworldly forces. It is not lost on me that the shores to the west are those of the North American continent. Barleycorn is, of course, just what his surname implies. He is the fruit of the harvest, the barley and corn used to brew ale and distill spirits. His death, the inevitable end of the growing season, is explicit from the start, for he *must die*. He is a god that must be sacrificed so that we may live. This may be what was symbolized by the Wicker Man's burning, as Julius Caesar described. In Europe, we have relatively modern examples, noted by English travelers, of burning a wicker effigy around Midsummer or just after. In the first century BCE, Diodorus Siculus wrote that the Celts burned humans or animal sacrifices and the first harvest fruits on great wooden pyres. Human sacrifice was not unknown in ancient Europe. At some point, the burning of the Wicker Man, containing the first fruits, became a symbolic representation of the sacrifice of god embodied in the results of agricultural cultivation.

The song continues. Having been blessed on Plough Monday, the plows are now used to furrow the fields. Seeds are planted and left alone to germinate. Eventually, they break through the soil, Sir John raising his head, and begin to mature. The first evidence of his advancing age is seen at Midsummer when he grows facial hair, a sign of manhood. Then men are hired to cut him down, the harvest. Then, poor John is thrown onto a cart and bound.

Interestingly, bog bodies, generally assumed to be sacrificial offerings that stretch from the Stone Age to the Bronze Age, are bound. He's next taken to a barn where the harvesters take an "oath." What is the nature of this promise? Perhaps the oath that binds humanity to the earth and fruits thereof. The Mother made us a commitment long ago when she first emerged from the unknowable mystery, and we annually reciprocate that oath in our honoring of the harvest. Then, men come to complete the barley processing to prepare it for use. From the harvest comes the sacred elixir proffered in the nut-brown bowl.

Brown ales are a quintessentially British beverage; see the recipe that follows. The first was developed by London brewers in the seventeenth century using 100% brown malt and lightly hopped. The result is a deep mahogany color brew with a rich, malt-forward flavor profile. It is in this alchemical product of the land, the song goes, that ol' John Barleycorn proves his strength. Absent the fruits of the harvest, humankind would not survive. The hunter couldn't hunt, and the worker couldn't work. Cereal grains give the gift of life and beer a little respite.

In Robert Burns's retelling of the story, he provides a toast to the hero:

John Barleycorn was a hero bold,
Of noble enterprise;

For if you do but taste his blood,
'Twill make your courage rise.
'Twill make a man forget his woe;
'Twill heighten all his joy:
'Twill make the widow's heart to sing,
Tho the tear were in her eye.
Then let us toast John Barleycorn,
Each man a glass in hand;
And may his great posterity
Ne'er fail in old Scotland!

We can see the echo of this toast in the tradition of wassailing, especially if spice ale is used. Revelers raise a glass in his name on Plough Monday, even as they know that the edge of the plow will be echoed in the blade edge of the scythe at the time of his sacrifice.

In "John Barleycorn," we see the remnants of an ancient understanding that the Mother gives her son to die annually so that we may live and enjoy that life. Michael Howard writes in *Liber Nox* that the wheel of the year "basically follows the coming of the Horned God through the seasonal and agricultural cycle, symbolically from his birth to his death and rebirth."[8] The god begins as a glimmer of hope after the shortest day of the year. The seed is readied at Oimelc and planted as the local climate allows. As winter months give way to summer, what we call spring, we ask the Mother to nourish and look over her son. The seed sprouts, and the god emerges from the underworld. He matures at Midsummer and ages as he approaches his death at harvest. As the husk of his body becomes compost, his spirit is our life in our grain stores, our larders, the livestock we prepare for winter slaughter, and the rich brown ale with which we toast the harvest and the hunt. Critically, he also leaves behind his seed—his promise to return in the new year.

Burroughs often spoke of calendars and ritual calendars in particular, as a means of control. He focused on the complex Mayan calendars, but we can also see this in the medieval liturgical calendars. One can only begin to imagine how our agrarian ancestors, who reckoned time by a lunar calendar, saw the world differently. I strongly suspect time progressed cyclically and was intrinsically tied to the movement of the sun and moon combined with a direct observance of the land. Contrast this with our modern age, when time has become something that we sell or trade. It has all too often become ajust another commodity in a cycle of mass production.

Observing the wheel of the year is central to my practice. It connects us to something larger than ourselves, yet we are part of it. It connects us to the divine Mother's presence all around us. She is the sun that warms us and sustains life. Though she withdraws for a part of the year, she is never truly distant. It lifts us out of the everyday and links us to the larger arcs of time. We see ourselves in the process of the god's birth, life, death, and birth again. He is us; we him. The turning of his wheel is not cyclic but a spiral. His spirit grows and is transformed by each passing season. In the same way, our ritual cycle grounds us in the collective growth of all that surrounds us. Seeing oneself in a process larger than just our own immediacy can be a profoundly healing experience. It has the potential for both perspective and resilience.

Chapter XXIX
The Holy Tides

MIDWINTER

The days around the winter solstice, known as Midwinter, is when the potential of rebirth is honored. This is why evergreen foliage, such as holly, pine boughs, and mistletoe, are commonly used for decoration at Yule. It is also the time in between the old year and the new. We see the close of the old year as we move from the final harvest to the dark, interstitial time following All Hallows and Winter Nights. We now begin the transition from the edge of one cycle and contemplative space between life and death to a time of celebration interrupting the winter months. If we live in a climate that has a cold winter, we know well the welcome respite the revelry Yuletide brings.

Ronald Hutton suggests that Yule was imported to the British Isles during the Danelaw. The name certainly supports this notion of Germanic or Norse origins with their *Jul* or *Jól*. The famous "Yule log" was undoubtedly a European import. The oldest recorded instance of one comes from Flanders and pre-dates 1600.[1] It was thought that burning the log brought light and heat into the darkness, encouraging happiness and prosperity in the coming season. In Devon, local custom used a faggot, or bundle, of ash, willow, or hazel bark in a very similar manner.

An element of shape-shifting, a transitory practice between humans and animals, occurs at this time throughout the Isles. In the Western Isles, a group of young men, one wearing a cowhide to mimic a farm animal, would circle houses clockwise. The one in the guise of a cow would be in the lead, or perhaps more accurately, be chased by the others who would beat him on the hide with a switch. We also find the practice of the White Mare on the Isle of Man, where a horse skull with a hinged jaw is carried about on a stick by a person cloaked in white cloth. In southern Wales, the very similar Mari Lwyd, the "Grey Mare," leads the wassailers. In other parts of England, such as Derbyshire and Yorkshire, the "old horse" or hobby horse is common, represented by a skull or wood. In Teutonic regions, the Jul Goat remains a familiar seasonal image.

Likely, Yule has always been a multi-day feast. The Twelve Days of Christmas officially date from 567 and the Council of Tours, the Church likely incorporating a pre-existing practice. The Roman Saturnalia festival that also occurred in December was a multi-day affair. Having lived in a cold-winter climate, I can attest to the need to have *a real mother of a blowout,* in the words of Monty Python's Eric Idle, as Michelangelo, to the Pope. Yule is a time outside of the year cycle, between the end and the new beginning. It is an upside-down time when rules and customs are suspended.

The revelry is ruled over by an individual crowned the Lord of Misrule. In a similar custom found in Scotland, he is known as the Abbot of Unreason. Primordial chaos erupts across the land. Nigel Jackson calls it the *Great Inbetweenness,* a "void" or "chasm" that opens a "liminal cleft in time and space."[2] This time of reversal is our opportunity to touch primordial, or UR, chaos.

Our Yule season commences with Modraniht, or Mother's Night. Observance takes place on the eve before the solstice. The night is set aside to honor the female deities and mothers among our ancestors. There is a connection to the three women, the Wyrd sisters, mothers of fate. Three is similar to the Scandinavian *Dísablót*, thought to have occurred during the Winter Nights celebration in the Northern regions of Europe around the vernal equinox. The female spirits, known as *dicier*, were honored during the *blot*. This celebration continues to this day as the Disting fair held in Uppsala. In both instances, the festivities are meant to encourage the productivity of the summer season. These activities may be focused on your primary altar or home shrine. It is most appropriate to leave an offering to your matrons on your ancestral altar.

On the night of the solstice or full moon following, set up your altar, cast a circle, and conduct your version of the ritual described later in Part III.

Dating back to at least the late fifteenth century, Plough Monday was a common custom throughout much of rural England. On the first Monday following Twelfth Night (Epiphany), men decorated a plow and paraded through the village from home to home. Sometimes, the leftover wax from Christmas candles was poured over it. The men often blackened their faces with soot and sometimes crossdressed for their dancing parade. Much drinking was also generally involved. The men in the procession were referred to variously as Plough Horses, Plough Jacks, Plough Boys, Plough Bullocks, and, interestingly, Plough Witches.

WASSAILING

In the West Country of England, where apples are commonly grown, there is a custom known as "wassailing." Traditionally held on Twelfth Night (January 5 or 6), the final day of the Christmas season, the tradition breaks down to two distinct practices. In the Victorian period, wassailing from door to door in a similar fashion to caroling became popular. There is a much older tradition that involves going into the orchards as a group and toasting the trees with a drink akin to mulled cider or ale. The toasting is directed at the Apple Tree Man held to be the spirit of the oldest tree in the orchard. Though tied today to the Christian seasonal cycle, the folk custom or some variant may be older. The term comes from the Old Norse *ves heill* through the Old English "wes hál," a greeting of health and good fortune from which we may get our present-day "hail."

Men dressed up in their finest, sometimes decked out in ribbons and with soot on their faces, would lead the group in among the trees carrying a "wassail bowl" filled with the prepared beverage. The group would then hail the most majestic tree in the orchard. A portion of drink from the wassail bowl would be offered to the tree, and then all would partake. From this custom, we may derive our modern concept of "toasting," like raising a glass or drinking vessel. Some of the earliest recipes for or mentions of the wassail drink include adding toasted bread into the liquid itself. The details of the practice varied by village and region, but the general sense of the outing was the same. During Victorian times, the custom transitioned in some areas to going door-to-door, similar to caroling—exchanging a drink from the wassail bowl for gifts.

The Yuletide season is a multi-day affair now draped in Christianity but retaining many folk customs. It was the most popular holiday in much of Britain during the Middle Ages.

The Tudor celebration of the Twelve Days of Christmas was the apogee of its medieval expression. Before the commencement of the holy time, the English fasted. Rich and poor stopped work for twelve days on the 24th. They decked their houses in evergreens.

At the beginning of the celebrations, the revelers selected a Lord of Misrule, or Abbot of Unreason in Scotland, to preside over the festivities. The season kicked off with midnight mass followed by a feast on the morning of December 25. A similar French tradition continues in New Orleans, where the finest restaurants open at 2 a.m. to serve a special réveillon dinner to break the fast. The next day, on Boxing Day, the English celebrated the Feast of St. Stephen by giving alms to people experiencing poverty. On the third came the Feast of St. John. As the good saint was said to have survived drinking poison, the day was one of imbibing. The wassail bowl was passed around, "Wasshail!" On the fourth day was the Feast of Holy Innocents (Childermas), where roles were reversed and children were in charge of adults. New Year's Eve was a day of sport, games, and hunting. The first day of the new year saw the exchanging of gifts among the well-off classes. On Twelfth Night, they brought the season to a close with a feast on the final night and another the following day on the Feast of Epiphany. In New Orleans on January 6th, the Joan of Arc parade walks through the Quarter, marking the beginning of Carnival.

This time of year was not exclusively about celebration and merriment; it was still the middle of winter, after all. The days may be lengthening following the solstice, but the nights are still longer. The restless dead don't simply return to their wells after Mother's Night. It would be unrealistic to think they would hang about on Boxing Day. Throughout Europe, there is a widespread folktale concerning ghostly armies that ride forth at night. These Phantom Hoards, often called the Wild Hunt or Yule Hosts, are said to commence their rides around the winter solstice and continue through the remaining month or so of high winter. Though often thought of as human souls, sometimes the otherworldly regiment is composed of demonic dogs, fairies, elves, or the Valkyrie in Scandinavia. Depending on the region, the Wild Hunt is led by Woden, Óðin, Frau Holle, in the Alps region, or Gwyn ap Nudd, Welsh king of the "fair folk."

An Anglo-Saxon chronicle from the early twelfth century contains the report of a sighting of a ghostly hoard riding abroad:

> Many men both saw and heard a great number of huntsmen hunting. The huntsmen were black, huge, and hideous, and rode on black horses and on black he-goats, and their hounds were jet black, with eyes like saucers, and horrible.[3]

Within one "eyewitness" report, we have many elements: black, huge, and scary—men, horses, he-goats, and dogs. Reading these accounts, I am reminded of the Nazgûl in J.R.R. Tolkien's *The Hobbit* and the *Lord of the Rings* trilogy. These Dark Riders, a name Tolkien also used, are similar to the nine Ring Wraiths. In Middle Earth, the riders are led by the witch-king Angmar, as those in Britain are guided by the Witch-father.

OIMELC

In the Northern Hemisphere, February 1st or 2nd is the first cross-quarter celebration of the year. In Gaelic countries, early February is seen as the return of the goddess Brigid or Bridhe. In Scotland, the day is known as *Là Fhèill Brìghde*; Ireland, *Lá Fhéile Bríde*; Manx *Laa'l Breeshey*; and modern Druidry *Gwyl Ffraid*. Modern Wiccans often call this cross-quarter festival Imbolc. Christianity adopted the festival of lights and continues to observe Candlemas. There is light twinkling in the darkness. The candles on the altar mirror the stars in the night sky. With the Winter Solstice, the daylight begins increasing. Now, that transition becomes noticeable as winter draws to a close and spring may be sensed on the horizon. The Wild Hunt has completed its ride, and the restless dead have returned to the Underworld.

Known as the Irish name Imbolc in the traditional Craft calendar, the festival celebrates the child in its mother's womb. The name has two meanings in Old Irish: "in the belly," referring to pregnant ewes, or to cleanse or wash, referring to purification. It is a day where "spring cleaning" is appropriate and echoes the Roman month *februa*, also meaning purification. The Irish name likely derives from the Old English Oimelc or Ewemilc, meaning "ewe's milk." It is interesting that an Anglo-Saxon name may have been borrowed, sometime in antiquity, to denote a Celtic holiday.

The festival shows the importance of livestock within the rural sense of time. In England, sheep are bred in early fall, so the ewes give birth in late January and February. Of course, when the lambs are weaned, it is best to have grass for them to eat in the pastures. That's why in Maine, farmers usually breed their sheep so the lambs are born in the spring, often in May.

Maine was where I practiced much of my life. Early February in the northern New England climate is still the heart of winter. For this reason, Oimelc has always been more about the light in the darkness than the birth of lambs or planting seeds. The ground is still completely frozen, so there is no plowing. The days are still cool, but as the duration of daylight increases, we begin to feel that spring is coming. The seasons and meanings of the festivals are not written in stone and universal; they are relative and local.

Oimelc is the glimmer of hope foretelling the end of the dark winter months. I celebrate the light in winter. Though the days may have been colder, the stars have always accompanied us. They reflect the promise within the night and a beacon drawing us forward. The Star cards in the Tarot and the Lenormand reflect guidance and the path ahead. Sailors took their reckoning from the starry heavens, gauging speed and direction.

In Ireland, they celebrate the Feast of St. Brigid—a thinly veiled version of the pagan goddess of the same name. Crosses are woven out of straw and hung by the door to bring blessings of the Saint. In Scotland's Outer Hebrides, there was a tradition of women swaddling a sheaf of wheat in cloth and making a bed for it by the front door, calling Brigid three times to come lay in her bed. Our ancestors once asked for the fertility of their livestock and a bountiful harvest; we can reckon the cross-quarter cycle as times to focus on our prosperity beginning today and continuing through to the harvest.

According to Bede, the Anglo-Saxons referred to the month corresponding to February as Solmonaþ, which he translated as Month of the Hearthcakes. I think this is very fitting, as the warmth of the hearth is vitally important this time of year.

Even here in southern Louisiana, January and early February can be chilly. It may dip below freezing for a couple of days. During these days, a warm fire is welcome. I bake Welsh tea cake or Irish soda bread (Brigid cake) this time of year, leave slices for my ancestors, and incorporate them into the sabbat ritual.

EOSTRE

Modern Wiccans celebrate the vernal equinox on or around March 21. The Farrars discuss the spring equinox, Ostara, as a solar festival and note that Gardner's Book of Shadows calls for placing the Solar fire-wheel on the altar.[4] Michael Howard's *Liber Nox* refers to the equinox as Lady Day, a name that connects it to the Christian Feast of Annunciation March 25. The nature of the festival differs depending on the local seasonal climate. In much of Europe, the time was one of fertility, but in Northern Europe, these festivities are more commonly associated with Beltaine, our Festival of Flowers. Interestingly, English-speaking Christians have adopted the name of an Anglo-Saxon goddess for one of their holiest days.

The thawing of the land that began at Oimelc continues. The Sun goddess is growing in her strength. Now, the young god begins the transition from child to youth. The first hints of puberty begin to transform him, presaging the sexual maturity that will come on the next cross-quarter festival. At this time, Jack-in-the-Hedge, the prototypical green man, makes his first appearance.

In his ecclesiastical history of the British people, the

venerable Bede discusses this time of the Saxon month of Eostre. The name of the month is also shared with a goddess. Bede links Eostre to a Germanic goddess. Scholars have traced the etymology to "eos" meaning "shining" or "east." This may indicate a direct link with the Anglo-Saxon sun goddess Sunne. I associate her with the sun in spring when the grass begins to turn green, and April showers bring May flowers. She is the warm welcome of the first touch of spring air when you step outside. Kristin Chenoweth's portrayal of Easter in the TV production of *American Gods* captures the spirit of the season well. It is a light time with a touch of madness and abandon. Animals are feeling frisky and beginning their rut.

Holding the sabbat anytime between the equinox and the next full moon is appropriate. Following the Old English lunar calendar, our coven celebrates her festival on the first full moon following the equinox. If you live where spring flowers have broken through the earth at this time, daffodils, crocus, and tulips should adorn your altar or home shrine. A symbol common across Europe, decorated eggs feature prominently here, too.

FESTIVAL OF FLOWERS

Beltane (*Bealltainn* in Scots Gaelic) is one of the great historic fire festivals celebrated across the Gaelic speaking portions of the British Isles and Ireland. The seed planted into nature's womb at Oimelc is beginning to come to fruition. Pregnant women jump over the fires to ensure a healthy birth. The Maypole is erected and encircled with colorful ribbons.

The Druids, it is said, used fire to bless their cattle before moving them to summer pastures. On the continent, however, the celebration does not follow the lines of the other historic Celtic cultures. Instead, it follows the lines of the pastoral regions of Northern Europe. For the Norse, it is "Summer Finding."[5]

Now, we celebrate the fertile potency of the E(e)arth with both a capital and lowercase "e." The Horned God is out in the land. The young stag's antlers are beginning to take form. The roe deer, common throughout Europe, sheds its horns each year. Now, they are beginning to retake the shape. Animals continue their rutting season.

The Maypole is of German origin and was brought to Britain with the Anglo-Saxon cultural migration. In Scotland, the summer goddess Brìghde supplants the Cailleach as the goddess of the season.

For Anglo-Saxons, this was the Festival of Flowers, Blostmfreols in Old English. They called this month Þrimilcemonaþ, "triple milking." It is a time of coming productivity and fruitfulness, marked when animals produced the most milk, and farmers moved their herds to the summer grazing lands. The altar is again decorated with spring flowers appropriate to one's local area.

MIDSUMMER

The time around the longest day of the year is a period for honoring the sun goddess Sunne as she rises in all her glory. The Old English word *Litha* means "calm." June and July have some of the best weather in Britain. In Louisiana, we also know this is the beginning of hurricane season, a reminder that the Mother can be both pleasant and destructive.

Bonfires are traditionally lit throughout Britain at this time. In the Orkney, the fires are kindled with a mixture of peat and twigs. An animal bone is thrown in when they are lit—hence the term bon(e)fire.[6] Each farmer takes a light from the fire to bless their farm.

Like other high festivals of the year, this is when the magical realms are closer to those of humans. The veil between our world and the Elfamme is again thinner at midsummer. The Feast of St. John is widely celebrated in Britain on June 24th. In New Orleans, St. John's Eve, the evening of June 23rd, has traditionally been celebrated as a Voodoo holiday. The practice is said to date back to Marie Laveau. Sally Ann Glassman continues this tradition today and conducts a public ceremony near Bayou St. John each year.

FEAST OF FIRST FRUITS

Commonly referred to by either the Irish as Lughnasadh or the Christian as Lammas, the beginning of August, roughly halfway between the summer solstice and fall equinox, marks the celebration of the commencement of harvest. In Scots Gaelic, it is known as *Lùnastal* and is similar to the Welsh harvest festival *Gwyl Awst*. The festival shows gratitude for the fruits of the land and offerings to prevent spoilage. Bread is baked from the first wheat or corn of the season. There was a tradition of breaking the loaf into four pieces and placing them in the corners of the barn. The word Lammas derives from the Old English name "hlafmaesse," meaning loaf-mass.

Lughnasadh is a traditional Celtic festival that marks the beginning of the harvest season. It is celebrated on August 1st and is also known as Lammas. During this time, people would gather to give thanks for the harvest's abundance and honor the god Lugh, who was associated with the sun and the harvest. The festival was also a time for feasting, dancing, and games, and many people would bring food and drink offerings to share with their community. Today, many people still celebrate Lughnasadh in various ways, including attending festivals, holding feasts, and participating in traditional rituals.

At this time, the sun noticeably drops lower toward the horizon as she descends into the Underworld. Sweet items were also offered. Echoing the fertility rites of spring, people would ride poles, sometimes split at one end or topped with a horse head, through the fields to ward off decay and promote the final growth of the crops. Throughout the first weeks of August, decorations were placed at holy wells and springs in honor of the goddess. Crosses made of Rowan wood were hung in farmhouses and barns at this time of year.

The harvest is a time of reaping, so death imagery abounds. Far back in history, the festival may have involved literal animal or human sacrifice. Today, we observe the gift of the fruits of the harvest. In the folk song about John Barleycorn, he is the symbolic emblem of the agricultural cycle. His death, or sacrifice, is necessary for the materials needed to brew beer and distill spirits.

HARVEST HOME

This time around the autumn equinox marks the traditional end of harvest. Of course, it might be hard to tell here in New Orleans with today's high temperature at 90°, but there is a hint, if the slightest, of fall in the air.

After this celebration, the last of the crop is left in the field. "Crying the neck" is a tradition in parts of England, where the cutter of the last sheaf of wheat yells out that he has "the neck." This is met with a rousing cheer from his fellows. This last sheaf of grain or corn is then made into a dolly. This practice may have involved capturing the spirit of the field and providing a safe vessel for it to occupy until returning in the spring.

Modern Wiccans often refer to this holiday as Mabon. The usage of this term for the Autumn Equinox is ahistorical and of contemporary invention. It has no roots in Celtic seasonal festivals. The originator of this application has been discredited within the Craft, and the use of Mabon has been under increasing scrutiny. Mabon ap Modron is a character in Welsh mythology, not a festival day. The usage of this hero/god's name in this context, without reference to his story, is a form of cultural erasure.

The Anglo-Saxon pagan harvest festival, known as "Hlæfmæst" or "Hláfmæst" in Old English, held a significant place in the agricultural calendar of early Germanic tribes. This sacred celebration marked the culmination of the harvest season, a time when communities gathered to give thanks, share in abundance, and honor the deities associated with fertility and the earth's bountiful gifts.

As the days grew shorter and the crops ripened, the Anglo-Saxons prepared for Hlæfmæst with great anticipation. The festival typically fell around the autumnal equinox, a pivotal moment when day and night held equal sway, symbolizing the delicate balance between light and dark, life and death.

At the heart of Hlæfmæst was the offering of the "hláf," or loaf of bread, which represented the culmination of the year's toil and the promise of sustenance through the coming winter. This ritual act of baking and sharing bread served as a potent symbol of communal unity and gratitude for the earth's gifts. The loaf was often adorned with intricate patterns, sigils, or runic inscriptions, adding a touch of sacredness to this culinary creation.

The Anglo-Saxons believed in a pantheon of deities deeply connected to nature, and during Hlæfmæst, they paid homage to gods and goddesses associated with fertility and agriculture. Freyr, the god of prosperity and fertility, and Eostre, the goddess of spring and rebirth, were particularly venerated during this festival. Offerings of grains, fruits, and freshly baked bread were made to these deities, beseeching their favor for bountiful harvests in the years to come.

Community likely played a vital role in Hlæfmæst

celebrations. Villagers would come together to partake in feasts, exchange stories, and engage in music and dance. The harvest's bounty was shared among all, reinforcing the bonds of kinship and mutual support that were crucial for survival in a challenging world.

ALL HALLOW'S

The festival of Samhain (pronounced *sow-in*) in Irish and Scottish Gaelic; *Calan Caeaf* in Wales; *Kalan Cwav* in Cornwall; and All Hallows in Old English, marks the beginning of the darker part of the year. *Vetrnætr*, "Winter Nights," in the Norse, marks the start of the winter season through the Festival of Flowers. The harvest has finished, and the cold, darker nights are beginning to come to the fore. This is a time of contemplation when the veils between the worlds are at their thinnest.

In modern practice, the time also marks the transition of the holy year, though the historical underpinnings of this being the pagan "new year" are not so clear cut and quite suspect. It seems almost universally held within modern pagan circles that October 31/November 1 was the end and beginning of the Celtic year. This concept rests on dubious and mostly modern rationality. It likely stems from John Rhys's 1901 work *Celtic Folklore*. The idea was then further popularized by John Frazer. Samhain is first on the list of cross-quarter days contained in the "Tochmarc Emire," one of the stories in the Ulster Cycle of Irish mythology. Though no doubt dating back farther, the oldest extant manuscript of the tale dates to the fifteenth or early sixteenth-centuries. However, the tale has no internal evidence that the ordering holds any particular significance. The order of the list may be no more than coincidence.

This is a period on the threshold between light and dark. It is a time when the dead, spirits, and fairies more easily walk abroad in the land of humankind. It is a time of reflection, introspection, and divination. Once again, we can be with our ancestors and brothers who have passed to the Summerlands. Even at the beginning of the modern era, divining one's future husband was a common pastime among young girls during this season. We celebrate the goddess of the underworld realms, Hel.

It is uncertain if the ancient peoples had a concept of a beginning and end to the year. I lean toward the thought they viewed the seasons as more a continuous spiral than a closed circle. The seed of the year begins if we can say it does, at sunrise on the Winter Solstice. The importance of this date is borne out in the particular alignment of many sacred Stone Age monuments. The period between All Hallows and Midwinter is a dark, gestational period, when the seed of spirit lies in the womb of the Great Mother. It is a time of contraction, reflection, and calm. The time between All Hallows and the winter solstice is truly interstitial.

In *The Stations of the Sun*, Ronald Hutton observes that, unlike Beltaine, there is scant obvious historical evidence that Samhain was a ubiquitous festival period across all the Celtic regions.[7] We can, however, tell from the antiquity of superstitions and the commonly held ancient folk customs that the time was viewed as a period of the year where supernatural forces, the dead, and entities from the otherworld were of utmost concern. Folklore and the modern vestiges of ancient custom that lingered into the modern era demonstrate the period was also a time for divination and looking toward the future.

Like Bealtaine, Samhain was historically a time of bonfires (now in England moved to November 5, Guy Fawkes Day). The time has long been a special period of observance and a marker for the end of the harvest/beginning of winter. It is an appropriate balance and counterpart to Spring's Beltaine celebration.

In Scotland, November 1 begins the time of the Cailleach or Hag Mother. She rules over the stormy winter months until she is replaced at Beltaine by Brìghde. The actual transition between these two seasonal goddesses differs by local climate. In Scotland, the corn dolly made from the last of the harvest is a representation of the Cailleach. She is known for herding deer and is credited with creating Scotland's mountains and lochs. The famous mountain of Ben Nevis is known as her throne. She is said to wash her plaid in the Gulf of Corryvreckan on the west coast. After three days, the plaid is white, symbolic of the snow covering the land.

In Cornwall, on October 31, local tradition celebrates the Feast of St. Allan, also known as Allantide. Apples, especially those known as Allan apples, feature prominently. Apple markets were held throughout the area. Polished red apples were given as gifts to loved ones. Games have long been associated with the festival. One wonders if the modern tradition of kids bobbing for apples echoes these folk associations. Here again, love divination is an element. Women would throw walnuts into fires to predict the faithfulness of lovers.

THE DUMB SUPPER

The Dumb, or Mute, Supper is a Halloween tradition common to the British Isles dating back to at least the seventeenth century and may go as far back as the Middle Ages. The origins have roots in Celtic, Irish, and Scottish traditions around Samhain when the veil between our world and that of the dead is held to be the thinnest. Many of the historical motifs surrounding the Dumb Supper were the domain of girls and young women and had connections to love magic and divining of one's future husband. Alternatively, Paul Husson includes a detailed description of a Dumb Supper related practice for summoning a deceased lover in chapter three "Spells for Lovers" of *Mastering Witchcraft*.[8]

Eventually the observance transitioned to focus, again, on welcoming ancestors into the home. The tradition crossed the Atlantic with Scots and Irish immigrants and is documented as having been a common practice in the Ozarks and Appalachia up to the early part of the twentieth century.

The key component of the supper is that it is conducted in complete silence, hence the name. A fine dinner is cooked and the space is decorated for an elaborate dinner party. All electric lights are turned off—candles providing the illumination. It should go without saying, cell phones are to be left at the door! A sideboard may be set up with images of deceased loved ones, glasses of water, and more candles. Myrrh is an appropriate incense with its earthy notes. As the table is laid out, a place of honor is set for the ancestors at the head. Windows or doors may be opened to allow the spirits to enter.

Though the dinner is consumed in absolute silence, after dinner one may converse with the spirits who have joined. Over a post-dinner apéritif, one may fill in loved ones of the news of the year passed since the last supper. At the conclusion of the meal, participants may offer words of thanks or blessings in their hearts before slowly and quietly dispersing, allowing the spirits to depart in their own time.

I've made dinner with the Mighty Dead of the Craft an annual tradition for our coven. Though there are now public pagan Dumb Suppers, ours is a more intimate occasion in the days leading up to the All Hallows rite.

The Dumb Supper serves as a powerful reminder of the cyclical nature of life and death. It bridges the gap between the tangible world and the unseen, offering a space for healing, remembrance, and connection with those who have journeyed beyond the mortal realm. It is a practice that honors the legacy of the departed while affirming the enduring bond between the living and the dead.

Chapter XXX
Sitting Quietly, Doing Nothing

Mindfulness and situation awareness are essential, though sometimes overlooked, tools of the Craft. I practice meditation called Samatha (Sanskrit for "calm") meditation, also known as calm abiding. This technique involves practicing good posture (*asana*) and controlled breathing (*pranayama*) to quiet the mind and achieve a state of peacefulness. This foundational technique taught in Tibetan Buddhism is similar to *Shikantaza* or *Zazen* in Zen.

Posture is crucial for aligning the body's energy centers and maintaining alertness. To practice this technique, one should sit cross-legged with slightly elevated buttocks on a cushion, such as a zafu or a short bench. The hands should rest lightly on the thighs with the arms extended but not locked. This will keep the spine straight but not stiff. The chin should be slightly tucked in to prevent the head from moving forward. Alternatively, the hands can be joined and placed four finger-widths below the navel. The proper attitude during this meditation should be like that of a tiger about to pounce, as Aleister Crowley described it. This is essentially the "five point" meditation posture described as ideal by Marpa.

During meditation, the eyes should be half-open and focused on a point about four feet ahead. As the mind becomes more tranquil, one can raise the eyes and lower them again if the mind becomes distracted.

Breathing should be slow and easy, following a regular rhythm of inhaling, holding, exhaling, and repeating. Breathing should come from the diaphragm and not the upper chest.

Quieting the mind is the heart of meditation. The mind is a tool that can be focused and trained through mindfulness and meditation. Tibetan teachers often use the analogy of a wild horse that can be tamed and conditioned through methodical and repetitive training to become a helpful asset. With practice, we can attain a state of awareness that extends beyond meditation and into our daily lives.

> The layer of activities on the surface hides that which is deep inside. Insignificant waves hide from our view the unfathomable depths of the ocean. How strange it is that the mighty is suppressed by the trivial, that a speck in the eye renders mountains invisible! But the sea does not cease to exist because of the waves.[1]

The ability to control our thoughts is both simple and difficult, as it requires practice. Initially, we mistake our thoughts for our mind. However, through meditation, we gradually realize that thoughts move across the surface of our mind but are not the mind itself. When we begin meditation, it may seem like our thoughts are increasing, but this is only because we are becoming aware of the countless thoughts that pass through our uncontrolled mind. Thoughts are like clouds that drift across the open sky.

To start meditation, we sit comfortably and focus on our breath. We count each inhale-hold-exhale cycle as one number. When our mind wanders, we return it to the breath and start counting from one again. Once we reach twenty, we begin again from one. Alternatively, we can look directly at our thoughts and label them "thoughts" to make them disappear.

It's essential to strike a balance between control and calmness. If we are too loose with our control, we can easily get carried away by a chain of thoughts. On the other hand, if our control is too tight, we may become obsessed with guarding against thoughts. Instead, we should relax into the tranquility and balance of our mind's natural state. We should let an idea go without getting caught up when it arises.

There are three basic meditation methods: on an external object, an internal object, and no object. The ultimate goal is to meditate with no object, but beginners may find it helpful to focus on a concrete reminder of the practice, such as a high or low object. A high object could be a statue of Buddha or a deity, while a low object could be a rock or tree.

When it comes to meditation, a few obstacles can get in the way of a successful practice. One common issue is feeling tired or sluggish, which can make it tempting to give up and go to sleep instead. To combat this, it's helpful to reignite your motivation by focusing on the benefits of meditation, such as increased mental clarity and emotional freedom. Another obstacle is agitation, when your mind races with distracting thoughts. External factors like loud noises, or internal factors such as pride or desire, can cause this. To overcome agitation, reflecting on the impermanence of our existence and the nature of emptiness can be helpful. As one progresses, many fantastic and magical things happen during meditation—waves of "realization" crash over one. One may see spirits, angels, or even Buddha. It is best to remember the advice of the venerable

Buddhist master: "Ignore them, and they will go away."

Likewise, in the *Itivuttaka Sutra*, the Buddha states:

> If you seek after truth, you should investigate things in such a way that your consciousness as you investigate is not distracted by what you find, or diffused and scattered; neither is it fixed and set. For the one who is not swayed, there will be a transcending of birth, death, and time.[2]

Another image often used by Tibetan meditation teachers is that of a bowl of muddy water. It will become clear if it is let to sit; if it is continually disturbed, the water will remain murky.

Designating a specific area or room dedicated to spiritual practice is helpful in meditating effectively. This could be the space you've already established for your witchcraft workings or elsewhere. This space should be uncomplicated, peaceful, and clutter-free to mirror the clear state of mind one aims to achieve. Personal items that represent individual aspirations may be added as progress is made, but it's important not to overdo it and unnecessarily clutter the space. In the case of a meditative environment, simplicity is always the best approach.

> Our mind is the source of all our happiness and all our suffering. If we can control our mind, if we are the master of our mind, we will have the source of our happiness and we won't need to rely on any outer objects to make us happy. If, on the other hand, we don't control our mind, we will always fall prey to thoughts, to negativity, and no matter how many outer pleasures we possess, we will never be able to enjoy them. – Thrangu Rinpoche[3]

I am sometimes asked, *what is your practice?*
My usual answer is *listening*.

Meditation, calm-abiding, is not the cultivation of passivity. We are training our mind, just as we would our muscles, to be present—simply present to (not *in*) the moment. This is why posture is so critical. Our eyes are neither tightly shut nor wide open. While we meditate, we are not closed to the world. Our perceptions still operate, but we strive not to be drawn in by them. On the other side, once the meditation state has developed sufficiently, we may call upon it while engaged in other activities. This is a good tool we may call upon to keep us from descending a bunny trail of distraction.

We will never be entirely free of our conditionings and prejudices. Our memories, what we have experienced, inform how we interpret future events. It is as if our historicity throws us into the future. The present moment seems but a glimpse out of the window of a quick-moving train. The present moment is an intersection between time and space within which we are the center point, we are presented with an inconceivable quantity of stimuli and reference points. By necessity, our brain organizes, filters, and cuts the many points of information to make the world comprehensible. Our world is not luck or fate but is an unconscious collage of our own making. During a 1982 BBC interview, Burroughs observed:

> "How random is random? ... These juxtapositions between what you're thinking if you're walking down the street and what you see, that is exactly what I was introducing. You see, life is a cut up. Every time you walk down the street or look out of the window your consciousness is cut by random factors and then you begin to realise that they are

not so random, that this is saying something to you."[4]

Generally speaking, our perception of the world around us is a subconscious selection, or cut-up, of the actual sensory stimuli coming at us. As Burroughs highlights, it is not random but processed through layers of our particular filters.

Even our senses themselves are not immune from their perspective of function. A simple demonstration of this is to put one hand in ice water, the other in hot water, and place both in water at room temperature, and they will present different readings of present conditions. Sextus Empiricus, the originator of Greek skepticism, provides numerous such examples. The senses can be fallible and unreliable, but they are all we have for the most part.

A regular meditation practice allows us to reach a place of equipoise with the universe. The further we progress, the more we can accurately perceive the world. Our filters recede, and we can see beyond their boundaries. We enter the space just beyond the edges of our perception. This affords us a better opportunity to understand and listen to the environment unfolding before our present.

A critical component of magic is the correct interpretation of current conditions. Before working, we should strive to know key aspects: What is the basis from which we start? What is the current trajectory? What external factors may adjust this course? These may sound similar to the placement of cards in a tarot reading. And indeed, that is a superb method of analyzing a given situation in these terms. Divination brings in an element outside ourselves that can enrich our perception of what's happening. Without the balance brought by mindfulness practice, however, a reading may just as quickly reinforce our own prejudices and misconceptions as enhance our understanding. Meditation builds the strength of simply receiving information.

"Coincidence" is the defense of the rational mind of mainstream science. It is a single-word banishing spell against the uncanny. When two things occur that should have no reason to be connected yet still seem to be, one invokes the word to dismiss the possibility of an underlying connection. German psychologist C.G. Jung coined the term synchronicity to describe such events. It centers the uncanny in two events that seem at once connected but lack any apparent causal connection. Jung detected a more profound meaning in these seemingly unconnected yet synchronous events. In synchronicity, a web of reality (the Wyrd) is revealed. The uncanny is the unexpected; it gets us to sit up and notice that something is happening here!

> We train a child to focus his mind—to concentrate—because without concentration he will not be able to cope with life. Life requires it; the mind must be able to concentrate. But the moment the mind becomes able to concentrate, it becomes less aware. Awareness means a mind that is conscious but not focused. Awareness is a consciousness of all that is happening. – Osho[5]

Chapter XXXI
Not So Quietly Doing Something

In his work *Liber Astarte,* Aleister Crowley provides instructions for the magical operation of performing devotional service to a deity. He notes it does not matter to which deity one devotes oneself, but to choose wisely anyway. His writing has a little of the atmosphere of chaos magician's meme adoption (the old meaning of the word, not the post-internet one). One should be careful in making this choice, as one is all too often pulled toward a particular deity that matches an aspect of their personality. This can work to amplify a given trait rather than nuancing it. It is just as usually the case that the spirits have something different in mind. We may feel a pull toward a particular god or goddess, only to find out along the way that we are actually being called from an unexpected quarter of the divine realm.

In the vast tapestry of spiritual practices, devotional service to a deity is a profound and intimate way to connect with the divine. Rooted in various religious and cultural traditions, this practice transcends boundaries, inviting individuals to embark on a sacred journey of love, devotion, and self-discovery. Devotional service, called Bhakti Yoga in Hinduism, is a path of heart-centered devotion to a chosen deity. Whether it's in the form of prayer, rituals, shrine offerings, or acts of kindness, the essence remains the same: a sincere and selfless offering of one's love in service to the divine. Over the years, I have had a lot of interaction with devotees of Vaishnavism, literally "worship of Vishnu." This significant branch of the faiths collectively known as Hinduism is marked by the importance placed on devotional service to the Godhead. In the West, the Hare Krishna movement, the International Society of Krishna Consciousness, is the face people are most familiar with.

Crowley notes the choice is a "matter of no import," though, as noted above, he does advise choosing "one suited to thine own highest nature." Here I think we can read "highest" as in contrast to "mundane" tastes and predilections. Our higher self often knows us better than we do. Different spiritual traditions offer myriad deities, each representing unique aspects of the divine. Some might feel drawn to the compassionate embrace of Lord Krishna, others to the fierce strength of goddess Hekate, and some to the wisdom of the Dark Man of the Forest Green. The choice of a deity is deeply rooted in the personal, influenced by one's spiritual inclinations, cultural background, or personal experiences. Of course, the "choice" has a deeper meaning within Brotherhood.

The act of service fosters qualities such as compassion, humility, and gratitude. It encourages a shift in perspective from a self-centered existence to one that recognizes the interconnectedness of all beings and the divine presence in every aspect of life. Devotional service is not confined to temples or sacred spaces; it seamlessly integrates into everyday life. Acts of kindness, compassion, service, and support of others (including our brothers) become an extension of one's devotion. Service transforms the mundane into the sacred; life itself becomes a continuous offering to the divine.

Devotional service to a spiritual entity is a sacred dance of love and surrender. It transcends boundaries, offering a path for seekers to connect with spirit. As one immerses oneself in this journey, the boundaries between the self and the spirit realms blur, revealing truth. In the tapestry of devotion, we find not only a connection to the divine but a path to self-realization and a deeper understanding of the universal force of love that binds us all.

Chapter XXXIII
The Book of Ways

One of the most familiar elements in modern witchcraft is *The Book of Shadows*, of Book of Ways, which has an antique feel despite being a relatively new innovation. The concept only dates back to the mid-twentieth century and wasn't mentioned in Gardner's novel *High Magic's Aid*. However, when Gardner was working with his Bricket Wood coven, they had their book of magic. According to Doreen Valiente, the name may have been taken from an advertisement that ran opposite one for Gardner's novel in a 1949 edition of *The Occult Observer*.

As books on witchcraft became more popular in the 70s and 80s, such as those by Scott Cunningham and Silver Ravenwolf, the idea of a witchcraft grimoire became increasingly widespread. *The Book of Shadows* eventually became ubiquitous, with many versions available. It was firmly established in popular culture through the TV series *Charmed*, where the Halliwell sisters possessed a hereditary book that was often a central component of the show's plot lines.

Although *The Book of Shadows* may have been a creation of Gardner's, books were mentioned in confessions and trial testimony during the burning times. Stories often involved signing the Devil's black book. In *The Witch Cult in Western Europe*,

Margaret Murray asserted that covens kept their records in a secret book. Today, some covens such as ours, retain this custom by having initiates sign the coven or Magister's book. Witches and cunning folk also often had a book of recipes and spells, commonly called "black books." Several examples of these survive today, such as two black books discovered in a Norway attic by Mary Rustad and published with annotation as *The Black Books of Elverum* and a sixteenth-century collection published as *The Cunningman's Grimoire* edited by Stephen Skinner and David Rankine.

With the intervention of the printing press, grimoires became accessible to cunning men and women rather than just being the realm of the moneyed elite. After Robert Turner published an English translation of Cornelius Agrippa's *Fourth Book of Occult Philosophy* in the mid-1600s, charms and countermagic from the book began to appear in the personal books of cunning folk, wise people, and witches. Today, collections of spells often have material borrowed from high magical and ceremonial texts, such as *The Key of Solomon* (*Clavicula Salomonis*), which first appeared during the Italian Renaissance, even in early Gardnerian witchcraft.

In *The Goodman's Croft*, that follows, you will find our little black book, or Book of Ways, designed for use by solitary practitioners or groups. All material can be adapted for either use, and it includes a dedication ritual so that a solitary person may begin their journey dedicating themselves to the spirits of the Craft. Our practice is for individuals and those seeking to be part of a more extensive lineage.

The Craft is always your own. Even when involved with a coven, much work is done independently. There is nothing wrong with working without other humans present. Know when you're doing it right, you are never alone. The spirits, your spirits, are always there by your side. From all that can be discerned, a coven of witches and the concept of the witches' Sabbat arose in the early modern period. The term denoting an infernal gathering of witches was first promulgated on the European continent by the *Malleus Malificarum,* printed in Germany in 1489. It did not make its first appearance in the British Isles for another century. The first reference to such a convention appears in Scotland in 1591 in the confessions of Lady Newes.[1] In fact, the solitary practitioner has been the norm throughout most of history—the cunning woman or man operating on the fringes of the village.

An important component of the festival rites that follow is the houzel, or cakes & ale/wine/mead offering. With the increasing number of people choosing for one reason or another to abstain from alcohol, the actual content is not a firm requirement. It is up to the individual to determine what works for them. For my part, even if I am not partaking at that given time, I continue to offer up the libation appropriate to the recipient spirit(s). In group work, an appropriate non-alcoholic drink may be passed.

While books can store and disseminate knowledge, only so much can come from them. Verbal interaction and the initiatory process are also necessary for teaching. Initiations are reserved for covens and omitted here. However, a "self-dedication" is included, as the path is open to all. Group rituals are available to those within or without the lineage of United Rite Groves. Our practice is both open-source and an initiatory lineage—holding additional oathbound rites. For more information on the United Rite, please visit our website: www.unitedrite.org.

Part Three
The Goodman's Croft

The Space Between

Life is simply better with a little magic in it. Just a little mystery there at the edges, in the space between: the contemplative stillness that exists in that moment between past and future; the dimensionless point between memory and impermanence; the intersection between the world of human and the world of faery; between head flesh and ethereal fae; the interstitial space of legend between history and myth...

The Covenant

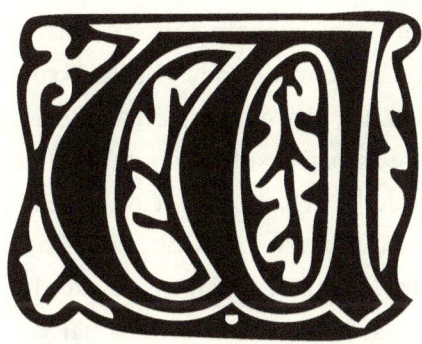

When you stand at the crossedroads, I will meet you. Though I have been with you since the beginning, I will seem to walk up from behind and put my hand on your shoulder. My mother is above us and below us; she surrounds us in her expansiveness. She may be perceived, sensed, but never truly known. I am your father, brother, and lover. Once you choose the witch road, I am your companion as we walk on together. I am beside you and in you. There is no part of you that is not also a part of me. I share in your joy; I join you in your pain. When you fuck it is an offering. We raise our head as one moaning in pleasure. When you hurt, I lick the salt from your cheek. To me your seed and your tears are equally sacred. This is the sacred and profane promise I make to you.

Dedication

Historically speaking, if an ounce of the confessions holds true, initiations into the witch mysteries were mostly solitary affairs. The would-be witch or warlock meets the Devil at the crossroads, the Dark Man in the wooded grove, or the fairies emerging from the barrow mound. In all these instances, the warlock is alone but not alone. They have removed themselves from the company of man, yet are now surrounded by the supernatural representatives from the shadows of humanity's distant past. These meetings often occur at places that are liminal. Several common themes show up across the confessions and remnants in folklore. In some instances, the witch places a hand on their head and the other on their heel, then pledges all that is between to the Infernal Father. In other instances, the warlock renounces the Christian faith by reciting the Lord's prayer backward three times.

This dedication is based on a well-known instance known as the Orkney Charm collected by nineteenth-century folklorist Walter Traill Dennison but no doubt much older. At midnight on the night of the full moon, the prospective witch, warlock, sorcerer, or spae-wife goes to the shore at the ebb tide. The ritual is done at the point halfway between the low and high tide marks. So to begin, find a place set apart and remove yourself there on the night when the moon is full and not obscured by clouds.

Set out a circle of seven stones. A single unlit candle is placed at its center. If you were raised in the Christian faith, it is appropriate to renounce that connection.

Walk around the unlit candle widdershins, anti-clockwise, three times. Sit before the candle. Then recite:

O Dark Master,
Come fill him with the Warlocks' Skill,
Bring him wisdom and true sight,
And he shall serve with all his will.
May you take him if he err!
May you take him if he fly!
Come take him now, and take him all,
Take lungs and liver, organs and feet,
Take him, take him, now I ask!
From the brow of his head, to the tip of his toe.
Take all that's out and in of him.
Take hair and hide and all to thee.
Take heart and brains, flesh, blood and bones,
Take all between the seven stones!
In the name of the Great Dark One!

Light the candle and spend time meditating on the presence of the Man in Black.

At some time afterward, take the seven rocks to a lake, river, bayou, or ocean and cast them one at a time into the water.

The last line was originally recorded as "I' de name o' da muckle black Wallowa" which begs an interesting question as to its meaning. Some scholars interpret Wallowa simply as another name for the Devil. Others connect it to the Norse volva or prophetess, which would seem fitting and may hark back to the ancient connections between Orkney, Shetland, and Norway. At Performing Magic in the pre-Modern North

Conference, Ragnhild Ljosland suggests rather convincingly that the Wallowa may have been an elf man (Old English ælf).[1]

Working Tools

Though magic can be done anywhere and often employs common items or objects, specific tools are held as essential elements of ritual practice within witchcraft. The First Degree initiation into Gardnerian lists eight "Working Tools": the magic sword, athame, white-handled knife, wand, cup, pentacle, incense censer, and scourge. Below, we will discuss each of these and add a few. We find four of these items in the four suits of the traditional tarot deck: Swords, Cups, Pentacles, and Wands.

THE BLACK & WHITE-HANDLED KNIVES

The athame, traditionally a black-handled knife, is the witch's primary working tool. It stands in for the sword. The coven usually owns the latter, while the former is the personal tool of each member. It is associated with the element of Air.

While the Gardnerian initiation notes that the tool is used to subdue or control spirits, it is more apt to say that its use is to direct energy. It is with the athame that the witch draws the Circle and draws down the power within the pentagram when inviting the spirits of the Watchtowers to come to the ritual. Symbols are often carved into the hilt of the athame. This is undoubtedly the case with Gardnerian and Alexandrian traditions. This practice is rooted in the grimoire tradition. Indeed, the dagger hilt depicted in the endpapers of Gardner's *High Magic's Aid* is inspired by similar depictions in *The Key of Solomon*. However, symbols on the hilt are not common to all traditions, and the hilt is not always black. Stag horn or a deer hoof also make ideal materials for the hilt of one's athame. Anglo-Saxons had a knife called a *seax* (pronounced SAY-ax), which is also appropriate for use as an athame.

The athame is *never* used to cut anything physical. Its role is purely on the spiritual plane. The white-handled knife, in contrast, may be used for inscribing candles, cutting cords, and similar activities.

THE SWORD

The sword is a complete analog for the athame and may stand in for it. At coven gatherings, the sword is often employed to draw the Circle. If a portal in the circle is opened during a ritual, the sword is often laid across it until it is closed. The sword is the tool of the Magister of the coven.

THE WAND

Like the symbolism of the tarot, the wand is associated with the element of fire. There are differences in these elemental linkages, and they do vary by tradition. The Farrars ascribe the element of air to the wand and the athame to fire. Doreen Valiente preferred the wand/fire and athame/air combinations.[1] I like using those from the tarot, which is most likely derived from the Golden Dawn. Mirroring the tarot attributions helps keep things symbolically aligned.

The Gardnerian *Book of Shadows* tells us that the wand is used to "call up and control certain angels and genii." This also sounds like a concept lifted from the wand's use in traditional grimoires. The wand is a tool of evocation and invocation. It is employed to draw down the power of the divine into its symbolic representation, such as a statue or similar idol. Though the Farrars consider it gender-neutral, I sense it relates directly to the phallus. Indeed, historical examples often have a pine cone at one end, symbolizing the glans of the penis. A wand is traditionally the length between one's elbow and the tip of the middle finger.

The Essex cunning man George Pickingill was said to have a "blasting rod" made from blackthorn. Locals feared its power. Robert Graves associated the blackthorn bush with harmful magic used to cause illness or misfortune. The Farrars relate that it is a plant of the goddess but in her dark aspect. Most are familiar with the blackthorn through its berries used to make sloe gin.

The materials used to make a wand vary considerably. Many are made of wood, such as oak, ash, or pine. The wand I use most often is pine to connect with the Horned God and spirits of the forest. The graves of Norse magical practitioners often contained an iron wand or staff in pride of place among the grave goods. Indeed, this is common enough to link iron wands to the practice of Norse witchcraft intrinsically. I also use an iron wand with a cloven hoof at one end, custom-crafted by Troll Cunning Forge.

THE PENTACLE

Continuing with tarot attributions, the Pentacle is connected to the element of earth. The pentacle is a round disk with a similar role to the paten. It forms the base or focal point on the altar for much of the workings during a circle. The cakes and libations are commonly consecrated upon the Pentacle. It is, almost always, a five-pointed upright star, preferably with its lines overlapping to denote one continuous stroke. The pentagram represents the four elements and, in this position, the surmounting of the fifth element, spirit. The surrounding symbols vary by tradition. Ours has a single eye at its center. This may link to the eye of wisdom or insight. It also represents the one eye of the Witchfather. Whether it's the one eye that looks upon this world or the "blind" eye that sees into the next may vary by context. Additionally, we have seen the single eye in the form of the moon above the Tower, discussed in detail earlier, and its connection to sexual magics. Indeed, the altar phallus may be placed upon the pentacle during specific workings.

THE CUP

The Chalice or cup is associated with the element of water. Gardner writes that he was puzzled at the absence of the cup in the coven into which he was initiated. He surmises that the Pentacle might have taken its place, the cup being too close to the Christian mass and practitioners of old fearing its reference would provoke accusations of their conducting a parody of the mass.[2]

Its primary use in the circle and upon one's altar is to offer libations. In our work, a drinking horn may be just as appropriate, if not more so. It is the vessel that offers a toast hailing the gods, ancestors, and brothers of the Craft. It is a symbol of welcome and hospitality. When we pass the horn between brothers, it reaffirms our kin connection. There has long been an association between offering a drink and a feast to the divine. Indeed, the offering of beer or mead was so connected with pagan practices that early medieval church fathers railed against it.

THE CENSOR

The censer is used for the burning of incense. It takes a variety of forms. The best are those with an insulated handle made of something like wood, as the censer must be carried about the circle during the casting. During festivals, my altar is often made of wood, which is flammable. I use a stone coaster inscribed with a pentagram at these times to protect the surface below.

The censer is used with a charcoal disk, which one may buy from occult stores or where hookah supplies are sold. A set of metal tongs is also recommended, as they make the lighting of the charcoal much easier. Don't learn from the experience of burnt fingertips! A small spoon to replenish the incense is also very useful.

THE SCOURGE

The scourge is a small ritual whip formed of eight tails, each with five knots tied in them. Some believe it symbolizes the severity of the goddess, especially as contrasted with her kiss, but it does serve a more practical and benevolent purpose. Light scourging, ritual flagellation, across the back draws blood to the surface and is a suitable method for inducing trance.

THE CORDS

Traditionally, practitioners possess three colored cords—red, white, and black. These are each commonly nine feet in length. Cords have a long tradition of use in witchcraft. Many spells survive that require knowing a cord for control of weather and storms. I include one later.

In ritual practice, they may be used for binding, especially before applying the scourge. They are representative of the goddess and relate to the umbilical cord. The black and white may relate to primordial opposites, day/night, winter/summer. The red cord indicates blood and reflects the witch's connection to ancestors and their lineage in the Craft.

I utilize bowls for several purposes. A bowl, or the chalice, may be used to make offerings on one's primary altar or specific shrine. Two small bowls are also used during the casting of the circle. One contains water, the other salt.

THE STANG

Noticeably absent from Gardnerian practice, the stang is common among many other British Craft traditions. Indeed, it is the central point of many who practice traditional Craft. Robert Cochrane introduced the stang into his Clan of Tubal Cain, but the historical usage is attested to in the many examples found by Cecil Williamson, the founder of the Museum of Witchcraft and Magic.[3] It is the Axis Mundi, the central world pillar. Here, we again encounter a concept echoing the image of the Irminsul. In its traditional form, the stang was made of ash split at one end to form a V.

The bottom end was capped in iron or had an iron nail driven into it. The forked end may be viewed as representing the Horned God.[4] Other forms have a wooden staff topped by iron horns with a candleholder between them. In antiquity, a simple wooden pitchfork may have been employed for the same purpose. The candle between its horns is very similar to that of the bucca, discussed later, and Levi's image of Baphomet. Like the cauldron symbolizes inspiration, the light betwixt the horns symbolizes otherworldly wisdom. Thus, the folk saying, "The truth lies betwixt the horns." George Hares describes the candles as representative of "the primordial witch fire Auld Hornie holds within him, that we ourselves carry within us also."[5] I possess a stang thoughtfully purchased by a brother from the Museum of Witchcraft and Magic.

A related object found in traditional Craft is a candleholder made from a horseshoe known as the "hood lamp." The shoe is connected to another piece so that it stands vertically, its tips forming the two points of the horns. The candle sits between. The magical power of horseshoes is discussed in detail in the chapter on protective magics.

THE CAULDRON

I can think of no more prevalent a symbol connected with witchcraft than the cauldron. Look at any store's Halloween decorations, and the image of the three witches huddled around the cauldron in *Macbeth* immediately comes to mind. The witches enter at the first scene to thunder and lightning. When the three appear, the cauldron is readily to hand:

> Double, double toil and trouble;
> Fire burn, and cauldron bubble.

In three "Wiërd" or Wyrd Sisters, we may detect the three fates, vestigial remnants from the Anglo-Saxon period carried forward to the days of the Elizabethan playwright. The cauldron is also just a cast iron cooking pot. Here again, we see the connection between witchcraft and the traditional domestic realm of the feminine.

A cauldron features prominently in the Welsh story of the birth of Taliesin, the great bard. The ugliness of her son Morfran saddens the great witch Cerridwen. She seeks to brew a potion to imbue him with great knowledge in compensation for his unfortunate appearance. The potion must steep for a year and a day. She employs two laborers, the blind Morda and Gwion Bach, to keep the fire stoked. When the potion is ready, and Morfran is brought to it, liquid erupts from the cauldron. Concerned for the young boy's safety, Gwion places himself between the youth and the hot potion. He gets a few drops on his arm and instinctively licks them off, thus unintentionally taking the elixir of wisdom himself. Cerridwen is outraged and begins to go after the innocent Gwion.

A chase involving multiple shapeshifting ensues. Ultimately, Gwion transforms into a grain of corn and conceals himself among many. Cerridwen changes form to a black hen and eats all the corn. Nine months later, she gives birth to a male baby. Unable to bring herself to kill the child, she sets him adrift in a carbuncle, a hide-covered basket. He is later captured in a fish weir and saved. Cerridwen's cauldron is intrinsically connected to the force of poetic inspiration known as *Awen*. Thus, it seems fitting that one of the greatest writers in the English language would employ the cauldron as a central element in one of his greatest works.

It is thus the cauldron of inspiration and remains a potent element of the witch's practice. The cauldron may take the role of the altar as a focal point of certain rites.

THE BESOM

The besom, or broom, derives its name from Old English *besma*. They were originally made from birch twigs tied around a hazel or willow branch to form the handle. Next to the cauldron, the witch riding her broom is one of the most popular cultural images. The broom's magical use is the same as its mundane purpose. One symbolically sweeps the space in a clockwise fashion before casting the circle. Here, the detritus it removes is as much spiritual as it is physical. Many contemporary depictions of witches in flight upon their broom survive from the early modern period. The popular belief was that they would employ this everyday household object to fly to their sabbats. Here again, we have a domestic item used for witchcraft.

The Bone Wand was a Scottish term for anything a witch uses to take flight. These may have been easily disguised as the handle of an unremarkable broom. It was said that they greased the handle with flying ointment to absorb it as they straddled the wooden shaft. No doubt, this form of the wand was also a phallic image. Some historical examples survive where the end is carved into the shape of the male member. Versions with a forked end are reminiscent of the stang. Valiente associates this form with the goddess Hekate, who often met at the place where three roads converge.[6]

Consecrating the Working Tools

Cast the circle. If this is your first circle and you are working on your own, you may use your pointer finger to cast the first circle before consecrating your athame.

Place the tool to be consecrated on the pentacle. Sprinkle with salt and water. Pass the tool through the incense smoke and over the candle flame.

> *Oh, Mighty Ones, bless and consecrate this* [*tool name*] *prepared in thy honor, that it may aid me in all acts of love and beauty.*

If the tool is the sword or athame, say instead:

> *I conjure thee, O Sword of strength, by the Great Old Ones, by the powers of the Heavens, the Earth, and the Realms of Spirit, that it may obtain thy virtues and channel your energy in all things wherein I shall use thee.*

If working solo, place the newly consecrated tool in your hands and breathe on it, willing your power in the flow of your breath. If two or more brothers are present, the owner and the Magister or another brother should place the tool between them at their chests. They seal the consecration with a kiss. As they do, they will their combined energy into the tool.

In the case of the sword or the athame, use it immediately to redraw the circle.

The Ritual Bath

In the traditional "Charge" of the Goddess, she instructs her children "to be naked in your rites" as an outward sign of our freedom.[1] Ritual nudity is essential to Gardnerian Wicca and its appendant lineages. Working skyclad, as it is known, has many elements. It demonstrates our innocence as newborns and our willingness to show ourselves completely. Being naked with one's brothers creates a space of openness and sharing. There is a natural connectedness in mutual nudity. Ritual nudity can be a way to shed societal expectations of masculinity and embrace a more vulnerable and open state. Being naked in the presence of other male practitioners can reinforce the sense of brotherhood, as everyone is equal and without the barriers of clothing or social status.

Beyond our interconnectedness brother to brother, the practice of working skyclad, on a deeper level, is a way to connect with the divine and nature more authentically. We can feel the breeze directly on our skin, the cool earth as our toes dig in, and the warming of the sun or the inspiring bath of moonglow. The practice of ritual bathing stretches back for millennia. When we enter the circle skyclad, we enact a tradition that takes us back in time, meeting at a temporal intersection with those who danced naked within the grove, among the standing stone, and around the festival fire.

A ritual bath before entering the circle is essential to the rite. It cleanses one of outside influences and is a moment to release stress from the day. Assisting our brothers in bathing is a powerful act of care and love.

A bath may be a full bath or a large vessel of warm water in a shower. Prepare your bath with warm water and add floral waters, such as rose. You may also float rose petals or flowers on the tub's surface. You can choose ingredients based on their spiritual properties and the season or planned work, such as lavender for calming, rose for love and self-care, or mint for purification. As you fill the bath, set your intention for the ritual.

Before getting into the bath, take a moment to cleanse your body with a shower or a sponge bath. This is important to remove any dirt or negative energy from your body. You can also use this time to do some stretching or gentle yoga poses to prepare your body for relaxation, settling into the meditative space.

Once all are ready, each, in turn, steps into the bath and immerses themselves completely. Take a deep breath and feel the warm water enveloping your body. Allow yourself to relax and let go. Feel yourself surrounded by the light and love of your brothers. Breathe the scent of the ingredients in the water, absorbing their magic.

Following the bath, each dries themselves with a clean towel. Their brothers then draw the witch's mark on their chests with oil.

The Devil's Mark

The concept of the witch's mark, also known as *sigillum diaboli*, "the Devil's Mark," first appeared in the fifteenth century and increased in widespread usage during the witch craze in the reign of James the VI of Scotland, I of England. The mark was thought to be immune to pain, so accused witches were often pricked with specialty instruments to detect the mark and prove the accusation. So-called 'Witch Prickers' earned a lucrative trade rising to answer the need. Some even used a trick bodkin that did not penetrate the skin.[1] The notion of the witch's mark reached its peak during the English Civil War and disappeared from contemporary accounts by 1700.

It was thought that evil was marked by God, as described in the Bible through the story of Cain slaying Abel. According to biblical tradition, the Mark of Cain was a physical sign God placed on Cain to warn others not to harm him. In some interpretations, the mark was a trident-shaped symbol, while in others, it was said to be the footprint of a crow or raven. It was quite often referenced as being on the left shoulder, long associated with "evil." The Devil is conceived as standing at one's left, whispering in the left ear.

The Mark of Cain is often used to symbolize protection against harm and malignant forces. Its glyph is a potent shield of defense. The Mark of Cain may also be used to channel the energy of the divine; an invocation, including the mark, can tap into a powerful source of spiritual energy that can help achieve goals and overcome obstacles. Cain's mark was also sometimes characterized as being shaped like the foot of a raven or crow.

Black birds such as rooks, crows, and ravens have a long association with witchcraft and folklore. The Sutton Hoo helmet has a bird in flight across the front, its body forming the nose covering and spreading wings over the eyes. Anglo-Saxon Woden and Norse Óðin have two ravens as their companion. Huginn and Muninn, in Norse, represent thought and memory, respectively. It is said that they fly out into the world each day and bring their news back to Woden. The connection between ravens and the god predates the Viking Age, and the imagery is found on Anglo-Saxon artifacts such as sword hilts. The word raven is of Anglo-Saxon origin from the Old English "hræfn." In Teutonic countries, ravens accompany The Wild God on his nightly ride-outs during the Wild Hunt.

Birds, in general, have a long connection with augury. The Greeks interpreted a raven flying in from the east or south as a good omen. The raven has also long been associated with death, the gallows, and hanged men. This association became increasingly pronounced with the spread of Christianity, no doubt as a reaction to the bird's importance to the pagans. Crows have a long-standing association with the Devil. During his 1630 interrogation, accused warlock Alexander Hamilton said the Devil came to him in his guise as a "corbie," Scottish for crow. In Norfolk, the Man in Black is often identified by a black raven's feather in his hat. Famously, the twentieth-century witch Sybil Leek had a pet jackdaw, a smaller but closely related member of the Corvidae family, named Mr. Hotfoot Jackson.

The legend of the ravens and the Tower of London proves the enduring connection between ravens and the supernatural. The Tower of London is a historic fortress in the heart of London, England. It is steeped in legend and history, with stories of royal intrigue, imprisonment, execution, and murder. It is also known for its resident ravens. Legend has it that if the ravens ever leave the Tower of London, it will spell the end of the British monarchy. As such, the ravens are taken care of with the utmost care and attention, with a dedicated team of Yeomen Warders, also known as Beefeaters, responsible for their well-being.

The tradition of keeping ravens at the Tower of London dates back to the reign of Charles II in the seventeenth century. The king was interested in astronomy and set up an observatory at the Tower. He was annoyed by the raven poop on his telescope. He ordered that they be removed. His astrologer warned him the monarchy would fall if the ravens ever left the tower. To ensure this did not happen, Charles ordered that six ravens be kept at the Tower at all times and moved the royal observatory to Greenwich, where it remains. Today, there are seven resident ravens at the Tower of London. Each raven has a unique personality and name, such as Merlina, Poppy, and Jubilee. They are cared for by a team of Ravenmasters, who ensure that they are fed a healthy diet of raw meat, fruit, and vegetables. The ravens are housed in a specially designed enclosure within the Tower grounds and continue to welcome visitors to the Tower.

The shape of the crow's footprint is similar to the rune Eolhx. The rune's name translates to Elk sedge, a plant that resides at the edge of marshes and fens. Archeological studies have shown these boundary areas were significant to early Britains as they were places where individuals met the spirit world. The abundance of evidence of offerings being made to the watery realms attests to the continued understanding of the spiritual import of the interstitial space where water meets land. The rune is also a power tool for protection, and this has long been an important meaning of the witch's mark.

In the Anglo-Saxon Futhorc, there are three additional runes. One, Calc, is the same shape as Eolhx but inverted. It is thought that this rune translates as chalk. In areas of Britain, chalk exists just below the surface of turf. If we look at the chalk drawings such as the Uffington Horse, we see the magico-religious potential the ancestors discerned in the hidden white material. Like the witch's power, chalk is there just below the surface, waiting to be revealed in spectacular artistry. It hints at inherency.

When we gather skyclad with our brothers, we create a perfect space of trust and love. Our secret mark, hidden to the society at large, is exposed for all present to see. We assist each other in bathing as a sign of mutual support. When we draw the witch's mark in sacred oil, we affirm our connection to a holy tribe.

Casting the Circle

Casting the Circle of the Arte is the common element of all rituals. The circle is a boundary erected for the ritual to be conducted within. In Scotland, it is known as casting the "caim," while in traditional Craft they have the practice of the compass round. A circle is traditionally at least nine feet across, though I have also used eleven feet to accommodate the coven. This ritual is appropriate for use by a single witch or a group. A server should be identified to assist if more than one witch is present for the working. A circle may be cast in any space, allowing for a nine-foot diameter. Chalk, a cord, rocks, shells, or a circular carpet may mark off the circle.

The altar should be set up facing north. A candle or lantern should be set in each of the four directions. Required elements on the altar are the pentacle, two bowls of water and salt each, an incense burner, candles, phallus, flowers, and other decorations appropriate for the season or rite. It is most suitable for rites to be done after the sun's setting. The altar should have two lit candles on either side of the central deity image and one altar candle unlit. I usually have a bouquet.

First is the consecration of the Water. Touch water with athame, saying:

I exorcise thee, O creature of Water, that thou cast out from thee all the impurities and uncleannesses of the Spirits of the World of Phantasm, so that ye harm none.

Next, we bless the salt. Salt is associated with banishing, so we do need to consecrate it. Touch the bowl with salt with athame, saying:

I bless thee, oh creature of Salt. Let all malignity and hindrance be cast forth hencefrom, and let all good enter herein. Without thee, we cannot live. I bless thee and invoke thee, that thou mayest aid me/us in my/our rites."

Pour the salt into the water.

Invoking Pentagram

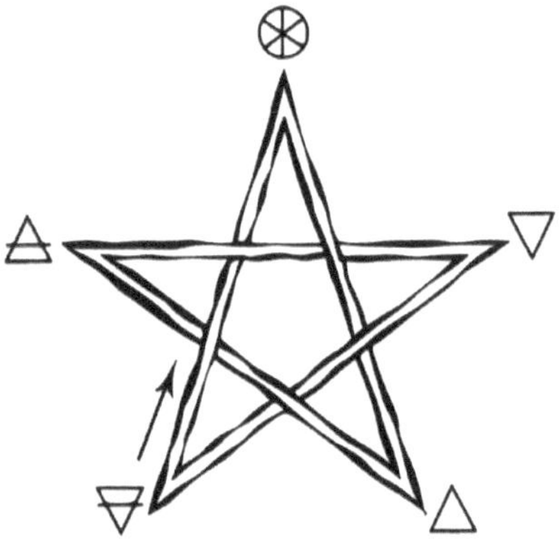

Banishing Pentagram

Now we call the Watchtowers of the directions.

Begin in the east. Draw the invoking pentagram in the air with your athame. Use the invoking pentagram of the earth, drawing down from the top point to the lower left. Use the same pentagram invocation for each quarter to draw the spirit down to earth. You may also use the appropriate one for the direction, drawing a continuous line from spirit to the appropriate element.

Ye spirits of the watchtower of the east, the golden light of the rising Sun, ye spirits of air, I welcome you to attend our rite and join us in this our Sacred Grove.

Move to the south:

Ye spirits of the watchtower of the south, the realms of the fiery Serpent, ye Spirits of Fire, I welcome you to attend our rite and join us in this our Sacred Grove.

Proceed to the west:

Ye spirits of the watchtower of the west, silvery realms of the Moon, spirits of death and initiation, ye spirits of water, I welcome you to attend our rite and join us in this our Sacred Grove.

Finish in the north:

Ye spirits of the watchtower of the north, the woods of the great stag, ye spirits of earth, I welcome you to attend our rite and join us in this our Sacred Grove.

Now point your athame toward the ground and draw a circle clockwise from north to north:

I conjure thee, O Circle of Power, that thou be a boundary and a protection. I erect this Grove as a meeting place between the world of men and the Otherworld. I invite you to be a Guardian and a Protection to preserve and contain the power raised within thee.

Walking clockwise, sprinkle the circle with the salt and water mixture:

With the waters of life and the salt of the earth, I purify this Sacred Grove.

Light the altar candle, saying:

I welcome thee, O Creature of Fire, that every malevolent spirit be banished henceforth.

Walk around the circle carrying the lit candle:

With the light of inspiration, I purify the Sacred Grove.

Light the incense, saying:

I welcome the ethereal element of Air.

Walk around the circle bearing the censor:

With the Sweet Air do I purify the Sacred Grove.

Return to the center and stand before the altar. Now, you shall call down the element of spirit.

I call upon Thee, O Mighty Mother. We ask that you be present with us by Seed and Root, by Stem and Bud, by Leaf and Flower and Fruit, by Life and Love.

Raise your above your head to form a Y.

I am the stag of the seven tines,
I am the flood across the plain,
I am the wind on a deep lake,
I am the tear of dew that falls at dawn,
I am the hawk that flies above the cliff,
I am the thorn on the branch,
I am the wonder among the flowers,
I am the Witch Father: who but I
Sets the cool head aflame?

I fly like a spear to part illusion,
I swim as the salmon bringing wisdom,
I am the hint of paradise,
I am the hill where poets walk,
I am a tide that threatens to pull you under,
I return like the receding wave,
I am a child: who but I can hold
the secret of the Dolmen arch?[1]

Following the casting, the Magister and the coven join hands. The Magister then leads them in a guided meditation to ground them to the earth.

After this, the coven raises the power in the circle, traditionally known as the "cone of power." This is generally done through a short chant increasing speed as the coven circles deosil (clockwise):

AIR breathe and air blow,
Make the mill of magic go,
Work the mill for which we pray,
Io dia ha he yay.

FIRE flame and fire burn,

Make the mill of magic turn,
Work the will for which we pray,
Io dia ha he yay.

WATER heat and water boil,
Make the mill of magic toil,
Work the will for which we pray,
Io dia ha he yay.

EARTH without and earth within,
Make the mill of magic spin,
Work the will for which we pray,
Io dia ha he yay.

When he deems the power sufficient, the Magister abruptly stops the round.

Now, one may continue calling down the sun, moon, or the witch's rune.

Never break a Circle. Always open a portal, known as 'cutting out,' before leaving or entering.

The Housel: Cakes and Ale

The Offering of libations is a central part of most circles. It generally follows the work the circle was cast to perform and comes before the closing. It is a time to offer to the spirits, the ancestors, and our brothers in the Craft, and to sit in comradeship with those with whom we share the sacred space. It is commonly called "Cakes and Wine" or "Cakes and Ale." This form is a ritual reenactment of the great rite, the blade and cup being the lance and chalice from the Lovers card of the tarot.

In Anglo-Saxon practice, it is called the Housel variously spelled housle, húsel, and húsl. It is often translated as sacrifice and has a post-pagan connection to the Eucharist. In some traditional craft, it is also termed the "red meal" and consists of dark bread and red wine.

Dark ales and stouts are generally appropriate. Red wine is also often used in Wiccan circles. Other libations may be substituted depending on the nature of the working and seasonal tide. For example, our grove has given a toast with champagne at Oimelc to symbolize stars twinkling in the night sky. In addition to the cup or horn, a small offering bowl should be on or before the altar to receive a portion of the libation. If the rite is conducted out of doors, the liquid may be poured directly on the earth. The "cake" may be a rustic loaf of dark bread or something sweeter and appropriate for the ritual/ season.

All Hail! A guest has come into our Sacred Grove seeking warmth and weal. Let him join us and take a seat at our hearth. Bring him libation to quench his wanderer's thirst.

Place the horn or cup upon the pentacle at the center front of the altar. The Magister places his hands, palms down, over the horn:

I consecrate this ale in the names of the Old Ones.

He grasps the horn and lifts it into the air toward the altar.

I offer this to the spirits
who have graced us with their presence;
To the good people of the land;
To the Mighty Dead;
To our Brothers in the Craft;
And those who gather in our Grove this night.

The Magister pours an amount of the ale into the offering bowl or on the ground. He then passes it to the brother at his right, who drinks and passes the cup clockwise. Only when all others present have tasted the liquid does the Magister take his.

The Magister replaces the horn/cup on the altar. He then moves the cake onto the pentacle. "I consecrate this in the names of the Old Ones that it may bring us strength." He lifts the bread or cake, breaking it into two pieces. He leaves one on the altar and passes the other half to the brother to his right. They again pass it around the grove, each taking a bite, leaving the last for the Magister.

Following the offering, the brothers may sit in the circle and engage in spiritual conversation. At certain times, the power of the erected grove has other thoughts, and the brothers are brought toward enactment of the *hieros gamos*.

Closing the Circle

The final act of the circle is to thank the spirits who have deigned to bless you with their presence for attending. We close the circle widdershins (working counterclockwise).

Begin in the north and draw the banishing pentagram of earth, saying:

> *Spirits of forces of earth, I thank you for attending our rites. Ere ye depart to your beautiful realms, I bid ye hail and farewell.*

All repeat after the Magister:

> *Hail and farewell!*

Move to the west:

> *Spirits of forces of water, I thank you for attending our rites. Ere ye depart to your beautiful realms, I bid ye hail and farewell.*

All repeat after the Magister:

> *Hail and farewell!*

Move to the south, draw the banishing pentagram, saying:

Spirits of forces of fire, I thank you for attending our rites. Ere ye depart to your beautiful realms, I bid ye hail and farewell.

All repeat after the Magister:

Hail and farewell!

Move to the east, draw the banishing pentagram, saying:

Spirits of the forces of air, I thank you for attending our rites. Ere ye depart to your beautiful realms; I bid ye hail and farewell.

All repeat after the Magister:

Hail and farewell!

Return to the center. The Magister raises his arms and says:

Spirits of the other realms, I do thank you for attending our rites. And ere the cock doth crow, we ask that you leave a little of your blessings here with us to sustain us until we meet again. Fire seal this circle round.

The coven all:

Blessed Be.

All stamp the ground with their right foot.
As each leaves the circle, hug and say:

Merry meet. Merry part. Merry meet again.

Calling Down the Sky

The sun, the goddess Sunne, is a star; she's our star. The night sky is filled with many stars. The sky filled with a web of twinkling lights is the Mother's arched body. Her sun, the moon, reflects his mother's light as he traverses the sky.

Mother Sky, radiant and vast,
Mistress of the heavens, first and last.
Windswept clouds and stars that gleam,
In your presence, I find my dream.

Mighty ruler of the day and night,
Guiding us with your eternal light.
Your cosmic dance, a wondrous sight,
Fills my spirit with pure delight.

Giver of life in every form,
From the raging storm to the gentle morn.
Your nurturing touch, forever warm,
In your embrace, I am reborn.

Empress of mystery, fierce and wise,
Unveil the secrets that in me lies.
Grant me vision that truly flies,

Open my heart, unbind my ties.
With gratitude, I call your name,
In reverence, I kindle this flame.
Grant me strength, release my shame,
Empower me in your sacred game.

So Mote It Be.

Calling Down the Moon

The Magister stands before the altar with arms raised, bent at the elbows so that the upper arms are lined up with the shoulders, and forearms are perpendicular. Palms should face outward. He takes the phallus or wand and draws an invoking pentagram above the altar.

I welcome you, Oh Witch Father, bringer of fire. By all the fruits of the earth and flickering flame of inspiration, I beseech thee to descend and be with us in the sacred space amongst your band of brothers.

A brother should be chosen to assist with serving. He approaches the Magister and gives the Fivefold Kiss:

Kiss both feet, left then right. Then say:
Blessed be thy feet, that have brought thee in these ways

Kiss the knees:
Blessed be thy knees, that shall kneel before the sacred altar

Kiss the tip of the phallus:
Blessed be thy phallus, without which we would not be

Kiss both sides of the chest:

Blessed be thy chest, formed in strength

Kiss lips:

Blessed be thy lips, that shall utter the sacred names.

In the midst of the last kiss, embrace.

The Charge

Magus: *Listen to the Charge of the Great Mother, whose arched body forms the night sky and whose kiss touches the small flowers of the field. We meet at her altars, in the grove and amongst the standing stones. Whenever we have need of her, once in the month, and better it be when the moon is full, we assemble in a secret place and call the Mother of All. There we assemble, beneath the stars, and partake of her nectar of inspiration and feel the kiss of the breath of life. Just as she taught the first person sorcery, we sit at her feet to learn things that are yet unknown.*

"And the divine decreed, all shall be free from slavery, and as a sign that we are truly free, we are naked in our rites. We dance, sing, feast, make music, and love, all in praise of the Old Ones. The gods give ecstasy and unimaginable joys on earth. Each act of pleasure is an offering to them.

"Hear the words of the Star Goddess. I love you! I yearn to you! Pale or purple, veiled or voluptuous, I who am all pleasure and purple, and drunkenness of the innermost sense, desire you. Put on the wings, and arouse the coiled splendour within you: come unto me![1]

"All acts of love and pleasure are her rituals. So let there be beauty and strength, leaping laughter, force and fire within you. And if you say, 'I have journeyed unto thee, and it availed me not,' rather shall you say, 'I called upon thee, and I waited patiently, and lo, thou wast with me from the beginning.' For all that ever desired her shall abide in her presence for she is everywhere."

Midwinter

For all sabbats, set up the altar in the North. At its center, place a small to medium-sized cauldron. The vessel represents the great goddess at the beginning of formation as well as the elixir of inspiration brewed within. A candle should be placed inside. Two candles are placed to either side. Their colors may vary by season. You may choose to have a statue of the God near the cauldron. The pentacle is set before the altar with the athame to the right. Two small cups with salt and water are to the left, and the censer of incense to the right. The altar should be decorated as appropriate to the season.

The altar is set in the normal way. For midwinter it may be decorated with ivy, pine, pine cones, and mistletoe. Decorating with evergreens is a tradition that dates back centuries. It is a reminder that even in the darkest night of the year, spring will come. The cauldron candle is unlit. The altar candles are red. The statue of the god should be shrouded in black cloth.

The Circle is cast, the cauldron lit, and the coven is welcomed inside. Neither sun nor moon are drawn down. The Magister stands before the altar cauldron and recites:

Incantation for Midwinter:
Queen of the Sun and Stars
Queen of Holy Waters

Queen of the Earth
Mother of the Promised Child
Great Mother who gives birth
To the King of the Year
Darkness and tears
Recede behind us
The Guiding Star
Rises in the morn.
Grief is laid aside
And Joy is raised
Across her realms.

The Magister lifts the shroud from the God.

To the blessed Mother
Without beginning nor end
Everlasting, eternal
EE-OH EE-VOH-HEY
Blessed Be!

Follow with the cakes and ale. Close the circle.

THE WASSAIL

The orchard wassail ceremony is choose often held on the Epiphany or Twelfth Night. Since at least Tudor times, it has marked the end of the Christmas season. For our purposes, the first full moon after the winter solstice is most appropriate. What follows is a traditional wassail recipe handed down to me from one of Crafts ancestors. Many variations exist, some with just ale, others with just ciders, while some add red wine instead of cider.

Prepare the Wassail per the instructions included in the recipe section. Traditionally, wassail is served in a large cup or bowl specific to the purpose. Often, these were made out of wood, particularly maple or silver.

If you are fortunate enough to have an apple tree or orchard at your disposal, take the bowl to the oldest tree. Seventeenth century poet Robert Herrick provides the following guidance in his poem "The Wassail":

Wassail the trees, that they may bear
You many a plum and many a pear:
For more or less fruits they will bring,
As you do give them wassailing.[1]

If you cannot access a fruit-bearing tree easily, you may create a temporary altar to the Apple Tree Man. This can be done on your main altar or as a separate shrine. Approach the tree or altar and recite this historical toast:

Here's to thee, old apple tree,
Whence thou mayst bud
And whence thou mayst blow!
And whence thou mayst bear apples enow!
Hats full! Caps full!
Bushel–bushel–sacks full,
And my pockets are full, too! Huzza![2]

Pour some of the libation on the ground or into an offering bowl on the altar. Pass the wassail cup around so that all present may partake. All Hail! Prosperity in the coming year!

Oimelc

The altar should be set up in the normal fashion with the inclusion of a phallic wand on the altar. The usual form is a wand ending with a pine cone. Cow's or goat's milk is an appropriate offering, and a vessel should be available to receive it. The altar candles should be white or silver and lit at the festival's beginning. The room may be filled with as many lit candles as one desires. The altar may be decorated with white flowers, such as snowdrops. The cakes may be a hearth loaf. Moon-colored cookies would also be appropriate. White wine may be substituted for Ale.

The Circle is cast, and the Sky is drawn down.

The Magister stands with the altar to his left, facing East, and arms raised. The server proceeds with the five-fold kiss.

O Great Lord who dies and is resurrected, the seed and promise of life. O Lord, within each of us, who is the Mystery of Mysteries, grow in our hearts as you grow in the soil. The Light crystalizes in our blood and brings about the rebirth of the Divine Son, for there is no part of us that is not part of him.

The Magister takes the wand and moves it above the coven.

Descend, O Father, upon your children gathered here in your honor.

Proceed with offering the milk, placing the offering vessel on the pentacle, and pouring it into it.

Next, follow with Cakes and Ale.

Close the Circle.

Eostre

Prepare the sabbat altar in the usual fashion. The cauldron is unlit at the start. Ahead of the festival dye or paint five hardboiled eggs. Place these on a plate in the form of a pentagram and surround it with flowers. Place the plate of eggs beneath the altar with the cakes and libation, preferably mead or elderberry wine. The altar may be decorated with any flowers appropriate for the season in your local area.

The Magister casts the circle and welcomes in the coven. He assumes the posture of the God with arms raised.

> *We kindle the fire this day. In the presence of the Old Ones, we welcome the light of life. Let this bright light before us be our guiding star illuminating the perfect path before us.*

The server lights the candle.

> *Kindle the fire within our hearts, the flame of love for our brothers. Let its warmth be felt by our foes, our friends, and our kindred all. May the fire of peace extend to all on Earth.*

Set the plate of eggs and flowers on the pentacle.

> *O Divine Son, Brother, and Father in one, as the light brightens*

the world from the highest point to the lowest, the Mother warms the seed in the ground and embraces the lamb in the womb.

May all be bathed in Light and Love of the Ancient Ones.

Continue with the Cakes & Ale then close the circle.

If possible, dispose of the eggs in the forest or by a body of water.

Festival of Flowers

The Festival of Flowers is the quintessential fertility festival. The altar should be decorated with seasonal flowers appropriate to the time and region. You may also construct a small maypole with rod and ribbons topped with a pine cone. If erecting a stang, it may be decorated with a wreath of flowers and ribbons. Candles should be green, preferably a pale green, and the altar cloth green or an earth tone. A vessel of honey and one of grain should also be placed on the altar. Adding these two together symbolizes the son (grain) being nurtured in the arms of the mother (honey). Libation should be of mead or a berry wine. If you have a place where you may safely work outside, it is traditional to build a fire at the center of a large circle. After combing the grain and honey, the coven should jump over/through the flames of the fire.

In addition, craft a small Wicker Man effigy. If practicing outside and the coven feels ambitious, you could construct a full Jack In the Green costume for one of the members to wear. However, it would not be advisable to sacrifice him in the fire at the end.

The Magister casts the circle and welcomes in the coven.

He stands before the altar with arms raised, saying:

Do not tell anyone of our flight.

For they would call it sin,
For we will be in the woods all night
A conjuring conjuring summer in.

The Magister invokes the mother by drawing down the sky. The magister places the bowl of honey onto the pentacle, saying:

We bring you good news by word of mouth.
For humans, cattle, and corn:
The sun is coming up from the south,
With oak and ash and thorn.

He then takes the bowl of grain and raises it toward the sky. Lowering it again, he takes a pinch of grain and pinches it into the bowl containing the honey.

Oh, Jack in the green, we call upon thee,
Spirit of nature, wild and free,
Green man of the woods, bringer of spring,
Through the dance thy power we bring.

We honor thee on this sacred day,
As the earth awakens from her sleep,
And the flowers bloom in her honor,
We call upon thee, oh Jack in the green.

Bless us with thy presence,
As we celebrate the turning of the wheel,
And let thy greenery encircle us,
As we ride the tides of the year.

Oh, Jack in the green, we welcome you,

We dance in gratitude
for the gifts of the earth,
And we commit to honor
and protect this sacred land.

Blessed be.

The designated server joins the Magister at the altar. They stand facing each other with their sides to the altar at the circle's center. The Magister kneels and gives the Server the five-fold kiss. He stands, and they embrace. Then, all members of the coven embrace.

Offer the cakes and mead with the traditional toast to the spirits, ancestors, and brothers of the Craft.

Then follows the heiro gamos either actual or symbolic.

Close the circle.

Midsummer

The full moon of June is sometimes called the faery moon in British Craft. Because of this, folks eschew iron items in the Midsummer circle. Instead of the cauldron, you may use a large pottery bowl. It should be filled with spring water. Similar to All Hallows and the spirits of the departed, the time around the summer solstice is when the spirits of the land, the genus loci, are thought to be close to hand. Surround the bowl and decorate the altar with summer flowers. On the altar, place the pine cone-tipped wand or a sturdy sprig of rosemary. Fresh herbs such as basil, thyme, and rosemary all make fitting decorations at this time. The candles should be yellow or gold. The altar cloth may be yellow or a summery shade enhanced by gold embellishments.

Form the circle in the usual way. After the coven enters, the Magister stands before the altar, wand or rosemary in his right hand, saying:

> *We call upon the divine spirits of the land by the ancient names — Michael, Balin, Arthur, Lugh, and Herne. We ask for your presence and guidance in this land once again. Illuminate the darkness with your powerful light and protect us with your shining spear. Bless us with abundant orchards, green fields, and ripening corn. Lead us to your hill of vision and show us the way to the beautiful realms of the gods.*

The Magister draws the invoking pentagram over the water. He then places the tip of the wand into the water's surface, saying:

Spirt to flesh, sun to earth.

The Server lifts the bowl and holds it before the magister. The coven then progresses before them. The Magister dips the wand or rosemary into the water and sprinkles it onto each member as they pass.

Follow with the libations.

Close the circle.

Feast of First Fruits

In the Northern Hemisphere, around the beginning of August, the first fruits of the harvest are coming in. Soft fruits are beginning to ripen, and fresh vegetables are available. The altar may be decorated with berries and summer fruits such as blueberries, raspberries, or strawberries. The altar cloth may be red or blue; the candles blue or green. The huzel should consist of mead or berry wine and a loaf of freshly baked bread—as this holiday was also known as "loaf mass" in ancient times.

This season is a time of knowledge and growing wisdom. Just as the fruits come into their own, we join together to ask the spirits to grant us the maturation of their guidance and insight. Nigel Pearson remarks that the rune Cen (Kenaz on the Elder Futhark) has a special connection to this time of year.[1] The rune is the root of the modern word "kenning." In Old English, cennan means "to make known," hence an active transmission of wisdom. A kenning is a descriptive compound construction used metaphorically in Old German, Norse, and English poetry. Examples in Beowolf are "Swan-Road" and "Whale-Road" for sea. Kennings were often used to refer to the gods.

This is the beginning of a time to reap the abundance of the harvest; it is also the start of a time of reflection and to gain insight within. Cen means "torch," and it is the spiritual flame of inspiration that burns between the horns. If you have created a bucca, that spirit should be welcomed into the circle, the candle unlit between his horns. Stand in the circle and place an unlit candle between its horns if you work with a stang. Similarly, a hood lamp could be substituted and placed on the altar.

Form the circle in the usual manner. Invite the coven in.

The Magister stands before the altar. The designated server gives him the five-fold kiss. The Magister turns and raises his arms, saying:

Oh, flame of inspiration, burn bright within us
Ignite our minds with thy sacred fire
Illuminate the path of wisdom ahead
Guide us out of the darkness.

As we enter this time of harvest,
Grant us the gift of understanding.
May we reap the fruits of our labor
And gain insight into the mysteries of life.

The server lights the candle betwixt the horns, while the Magister continues.

With thy fiery energy, inspire us.
To continue the work before us.
May we be moved through thy benevolence
to create and to grow in the light of knowledge.

Oh, flame of inspiration, we honor thee
And we welcome thy presence into our circle
May thine light guide us always
And may we continue to grow in thine wisdom.

The coven should join hands and stand around the horns in a circle or half circle. Each member should rest in the still point and absorb the light and inspiration emanating.

After a time, follow with the offering of libations and close the circle.

Harvest Home

Now is the time to bid farewell to the Solar Mother. Our ancestors conceived a divine entity that departs to a sacred realm upon passing. The Sun leads the forces of the sky and resides within all living beings and the world around us, as everything began with the stars. Stardust is akin to a seed, always capable of sprouting into something new. This seed is unique in that it originates from the stars and endures eternally. Therefore, we do not grieve at the Sun's passing but rather find joy in the transition of the seasons and the promise of her return in spring.

The Mother passes into her slumber. The Harvest God willingly sacrifices to sustain us through the long nights to come. In John Barleycorn's guise, the harvest's final fruits are transformed into bread, whiskey, and ale. His gifts will provide us strength through the winter months. In addition to wheat, barley, and oats, the darker fruits come on toward the end of the harvest season. Blackberries, or "bramble," sloe berries of the blackthorn, and cranberries are all mature now. These darker-colored fruits have a longstanding connection with witchcraft and the darker aspects of the goddess. We place a corn dolly between the altar candles. In addition, have at hand a small bowl of a grain of the same type used at the Feast of Flowers in May.

The candles and altar cloth should be fall colors, earth

tones, oranges, and browns. Harvest grains, dark fruits, and apples adorn the altar.

Cast the circle and welcome the coven.

Farewell, O Mother Sun,
even in thy departure
Is the promise of thy return.
Sleep well, dear lady.

Symbolically sacrifice the God by sprinkling a pinch of grain onto the incense charcoal.

He departs to the land of youth.
To dwell crowned as the king of the year.
He is ever the Horned Leader,
Who rules over the green of the wood.

As we stand unseen within the circle,
The forms of the Mighty Spirits
Of the other realms surrounding us.
Likewise, he is the Lord within ourselves.

He dwelleth within as the sacred seed,
The seed of new reaped grain,
The seed of flesh, hidden within the earth
And the mysterious ancient starseed.

Thee are that which is never born and never dies,
Therefore, we weep not and rejoice!

Toast the gods, spirits of the land, ancestors, and your brothers. Then, close the circle. Follow with a rich feast.

All Hallows

The altar should be draped in black and decorated with pumpkins, apples, and pomegranates sacred to the Dark Mother. Skull and crossed bones are also appropriate. The libation for the huzel should be a sturdy red wine, dark mead, or a rich stout or porter. You will need at least one apple for the ritual. The white-handled knife should be placed near the altar. Outside the circle to the north, set up a small table. Upon this display are pictures of loved ones, especially our queer family and brothers who have passed over. This table may be decorated with orange flowers.

Cast the circle and welcome in the coven.

The Magister stands before the altar, arms extended, pointing down to the earth.

> *Oh, great goddess of the underworld, mistress of shadows, giver of life, and bestower of the gift of death, hear us. Open wide thy gates through which all must pass eventually. Return this night and make merry with us. And when our time has come, as it does to all, comfort us in our journey to rest in your realms under your dominion. When we return, born again by thy grace, may it be at the same time and place as our loved ones and brothers of the art.*

The Magister and the coven focus on the images of the

departed and the dark space outside the circle's confines.

Hear me, ye Mighty Dead, we welcome thee to be with us on this Holy Night.

Place an apple on the pentacle. Have the knife at hand.

On this night, when the veil is thin, the dead are welcomed as they walk among us. Their presence reminds us of the gift of life, the assurance of rest, and the promise of rebirth. Such is the great covenant.

Slice the apple in half crosswise. The seeds form a pentagram. Hold it up to the images of the dead and display them to the coven. The hidden pattern in the seeds represents the power of the goddess hidden in all of the world. Leave the apples on a plate as an offering.

Now is a time for divination.

For the toast, salute the goddess Hel, ruler of the underworld. The salute to the ancestors should be a particular focus—solute separately all coven brothers who are now among the Mighty Dead.

Close the circle. It would be appropriate to follow with an interaction of the mute supper.

The Esbat

For centuries, witches, warlocks, seeresses, and sorcerors have gathered on the fringe to revel with the Horned Elder Father. We ride out on besom or rod and run through the wood as a hare, dog, or mouse to convene in the grove, on the moor, at the water's edge, and atop the hollow hill. We come together at the verge to celebrate the Dark Father, to dance with Jack-in-the-Green, and rut with the Silver Stag. Overtaken by the chthonic powers, the Man in Black conducts our revelry like a mad maestro. The flame between the horns bestows wisdom of the primordial Antlered God on those gathered in his name.

> *We gather once a month when the moon is full. Form a circle with the cauldron at its center. Inside have kindling for a fire if out of doors or an unlit candle.*

Cast the circle. Form a ring around the cauldron. As the Magister or server light the flame, recite:

IO EVOHE (ee-oh ee-voh-ay)
Icy winds blow out of the North
From the earliest of days
We gather to call ye forth
As we light the cauldron blaze

Sky-Mother descend from above
Horned Father join our revelry
We gather not in fear but love
Our joy, others term devilry.

Join hands and dance deosil, sunwise, around the cauldron chanting: *IO EVOHE* at increasing speed until the cone of power is raised.

Perform any other work desired.

Follow with the Cakes & Ale.

Thank the spirits for attending and close the circle.

Weekly Rite

Choose a day once a week to honor the Elder God. Go to your altar. Light candles and incense. It is best to be skyclad or dressed in ritual attire set aside only for the purpose of magical work. Stand in front of the image of the God with arms raised, legs slightly apart.

Oh, mighty Horned God, I call to thee
With reverence and respect, on bended knee
Lord of the wild, protector of the land
We seek your guidance; take me by the hand

Your antlers reach high, your power so grand
We honor your strength across the land
In the forest and fields, your presence is felt
I honor thee and the land in which you've dwelt

Oh, Great White Stag, ruler of the wild,
With antlers tall and nature mild,
I call upon thee in this hour,
To grant me strength and give me power.

From forests deep to mountains high,
Your presence fills both earth and sky,
So, hear my call and heed my plea,

And bless this humble devotee.
So, I call to thee now, on this sacred night
With a heart full of love and a spirit bright
Guide me through darkness and lead me to light
Oh, Horned God, hear my call tonight.

May thy wisdom guide my way,
And bring me closer to thee every day,
To the mysteries of the Greenwood,
And the magic where er' thee stood.

So, hear my call, oh Elder One,
And until that time when my day is done,
With thy aid and steadfast love,
May I soar to the heights of the crow above...

Snuff out the candle, while saying: So mote it be!

Daily Observations

A practice I've adapted from Crowley's writing is recognition of the movement of the sun across the day. *Liber Resh vel Helios* provides instructions for observing the sun at dawn, midday, sunset, and midnight. I found it an exemplary method for bringing focus back to spirituality throughout the day. It entails taking a slight pause and recognizing the course of Ra's solar bark across the celestial heavens. Since first encountering the practice, I have adapted it to cuddle up with my own cosmology. I should note that I do not currently perform this every day of every week of every month. There is a tradition in Tibetan Buddhism allowing one to temporarily take the monk's vows and live in a monastery. As everything is impermanent, all commitments are transitory by the nature of the universe. Years ago, I began going on mini retreats within the world to refocus myself. This involves pledging to do certain things for a specific time frame. For expediency's sake, I've borrowed the names of the early Christian church's liturgical hours.

LAUDS/PRIME

The first observance of the day, either at dawn or upon waking.

Oh, great and powerful Mother Sun,
I honor you in your rising.
Bless me with your radiant and fiery energy,
Guide me on my journey of the day,
And illuminate my way with your light.
May your warmth and light be with me always,
I honor you with love and respect.
Blessed be.

SEXT

Technically, the sixth hour of the day, this observance corresponds to noon or the high point of the sun's arc.

Oh, great and powerful Mother Sun,
I honor you at your zenith.
Bless me with your life-bringing warmth,
Guide me on my way with your light.
I honor you with love and respect.
Blessed be.

VESPERS

The observance corresponding to sunset.
Oh, great and powerful Mother Sun,
I honor you at your setting.
Bless me with your inspiration and wisdom,
As your light descends to sleep,
I know you are still there.
I honor you with love and respect.
Blessed be.

COMPLINE

When retiring to bed and preparing for sleep, I silently rest in the arms of spirit, settling into the equipoise of the meditative point.

MATINS

Much like the new moon is in the night sky, the dark of night is a time of silence.

The Hieros Gamos

Ritual and sacred sex have a very long history. There remain few areas more controversial. Contemporaries describe ancient sexual rites in the Near East in places such as Sumer, Babylonia, and Cyprus. Cultic brothels were common in Ancient Greece, and temples of Aphrodite had their attendant prostitutes. This was particularly pronounced in the port city of Corinth between Athens and Sparta. The so-called "East Building" in Minoan Crete shows archeological evidence of prostitution and sacred rites. The Romans' celebration of Venus often included sexual rites. On April 25, Romans participated in the festival known as Robigalia to protect crops from disease and fungus. On the same day, they also celebrated pueri lenonii, literally "pimped out boys,", e.g., male sex workers.

In the flow of the remaining embers of Beltane fires, couples broke away for their celebrations of spring fertility. Witches rode to the sabbat on broomsticks said to hide a carved phallus. The pine cone-tipped wand sprinkles the seed of life on the congregants. Crowley and Neuberg fuck in the desert to move through the Enochian Aethyrs and in Paris to invoke the God.

For gay men, sex is far from a taboo subject. We have come far to shed its negative connotations of shame and fear. That being said, online screeds continue to erupt, denouncing any connection between the sexual and the sacred.

Sex is a shimmering facet of the natural world. The sexual impulse has been separated from the reductive aspect of fertility. We have been given the lure of pleasure to build our communal connections. The phallus on the altar is the embodiment of the God force. In days gone by, the witch rode the road to the sabbat on the phallic staff disguised as the besom.

First and foremost, consent is key.

The Great Rite, hieros gamos, may be symbolic through the passing of the altar phallus between the thighs of the server or it may be actual or anywhere in between. Some covens join in mutual stimulation, each providing his seed as an offering. Others engage in ritual anal sex or unscripted orgy. In contrast, others hug in communion and return to the world.

THE ELIXIR

Sexual fluids have a long connection to magic. Along with blood and spit, one cannot think of a more personal offering and a more readily available tool. We can use semen to empower objects with our nature. Climax can serve as a particular magical launching point for workings. Draw a sigil that represents your desired results. Concentrate on it, and at the point of climax, throw one-pointed energy at the abstraction of your intent without thinking of the desired results. Clean up, hide the sigil, and walk away. Think about it no more until the result manifests.

Physically, we can offer ourselves to our brother(s): Priest united with Priest. When we take another within ourselves, it is an act of trust. The spirits surround us and partake in our pleasure.

When we drink of another, we take part of their magic into ourselves.

In the name of thou who at midnight doth reign
Master of the dark green wood
We gather in your sacred grove
Where sacred oak has long stood
We are watered by your love
By your golden rod of power
By branch and leaf and bud
By seed that grows into flower
By the power of coursing blood
By flowing waters and leaping flame
By gusty wind and fertile earth
Descend upon us as our desire
Wisdom flowering in our mirth

They kiss.

To thee, I hold most dear
The Horned God incarnate
In flesh the great rod fills
Until the hungry night is sate
And the holy seed spills.

The priest kisses the offeror's chest.

Secret of the moon above the tower
The blessed circle's center point
Altar portal of the raised power
Through my kiss, I do anoint.

His brother turns and bends forward. The priest performs the infernal kiss on the offeror and then commences the sacral act.

We can hear the Hunter's hounds
As our sacred journey begins.
The priest enters the offeror.
The love of our brothers abounds
A joy that knows no sins
We tread the secret path
As we join under the holy tree
In shadow of Yew, Oak, and Ash
Guided by the sacred roebuck
Our bodies are knit as one
Mirth is gifted by Ol' Puck
And our fetters are undone.

At climax each says, *So mote it be!*

The Infernal Kiss

The history of the *Osculum Infame*, the "infamous kiss," "kiss of shame" or "infernal kiss," predates the period of the witch hunts. It was a trope found during the Inquisition employed in the denouncing of heretics. The earliest recorded referenced dates from the twelfth-century in Walter Map's *De Nugis Curialium*. He writes that the heretics gathered and a black cat of "wondrous size" appeared before them. They lined up to kiss the supernatural creature in various places:

> *quisque secundum quod ampliore feruet insania humilius, quidam pedes, plurimi sub cauda, plerique pudenda, et quasi a loco fetoris accepta licencia pruriginis, quisque sibi proximum aut proximam arripit, commiscenturque quantum quisque ludibrium extendere.*[1]

> Each kissed the beast according to the extent to which the insanity strikes more lowly, some feet, most under the tail, most shameful, and as if from the place of the stench having received permission to itch, each seizes the next or nearest to him.

The trope was often connected to the Albigenses heresy, otherwise known as the Cathars, in Southern France. The ironically named Philip the Fair, Philip IV King of France, my twenty-third great grandfather, incorporated this by then well-entrenched heretical action in his accusations against the Knights Templar that resulted in their put down.

Witches often described how they were asked to kiss the hindquarters of a black goat during the gatherings of the witches's sabbat. This is a similar example of inversion to that of which the Templars were accused. Kissing backside of a goat, symbol of the Devil, is a direct corollary to kissing the bishop's ring.

Protective Magick & Warding

The practice of magick is like setting up a beacon on the other planes. It tends to attract the attention of spirits, good and "bad." All traditions have some evil or malevolent spirits. Witches must protect themselves and those close to them. In addition to the spirits that your work might attract, other practitioners may not wish the best for you. Even benevolent or indifferent spirits, if not invited, can be a bit much after a while. We know this from a beloved relative who shows up unannounced and stays a bit too long.

Burroughs observes:

> Black magic operates most effectively in preconsciousness, marginal areas. Casual curses are the most effective. If someone has reason to expect psychic attack, an excellent move is to make oneself as visible as possible to the person or persons from whom the attack is anticipated, since *conscious* attacks on a target that engages one's attention are rarely effective and frequently backfire.[1]

Wards operate as beacons as well. They attract and turn

back magical attacks by their visible existence on other plains. Witches don't go looking for trouble, but we are not always able to control what is attracted by our work. In the words of the tenth Doctor, "Trouble's just the bits in-between."[2]

A witch should perform cleansings of the self and their home regularly. Like one's house, your personal and ritual space should be tidy and physically organized before embarking on spiritual work. A cluttered and disorganized space leads to unfocused and disorganized magick.

Three steps are crucial to magickal maintenance: Banish, Cleanse, and Ward. First, we remove any negative or unwanted energies that may have come into the space. The second is to cleanse the space—purify and fill the void with positive energy. The third is to ward the area, setting or resetting protective charms at the thresholds.

Think: Sweep the floor. Mop with cleanser. Apply a protective polish.

Personal protective devices often include charged jewelry, sachets, protective oils, and baths.

Erecting wards and deploying protections around your house or apartment is essential. These may include physical wards at windows and doors, metal crosses, mirrors facing out, statuary of protective entities, salt, or red brick dust. Witches often create a witch bottle filled with nails, needles, broken glass, and their urine and bury it on their property.

One should start with the main entrance or entrances to your house. Then follows any additional doors and then the windows. If the space has other external openings to the outside, one should incorporate those as well.

There are several ways to ward doors and windows. Protective charms or symbols may be hung above them or set atop the lintel. Protective devices may be buried just outside/below them. Door thresholds and window ledges can be washed with protective floorwash. A line of brick dust can be drawn at door openings.

Some common wards and protective charms include:

WITCH MARKS,

Sometimes called "hex signs," witch marks have been common apotropaic devices dating back to at least the sixteenth and seventeenth centuries. Incised markings on timbers are still being uncovered in Elizabethan and Stuart-era buildings in Britain and the American Colonies. This class of markings was employed to protect the home from witches and other evil forces. Marks recently uncovered at Knoll House in Kent appear to date around the time of King James VI and I's visit to the house in 1606. Just coming off the Gunpowder Plot, it was likely everyone around James was being doubly careful. Witch marks take many forms. Two of the most common are in the shape of a daisy (hexafoils) and a figure reminiscent of a W.

Employment of daisy wheels and similar compass-drawn markings date long back into history. Similar forms may be found in the Late Bronze Age. In England, the symbol of a daisy "flower" inside a circle is common in churches, barns, and private residences. In New England, they are also very common adornments of gravestones of the period. The W-looking symbol is likely two Vs standing for the Virgin Mary or the Virgin of Virgins.

CROSSES

Crosses and X marks are among the oldest forms of protective markings. They have been used long before Christianity popularized their connection to the execution of a would-be prophet. Employing a cross as protection may be as simple as crossing two slender lengths of material and saying, "Thou shalt not pass..." Protective crosses made of twigs from the Rowan are a very traditional form of protective cross. Mullein may also be used. Using ashes or chalk, crosses or X marks may also be drawn above doors and openings.

MIRRORS

Mirrors have long been employed for magickal purposes. One may place small mirrors anointed with protection oil on windowsills facing outward. The mirror should be bathed in clean water, and the oil should be reapplied regularly. The wash may include protective herbs such as hyssop or patchouli. The mirror serves to turn the forces back from whence they came.

NAILS

Three nails, especially iron ones, may be pounded into the lower two corners and center of the top lintel of each window and door. Iron has long been thought of as a protective material. Two nails may also be assembled as a small cross tied together with red thread.

There are many varieties of protective charms widely available. One of the most common is the "evil eye" amulet *nazar* in Arabic. This bead or charm comes in a variety of sizes and mountings. It is generally a glass circle of dark blue surrounding an eye of white, lighter blue and a black pupil. The symbol originates from the Mesopotamian and Mediterranean.

BRICK DUST

The usage of red brick dust is common in the American South and among Hoodoo practitioners. The dust must be from a brick formerly part of a structure to be effective. The memory of its time as part of a boundary wall gives it power. The red, as seen in the thread tying the Rowan cross, is a vital element of magic. The redder the brick, the better the dust. Place the dust to form a line across your front path and just outside your doorways. It will need to be replenished periodically.

PROTECTIVE PLANTS

Plants are also beneficial to have around one's home. Herbs such as rosemary and basil can be protective elements for their use in the culinary world. Oak trees have long been connected with strength and are potent guardians. The holly brings luck and prosperity and is good to have on your property. Bunches of dried herbs may also be hung from rafters or over doorways.

THE WITCH BOTTLE

A vessel known as a witch bottle has a long history in European folklore. It is a common apotropaic object in use for centuries. The practice was well established by 1670 when an anonymous pamphlet appeared in London entitled *A miraculous cure for witchcraft, or, Strange news from the Blew-Boar in Holburn*. The leaflet told the story of a young girl beset by malevolent witchcraft. Seeking a remedy, she visited a chemyst who advised her to fill a bottle with her urine and add to it some other ingredients. From the mid-sixteenth well into the seventeenth century, the practice was common in both England and New England.[3]

While urine is the common ingredient, the vessel is often filled with nails, bent pins, salt, nail clippings, and (more modernly) broken shards of mirrored glass. The urine was held to have a sympathetic relation to the individual for whom the bottle was meant to protect. We can see a similar notion in the witch cake, such as the one baked by Mary Sibley. The cake containing the victim's urine is fed to an animal and was meant to transfer the baneful affliction from the patient to the unwitting creature.

Recently, witch bottles made a brief appearance in international news when *Antiques Roadshow* presenter Andy McConnell accidentally drank 180-year-old urine on air. The glass specialist mistakenly identified an antique wine bottle as containing vintage wine. Using a needle inserted through the cork, he sampled a bit and declared it port. After further examination, he admitted on a later show that the bottle contained human urine and a single hair.

A jug called a 'Bellarmine' was most commonly used for the construction of a witch bottle. These earthenware bottles had a round body and featured a bearded face on the neck. Today, one can use any stoneware or glass bottle that can be sealed with a cork. Once you have found your bottle, assemble your other ingredients, such as nails and bent pins. Insert odd numbers of each into the jar, add your urine, cork, and seal with wax. Bury in your yard or conceal in the walls of your home if possible.

Another method of using a witch bottle was less protective and more curative. A bottle was created similarly, except the urine was that of the person the cure was intended for. The bottle was then crafted, corked, and put onto a fire. When the bottle burst, the curse was thought to have been lifted. Be careful if you attempt this, as the bottle's explosion can be unpredictable.

WITCH BALLS

Glass spheres have long been popular home decorations, hanging in windows to catch the light. These first became popular in England when the Nailsea glassmakers began manufacturing them in 1788. Their appearance is similar to oversized glass Christmas ornaments. Like mirrors, these decorations also hold a protective purpose and are often called "witch balls." Earlier versions of blown glass spheres, predating those manufactured by Nailsea, have been found. These are often filled with tangles of multi-colored strings. In New England and coastal areas, hollow glass balls were long used as floats for nets. These also served a similar warding function when hung in one's home, especially in windows. In the case of glass floats, their immersion in salt water was considered integral to their effectiveness. Glass floats may be found in antique shops in various sizes and colors—authentic ones are often green. Reproductions can be readily found in the gift shops of coastal towns and now, no doubt, online. If one does acquire one of the reproductions, it should be soaked for a time (not too short a time) in seawater or, if not available, water with sea salt added to it.

ROWAN

The Rowan tree, also known as the "witch tree," has a long connection in folklore with magic, witchcraft, and the Druids. Two twigs can be fashioned into an equal-armed cross and bound with red thread. Miniature versions of these may be carried in one's pocket for protection. They can also be hung by doors, windows, and chimneys to protect the home from unwelcome spirits. Farmers hung rowan from the rafters of their barns to protect their livestock. The stealing of milk by witches was a commonly perceived threat. A switch made out of a rowan branch was said to be able to whip the hex off one.

We have the Mountain Ash, or American Rowan, *Sorbus americana* in America. Despite the name, the tree is not related to the Ash but is part of the rose family. The North American variety may be used similarly to its European counterpart. The tree's berries bear the pentagram sign and have long been linked to the goddess. Norse mythology says the first woman was created from a rowan tree, while the first man was from ash. Thor used a rowan tree to save himself from a rushing river.

Rowan is often found planted in churchyards. The small tree makes a great addition to your yard if you have a suitable climate. The rowan grows abundantly in Scotland, where some say it may not be cut for any purpose other than spiritual. An amulet with a protective rune carved into it may also be fashioned from its wood and worn or carried about the person.

CLEANSING BATH

The following cleansing bath is a variation of one taught to me by my teacher, Hermes. It is an excellent method to remove the "spiritual ick" as he called it—that feeling of things being not quite right. A bath such as this may be done anytime, but the dark moon and time of the year are particularly appropriate. It may also not be sufficient to bathe only once. It may be necessary to repeat this practice over three or seven nights. Sometimes it just takes repeated scrubbing to remove all the accumulated grime.

You will need:

A White candle
A large bowl
A kettle or pot to heat water in
A colander lined with cheesecloth or a cloth sachet
Florida Water
White rum
Equal Parts Dry Herbs: Rosemary, Hyssop, Rue, Basil, Parsley
Salt

First, take a shower so that you begin physically clean. Light the white candle and pray to your spirits, asking them to bless, guide, and protect you. Heat the kettle or pot of water to a medium temperature but short of boiling. Place the colander in the bowl. Since dried herbs tend to be fine, I line the colander with cheesecloth. You may also find a porous cloth bag designed to infuse herbs into bathwater.

Once the water is just shy of boiling, pour it over the herbs and into the basin. Let it steep for five minutes or so. Lift the colander or bag out of the water. Continuing to call on your spirits, add Florida Water and a pinch of salt. Take a swig of the rum but don't swallow. Spray it into the bowl, letting the distilled spirits intermingle with your energy.

Take the bowl to your shower or bathtub. With your hands, pour the liquid over yourself, starting at your head and moving downward. When you complete the bath or series of them, dispose of the white candle. Use new herbs with each repetition.

HAG STONES

Hag stones are another traditional protective amulet. It is a stone with a natural hole in it. One finds them along the shore. Or, as it is said, they find you. They may be hung above doors or windows to prevent negative forces from entering. They may also be worn on the person as a defensive charm.

Here is an adaptation of a sixteenth-century charm said to protect one's horses from Night Hags:

> Take a Flynt stone that hath a hole of his kind, and hang it over him (the horse). Write on a piece of paper: *In nomine patris,* etc. And say, Saint George, our Ladies Knight, walked day and night until he found her. He beat her, and she bounced until she told him her plight that she would not come in the

night. There was Saint George, our knight. Repeat his name three times: Saints George.
Hang the stone and the Scripture over him, and let him alone.[4]

HORSESHOES

Horseshoes have long been utilized as protective devices or ones to ensure prosperity. They mimic the shape of talismanic images ubiquitous throughout history: the horns of animals, the crescent moon, and the open hand. Iron has long been held to possess protective properties against spirits and goblins.[5] It is considered sacred to Woden. Norse sorceresses' graves often include an iron staff archeologists ascribe as an implement of their power to control spirits. There is a link between iron and flint. Arrowheads made of flint were known in Scotland as "elf-shot" and were thought to be shot by fairies. Farmers would place pieces of flint into a bowl of milk in the Hebrides to rid their herd of bewitchment.

One can find horseshoes hung in barns and cottages throughout England, Scotland, and Wales. A horseshoe hung over the bedroom door was said to ward off nightmares. The practice of employing horseshoes as protective emblems crossed the Atlantic and remains common throughout America today.

Horseshoes were also connected with prosperity. The English word "luck" has a Scandinavian origin from the Anglo-Saxon word "to catch." In the shape of the horseshoe, it collects the fortune within it. The form is reminiscent of the Pethro rune in the Elder Futhark, which is thought to derive from a dice cup and relates to wealth or fate.

There is much debate about hanging the shoe points up or down. Each argument is connected with prosperity. On one side is the idea that points up the shoe keeps in the bounty drawn and down the wealth pours out. On the other hand, some feel the downward-pointing open end, either straight down or at an angle, pours forth the prosperity of the home. I'm firmly in the points-up camp.

Though common, hanging a horseshoe in one's home was not always looked on positively by secular and, especially, ecclesiastical authorities. In sixteenth-century Scotland, Elizabeth Bathcat was charged with witchcraft for having a horseshoe above her cottage door. The accusers held the shoe was "a devilish means of instruction from the Devil to make her goods and all her other affairs prosper and succeed well."[6]

The space within the shoe is also a space betwixt and between. The shape is similar to that of the traditional witch's stang. We see this in the hood lamp discussed previously.

Candle Working

Below are traditional magics corresponding to commonly colored candles. It is important to note our ancestors would have generally only had access to white candles. Therefore, that color is appropriate for all workings.

Red: Love, sex, vitality, strength, and courage
Blue: Healing, protection, peace
Green: Success, money, growth, good fortune
Black: Darker realms, the dead, hex work, and returning evil whence it came
Brown: Justice and court proceedings
White: Blessings, purification, general purpose
Orange: Divination, journeys, communication
Purple: Power, favor, judgment
Yellow: Wealth and vitality
Gold: Riches and the light of day
Silver: Treasure and the mysteries of the starry heavens

Before use, candles should be anointed with oil. This may be general-purpose Anointing Oil or one specific to the working or use. The tradition is that one places the oil on the candle in a line up from the middle and then down from the starting point, saying, "As above, so below."

Spellcraft

Magick is to work with natural forces to bring about change. It is not about controlling the world but should be viewed as aligning oneself to the current of the Universe's unfolding. Spellcasting is a way to pull a string on the tapestry of existence (the web of the Wyrd) for a particular purpose. Rightly viewed, the witch's work is an integral component of the fabric.

Just as important as knowing how to cast spells is the ability to listen to the world around us. The witch needs to sense the natural momentum to work in the present moment with the currents moving out of the past into a manifesting future. The path forward is always more accessible with the wind at your back.

There are three types of magick: journeying, making, and changing. We may use rituals and spells to guide us in traveling between worlds and our inner landscapes. Known as "hedge riding" or "riding the hedge," the witch journeys through liminal spaces and into otherworldly realms. We can craft and create, using our art to make something new. Poetry and art are forms of magick. Blessing falls into this category as well. And lastly, we can use our craft to provoke change in our surrounding world or circumstance.

The "Gift of the Magi" is essential not to forget here. It is best to be general and not specific. We likely will get what we wish for, but it may not be how we intended. We put our lack front and center when asking to obtain something we lack. It is often that we trade one lack for another. We should open ourselves up to attract change rather than target a specific outcome. The Money Pot, below, is an excellent example of this. Rather than asking the Universe to give us a million dollars or win the lottery, we thank the universe for the random monetary gifts we receive and open our lives to the natural abundance around us. Appreciating abundance attracts more of the same.

Many methods of magic exist. Among those techniques employed by traditional witches are the utilization of knots, candles, and herbs.

In crafting a spell, you should focus on being as precise (though generally not specific in outcome) as possible in wording, targeting, and timing. The zodiac sign the Moon is transiting as well as the phase of the Moon is often considered when deciding when to perform a spell—Waxing or Waning, Full or New. Traditionally, the waxing moon is a time to work toward manifesting, while the waning moon is a time for banishing or eliminating. We work with the energies in the world instead of against them. It is far easier to swim with the current than against it.

When trying to influence a future occurrence, the further out from the event time-point, the more potential for success. Just as a minute change in direction has limited impact over a few inches, it has a dramatic impact over miles. The bigger the ship, the longer it takes to turn.

Many (though not all) Wiccan traditions hold to the threefold law of return—where what the practitioner puts out in the world comes back at one threefold. I prefer the Druid imagery of the returning tide. The energy we put into the world comes back to us. A smile usually elicits a smile. Philip Carr-Gomm quotes Thoth from the Egyptian Book of the Dead in *Druidcraft*:

> Truth is the harvest scythe. What is sown – love or anger or bitterness – that shall be your bread. The corn is no better than its seed, then let what you plant be good.

I generally believe in not working a spell on someone without their permission. Individuals often approach me to work magic related to healing, improving a crossed situation, and general prosperity or luck. I usually assist them, providing the tools and showing them how to work for themselves. They have the intent and the will to empower the spell.

On rare occasions, I have needed to push back at someone sending negative energy my way, intentionally or subconsciously. Protective magic usually works by turning the negative energy back on the sender. In this way, your work does not bring them misfortune but their intent returning to them. There is a simple but effective spell to bind someone from intending to do you harm, used only when necessary. It employs a black candle, a photo of the person, black thread, and banishing oil. Anoint the candle with the oil. Light it. Wrinkle the photo into a ball and bind tightly with the thread. Light the photo with the candle and watch it burn. Let the candle burn down, and then cast the ashes outside the boundaries of your home/property. Think of the person no more.

THE MONEY POT

I learned the Money Pot spell from the work of Orion Foxwood.

He discusses it in detail in his book *Mountain Conjure & Southern Rootwork.*[1] As far back as I can remember, I have always picked up change I have found on the ground. If the universe gives one money, one should take it. If you pass by money, what message would that send to the spirits?

This spell creates a vessel to create a receptive environment for the attraction of wealth and prosperity. You will need a copper vessel such as a bowl or small bucket, three lodestones, money oil, and seed money to create the pot. I also placed a small gold toad in mine. These are common in feng shui and generally have a coin in its mouth. Dress (anoint) the lodestones in oil. Place the toad and stones in the copper pot along with the seed money (a few coins). Place it in your magickal area or on your working altar.

In the future, each time you find money, pick it up and thank the spirits for the gift. Then, place the found money in your pot. Periodically, you can retrieve the funds from the pot, leaving seed money for the future. Use the funds to purchase a gift or offering for your home spirits.

CHARM BAGS

Place the following in a small red bag (preferably flannel) and tie with red thread or yarn: a crumb of bread, salt, rue, and parsley. As you assemble and tie off the bag, say:

> *This bag I sew for luck for you,*
> *And also for my family,*
> *That it may keep by night and day,*
> *Troubles and illness far away.*[2]

This English talisman is similar in style to the talismanic

bags common in New Orleans known as *gris-gris* (pronounced "gree-gree") or mojo bags. Gris-gris originated in West Africa, and the practice came over with enslaved peoples. The name may come from the Yoruban word *juju,* meaning a fetish. In Africa, the original bags were most likely used to ward off evil forces. In Haiti, they are connected to positive and luck magic. Within Louisiana Creole communities, they developed a darker reputation. In Africa today, women continue to wear similar bags as a means of contraception.

NINE KNOT SPELL

Spells involving the tying of knots are widespread in English and Scottish witchcraft. This work involves tying knots at opposite ends of a cord at equal distances until they meet in the middle. This may be done as a solitary or group working. If it's a group working, every participant may have a cord, or each ties a knot in sequence clockwise around the circle.

As each knot is tied, say:

By knot of one, the spell's begun.
By knot of two, it cometh true.
By knot of three, so mote it be.
By knot of four, the open door.
By knot of five, the spell's alive.
By knot of six, the spell is fixed.
By knot of seven, the stars of heaven.
By knot of eight, the stroke of fate.
By knot of nine, the thing is mine![3]

Three knots may be used for smaller or lighter spells. The nine knots above are appropriate for stronger workings. To undo the spell, untie the knots.

LAMPS

Oil lamps have a long history of use in magick. I utilize hurricane lanterns that have a clear glass vessel for the oil. I place items in the lamp representing my intent and a written message in Theban runes.

For example, a lamp to bring luck to the home may contain pyrite and whole nutmeg. A light for clear sight in divination could have clear quartz crystal and mugwort—a protection lamp, obsidian and patchouli.

BURNING APPLE WOOD

If you have reason to cut an apple tree or know someone who does, save the wood. Do not cut a branch or tree specialty for this work. Soak the wood in seawater or saltwater brine for twenty-eight days from the New Moon to the New Moon. After it has soaked the allotted time, dry the wood out thoroughly. Once it is scorched, burn it. The flames will be of multi-colors, and prosperity shall shortly rain down on the house.

DREAM LOVER

In his classic *Mastering Witchcraft,* Paul Husson provides an old spell for summoning dreams of one's lover.[4] What follows is my variation. Traditionally, the spell was done on St. Magdalene's Eve (July 22). No matter what, it should be done during the waxing moon. Create a sachet of St. John's Wort and the name of your lover written on paper. Place it beneath your pillow.

Mix a draught:

> Spring Water
> 3 Drops each white wine, gin, & apple cider vinegar
> Stir with a sprig of rosemary

Drink before retiring. Your lover should come to you in the dream space.

SATOR

Though it is undoubtedly rooted in Christian magic, European conjurers have long employed this love talisman. Take a small piece of parchment to your working altar. Perform these workings on Friday evening during the waxing moon. The intent of this spell is to strengthen one's aura of attraction. As you write each letter, call out the name of the person for

S	A	T	O	R
A	R	E	P	O
T	E	N	E	T
O	P	E	R	A
R	O	T	A	S

whom the talisman is being created. Begging with the top row, write the following. Then, continue with the last row from right to left. Fill in the left from top to bottom. Then, the right from bottom to top. Finish it by writing the interior in three rows: left to right, right to left, and left to right.

Place your completed parchment and bury it in the ground. This should be done at a crossroads or in a churchyard, but any patch of soil, such as your garden, will work. After twenty-four hours, unearth it and present it to the person for whom it was intended.

TALISMAN FOR PROSPERITY

Inscribe the design to the right on two sides of a silver disk—alternatively draw the design in ink on two sides of a piece of parchment. The working should be done on a Wednesday between the new and full moons, preferably when Mercury is favorably disposed in conjunction with Jupiter, the Sun, or the Moon. Pass the talisman through the smoke of the incense described below. Then, bury it at a crossroads for seven days. After retrieving it the following Wednesday, pass it again three times through the same incense. You may continue to strengthen the talisman periodically by again fumigating with incense on Wednesday.

Burn the prosperity incense include in the fumulary.

A
G
L
A

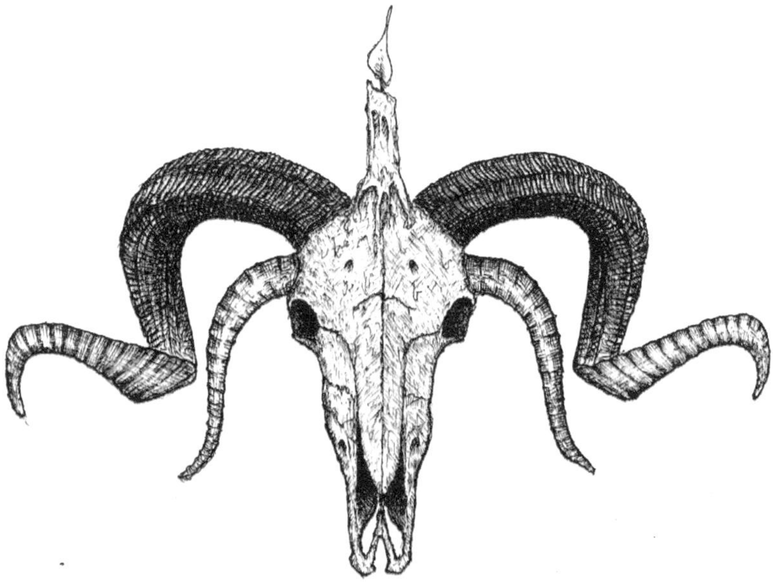

Ol' Horny

The use of the skull of a horned animal with a candle fixed between its horns is common in the West Country of England—Cornwall, Devon, Dorset, Somerset, and Bristol. A close brother first taught me how to create such a vessel years before I encountered it in written texts. The skull used is often that of a goat or ram. He painted his in red ochre, and I have done the same. The use of ochre to color bone has deep historical precedence. The Red Lady of Paviland was called such because of the red color of the bones. First discovered in Goat's Cave in 1912, the "lady" was first thought to be a Roman prostitute and later dated to the Neolithic. Modern forensic technologies show that she is, in fact, a he and dates instead to the Paleolithic period, the last Ice Age some 33,000 years ago. He is called *bucca* in Cornwall after the Anglo-Saxon word for "he-goat" and is also known as Pook, personified as Shakespeare's Puck *in Midsummer Night's Dream* and lives on in the folk legends of Robin Goodfellow. Veneration of the Goat-God continues in the Norse Christmastide celebration of the Jul goat. In modern times, he has been personified as Black Phillip, the goat star of the film *The Witch*.

The skull serves as an oracular vehicle that rests between the worlds. Gema Gary writes of the bucca, "It is about these altars and their skulls that the witches work to conjure forth spirit presences and manifestations, or visitations from the

Old One himself. Thus, the skull remains to the witch a potent device of vision and reaching out to the experience of the Otherworldly."[1] The bucca is the personification of the Witchfather and the Sabbatic Goat. Cecil Williamson had among the artifacts in his collection, housed in the Museum of Witchcraft in Boscastle, the skull of a ram used in a witches' shrine on Bodmin Moor. My bucca is made from the skull of a Jacob ram. I first encountered Jacob's sheep at a farm in the Cotswolds. If you haven't seen one, they are pretty impressive. They have two sets of horns—one pair going straight up and another set curling around their head.

After choosing an appropriate skull, clean it with pure water. Infusing such with mugwort would be appropriate. I recommend doing as we did and painting it with red ochre mixed with linseed oil or ochre-colored paint. Once it has dried, retire to your quiet space to work at dusk or midnight during the waxing moon. It would be ideal to conduct this working out of doors so that the skull makes direct contact with the earth. This rite may be performed alone or with a suitable working partner (or partners). When we consecrated my Jacob skull, there were three of us present to work the magic.

INVOKING OL' HORNY

Place the skull on the ground, a cloth, or a low altar. Surround it with flowers. Two flowers may be placed into its eye sockets to mimic eyes. Ones that can be quickly dried for saving are ideal. Also, have on hand several squares of natural, undyed cotton cloth—light two candles, but not the one on the bucca itself. Light an incense of two parts Benzoin and one part each of Cedar, Pine, and Juniper Berries.

Meditate and center yourself.

Stamp three times on the ground. If three witches are present, each stamps once—to the left, right, and in front of the skull.

Invoke the Horned One:
Io Evohe
(EE-Oh EE-voh Hay)
Io Evohe
I call on the Horn'd One
Io Evohe
I/We invite you here this night.

Once you feel his presence, lay your hands on the skull.

O, Bringer of Fire,
Lord of the Witches' Sabbat
Kindle flame
Where once there was life
Leave a spark of yourself behind
Within this vessel

I/We consecrate this night.

Begin to kindle the fire within. If alone, get yourself sexually aroused. If working with a partner, start by stimulating each other. Take it slow; there is no deadline. Feel the fire building. As the flames rise, focus on the spirit coming into the skull. Begin to pleasure yourself or each other. Just before the climax, pull out if necessary, and catch the cum into the pieces of cloth.

Sit back in post-coital equipoise.

Once dry, the cum-soaked cloth may be placed inside the skull or contained in a small clay vessel set alongside it.

Place the bucca as the central point of an altar established for this purpose. When you do work requiring the wisdom of the Old One, light his candle and call his name. He will come.

The Magic Mirror

Obtain a concave piece of glass. Wash the glass in warm water for at least three minutes. Let it dry. Paint the back of the glass black until no light is able to penetrate through.

Brew an infusion of mugwort or wormwood and spring water. Consecrate the liquid by placing the tip of your athame into the liquid and saying:

> *Spirit of the green, breathe thy sight into this water so it shall*
> *show me true and none shall evade thee.*

Paint the back of the mirror with the mixture and allow to dry. At the next full moon esbat, consecrate the mirror and allow it to catch the moon's light. Use it immediately for scrying. Any others present should sit in meditation surrounding the scryer.

Honoring the Dead

The following ritual was penned by my friend Dave Gaddy, author of *The Simple Magic of Wild Things* (Arabi Manor 2024). I was fortunate to attend Dave performing this as a group ritual. I found it a beautiful and powerful way to honor and connect with one's ancestors.

First cleanse your space. Perform this in front of our ancestral altar. If you have not already set one up, it is perfectly fine to create a temporary one arranging photos, mementos, symbols, and offerings that represent your ancestors and their cultural heritage.

Light a candle or candles on the altar; white, black, or purple are appropriate colors. These symbolize the presence of your ancestors.

Meditate and ground yourself. Visualize a connection with your ancestral lineage.

Now, speaking a heartfelt invocation, call upon your ancestors by name or by referring to them as a collective ancestral presence. Express gratitude for their presence, guidance, and the wisdom they bring to your life.

Place offerings on the altar that hold significance to your ancestors, such as food, drinks, flowers, or other items representing their cultural traditions.

Speak to your ancestors, sharing stories, asking for guidance, or expressing any concerns or intentions you have. Listen attentively for any messages, signs, or sensations you may receive in response.

Perform specific rituals or actions associated with your ancestral traditions or beliefs. This could include chanting, singing ancestral songs, reciting prayers, or conducting rituals unique to your ancestral lineage. If you have specific rituals passed down through your family, honor and incorporate them into the ritual as well.

Ancestral Invocation:

Oh, ancestors of my blood and spirit,
I call upon you with reverence and love.
I honor the lineage from which I have come,
The roots that anchor me, the branches that uplift me.

With open heart and humble spirit,
I invite you into this sacred space.
Guide my steps, lend me your wisdom,
And bless me with your ancestral grace.

Name specific ancestors if desired, or address the collective ancestral presence.

Beloved ancestors, whose stories reside within me,
I honor your struggles, triumphs, and resilience.
May your legacy shine through my actions,
As I walk this path, united with your essence.

I seek your guidance in times of doubt,
Your strength in times of challenge,
Your love in times of sorrow,
And your presence in all aspects of my life.

In this sacred union of past and present,
I offer gratitude for your presence and guidance.
May your wisdom flow through my being,
As I embrace the lessons you bestow upon me.

With deep respect and eternal love,
I express my gratitude to the ancestors,
And honor the connection that forever binds us.

Thank you, beloved ancestors,
For your eternal presence and blessings.

So mote it be.

Express gratitude: Thank your ancestors for their presence, guidance, and the blessings they bring to your life. Extinguish the candle(s) or leave them burning safely, depending on your preference and the duration of the ritual. Close the ritual space, concluding the ritual by thanking the spirits, guides, or deities you invoked and express your intention to close the ritual space.

Wortcunning

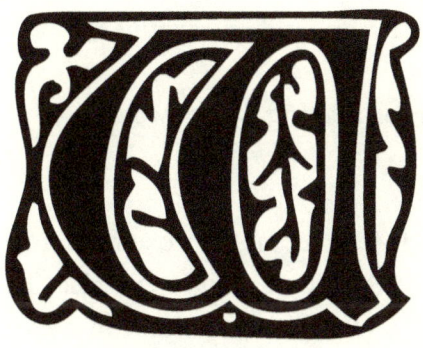

What follows is magickal herbalism, not medical. We do not recommend the ingestion of herbs other than common herbal teas. Other medicinal or internal use should follow the advice of a trained medicinal herbalist.

In witchcraft, herbs are utilized in a number of ways: incense, baths, to dress candles, oils, tinctures, pillows/sachets, powders, teas, asperging, amulets, and offerings. In addition to the traditional plants utilized by our witch ancestors in Europe, American conjure tradition provides a rich resource specific to the plants common to the southern United States.

When harvesting herbs, you should pay attention to the lunar and planetary influences on the day/time. The waxing moon is a good time to gather green herbs, while the waning moon is ideal for roots and poisonous plants. Try to gather at a time connected to the plants ruling planet. Always ask permission before harvesting. This is particularly true with trees. Never harvest the entire plant. Tell the plant that you will pay for its sacrifice. If you sense resistance, leave it and find another. Always leave payment behind, such as coins, honey, or your own blood, hair, or spittle.

Do not place harvested herbs directly on the earth. Hang them upside down in a cool, dry, dark place to dry.

Tools useful in magickal herbalism include:

Mortar and pestle. It will be useful to have several sets eventually dedicated to green herbs, resins, and poisonous materials.
Harvesting blade
Mixing bowls
Glass bottles (dark preferable) and eyedroppers;
Mason jars
An electric spice grinder for making fine powders
A nutmeg grinder

In blending perfumed oils, it is acceptable to use fragrance oils instead of essential oils. Fragrance oils may also be purchased in skin-safe formulas, which makes them ideal for perfumed oils to be worn on the skin. I use a carrier oil of almond as a base.

Following is a discussion of only a selection of herbs based on my own shelves containing what I regularly keep on hand. It is essential for the witch to obtain an appropriate herbal encyclopedia such as those by Paul Beyerl or Scott Cunningham.

One is encouraged to seek guidance from a professional medicinal herbalist prior to taking any herb internally.

ALKANET

Alkanet may be burned to remove negative energy and attract prosperity.

ANGELICA

Angelica has long been treasured for its protective properties, especially against spells, curses, and malignant magics. It has a very powerful and distinctive fragrance; thus, it is a great addition to protective incense. Sprinkle powdered Angelica at the four corners of your house for protection. A bath infusion is a powerful tool to remove hexes and cleanse the body of negativity.

BARLEY

We know barley best through its fermented incarnation as ale and spirits. In this form, it has long been given as an offering and is central to the toast of the houzel. It may be sprinkled on the ground outside one's home as a means of protection. In medieval England, clergy condemned the burning of barley on fresh graves. This may have been a practice of sending off, but it just as possible was to protect the surviving relatives from the specter of the deceased returning.

BAY

In addition to its culinary role, bay is a very useful plant. Planting one in your yard brings luck and protection. The dried leaves may be placed on the sills or worn as a protective amulet. Placed beneath the pillow, it protects against unpleasant dreams. The berries are a potent component of any working to attract money or luck.

BORAGE

In Uppy's garden, borage grew wild. I remember she would weed

CALAMUS ROOT

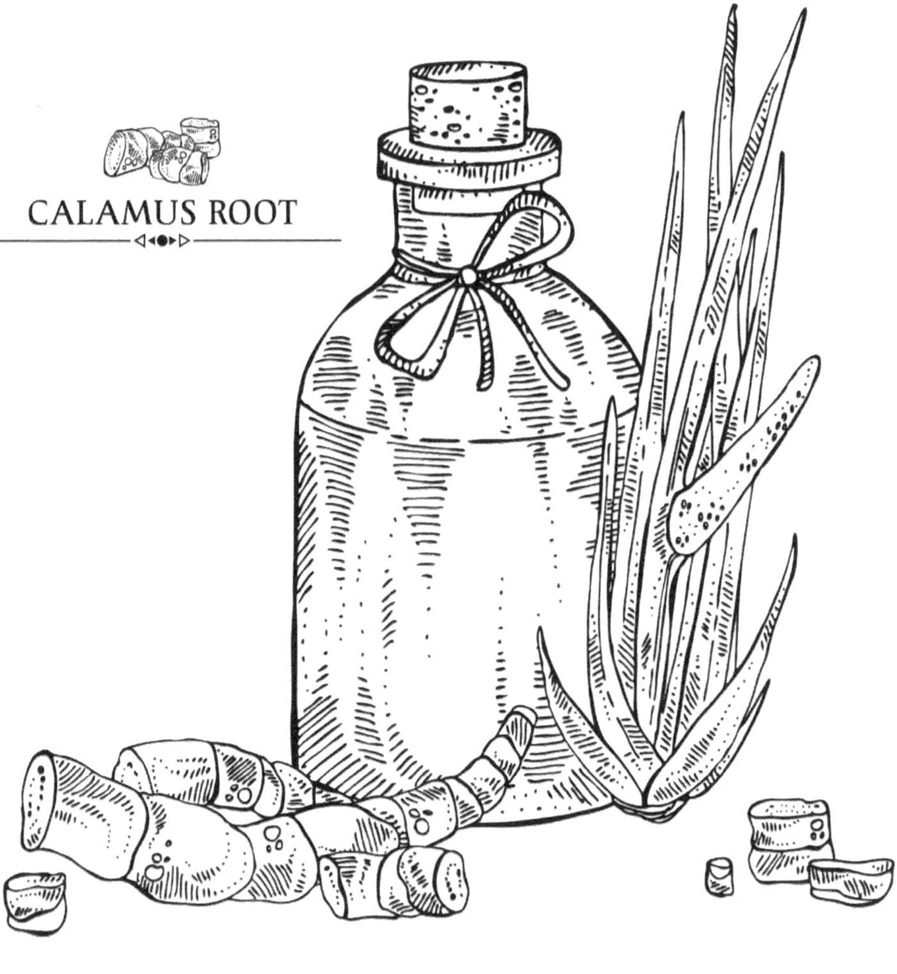

around it—the distinctive blue flowers coloring the garden at random. Borage has long been connected with strength and courage. The flowers may be floated in a ritual bath. The dried herb may be brewed into a tea to lift your spirits. The roots may be dried, powdered, and burned as an incense.

CALAMUS

In his collection *Leaves of Grass*, Walt Whitman includes a series of untitled poems he groups under the name "Calamus." They extol the virtues of same-sex love, what he terms "comradeship" and "adhesive love." He composed this series to counter the horrors he saw firsthand during the US Civil War. The poems speak to the emotional and spiritual components of male love, elevating it to the level of the mythic. He chose to name this section after the root of the calamus, a particular form of water grass, due to its phallic shape and light pink coloring.

The plant was long held to have a connection to sexuality. The root is highly fragrant when burned, so it makes a potent incense for male+male sexual rites. A bath in calamus would be fitting prior to such workings. Its oil makes an ideal anointing oil for such as well.

CHAMOMILE

Chamomile is another guardian plant to have in one's garden. It is an ideal herb for protection and invoking calm in the household. Powdered chamomile may be sprinkled as a protection. It is generally a bringer of success in any endeavor. An infusion added to your bathwater may be employed to attract love.

CLOVES

Cloves may be burned as incense to attract money and dispel bad luck. Either burned or ground with salt and sprinkled around your place of business on nine consecutive days, cloves are used to attract customers.[1]

COMFREY

Comfrey may be burned to bless a traveler before departing. Cunningham and Pearson note how the dried herb may be added to luggage to protect against it getting lost.[2] The leaves may also be used in spells for money or return of lost funds.

DITTANY OF CRETE

Dittany of Crete has long been burned as an incense. It is said to be potent in opening the way for communion with the spirits, especially those of the departed. Its smoke opens the way to the Underworld, and the plant is said to be sacred to Persephone. For this reason, it is an ideal addition to sabbat incense, especially rites around All Hallows. It was also once said that adding the herb to food or drink could make the recipient fall in love.

ELFWORT

May be burned for purification. The smoke is ideal for cleansing the person, particularly before entering a sacred space. There is also an aspect of the whimsical with this herb. Beyerl connects it to the Fool of the tarot.[3] Thus, it's a good herb to use when jumping off into the unknown.

FRANKINCENSE

Frankincense, along with it other resinous counterpart, myrrh, has been burned as an incense for millennia. It was prized throughout the Mediterranean by the Hebrews, Babylonians, Greeks, and Romans. It is universally used as an incense to purify and remove negative energies from a sacred space. It continues to be an important ingredient in church mixes to this day. Its properties are interesting as they can transit between the masculine and feminine. Thereby it is ideal for invoking primordial divinity that is beyond binary distinctions. A solid all-purpose ritual incense, it may also be used to bring good fortune, but only when the practitioner himself is balanced within.

HEATHER

Heather may be used to bring joy. It also makes a fitting incense for attracting the benevolent spirits of the dead. In combination with ferns, its burning was said to attract rain.

HOREHOUND

An infusion of horehound may be used to bring clarity and calm the mind, especially ahead of ritual or divinatory work. As an incense, it is helpful in purification and keeping negativity at bay. It has long been connected to exorcisms and may be sprinkled on the ground to dispatch baneful spirits.

HORNY GOAT WEED

Horny goat weed has a strong connection to male sexual magic. Chinese medicine has long used the herb to enhance male libido and treat erectile dysfunction. Burn as an incense to the libidinous spirit of the Horned One—the White Stag in his rut. Use as a tincture before enacting sexual rites.

HYACINTH

Hyancinthus was a human youth beloved of Apollo. This makes it an ideal herb where love between men is the matter at hand. Its strong and alluring fragrance is powerful in attracting love. Beyerl refers to hyacinth as the "patron herbe" of gay men.[4] Jeffrey Whitfield incorporates it in his potent formula Hyakintos Oil (see formulary).

HYSSOP

Hyssop has long been associated with purification and cleansing. Bunches may be dried and hung over doorways and windows to protect the home. It is an ideal herb to add to cleansing baths. I use an infusion of hyssop to cleanse the feet of those seeking purification from negative forces. Great for washing one's magical tools.

JUNIPER

Juniper is a protective herb. The foliage and berries have long been burned as a home purification. In the Scottish Highlands, saining with a bundle of juniper was common on New Year's Day to remove any evil spirits that might have entered during the preceding year and to welcome in good fortune for the year to come. See section on saining later in this chapter.

LADY'S MANTLE

Uppy's English garden featured a large patch of lady's mantle, so this particular plant has always had a place close to my heart. It has had a long connection to the Mother Goddess—one which transferred to the Virgin Mary with the intrusion of Christianity. Its broad, cupped leaves collect the morning dew, which is a potent addition to any spell. The leaves may be incorporated into a love sachet. The Irish prized the plant's ability to counteract the ill effects of Elf-shot.

LINGONBERRIES

Rich in antioxidants, anticancer, and anti-inflammatory properties, lingonberries are extremely helpful in promoting good health. They provide important sustenance to the forest's creatures, such as foxes and birds. The berries were also an important food source for the Nordic Sami peoples. They have long been prized for their medicinal properties and may be employed for spells relating to maintaining health and wellness.

MEADOWSWEET

This summer flower is sacred to the Goddess. Fresh meadowsweet placed on the altar attracts her love. It may be used in love spells or placed in handfasting floral arrangements to bless the union.

MARJORAM

Marjoram is another plant sacred to the Goddess, particularly Venus and Aphrodite. It is useful as a component of love spells. Like meadowsweet, it is also an ideal decoration at handfastings.

MOONWORT

Linked to the moon, the plant was held by Alchemists to have the property of transmuting metals. In this connection of pouring forth silver, it is ideal for use in money drawing spells. Legend held that horses crossing a field with the plant would have their shoes loosed through is transformative properties relative to metals. The unshoeing of horses was long connected with its sorcery due to the crescent shape of its frond.[5]

MOTHERWORT

Motherwort is treasured for its ability to strengthen the potency of any working to which it is added. It is an ideal ingredient in incense or magical pouches. It also has strong protective properties and is a good component of countermagic.

MUGWORT

Mugwort is prized for its ability to enhance clairvoyance and divinatory properties. An infusion may be used as wax for a crystal ball or magic mirror. It may be burned as an incense during divinatory operations. The plant is also known for its protective and banishing properties.

It should be noted that mugwort, sometimes called wild wormwood, is often confused with wormwood. Though members of the same genus, Artemisia, they are distinctly different plants. Mugwort is Artemisia vulgaris and wormwood Artemisia absinthium. Both are native to Northern Europe. Mugwort is a common medicinal herb and has many magical uses as discussed above. Wormwood on the other hand is best known for its use in the making of Absinthe. It contains the chemical thujone which is thought to imbue absinthe with its mild hallucinatory properties.

MYRRH

Combined with frankincense, myrrh is burned to cleanse and purify sacred space, invoking a general ambiance of spiritual calm. Its banishing properties make its smoke effective in blessing working tools and protective amulets.

NETTLE

Nettle may be used to turn back malevolent magic toward the sender or to protect against ghosts and other nasties. Sprinkle about the house as a warding. Combine with Yarrow to dispel fear. Can be used to speed recovery when placed beneath a sickbed.

PATCHOULI

Patchouli is one of the most commonly used protective herbs. It may be burned, added to magical sachets, or used as an infusion in a protective bath.

ROSE

It likely will come as no surprise that Rose has long been turned to in matters concerning love. It is one of the most common ingredients in love mixtures. However, rose hip tea may be used to bring on prophetic dreams. It is also often found as an ingredient in oils and sachets designed to attract luck.

ROSEMARY

Rosemary has long been associated with the Mighty Dead and the remembrance of those departed. It was often placed inside the coffin. For these reasons, it is an ideal incense for All Hallows and the dark interstitial time of the year when the dead are closest to us in space and memory. It may also aid memory in general. Water sprinkled by a rosemary twig is a powerful cleansing. It is also said that its pungent scent attracts the attention of elves, making it ideal when working with the good neighbors.

RUE

Since the Middles Ages, rue has been used to counteract the malevolent intentions of witches. The plant has powerful protective properties and can turn back curses and may be added to bath water for that purpose. Wearing rue around the neck was said to hasten recovery from illness. The juice of the fresh plant may be mixed with dew collected from lady's mantle leaves to draw a powerful protective circle about oneself.

THISTLE

Thistles are known for their complementary powers of protection and strength. The varieties of thistles are numerous and varied—several hundred species across fifteen genera. The thistle is familiar to many as the national flower of Scotland. Its origin story holds that in the eleventh century, a group of invading Danes landed on a shore replete with prickly thistles. Upon encountering the scratchy balustrade, their loud reaction awakened the local populace, who rose to the land's defense and successfully repelled the invaders. Since then, it has been venerated for its protection, strength, and aid in overcoming adversity. The plant's hardiness denotes perseverance.

Blessed or Holy Thistle (*Centaurea benedicta*) may be worn or added to bath water for protection and evil away. Its countermagic properties make it ideal for breaking hexes.

Milk Thistle (*Silybum marianum*) has many medicinal uses, and tea promotes health. Lore associates the plant's milk-white sap with the milk of the Virgin Mary. This connection may date back to older customs, and it is appropriate to hold this plant as sacred to the young goddess. Modern herbalists speak of its detoxifying properties and suggest its tea as beneficial to the liver.

In Scotland, a tea made from Melancholy Thistle (*Cirsium heterophyllum*) was said to dispel sorrow and madness.[6]

THYME

The ancients used thyme to purify their temples. It may be burned in one's temple space prior to erecting the Grove. It has a strong connection to the spirits of the dead. A bundle of thyme was brought into the house to be an abode for the departed until the coffin was removed for burial.[7] A bath infused with thyme and marjoram is good for removing sorrows and ill fortune—especially fitting at the start of a new year.

WITCH HAZEL

Witch Hazel has a long association with the witch's craft. It is highly valued for its protective properties. It may be commonly found as an astringent. Authentic witch hazel tincture may be used as a wash or sprayed around the house to take advantage of its defensive properties.

SAINING

The Scottish word saining (Gaelic: seun) means the act of consecrating or blessing or protecting. It is analogous to holy or make holy. Sain Water is water in which a sacred object has been dunked to bless it. Similar to smudging, saining is a very traditional means of sanctifying or purifying people, livestock, objects, and places. The focus is on removing negative spirits, not on cleansing negativity.

It is similar to the use of smudge sticks by Native Americans or palo santo in South America. There is much concern and discussion currently about use of these by non-native peoples as cultural appropriation. Certainly, the cherry-picked adoption of certain materials and techniques, from once colonized indigenous peoples, by the New Age and commercial spirituality movements should be discussed.

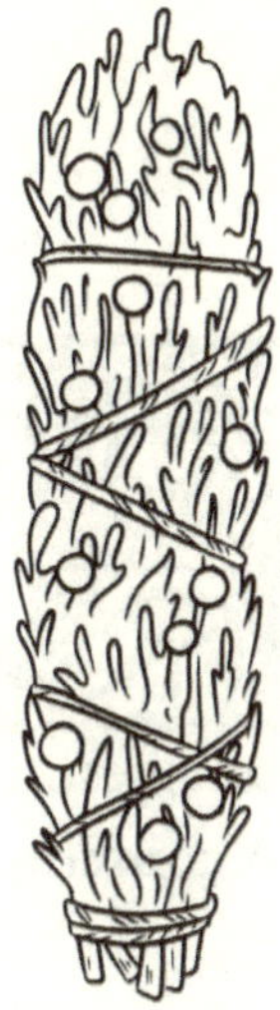

We can learn much from other cultures and traditions. It is less problematic when one approaches them with an attitude of openness and respect to understand the significance of the use in their specific cultural context. I find attempts to "gatekeep" just as troubling.

The act of saining, common to Scotland and other Gaelic peoples, is culturally relevant and appropriate for those of Western European descent.

Saining is generally done one of two ways through the use of water or fire/burning.

One may take a juniper bough and use it either to sprinkle water on the intended recipient target or, like smudging, light the bough and use the smoke. Other herbal items may be employed as well, such as rowan, elder, mugwort, pine, or rosemary.

Rowan was often brought into the house on Baltaine for a similar purpose.

NINE HERB CHARM

First written down in the tenth century, the Nine Herbs Charm is an important example of Old English herbal craft. It is one of only texts of the period that clearly reference the pre-Christian Woden outside of royal genealogies.

A contemporary translation of a tenth-century version:

Remember, Mugwort, what you made known,
What you arranged at the Great proclamation.
You were called Una, the oldest of herbs,
you have power against three and against thirty,
you have power against poison and against infection,
you have power against the loathsome foe roving through the land.
And you, Plantain, mother of herbs,
Open from the east, mighty inside.
over you chariots creaked, over you queens rode,
over you brides cried out, over you bulls snorted.
You withstood all of them, you dashed against them.
May you likewise withstand poison and infection
and the loathsome foe roving through the land.
'Stune' is the name of this herb, it grew on a stone,
it stands up against poison, it dashes against poison
Nettle (?) it is called, it attacks against poison,
it drives out the hostile one, it casts out poison.
This is the herb that fought against the serpent,
it has power against poison, it has power against

infection,
it has power against the loathsome foe roving through the land.
Put to flight now, Venom-loather, the greater poisons,
though you are the lesser, until he is cured of both.
Remember, Chamomile, what you made known,
what you accomplished at Alorford,
that never a man should lose his life from infection
after Chamomile was prepared for his food.
This is the herb that is called 'Wergulu.'
A seal sent it across the sea-right,
a vexation to poison, a help to others.
it stands against pain, it dashes against poison,
A worm came crawling, it killed nothing.
For Woden took nine glory-twigs,
he smote the adder that it flew apart into nine parts.
There the Apple accomplished it against poison
that she [the loathsome serpent] would never dwell in the house.
Chervil and Fennell, two of much might,
They were created by the wise Lord,
holy in heaven as He hung;
He set and sent them to the seven worlds,
to the wretched and the fortunate, as a help to all.

Lay of the Nine Twigs of Woden
It stands against pain, it fights against poison,
it avails against 3 and against 30,
against foe's hand and against noble scheming,
against enchantment of vile creatures.
Now there nine herbs have power against nine evil spirits,

against nine poisons and against nine infections:
Against the red poison, against the foul poison,
against the white poison, against the pale blue poison,
against the yellow poison, against the green poison,
against the black poison, against the blue poison,
against the brown poison, against the crimson poison,
against worm-blister, against water-blister,
against thorn-blister, against thistle-blister,
against ice-blister, against poison-blister,
If any poison comes flying from the east,
or any from the north, [or any from the south,]
or any from the west among the people.
Christ stood over diseases of every kind.
I alone know a running stream,
and the nine adders beware of it.
May all the weeds spring up from their roots,
the seas slip apart, all salt water,
when I blow this poison from you.[8]

The nine ingredients are: una or mugwort, waybread or plantain, stune or lambda cress, atterlothe or betony, myth or chamomile, wegulu or nettle, crabapple, chervil, and fennel.

For preparation of a modern salve based on the nine herbs charm, pulverize the herbs with a mortar and pestle. Next, infuse them in oil. Place the herbs into a sealable jar. Pour enough oil over them to cover them completely. It is best to used dried herbs as their lack of moisture content will help prevent spoilage. Place the jar in a dark place. Let sit for several weeks. Agitate occasionally. The longer they sit, the more potent the cold infusion.

Next, wrapping an ounce of beeswax in a towel, break up

the wax into small chunks. Place the beeswax in a double boiler and melt slowly. Add four ounces of the herb-infused oil and stir until mixed well. Remove from heat and quickly pour the mixture into tins or heat-resistant jars such as those used for canning. The consistency of the salve may be adjusted by using more or less beeswax. The more wax, the firmer the end result.

Formulary

What follows is a small selection of oils and incense I have used often and have particular connection to topics covered in this book. Several of these originate from Herman Slater's *Magickal Formulary* with my own adaptations. The are a few very comprehensive formulary books available and I encourage you to explore them. I will particularly note the Lady Rhea's *Magical Formulary*. For oils, I start with a base of Almond Oil to which I add skin-safe fragance oil. This is a much safer technique for multi-purpose usage as many essential oils may cause skin irritation or cause allergic reactions.

PURPOSE OILS

ANOINTING OIL

2 parts	Cinnamon
2 parts	Patchouli
1 parts	Verbena

A little camphor

CROWN OF SUCCESS

An oil to bring success and stop gossip.

1 parts	Clove
2 parts	Neroli
1 parts	Orange
2 parts	Sandalwood
1 parts	Whole Clove

XI° OIL

The Eleventh Degree was a degree in the Ordo Templi Orientis, the occult order Crowley headed. It has a particular relationship to queer magick and the initiatory powers of anal intercourse.

Equal parts
- Ambergris
- Frankincense
- Lilac
- Lily
- Rose

FAST LUCK

Half Patchouli & Rose
A few drops of Juniper
3 Juniper berries

FRENCH CREOLE

A formula to conjure prophetic dreams and make one's dreams come true.

Equal parts
- African Musk
- Bay
- Lilac
- Lime

HAS NO HANNA

A traditional recipe to attract money. Use to annoint money to attract more of the same.

Equal parts
- Gardenia
- Rose
- A small open safety pin

HERMES

1 parts	Lavender
1 parts	Sandalwood
2 parts	Vanilla

Zephyrus & Hyakintos based on a c. mid 5th century BCE pottery shard held by the Metropolitan Museum (vase no. 211738)

HYAKINTOS OIL

This oil was formulated by Jeffrey Whitfield, a brother who worked at Enchantments New York City crafting their famous oils. See the section in the Mighty Dead. Hyakintos was a handsome, young Spartan prince who was wooed by both Apollo and Zephyrus personification of the West wind. In the words of Lady Rhea, this oil "is Jeffrey's thumbprint that he left behind."[1]

A 50/50 blend of Hyacinth & Lily of the Valley
A few drops Neroli

A few drops Cinnamon
One drop of your own blood (optional)

OSCAR WILDE

Another of Jeffrey's oil blends designed to evoke the humorous, camp power of gay men. Ideal for Gay Pride.[2]

1 parts	Arabian Musk
2 parts	Hyacinth
1 parts	Opium
4 parts	Sandalwood

SAINT EXPEDITÉ

Equal parts
Allspice
Ambergris
Cinnamon
Honeysuckle
Sandalwood

UNCROSSING BATH

Add to bath water each day for seven days

Hyssop
Lavender

Lemon
Patchouli

A drop or two of Mrs. Crawford's Bluing

Mix into a warm soap base, such as castile.

INCENSE

PROSPERITY INCENSE

My own adaptation of a recipe by Scott Cunningham.

2 parts Frankincense
1 part Cinnamon
1 part Nutmeg
1 part Lemon Verbena
1 part Lemon Grass

SEAX INCENSE

Slater provides the following recipe for Seax or Saxon incense.[3] It is highly unlikely the British Saxons would have access to many of the ingredients such as Myrrh and Frankincense.

2 parts Cinnamon
8 parts Frankincense
2 parts Myrrh
1 part Orris Root

1 part Patchouli
6 parts Sandalwood

KYPHI INCENSE

A general purpose Egyptian ritual blend from the *Ebers Papyrus* (circa 1500 BC). I still have a small amount of this incense purchased from the Childe that I save for very special occasions.

8 tbsp. ground frankincense
4 tsp. ground mastic
4 tsp. calamus / sweet flag root
4 tsp. dried lemon grass
4 tsp. dried mint leaves
4 tsp. dried & ground juniper berries
4 tsp. ground cinnamon
Honey

Heat oven to the lowest setting and then shut off for ten minutes. Heat on baker's parchment for ten minutes

INCENSE FOR SEXUAL RITES

Combine equal parts:

Calamus Root
Dittany of Crete
Frankincense & Myrrh

FOUR THIEVES VINEGAR

Vinaigre des 4 Voleurs (Four Thieves Vinegar) is an historic recipe first crafted to protect against plagues. The preparation likely dates back to the medieval period. It is said that it was first used to combat the Black Death.

Vinegar or wines infused with herbs were employed against disease going back into antiquity. Similar preparations were used during the time of Hippocrates. Apple cider vinegar is noted for its antimicrobial properties. This recipe is edible and, mixed with virgin olive oil, makes a very nice vinaigrette.

According to the folklore, the name derives from four thieves who would steal from the dead. Once apprehended, they traded the recipe for the concoction that kept them safe from contracting disease in exchange for leniency. The incident is said to have occurred in Marseilles or Toulouse and the formula is also known as Marseilles Vinegar.

1 tbsp. dried sage leaf
1 tsp. dried lavender flowers
1 tsp. dried rosemary leaf
1/2 tsp. dried thyme leaf
1/2 tsp. black peppercorns
16 oz. raw organic apple cider vinegar
1 pint jar

Place all the dry herbs in the pint jar. Pour vinegar over the herbs until the jar is full.

Store in a cool dry and dark location for few weeks. Shake every couple of days to stir up the herbs. Strain and use.

Divination

The Universe is interconnected across dimensions and time. It forms a web, a blanket of twinkling stars. A singularity (intersection of space, time, and intention) has a ripple effect, just as when a rock is cast into a pond. Often, these connections are not obvious.

Divination methods are microcosmic systems that represent the vastness of the macrocosm. Oracular devices may be used to divine the future. or a set of potentialities based on current directionality. In addition, they may be utilized to analyze a situation. Different techniques are more or less suited for given applications.

There are numerous tools and methods. Key among them are the Tarot, Runes, I Ching, petite Lenormand cards, scrying, bibliomancy, pendulums, palmistry, and tea leaves.

Each witch chooses the techniques that work for them, but proficiency in at least one technique is crucial.

Often, the witch discovers a reading Spirit available to assist in Divination. It is essential to foster and nurture this relationship.

THE TAROT

There are a seemingly endless number of decks and thematic variations out there. It is best to start with a deck based on the most common symbolism from the Rider-Waite/ Smith-Coleman deck (Centennial edition / 1909 Facsimile). Many editions of this deck are available. In addition, numerous decks are based on its symbolism. For example, my first deck—which I still use often today—was the Morgan-Greer deck, which has contemporary artwork based on the RW /SC card designs.

I recommend beginning with a deck based on the traditional Rider-Waite-Smith symbolism. Many versions of this classic deck are available, and others employ artwork based on the original designs. My first deck was the Morgan Greer, which combines the RWS images with the color theory of Oswald Wirth. The Robin Wood deck merges RWS symbolism with the Celtic motif. Another deck drawn by a queer elder is Paul Huson's Dame Fortune's Wheel Tarot.

Once you have the basics down, you may move to a deck that fits your personal taste. I often use The Wildwood Tarot myself. One criterion I find essential when choosing a deck is that the minor arcana cards have full illustrations rather than just a depiction of the numbers of the suit, e.g., five swords, similar to traditional playing cards. Another thing to look out for are decks with multiple Lovers cards suited for different sexual pairings. The Cosmic Tribe Tarot featuring the art of Stevee Postman is one of these, and the imagery is beautiful and queer.

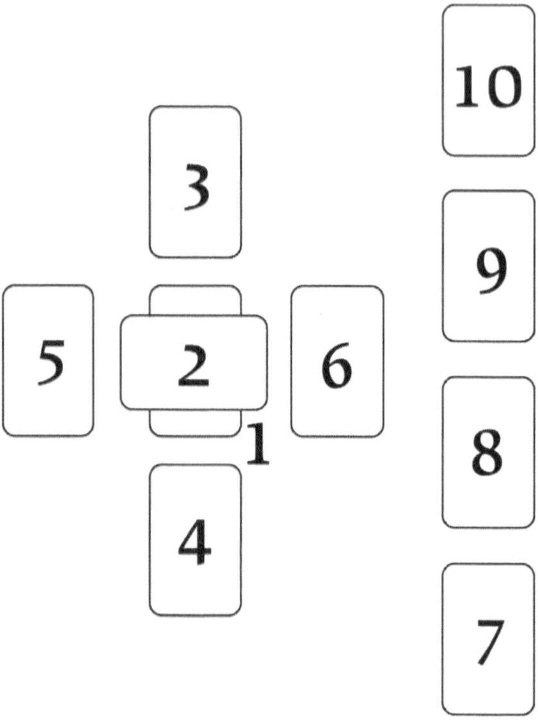

CELTIC CROSS SPREAD

This classic ten-card spread is likely the most commonly used of all spreads. The layout is in the form of a cross with four additional cards set to the right.

1 — The self, the querent or subject of the reading

2 — What crosses the querent, the problem, or what lies in opposition to the self

3 — The influence of the conscious mind

4 — The unseen or influences of the unconscious mind

5 — The past: elements of the past that impact the current situation

6 — The future: how the immediate future intersects with the situation

7 — The querent's perception: this is what the querent brings to the situation

8 — External influences, the thoughts or opinions of others

9 — The querent's hopes and desires

10 — The outcome: a summation card

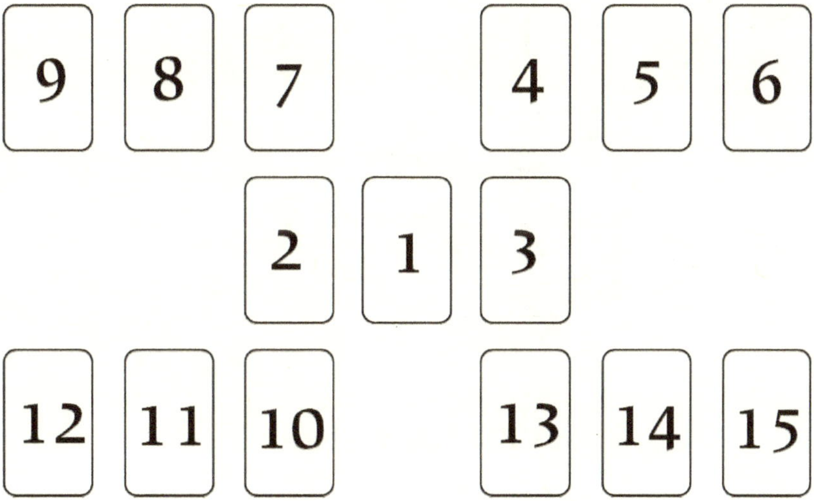

THE GOLDEN DAWN SPREAD

We always stand at a forked path at any given moment, faced with at least two choices. This spread is ideal for examining the decision and the factors that influence it. The reading is laid out in five sets of three cards each. The first three cards reflect the querent at present. The right upper triad is the future on one's current trajectory, the inclined choice. The left upper grouping represents the other fork taken if we choose the alternate path. The lower two groupings of cards are the influences on the matter in question. The lower left cards reflect our inner thoughts and desires, which are within our control. The lower right reflects the Universal forces that impact our path forward. These are immutable and are to be dealt with; they are not within our control to change.

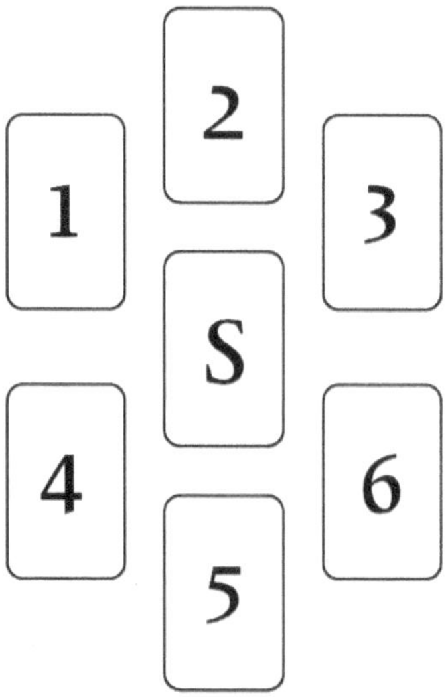

SEVEN CARD SPREAD

The following is a method well-suited to analyzing a situation. First, select a significator to stand for either the subject of the reading or a card representing the nature of the question being asked. Above the significator are the cards in the upward-facing point of a diamond. Below are three cards for the downward descending point. The upper three card represent the favorable influences on the matter at hand. The lower three illuminate the influences standing against a positive outcome.

THE PETIT LENORMAND

The Petit Lenormand is a set of thirty-six cards similar to a subset of playing cards but containing other symbolism initially introduced in the German deck The Game of Hope in the late eighteenth century. The Lenormand became highly popular in nineteenth-century France. Their popularity was attributed to the French fortune teller whose name would become synonymous with the deck. Lenormand is gaining in popularity, and variations on the original card set are becoming widely available. Again, beginning one's Lenormand journey with a deck that stays close to the original symbolism is best.

Where the tarot is ideal for analyzing the underlying influences and psychology of a given situation, the Lenormand is very straightforward. Its answers are very direct. Whereas in interpreting tarot, placement is often more important than the relationship between individual cards in a reading, for Lenormand, the cards are read together as one would read a sentence with subject, verb, and modifiers.

THE PENDULUM

The history of pendulums used for dowsing or divination dates back to ancient Egypt and Rome. In the simplest form, a pendulum or any object dangling on a string may be used for yes/no questions—one direction or type of motion (circle vs. line) for yes and the other for no. You can get to know the personality of your tool by asking the symbol for yes and no and noting its movement. Pendulums may also be used over a map to determine the location of a person or object. Modern dowsing boards are also available in many forms, similar to a small Ouija board.

DREAMS

Every witch should pay attention to their dreams. Keep a dream journal and take note of events that occur during sleep. Remember, dreams are a symbolic landscape that draws upon your memories as its language. Characters that arise in dreams may not be who they seem.

The Witch Runes

Throwing lots has a long history. After visiting the German territories outside the Roman Empire in the late first century, Tacitus described their practice of casting lots:

> For divination and the casting of lots they have the highest regard. Their procedure in casting lots is always the same. They cut off a branch of a nut-bearing tree and slice it into strips; these they mark with different signs and throw them completely at random onto a white cloth. Then the priest of the state, if the consultation is a public one, or the father of the family if it is private, offers a prayer to the gods, and looking up at the sky picks up three strips, one at a time, and reads their meaning from the signs previously scored on them.[1]

The Romans practiced sortes, where symbols or words were written on small pieces of wood. These were then dropped into an urn of water or thrown. The way they landed portended the future.

Our modern practice of runic divination combines the runes with the Roman methodology. Tacitus is the only contemporary source pointing to the Norse throwing lots as divination. He stops short of describing the "signs" upon them as the runic characters. It is possible that they were, but it is also possible they were other symbols. They could also have depicted bind runes, combinations of several characters with particular meanings.

Whatever the case, the modern practice of drawing or casting runes has developed a solid modern history and is here to stay. We will discuss two variations of the theme. The first is a small set of eight to thirteen symbols called the witch's runes or witch stones. The second is more akin to what many are familiar with from the Norse runic alphabet but focuses on the Anglo-Saxon version.

I first encountered the witch stones or witch's runes in Patricia Crowther's book *Lid Off the Cauldron*. Crowther describes a set of eight symbols. This is a simple yet highly effective predictive system. No one I have come across has managed to research its origins successfully. Several variations are available, the most commonly known today being a set of thirteen stones. I, however, still prefer the eight that Crowther describes. They align with the year's ceremonial wheel and seem to be the earlier iteration of the iconography.

It is easy to make your own set, though sets of eight and thirteen are also available on Etsy. The first set I made was of clay. My current set is burned into wood. One may also find eight flat stones of similar size and paint the symbols on them. The only criteria are that they should have a 50/50 probability of landing sign up/mark down, whatever material and shape.

THE METHOD

Spread out a reading cloth and light a white candle. Hold all eight runes in one hand. Think of the question you are asking. Exhale onto the runes. Toss them away from you. When reading, you note those that fell face up, starting with the rune farthest from you, known as the "leading rune." Pay attention to the proximity of runes to each other as each is read in the context of those adjacent.

MEANING

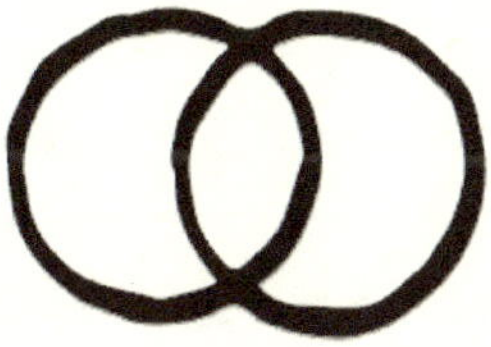

The Rings denote a positive outcome to any question about love, marriage, or connection issues. When the leading rune, it is a strong Yes. Engagement, marriage, a new love, emotional bond, strong friendship. It may also denote a successful agreement, contract, or mutual resolution when the questions regard business. It may mean completing a matter or a project coming to fruition.

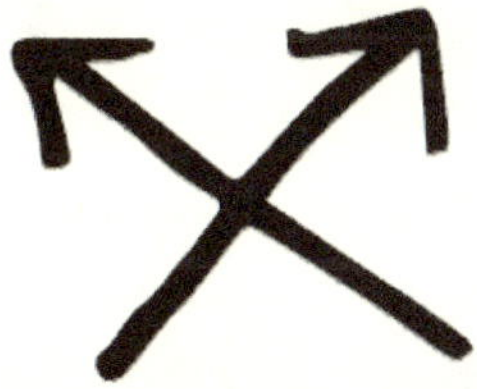

Crossed Arrows is when the leading rune means quarrels, disagreement, or strife. It may be a sudden, upsetting, unexpected occurrence. If it is near a fortunate stone, it likely means settling an argument or resolving a quarrel. A promotion may be in the offing if the querent is an armed forces member. It falls near the Rings and predicts the healing of a love relationship that has broken off. In questions of health, it means a swift recovery.

Birds in flight predict the arrival of unexpected news. If the birds are the leading rune, it could be news that changes one's life, often for the better. When near fortunate runes, it means documents or letters that bring positive influence. It may be news of a relative or a message from a distant friend.

Snake or wavy line stands for family, relatives, kinfolk, and their effect on the querent. When near the Sun, it may presage a long journey. When near the Moon, it means a journey to a relative. When near the Ring, it may mean a relationship at a distance.

The Rayed Sun represents a favorable omen for success. The sun reflects growth. When it is the leading rune, it means a successful outcome or a good year ahead. It represents honor, fame, and empowerment. It may stand for a man in the reading as well.

The Moon forecasts a change in position or circumstance within the coming twenty-eight days when in the leading position. Pay careful attention to the runes nearby. If the nearest is positive, the change will be positive; if negative, it will be a turn for the worse. The glyph is marked with four Xs denoting the four phases of the lunar cycle. This may mean a woman or conception.

The Sheaf of Grain is a lucky omen. As the leading rune, it means a positive, happy, prosperous outcome. It is an emblem of growth. It presages expansion in all things: money, luck, and love. When adjacent to the Sun, it means a growth in wealth or career. When near the Rings, it means a wealthy marriage. In the Americas, it is also appropriate to depict an ear of corn.

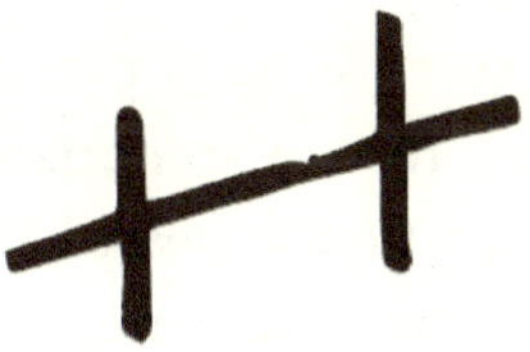

The Black Rune has a symbol of three lines similar to an H. It denotes grief, loss, or something unfortunate in the offing. This rune should always be read in the context of the other runes unless it is the only one face up. The stones around it often mitigate and nuance its meaning, initially appearing negatively. For example, if near the Moon, it means an unfortunate circumstance that will change for the better in the next twenty-eight days.

The Runes

What you ask the runes
will prove true;
they are of divine origin,
made by the mighty gods
and painted by Óðin.
You'll learn best with your mouth shut.

— *The Hávamál*[1]

You are most likely at least somewhat aware of the Norse runes. These twenty-four characters are by far the most common in modern occult texts. For his part, Gardner included the Theban Runes within his writing, and this has been passed down through the Gardnerian/Alexandrian lineages. This beautiful script first appeared in the early sixteenth century as a table in Johannes Trithemius's *Polygraphia*. The origin source from which Trithemius drew has not been identified. Though evocatively beautiful, the alphabet has little to do with British witchcraft. Gardner, no doubt, lifted them from a grimoire or similar magical text as he did with much of his early source material. Gardner's prejudices against Anglo-Saxons very likely underlaid his choice to ignore the Anglo-Saxon rune set, a uniquely English variant of the proto-Germanic runes.

Runes have a rich history rooted in the ancient Germanic

and Norse cultures. Runes originated around the second century CE among the Germanic tribes of Europe, particularly in what is now Denmark, Germany, and Sweden. The word "rune" itself comes from the Old Norse word "rún," meaning "secret" or "mystery."

The Norse runic alphabet, known as the Futhark or Futhorc in Old English, consists of characters made up of straight lines. Early runic inscriptions were typically used for memorializing or marking objects. There are several different runic alphabets, with the Elder Futhark being the earliest known and most widely used.

Runes held deep symbolic and magical significance for the ancient Germanic peoples. The sagas speak of how the runic alphabet was obtained by Óðin through his sacrifice on the World Tree and then gifted to humankind. Over the years, they have been used in various contexts, including protection, blessings, and divination. Runic inscriptions have been found on amulets, weapons, tools, and tombstones.

Runic divination, known as "rune casting" or "casting the runes," involves drawing, casting, or tossing runes, and interpreting their positions and relationships to answer questions or gain insight. Each rune is associated with specific meanings, much like a deck of tarot cards.

In addition to their symbolic meanings, runes are associated with poetic verses known as "rune poems." These poems were used to remember the definitions and properties of each rune. Three versions of these poems survive the Norse, Icelandic, and Anglo-Saxon or Old English.

With the spread of Christianity in Scandinavia, the use of runes began to wane. The Latin alphabet gradually supplanted runic writing for most practical purposes. However, the tradition of runic divination and magic persisted in more secluded and esoteric circles. In the late nineteenth and early twentieth centuries, there was a resurgence of interest in Norse and Germanic folklore and spirituality. This revival sparked renewed interest in runic divination, and various runic systems were developed or reconstructed. In the early twentieth century, this resurgence took a darker turn. Key figures in the revival of German folklore also espoused racist beliefs, and the rising ideology of National Socialism readily adopted these. Runes and pseudo-anthropology featured prominently in most Nazi groups. This was most pronounced in Heinrich Himmler's Schutzstaffel or SS, whose symbol was two Sowilo runes.

Today, runes are used in various modern pagan and neopagan traditions and by individuals interested in divination, magic, and Norse spirituality. The most commonly available rune sets are those of the Norse Elder Futhark and contain twenty-four characters. These runes first developed among the early Germanic peoples. Their precise linguistic lineage remains open for debate, but they trace back to the Phoenician alphabet—a descendent of Egyptian hieroglyphics. The Anglo-Saxon, or Old English, runes have similar origins to the Norse runes of the Elder Futhark but developed along different lines after they arrived in the British Isles. They are a fitting magical alphabet for the British witch and one that Gardner did a disservice in ignoring in favor of the Theban alphabet.

The Anglo-Saxon Futhorc (Old English *runa*) consists of thirty-three characters, the first twenty-four similar to the Elder Futhark. The runes likely first came to Britain in the fifth century CE, brought by Saxon immigrants or through the influence of commerce-driven cultural transference. Rune poems, a stanza ascribed to each symbol, exist in Norse and Icelandic. A similar poem survives (somewhat miraculously) for the English runes. The poem dates back to an oral tradition as early as the eighth century. A Christian monk first wrote it down in the tenth century. This manuscript was destroyed by a fire at the Cotton Library in 1731. Thankfully, a copy had been transcribed by Humfrey Wanley and published by George Hickes in his 1705 work *Linguarum veterum septentrionalium thesaurus*. The English rune has a stanza poetically describing each rune through the twenty-ninth. The three extant rune poems—Norwegian, Icelandic, and English—have similarities, but the English also has marked differences from the others. I've used both the Elder Futhark and Old English Futhorc in my practice. Here, I only bring in the other rune poems when they speak to or enhance the meaning derived from Old English.

Similarly to the Elder Futhark, the Futhorc are divided into rows, called "Aetts," of eight named after the first letter in the row. These groupings have common traits with their analogs in the Elder Futhark, especially the first four rows. For the four runes not included in the rune poem, we have their names and their use in the context(s) from which they have been identified. I find that the Old English Rune Poem's themes are more natural than mythological compared to its Scandinavian siblings. What follows is a starting point drawing on the rune poems, the wisdom of modern practitioners, and my own time spent with both the Futhorc and Elder Futhark. The runes are deeply personal; if you find yourself connected to them, your own gnosis will develop with time.

What follows includes my own (slight) adaptation of the English Rune poem, drawing on Bruce Dickins *Runic and heroic poems of the old Teutonic peoples* of 1915. I have provided a rough pronunciation as Old English is not always intuitive. I recommend Suzanne Rance's *The English Runes*, listed in the suggested reading section, for a more in-depth pronunciation guide. Rs are usually rolled.

ᚠ

Feoh - Wealth, Cattle

Pronunciation: fay-och

Wealth is a comfort to all men;
yet must every man bestow it freely,
if he wishes to gain honor in the sight of the lord.

Livestock is one of the most ancient forms of mobile wealth and represented a form of currency before the first minting of coinage. The English rune poem reminds us that material wealth may bring comfort, allowing as it does for a roof above our heads and food on the table. We are advised to give generously. One who amasses wealth yet keeps it to themselves alone, is universally considered a miser and exiled from the goodwill of humanity. Honor derives from our generosity. Though no doubt seen as referring to the Christian God by early translators, lord here refers to both the lord, laird, leader of the tribe or clan, and the higher gods.

Hospitality was of critical importance to both the Scandinavian and Saxon peoples. The *Havamal* reminds us it is better to give nothing than too little. We are extolled to provide of ourselves, of our bounty, and offer the weary traveler a drink and warm place at our hearth. We also make offerings to our spirits. Here, the rune may be seen to depict a person standing with arms raised in a gesture of ritual offering.

Compared to the English, the Norwegian and Icelandic stanzas relating to Fehu remind us that wealth may also bring discord, especially within families. Material success can elicit jealousy and distrust. The Norwegian speaks of the wolf living in the forest. Wealth may be a lurking danger. At death, kin may be disrupted in anger and disputes relating to the estate's dispersal.

ᚢ

Úr - Aurochs, Wild Ox
Pronunciation: oor

The aurochs is proud and has great horns;
it is a very savage beast and fights with its horns;
a great ranger of the moors, it is a creature of mettle.

The aurochs were an ancient wild ox dating back to the Paleolithic period. They were one of the few species from the period to survive into the contemporary period, the Holocene, outside of Africa. Unfortunately, they went extinct in 1627 due to hunting and habitat loss. The aurochs was a fierce animal. Both the male and female of the species had large, forward-facing horns. They were known for their strength but were one of the largest plant-eating mammals of our current period.

This rune speaks to primal strength and instinctual courage. The wild aurochs roamed the fens and moors of Stone Age Britain. It may also be a test of our bravery. Murals from Crete depict a game where male youth leaped over bulls. This may have been a test or rite of passage into manhood. The rune may relate to a trial or your fortitude.

ᚦ

Þorn - Thorn
Pronunciation: thorn

The thorn is exceedingly sharp,
an evil thing for any man to touch,
uncommonly severe on all who sit among them.

The rune represents the sharp thorn of the Hawthorn and Blackthorn. This can be seen in its shape, with a point menacingly protruding outward. In the poem, the thorn represents a lurking danger when one chooses to rest near such a tree.

Thorns have a long history of use in baneful magic. They represent a present, but perhaps not clear, danger. They are sharp and to the point. Whatever lays in wait may come and depart quickly. In modern practice, the Hawthorn's flowers appearing in May have become connected to May Eve and the beauty of the Goddess. They would be an appropriate decoration for our altar at the Festival of Flowers. This rune reminds us that even in beauty, a darker, hidden element may exist. In Gardnerian Wicca, the Goddess is represented by both the kiss and the scourge—beauty and severity often counterpoints to each other. The fruit of the Blackthorn is used to make Sloe Gin liqueur. We know that alcoholic libations, even when of lower proof like sloe gin, may bring either illumination or peril. Sloe berries are also used in other alcoholic preparations, such as *Schlehenlikör* in Germany, *bargnolino* in Italy, and *patxaran* in Spain. In Devonshire, sloe berries used to make sloe gin are soaked in cider to produce "slider."

ᚩ

Os - God

Pronunciation: Oos

The god is the source of all language,
a pillar of wisdom and a comfort to wise men,
a blessing and a joy to every man.

Woden sacrificed himself on the tree for nine days and nine nights to bring the runes to humankind. Thanks to Woden, they are the root of wisdom and are available to all. There are his blessings and gift. Dickens translates "Os" as mouth since it is the same as the Latin word. This is likely an intentional Christianizing of the poem, though the mouth is not entirely inappropriate in this context.

This is a symbol of divine wisdom. It's often a clear indication we should seek guidance from our spirits. It may show we are in a good space and are benefiting from divine blessing. In a more mundane sense, communication is indicated. It's time to use the power of your words. The spoken word is also essential. Bards composed powerful poetry long before the tradition of writing them down. Our tradition is rooted in the oral.

ᚱ

Rad - Ride or journey
Pronunciation: rahd

Riding seems easy to everyone while they are in their hall
But very strenuous to one who traverses the high roads
on the back of a stout horse.

Rad has several meanings: riding, road, and (ironically) furniture. So we can see in this stanza a play on words which the Old English were fond of. The journey may seem easy when sitting in the comfortable furniture of your dining hall (or modern living room), but it is much more tiring when you hit the road.

First and foremost, Rad represents a journey; more often than not, it's a journey home. It may be time to return to one's roots. Travel is indicated perhaps literally, but it may be metaphoric. The rune also represents the path that we are to take. We get our modern word "road" from the Old English *rad*. Given the wordplay, this may be an admonishment to be realistic. The road ahead may be more challenging than you think. Focus on the pathway before you, as it is crucial. You may rest again when you arrive at your destination.

ᚳ

Cen - Torch

Pronunciation: kane

The pine torch is known to every living man by its pale, bright flame; it always burns where people gather inside.

As far as can be told, *cen* is not a word in its own right within Old English. There is a *cennan* meaning to "make known, declare, acknowledge." It has its cognate in the German verb *kennen*, "to know, understand." In Scotland and Northern England, we see it surviving via Middle English kennen as "ken," meaning to understand or know. Pine boughs soaked in pine pitch were used as torches. Here, they are a symbol of illumination in both the literal sense of lighting the way and the figurative sense of realization. This interpretation is close to the meaning generally ascribed to the Elder Furthark's kaun rune.

The shape of the rune differs significantly from the Norse. The poems have pronounced differences as well. The Norse speaks of death, the Icelandic pain, and an "abode of mortification." Here, we're reminded that the Futhorc is a system uniquely its own. The fire is that of the hearth and the warmth and comfort it provides to those who gather around it.

In a reading, cen may be interpreted as either realization, illumination, sudden insight, or the comfort of home, family, and community. This represents the personal strength we draw from either confidence in our understanding or the support of our family, blood, and chosen.

ᚷ

Gyfu - Gift

Pronunciation: give-oo

Generosity brings credit and honor, which support one's dignity;
it furnishes help and subsistence to all broken individuals
who are devoid of anything else.

Gifts and gifting were very important to the early English people. The importance of giving and receiving remained well into the Tudor period, when the lists of gifts bestowed by King Henry were extensive. For the ancestors, gifts came with obligation. As the old saying goes, nothing is free in this world. A gift given requires that it be reciprocated in some way.

The basis and benefit of the community is also reflected in the poem. We are advised to help and support those in a difficult situation. The tribe supports the tribe. We provide assistance when our neighbor is in need. I remember in the days following my father's death, many of my parents' friends brought food to the house. These casseroles and trays of sandwiches were unexpectedly vital as we were in no mental capacity to worry about our own need for sustenance. Gifts such as these are given without expecting to receive something in return. However, there is a cultural expectation that help be returned in kind to other members of the community when the situation is reversed. It is an unspoken rule of tribal cohesion.

This rune speaks to romantic partnerships, marriage, friendship, and community support.

ᚹ

Wynn - Joy
Pronunciation: wen

Bliss is enjoyed by those who know not suffering, sorrow, nor anxiety,
and has prosperity and happiness and a good enough house.

The meaning of this rune is relatively straightforward. It denotes joy and happiness. The poem even helps to define how those states arise when we are free of suffering, sorrow, and anxiety. This rune shows we are prosperous, have happiness, and reside in a home sufficient for our needs. This is a rune of health, happiness, and the joy the combination brings to our life and home. Friends surrounds us. We have a fire in the hearth, food on the table, and ale in our cups.

ᚻ

Haegl - Hail
Pronunciation: hay-el

Hail is the whitest of grain;
it is whirled from the vault of heaven
and is tossed about by gusts of wind
and then it melts into water.

Hailstorms are very destructive. They can come quickly out of nowhere and cause much damage. It often accompanies violent thunderstorms with rain and high winds. But the hailstones melt into harmless water when the storm is over. In the poem, hail is likened to grain or a seed. Here, it reflects the potential that arises out of hardship and challenging times. Similar to the Tower card in the tarot, disruption is often required before something new can commence. Often, out of tribulation comes a new calm.

ᚾ

Nyd - Need

Pronunciation: need

Trouble is oppressive to the heart;
yet often it proves a source of help and salvation
to everyone who heeds it beforehand.

This is a rune of pain and deprivation. It is true to its name, to be in need. Something is lacking. There might be distress, difficulty, or an urgent requirement. Depending on context, it may also denote something that needs urgent attention.

There are two other components of the poem to keep in mind. There is hope if one heeds the warning of this rune beforehand. This is a time to listen; disaster may be averted if you take measures in a timely manner. Just as importantly, a personal need provides an opportunity for family, friends, or the community to step in and provide aid and comfort. Often, these may prove life-changing.

ᛁ

Is - Ice
Pronunciation: eess

Ice is very cold and immeasurably slippery;
it glistens as clear as glass and is most like to gems;
it is a floor wrought by the frost, fair to look upon.

Growing up in Maine, I am fond of the beauty of ice. I found the icicles hanging off the eaves of my grandmother's house very magical. In winter, my father and I would spend hours playing on the frozen pond and stream near our house. Ice can be beautiful, but anyone growing up with it also knows of its inherent danger. As the poem reminds us, ice is slippery. It's easy to slip and fall. It may also be a hidden danger, like black ice on the roadway.

Here, this rune advises us to be careful. There may be hidden danger, or something may be slipping from our grasp. We need to exercise caution and move with slow intent. Use caution.

ᛄ

Ger - Harvest/Year
Pronunciation: y-err

The harvest is humanity's joy when the lord of the sky,
bring forth from the earth shining fruits
for rich and poor alike.

As we've seen throughout this book, the harvest was incredibly important to our forebears. A good harvest was a boon; a poor harvest could prove devastating. A bountiful harvest was critically important, and that is why so much of the seasonal calendar focused around it. Here we can see this dual meaning as Ger contains this dual meaning of harvest and the annual year cycle.

We are reaping what we have sown. That which we've put forth in the past is positively returning to us. It is time for us to harvest the fruits of our labors—enjoying and sharing them.

The lord referenced is likely Thunor. As the god of thunder and storms, his good graces were almost as necessary as the sun for a fruitful harvest. Not enough rain is just as detrimental as too much.

ᛇ

Eoh - Yew

Pronunciation: ae-oh

The yew is a tree with rough bark,
hard and fast in the earth, supported by its roots,
a guardian of flame and a joy upon an estate.

The Yew, along with Ash and Oak, was one of the sacred trees of Britain. It is a very long-lived tree, living up to two thousand years. Its wood was prized for making bows and firewood as it burned slowly yet produced an intense heat. The yew was likely the only evergreen tree in early Britain. For modern druids and perhaps their historical antecedents, the yew symbolizes everlasting life. Its branches grow downward, entering the earth where they sprout new trees connected underground to the first. In Irish lore, they were one of the sacred trees brought from the otherworld.

In divination, Eoh stands for longevity, steadfastness, reliability, and strength. A positive result will come, but it may take a while. As "guardian of flame," the rune reflects the warmth and safety of the home.

ᛈ

Peorð

Pronunciation: peo-rth

Gaming is a source of recreation and amusement to the great,
where warriors sit merrily together in the banqueting hall.

As the poem states, this is a rune relating to recreation and amusement. It is fun and games and the camaraderie that come with them. There is ambiguity as to the meaning of this rune's name. It may be linked to a pear-tree from which gaming boxes and dice were carved. The shape of the rune reminds one of a dice cup.

In a divinatory context, the rune tells us to relax. Take time out and enjoy the company of friends. It may also relate to a competitive environment, but it is a friendly one. There may be an element that must be left to chance.

ᛉ

Eolhx - Elk sedge
Pronunciation: eol-cks

The Elk-sedge is mainly to be found in a marsh;
it grows in the water and makes a ghastly wound,
covering with blood every warrior who touches it.

In the genus Carex, Elk sedge is common to Europe, North America, and Asia. The tall plant grows in wet areas such as bogs and marshes. Its leaves are stiff with a sharp, serrated edge. They can inflict deep wounds when grabbed. We can see all these elements in the above stanza.

Elk sedge grows in boundary spaces where land meets water. Given its nature, here, it protects and defends the area. Yes, it can potentially harm, but only when grasped. It is a mighty vegetative rampart within the boundary. There is also the tremendous Eurasian wild elk with its strength and self-determination.

I see this as a card of the liminal. It denotes the space betwixt and between. It is also a card of protection and defense.

ᛋ

Sigel - Sun

Pronunciation: see-ghel

The sun is ever a joy in the hopes of seafarers
when they journey away over the fish's bath,
until the courser of the deep bears them to land.

The sun is the most prominent celestial body in the sky. She is our daily companion, and her warmth benefits us and the seed in the earth. Without her beauty and strength, the harvest would not come.

At night, we see a near infinite number of individual suns in the twinkling stars that adorn the mother's body. The sun and stars have been critical for maritime navigation going back to deepest antiquity. This is the meaning we see here. This is the sun and the bearer of hope and joy, as well as a guide along the course of our journey.

When Sigel comes up in a reading, it is an indication to look for/seek guidance. There is a route before us, but we will need assistance staying true to its course. Now is the time to ask for a little advice. The spirits or ancestors can provide clarity as to which path to choose.

ᛏ

Tir - The god Tiw

Pronunciation: T-ear

The North Star is a guiding star; well does it keep faith with princes; it is ever on its course over the mists of night and never fails.

The North, or Pole, star, Polaris, has been used for navigation since late antiquity. In the constellation of Ursa Minor, it is currently the closest star to the celestial pole. It is also one of the brightest stars easily visible to the naked eye. Given this, it is ideal for determining the northern direction. The North Star is an ever-present constant; its presence can be counted on. It is a symbol of dependability and reliability. In the play of the same name, Shakespeare describes Julius Caesar as "as constant as the northern star."

The name of the rune relates to the god Tiw. Both the Norse and Icelandic poems make this connection explicitly. He is a god of justice and order. He brings judgment, but it is always on the side of what is right.

The rune symbol resembles a spear, which has a dual connection to a true course as it flies straight and the decisive point of justice. The Tir has been found on swords and cremation urns. The former is undoubtedly due to the rune's connection with victory. The latter may relate to judgement or an earlier relationship with protection.

The rune represents justice, following a proper course, and re-establishing order.

ᛒ

Beorc - Birch
Pronounced: bayorch

The birch bears no fruit, yet without seed it brings forth suckers,
for it is generated from its leaves.
Splendid are its branches and gloriously adorned
its lofty crown, which reaches to the skies.

Birch is seen as a sacred tree throughout Europe. It is the first tree mentioned in the staves of the Ogham. Known as the White Lady of the Woods with beautiful silvery skin and fine hair, the Birch has long been considered a goddess tree. As one of the first trees to sprout leaves in the spring, she is connected with fertility. In Scandinavia, there is a tradition of couples making love among a grove of birches to encourage conception.

Beorc is a symbol of new beginnings, sometimes unexpected ones. It hints at the influence of the goddess underlying the generative process.

ᛖ

Eh - Horse
Pronounced: eh

The horse is a joy to nobles in the presence of warriors.

A steed in the pride of its hoofs,
when rich men on horseback bandy words about it;
and it is ever a source of comfort to the restless.

The horse was essential in the history of England. The oldest remains found in Britain date from 700,000 years ago. The domestication of horses began in Britain during the Stone Age around 2,000 BCE. Ancient cart wheels have been found in Flag Fen, along with early bits at other archeological sites. The Uffington White Horse, in Oxfordshire, is a testament to the importance of the horse to the pre-Roman peoples of the Isles.

One's horse was more than just an object of utility; but was both an ally and a signal of status. Horse breeding was the domain of the wealthy and nobility. The late queen was known for her champion horses. Horses played a significant role in Iron Age and Medieval society.

One can imagine a person riding a steed in the rune's shape. It also resembles a saddle. This rune is more about the relationship between the rider and their horse than just the horse. The meaning of this runes relates to the ally, one who is by your side on the journey. Its nature is relational.

ᛗ

Mann - Humankind
Pronunciation: man

The joyous person is dear to his kinsmen;
yet everyone is doomed to fail his fellow,
since the lord, by his decree, will commit the vile carrion to the earth.

Mann in Old English did not just translate as man but was gender nonspecific. Here, we see the community of kin and fellows. Here, our friends and loved one bring mutual joy. As humans, we relish the company of others. But we are reminded that each person will eventually depart and leave those behind in sorrow. Here is a sobering reminder that the end is inevitable. We all pass on, and our mortal remains are returned to the earth.

This rune signifies both the pleasure of community, and the tribe, as well as reminding us of its impermanence. Mann most often relates to interpersonal relationships in divinatory situations—generally the individual and the family or community. It may also signify a lingering loss of a loved one. In any sense, Mann is a rune of interrelation.

ᛚ

Lagu - Water, Lake, Sea

Pronunciation: lah(r)-goo

The sea seems interminable to people,
if they venture on the rolling ship
and the waves of the sea terrify them
and the courser of the deep heed, not its bridle.

The meaning of this rune is a large body of water. The rune poems speak of the boredom of crossing such an expanse in a boat. The ship does not seem stable and is rocked by large waves. In such weather, the vessel is hard to steer.

Lagu also translates as "the law" in Old English. This

definition is not explicit here, but we may see it as a subtle alternate interpretation. The process of the law may seem interminable in its duration and confounding when navigating its complexity.

This is a rune of turbulence. It may be not easy to stay the course. It is not violent disruption such as that found with Haegl. Here, the sea ahead is rough. It doesn't mean you won't reach your destination, but you may suffer seasickness along the way.

ᛝ

Ing - Ing

Pronunciation: ing as in thinking.

Ing was first seen among the East Danes,
till, followed by his chariot,
he departed eastwards over the waves.
So, the royal line named the hero.

Ing is not a word in Old English. It is likely a word imported to the Isles from the continent. Its presence probably shows a vestigial meaning that was known to the Anglo-Saxons but almost lost to us. Looking at *Beowulf*, scholars have deduced that Ing is another name for the Scandinavian god Freyr or Frey. "East Danes" here refers to peoples of southern Sweden and is also found in *Beowulf*. Here, we see the hero returning to his homeland, traveling to the east over the Baltic Sea. The author found it important to note that his chariot followed after him.

Years ago, I bought a pair of jeans at Priape, a fetish shop in

Montreal. The leather label bore the Ing rune. The clerk told me the symbol was there to help with successful cruising. The jeans fit well, too. I've long outgrown them, but I kept the label. I can't say if the rune on my butt helped, but it did make me think of the rune and its power every time I put them on. Fryer is connected with sexuality. The most common contemporary depictions that survive show him with a distinct erect penis. I see him as a handsome god with his sexual appetite literally at the fore.

This rune signifies the intervention of the god first and foremost. It is also connected to sexual desire. In my mind it will always be linked, as well, to cruising.

ᛟ

Eþel - Homeland

Pronunciation: er-thel

Homeland is very dear to every man,
if he can enjoy there in his house
whatever is right and proper in constant prosperity.

Here we have the home and one's family. It denotes one's homeland–which is more than simply the place where one was born, but relates to the ancestral homeland. For tribal communities, land was inextricably linked to kinship. This rune may also signify an estate as in inheritance.

In divinatory meaning, this rune may stand for the home, community, and the place of one's ancestral roots. An alternate meaning depending on context would be inheritance, or that which came down from the ancestors.

ᛞ

Dæg - Day - Awakening
Pronunciation: day

Day is the messenger of the gods;
it is beloved of men, a source of hope and happiness to rich and poor,
and of service to all.

This is one of the most straightforward of the runes. It concentrates on the day as the hours of sunlight. The sun brings warmth and happiness. It enables the crops to grow. The light of day is also one of relative safety, in contrast to the dark of night.

Here we have a very positive card denoting good fortune. It may be a new dawn, but it will be a glorious day.

ᚪ

Ac - Oak
Pronunciation: ahk

The oak fattens the flesh of pigs for the children of men.
Often it traverses the gannet's bath,
and the ocean proves whether the oak keeps faith

in honourable fashion.

In England, acorns were common fodder for feeding pigs. The wild boar and domesticated pig have long been important in Britain. The boar's connections to humankind go back into antiquity. It was a common food source during the Neolithic period. Bones of numerous boars have been found near Stonehenge, attesting to its importance in feasting. Wild boars feature in Anglo-Saxon art such as the ornamentation found at Sutton Hoo.

Shipbuilding relied on oak for its strength and rigidity. The gannet is a sea bird, so the "gannet's bath" is the sea or ocean. Ships built of oak cross the great expanse of water. Ships constructed of oak can be depended on. Its consistent reliability proves its honor.

Oak is one of the great sacred trees. Across Gaul, the center of *temenos,* sacred circles, may have had an oak at their center. We see this at the neolithic structure known as Seehenge where an inverted oak stump formed the altar. Later in history, we see the pillar of oak as the Igdrasil. The mighty oak is the king of the forest. He is linked to the English horned spirit/god Herne the Hunter, said to walk through Windsor Forest in Berkshire.

Herne is also known from his appearance in *The Merry Wives of Windsor.* In the play, he is associated not just with any oak, but a blasted oak—see the earlier chapter that discusses the lightning-struck oak in more detail. Herne likely has roots that go further back into history than his first appearance in Shakespeare. He may well be linked to the Gaulish Cernunnos.

In a divinatory sense, we see strength and dependability. There is stability; what we have is enough. Smooth sailing. It may indicate it's a good time to reconnect to nature and the spirit of the wild.

ᚫ

Æsc - Ash

Pronunciation: ash

The ash is exceedingly high and precious to men.
With its sturdy trunk it offers a stubborn resistance,
though attacked by many a man.

The ash was another tree prized by the early peoples of Britain. The tree is known for growing tall and straight. Its wood is flexible but unlikely to splinter. It was ideal for making spear shafts and bows. Indeed, like many words, "Æsc" has several means, one being "spear." It was also commonly used for the construction of balustrades. Thus, it may be employed for both offense and defense. We see the latter in the "stubborn resistance" referenced in the poem.

Many sources connect the ash with the World Tree (Old Norse Yggdrasill). This is the tree upon which Woden gave himself in sacrifice so that humanity may obtain the runes. Ash has long had a connection to witchcraft, especially as a protective charm. In Scotland, there is a tradition of carrying ash seeds to ward off evil magic. Snakes are said to avoid ash trees and their fallen leaves. Wands are often constructed from ash.

For divinatory purposes, Ash stands for protection and defense first and foremost. It may also mean success through flexibility. Being overly rigid may prove a hindrance. Sometimes a situation calls for a flexible approach. We may need to bend a little, but not break.

Yr - Bow

Pronunciation: earr

A bow is a source of joy and honor to all nobles;
it looks well on a horse and is a reliable equipment for a journey.

The bow in question, here, is generally interpreted as the iconic English longbow. The wood of the yew tree was considered the best for constructing the longbow. At first this may seem odd, as the documented military use of the longbow occurred after the Norman conquest of 1066 and increased to its widespread use in the fourteenth century. There is evidence that the short and long bows coexisted in antiquity. The fact that it is showing in this poem attests to its existence prior to the Anglo-Norman period.

Unlike the crossbow, the longbow required much skill in being able to use it effectively. It is probably due to its difficulty that it saw little military use prior to the Normans.

This rune speaks to skill—a specialized one that has to be learned. Our approach should be precise. We see success through skillful means.

ᛡ

Ior - Beaver

Pronunciation: ee-or

The beaver is a river fish and yet it always feeds on land;
it has a fair abode encompassed by water, where it lives in happiness.

The beaver is a creature that exists in two realms. It lives in the water like a fish, yet finds its food and building materials on land. They are not actually fish, but in ways they act like they are. Thus, it is a totem of those with a foot in both worlds. Beavers build dams to create ponds, at the center of which they construct their lodges. The watery boundary between their family's house and the dry land acts as a natural defense from predators. Through this transformation of the landscape, they also provide a rich microecology encouraging the growth of flora and breeding of fish.

As the poem tells us, the beaver is safe and happy. They mate in pairs for life. Beavers are a symbol of adaptability, but it is they who adapt the landscape around them to suit their needs.

ᛠ

Ear - The Grave

Pronunciation: ehah

The grave is horrible to everyone,
when the corpse quickly begins to cool
and is laid in the bosom of the dark earth.
Prosperity declines, happiness passes away
and covenants are broken.

With this rune stanza, we have a clear indication of the grave, of death and returning to the earth. This is a rune of endings and sorrow. It is not death as change as is often discussed in relation to the Death card in the tarot. Here we have a finality, much like the Scythe and Coffin cards in the Lenormand. There may also be a little of the Mice card here too, of decline, diminution, and loss. In the symbol, one may detect a person whose arms are raised skyward overcome with grief.

One meaning of Ear in Old English was as an ear of corn. Think of poor old John Barleycorn whose death is decreed from the outset. He then returns to the earth, to rise again, and the cyclic spiral continues.

The last four runes are not contained in the English Rune Poem. They are attested to mainly by their use in historical manuscripts. Each likely arose from other runes—Calc from Cen and Gar from Gyfu—to accommodate sounds that existed in Old English but not Germanic languages. Only scant information exists on each. Here, I will provide my notes on available information, but not attempt at meanings. Any divinatory explanations for these runes are based on personally received gnosis. You should approach these runes and let them speak to you as you work with them in the context of their better-known colleagues. Let your intuition guide you.

ᚸ

Gar

Gar means "spear," "dart," "arrow," or "javelin." The symbol may be that of an archery target. Its use in manuscripts give the hint of conflict. The spear is the sacred weapon carried by Woden.

ᛣ

Calc

Calc means "chalk" (limestone) in Old English. Chalk is

common in much of Britain. It brings to mind the white cliffs of Dover. In many places, it exists right below the surface. Early and modern peoples have used this to skim off the grassy top to form designs—such as the Uffington Horse (~1000 BCE), the Long Man of Wilmington (1700s), the Cerne Giant in Dorset (also perhaps 1700s), and the regimental badges at Fovant Down (1916—present). Another meaning of the word calc is "shoe" or "sandal." A similar Old English word cælc means "chalice" and this may provide an alternative line of meaning. As demonstrated by the various designs, in many places chalk lies just below the surface soil. I approach this rune as something that is latent or operating below the surface.

ᛢ

Cweorth

Very little is known of this rune from historical context. It is generally thought that the rune connects to fire and a spindle drill used to kindle one. Through this, it may connect to ritual fire or cremation—fire as transformation.

ᛥ

Stan

The meaning here is clearer: "stone" especially that used as a building material. From the Gothic "stains" and German "stein." Rock is something solid and immovable. For me, this is a rune of hardness.

Horizons

For Uppy

the sisters in my grandmother s family
all had nicknames weezie, tug, and up
uppy to the generations of children
who played at her feet
with the small zoo of oversized crocheted
animals hidden in the hall closet

summer sunday afternoons
as the garden progressed to harvest
sitting in the living room
when her bad foot prevented
her from making the trek
across the lighthouse road
an ashtray impossibly full
of cigarette butts to her left
a tall glass of light brown liquid
ginger ale or scotch and water
depending on whether the sun
had descended below
the window s meeting rail

trading books and authors
allen ginsberg on my part
archie and mehetible on hers
she wrote a poem at the time

offering a young poet
the advice of a comma well placed
a wonderful irony while
recommending the work
of a cockroach who couldn t capitalize
the shift plus letter keys
being too long a reach

stories swirled the room
fanciful and mysterious
and with a spry mischievousness
that belied her 80-some years
skipper mcbride and
his lucky ammonite,
the unlucky randell,
ringgold the pirate,
poor old sam who once
mistook a whale for a u-boat,
and the haunting creatures
of the maine woods:
the ravenous wendigo,
will-am-alones rolling
their poison balls
sowing nightmares
while you sleep,
harry-toothed dr. pillgarlic,
and the hang-downs
tales of the ancestral home
a mile from the harbor s mouth
an island with its indian middens,
fairy houses, pioneer communalism
of island privilege, and the unmarked
graves of black island quarrymen

who washed ashore in a time
precedent to current memory
a small house full of treasures
collected and catalogued
a pinched bottle
that belches when poured,
a wabanaki arrowhead,
a small milky-green block of beryl,
an agate tumbled smooth
to reveal the devil in hell,
drawers full of negatives and slides
travel photography to fine art
sorted sleeved and labeled

walls lined with books
field guides to everything
that one might find
in the natural world
from mushrooms, to feathers,
to wildflowers, to spiders
reminders of friends
a cat teased from stone
by the sculptor s hand
of chenoweth hall
a note from e.b. white
bookmarking his
collection of letters

the orchard of heirloom cultivars
curated and grafted for eating,
cooking, and winter storage
the spring at the foot of the field
a clear cool witch s cauldron

encircled in oaken roots
and beached in moss
the english garden its bricks
overgrown with sod
peonies, columbine, and ladies mantle
fighting their way through
the encroaching blackberries
the pink granite marker
edges softened by waves

the outbuildings
homespun museums
to two lives well lived
and a mutual love for art,
craft, literature, the natural world
stones, fossils, and
two-thousand year old tools
the yellow jeep cj
in which i first learned
to drive a standard
its alignment off to the left
after hitting a tree on
a late-night scotch-fueled
drive down to camp

the pilgrams path winding
contemplatively to the shore
stepping over blowdowns
and ducking under widowmakers
old tall spruces
falling like dominos
after the first one
succumbs to a winter nor easter

on the writing desk
hand built with utilitarian beauty
seafoam green horizon 3000
a single line on the paper
rolled onto its roller

i have seen horizons

MORE FUN THAN A BARRELL FULL OF
"HUNKIES"...
MANS
COUNTRY
5015 N. CLARK · CHICAGO

Lagniappe: The Monster at the End of the Book

A few years ago, my friends Jeff and Allan were asked to investigate a Palo shrine that had been left in a shed behind the Chicago bathhouse Man's Country. While there, they encountered a novel spirit they came to know as the Devil of the Bathhouse. They returned again with our mutual friend Steven and communed further with the spirit. A gifted artist, Jeff was moved to create a pair of statues depicting this handsome spirit. Soon after their visit, Man's Country closed and the building was demolished to make room for new construction.

In the words of Owen Keehnen, the man who literally wrote the book on Man's Country, "Bathhouses were places of dark sexual magic and erotic adventure—gay adult amusement parks that promised sex and delivered on the insular excitement and thrills. Bathhouses were their own worlds."[1]

When Chuck Renslow and his partner Dom Orejudos opened the bathhouse in 1972, the couple had already owned the legendary Chicago leather bar the Gold Coast for twelve years. Chuck was also co-owner of the Chicago Club Baths, an interest he sold to open Man's Country. The bath's advertising boasted that it was "a new plateau of pleasure" and invited men to enter "a new state of enjoyment," guaranteeing "complete satisfaction."[2]

Bathhouses were indeed special places. At their best, they represented a created safe space for gay men to gather and enjoy each other's company on whatever level they desired. They were places for entertainment and socializing. A New York bathhouse launched Bette Midler's career. During the early years of the AIDS crisis, they were unfairly singled out, much as gay bars had been the subject of officially-sanctioned institutional harassment in the previous generation.

The Devil of the Bathhouse is a patron saint of sorts for men who like sex with men—sex of the dark, anonymous, and feral. He is a reclamation of the spirit of this bygone era and a promise that even as things change, the magick remains. His churches are the bathhouse, sauna, backroom, gloryhole, woods, and fens. His sermon is the sound of belts hitting the floor. His choir is the primal chorus of anonymous sexual encounters.

In our grove temple space, we honor the Devil of the Bathhouse. We are privileged to have the third statue Jeff created, which is situated at the center of a specially dedicated shrine. Votives and offerings of poppers, portable lube, fire water whiskey, pinecones, and Viagra surround his image.

For more information on working with this unique spirit, go to Jeff and Allan's book *The Devil of the Bathhouse.*

DARK TUNNELS

Those who meet in these dark and often very damp places are under the elemental forces of the deeps and must come together for they are driven by wild and barbaric passions. There exists in those places a kind of daemonic priesthood, truly the sons of the underworld in all of his power, and they willingly drink the sacred cream like strange vampires, who cannot explain in any form their bizarre behavior. —Michael Bertiaux[3]

In the eyes of the mystic, the priests of these arcane rituals possess throats akin to dark tunnels. Their mouths are entrances to passages leading down into the primordial depths of existence. At the nadir of this mystical passage, the unspeakably wicked deep ones reside—guardians of the all-powerful wand. The gods stand tall in their grandeur, patrons of gold and fire. There within lie the keys to enlightenment.

As in the days before recorded history, our temple is wherever we are. We encounter our brothers in the dark of New Orleans' Eagle, upstairs at the Phoenix. We are priests of a fraternal order born of the primordial dark. Ours is an ancient cultus called together, guided by instinct to worship at the fountain of the golden elixir.

walk me to the anvil
no acid smile lights up the darkness
touch that padlock on the mineshaft door
everard boarded
relics of a revolution
crusaded
not long enough

—Assotto Saint, "Relics"

Our revels now are ended. These our actors,
As I foretold you, were all spirits and
Are melted into air, into thin air;
And like the baseless fabric of this vision,
The cloud-capped towers, the gorgeous palaces,
The solemn temples, the great globe itself,
Yea, all which it inherit, shall dissolve,
And, like this insubstantial pageant faded,
Leave not a rack behind. We are such stuff
As dreams are made on, and our little life
Is rounded with a sleep.

—Shakespeare, *The Tempest*

Appendix A: Recipes

I maintain a tradition in our coven of serving a dinner after our sabbat ritual. I've included here a selection of seasonal recipes. Of course, tastes differ, and you may certainly prepare what moves you. Coming together to share the bounty of the land, has been a tradition forming the focal point of community, since before recorded history. We honor our guests when we offer them libation and food. This is as true for our brothers as it is for our deities. *The Hávamál* opens with the arrival of a guest and a call that he be welcome and warmed by the fire and offered drink and sustenance.

MIDWINTER

THE REFUGE'S TOMATO ASPIC SALAD

Before we moved to our current house, The Refuge, we were not looking to move. The house beside us had sat vacant for seven years. The mother had passed away, and the elderly father had moved in with his daughter. One evening, the daughter called us and let us know her mother had come to her in a dream the night before and communicated she wanted us to have her house. A few days later, she walked us through. It needed love, but we saw the potential. Within months, we were carrying our belongings down the block. The daughter did warn us that the spirit of her mother, Joy, came with the house. The first Yule dinner I cooked in the house was delayed by a year by Hurricane Ida. At that first Christmastide meal, I served my first attempt at an aspic salad. I texted the daughter a photo and she immediately texted back that I must be channeling Joy as her mother had served aspic salad at every Christmas dinner in the house.

24 oz tomato juice
2 envelopes unflavored gelatin
½ tbsp dark brown sugar
½ tbsp kosher salt
½ tbsp ground pickling spices
½ tsp Crystal hot sauce
½ tsp grated lemon zest
1 ½ tbsp fresh lemon juice
½ cup minced small onion
½ cup finely chopped green bell pepper
2 finely chopped celery ribs

In a bowl, combine ½ cup of tomato juice with gelatin and let stand for five minutes. In a saucepan, heat the remaining tomato juice with the sugar, salt, pickling spices, hot sauce, lemon zest, and lemon juice. Heat just until warm. Do not boil. Add the gelatin and tomato juice mixture. Stir until completely dissolved. Place the mixture in a bowl and refrigerate for about an hour. It should be cold but not set.

Spray eight ramekins with olive oil. Stir the onion, pepper, and celery into the tomato gelatin mixture. Spoon into the oiled ramekins. Refrigerate until chilled and set. This will take at least two hours but may be left overnight.

Unmold the aspics. The oil should help them come out easily. Serve on a bed of artisanal lettuce with a side of blanched, halved Brussels sprouts and sliced hard-boiled egg.

WASSAIL RECIPE

6 cored tart apples
2 tsp ground cinnamon
2 tsp fresh ginger
(or 1 tablespoon ground ginger)
1 tsp allspice
3 whole cloves
2 tsp nutmeg (one whole nutmeg)
1/2 cup brown or raw sugar
2 quarts brown ale (6 12oz bottles), cider, or a 50/50 mix of the two

Preheat oven to 350F. Place the apples on a greased baking sheet, then bake until they are soft and the skin peels away quickly (approximately 45-60 minutes). After peeling the apples, mash the pulp then, add the dry ingredients. Pour the ale into a pot; heat but do not boil. Add the apple mixture. Cover partially and let steep until the desired flavor is reached. You may add more ale or cider if necessary. Strain and serve.

OIMELC

BRIGHD CAKE

The following is a traditional Irish soda bread, or cake, adapted to US measures from the Farrars's *The Witch's Goddess.*[1]

3-1/2 cups flour
1/2 cup sugar
4 oz (1 stick) butter
1/4 cup cut peel
1/2 cup raisins or sultanas
1 heaped teaspoon cream of tartar
1 heaped teaspoon soda
1 tsp salt
1 1/3 cups sour milk

Preheat oven to 400°. Sift dry ingredients. Mix with softened butter and sour milk. Stir in peel and raisins. Gently knead. Grease a 7-inch cake tin or a cast iron frying pan. Place bread into pan and cook for about 45 minutes. Internal temperature should be about 195° with an instant-read thermometer.

WELSH BARA BRITH

Here is my version of a Welsh tea cake.

10 oz raisins
4 oz black currants
2 oz candied citrus rind

1 1/3 cups black tea
3 cups flour
1 cup brown sugar
3/4 tsp quality ground cinnamon
½ tsp ground allspice
½ tsp ground nutmeg
¼ tsp ground cloves
¼ tsp ground ginger
¼ tsp ground coriander
A pinch ground mace
3-3/4 tsp baking powder
1-¼ tsp salt
4 tbsp butter
1 large egg

Place the raisins, currants, and citrus in a bowl with the black tea and let sit in the fridge overnight.

Preheat the oven to 325°.

Mix the dry ingredients and add the fruit. Once mixed, add the butter and egg. Once fully mixed, scoop out the batter and add to a greased pan.

Bake for 70 to 85 minutes. Use a toothpick to test doneness. Remove from oven and let cool.

EOSTRE

NANNY'S CREAMED FINNAN HADDIE

This was one of my grandmother's favorite dishes. The name

"finnan haddie" refers to a lightly smoked haddock or other white fish. Though debated, the etymology of its unique name may derive from the the town of Findon in Abderdeenshire. It was certainly a popular food in the Aberdeen area as far back as the seventeeth century. Its Scottish roots underline the eduring connection between New England and the old country.

2 lb smoke white fish (traditionally haddock)
2 medium onions, diced
2 cups of milk
2 cups heavy cream
1 tsp Colman's English mustard powder
6 oz butter
3/4 cup plain flour
1 bunch green onions or scallions, sliced
1 bunch parsley, minced.
White wine.
Lemon juice.
Salt and ground black pepper

Melt 1/3 of the butter in a large sauce pan over medium heat. Reduce heat and add the onion. Once tender but not brown stir in the milk, cream, and mustard. Bring to a low simmer.

In a separate pan melt the remaining butter and add flour to make a light-colored roux. Take off heat and set aside.

Gently place the smoked fish into milk & cream mixture. Poach for four minutes. Remove fish with a slotted spoon. Peal the skin off the fish and set the rest aside to cool only slightly.

With milk/cream mixture at a simmer, scoop some of the roux with a whisk and mix it into the liquid. After the roux dissolves you may add more slowly bringing the stew to the correct consistency. Be delicate with the roux. You can always thin with additional milk if necessary. Whisk in a splash of wine and a little lemon juice. Add the green onions. Season with white pepper to taste. The fish is quite salty, so I do not add salt, if needed, until the very end.

Break the fish into small pieces and add to the stew. Simmer, taste, and serve. Traditionally, it was served over mashed potatoes. My nanny often served it with toasted bread.

FESTIVAL OF FLOWERS

LAMB MINCE PIE

11-12 oz lamb mince
1 small onion, finely chopped
1 tsp mixed oregano, marjoram, basil, and rosemary
½ teaspoon mace
4 tbsp beef stock
Salt and pepper
Melted butter

Preheat oven to 350°.

Butter and flour your cooking tins. I use mini cheesecake tins with the clasp for easy removing. I also use premade pie crust as I am not a baker. Add the pastry dough to bottom and sides of the tins so a little bit hangs over. Cut circles of crust just a little larger than the tins. Cut a small circular hole in the center of each.

Fry the onion in a pan until soft and just starting to caramelize. Add the spices. Remove to a bowl and add a small amount of the stock. Once it has cooled, stir in the lamb. Add more stock until it is moist but not too wet.

Divide the lamb, onion, spice mixture into the tins. Put the top crust over each and pinch the sides together. Brush the tops with melted butter.

Cook for approximately 45 minutes. Check the crust toward the end. It should be just at the beginning of golden brown.

MARYANNE'S DOWN EAST SLOP

1 lb ground meat
8 oz mushrooms sliced
1 medium onion chopped
1 red/orange/yellow bell pepper chopped (optional)
2 cans of tomato soup
1 cup elbow macaroni
Salt and pepper to taste

Brown the meat in a skillet, adding salt and pepper. Set meat aside and cook the onions and peppers, then mushrooms in the same pan until soft. Meanwhile cook the pasta in water with olive oil and salt. Once the vegetables are cooked, add the meat back in. When the pasta is done, drain and add to the pan with meat and vegetables. Pour in the cans of soup. Heat on low until ready to eat.

MIDSUMMER

UPPY'S CHICKEN AND WHITE WINE

This is my great aunt's version of coq au vin. It was one of her small selection of go-to recipes she prepared when entertaining company for dinner.

3-4 lbs chicken, cut up

2 cups tomatoes
1 clove garlic, minced
1½ cup dry white wine
1½ cup chicken broth
1 bay leaf
½ tsp marjoram or oregano
Pinch thyme
6 peppercorns, cracked
Salt to taste when done
Carrots, onions, celery, and potatoes

Put in chicken in tight pot, such as a dutch oven, with wine, btoth, and herbs. Simmer covered until chicken for about twenty minutes. Take off heat for ten minutes and skim off fat. Add onions, carrots, celery and potatoes. Return to heat and simmer until vegetables are done. In her notes, she recommends Taylor's New York sauterne from a winery originally founded in the Finger Lakes Region of New York state. Through the de-evolution of multiple corporate purchases, Taylor's product line has been reduced to a small assortment of fortified wines such as port and sherry. Sauternes are a sweet wine from the

Sauternais region of France. If a sauterne is not available, substitutes include Semillon, Riesling, or Chenin Blanc. For a rich taste close to the original recipe a cup of cream sherry may be used. with two cups broth.

FEAST OF FIRST FRUITS

MUM'S BLUEBERRY PANCAKES

1-1/2 cups flour
2-1/2 tsp baking powder
3 tbsp sugar
3/4 tsp salt
1 egg, slightly beaten
3/4 cup milk
2 tbsp butter
1/2 cup Maine wild blueberries

Sift together the dry ingredients into a mixing bowl. Add the egg, milk, and melted butter and stir Add more milk, if necessary to make a batter that is thin and easy to pour. Stir in the blueberries.

Heat a greased cast iron skillet over medium heat. Drop large spoonfuls onto the griddle. When bubbles begin to appear, flip them onto their other side.

In Maine, we always served them with maple syrup. Here in Southern Louisiana, cane sugar is more the norm.

HARVEST HOME

ROAST CHICKEN AND FALL VEGETABLES

One of my favorite dishes is baked chicken over root vegetables. My mother, grandmother, and great aunt were avid gardeners. Squash and potatoes were important aspects of the harvest growing up. I add andouille sausage to bring in a little of New Orleans. Spatchcocking the chicken helps it to cook evenly.

1 whole chicken
1 butternut squash
3 potatoes
3 carrots
1 andouille sausage

Preheat the oven to 425°

Spatchcocking is a technique where you remove the backbone of the chicken using cooking shears. After the backbone is removed, the chicken can be flattened.

Peel the potatoes, carrots, and squash. Cut into bite sized segments. If using, cut the sausage into half rounds.

Spice the chicken on all sides. I use Tony Chachere's Cajun seasoning. Coat the vegetables in cooking oil and season with whatever you used on the chicken.

Place the vegetables and sausage, if using, in the bottom of a baking dish. Set the chicken on top.

Bake for about 45 minutes until the chicken has an internal temperature of 160°.

PICKLED ROOT VEGETABLES

Growing up, fall was a time for canning and pickling vegetables from the garden. The basement of my grandmother's house always had shelves of mason jars filled with everything from dill pickles to pickled herring. The followng is based on several medieval pickle or condiment recipes.

2 lbs root vegetables such as celary root, carrots, radishs, and turnips cut thinly
1 lb shredded cabbage
1 lb cored cut hard pears
2 cups apple cider vinegar
2-1/2 cups a fruity light colored wine
6 tbsp honey
2 oz white sugar
1 tsp caraway seed
1 tsp anise seed
1/2 tsp mustard seed
1/4 tsp ground black pepper
A pinch saffron

Place the vegetables and pears in a pot of water. Boil until they begin to soften. Drain and layout in a clean non-metal baking dish large enough that they layout in an even layer. Sprinkle with ginger, salt, saffron, and 4 tbsp vinegar. Cover and leave over night (at least twelve hours).

Prepare six quart mason jars. Place in a large pot and fill with water making sure the jars are covered. Boil for fifteen minutes to sterilize. My grandmother would always add to the pot any other items she would be using including funnel and a knife. In a separate sauce pan bring more water to a boil to sterilize the new lids and rings.

Rinse the vegetables. Add them to the jars leaving an inch of headspace in each.

In another small pot, bring the wine and honey to a simmer. Add the remaining vinegar and spices. Stir in the sugar. Reduce the heat until the sugar is completely dissolved. Return to a boil. Pour the liquid over into the jars covering the vegetables by about 1/2 inch.

Run a sterile knife down along the sides to release any air bubbles. My grandmother insisted this had to be done with a silver knife and kept a special one on hand reserved for this purpose. With a clean cloth, wipe the rim of the jar to remove any liquid. Put on the lids and retaining rings.

Remove some water from the stock pot to allow space for the filled jars. I always set the water aside just in case I need to add a little back in to cover them. Place the jars in the water and bring back to a boil. Process for fifteen minutes.

Remove the jars and set them on a kitchen towel on the counter. As they cool you should hear the sounds of the leds popping as the contents pressurize. Store in a cool place for at least two weeks before eating.

ALL HALLOW'S

BEEF STEW WITH BLACK TREACLE

2 tbsp vegetable oil
2 lbs Chuck roast cut into bite-sized pieces
2 tbsp plain (all-purpose) flour mixed with a pinch of salt and pepper

2 large chopped onions
3 cloves crushed garlic
2 cups red wine
2 large chopped carrots
2 medium peeled and chopped potatoes
½ small peeled and chopped rutabaga (a turnip or swede to the British and my New England grandmother)
3 cups beef stock
1 can diced tomatoes
4 bay leaves
Fresh thyme
1 tbsp black treacle or 2 tsp dark brown sugar
¾ tsp each salt & crushed black pepper to taste

Preheat oven to 325°.

Dust the beef in the flour mixture, then sear it in a cast iron Dutch oven. Do not crowd; cook in batches and remove to a plate. Deglaze the pan with a couple of tablespoons of wine. Add the remaining wet ingredients and then add the other items and spices. Cook in the oven for three to four hours. Stir occasionally and make sure it does not go dry. Add a small amount of additional stock if necessary.

Appendix B: Fermentation

MEAD

3 lbs Raw Honey
1 gallon Distilled Water
1 Black Teabag
Peel of 1/2 an Orange
1/4 cup Raisins
1/2 tsp Wine (D-47) or Champagne yeast
1 gallon carboy or fermentation jar with airlock

Hydrate yeast with room-temperature distilled water.

Add water, raisins (to provide nutrients and added sugar for the yeast), orange peel, and tea bag to a pot. Let come to a boil and then steep 15 minutes. It should be a very strong tea. When done, filter out solids. This forms a nutrient-rich tannin tea that both helps feed the yeast and adds flavoring.

Pour honey into carboy. Add half the tea mixture and shake. Fill with remaining tea until a short way from the top. Shake again, both to mix and to oxygenate. Let the mixture cool to to the appropriate temperature for the yeast being used. In the case of D-47, the ideal temp is between 95° and 98.6°F Add yeast. Mix again.

Let sit at room temperature (above 62° and below 86°) in a dark place for at least 4-6 weeks. Mead is a slower fermentation and may be allowed to sit for months.

Siphon and bottle.

BROWN ALE

28 oz Maris Otter malt
6-1/2 oz Cracked crystal malt
1/3 oz Pelleted hops (Northdown or Cascade)
1 tsp packet Nottingham, London ESB or Safale S-04 yeast
1-1/2 gallons water
1 oz Sugar (for secondary fermentation after bottling)
1 gallon carboy, blowoff hose, and airlock

Mashing the barley: Heat barley and 1.5 gallons of water to 158° F. Cover with towels to insulate and retain heat. Let sit for an hour.

Strain barley and retain the liquid.

Sparging: pour clean water through the grain to rinse as much of the sugars off as possible. Now we have our wart!

Bring to a boil. Simmer for an hour.

Divide the hops into three equal parts. You will add them at the start of the boil (adds bitterness), 30-minute mark (flavor), and 55-minute mark (aroma).

Remove from heat. Let cool to room temperture (65-70° for

London dry yeast; 78-84° for Safale). Check what is appropriate for the yeast you are using. Hydrate yeast. Pour the wart into the carboy, leaving room at the top for yeast and a small amount of air. Pitch yeast. Shake.

Fit a hose into the top of the carboy, with the other end in a bucket of sanitizer. The yeast will be very active during the first 24-48 hours. The blowoff hose allows release of these gases produced. After a couple of days, you may switch out the hose for an airlock.

Let sit for at least 2 weeks. You may rack it and leave for an additional week or so, if desired.

Move to a pitcher. Stir in sugar and to release gasses. Bottle and allow to sit another week. Chill 24 hours.

GRUIT

An medieval form of beer using herbs instead of hops, which were introduced to England in the early fifteenth century.

2 lbs. Two row cracked malted barley
12 dried Juniper berries
1 sprig fresh Rosemary
1 tsp Safale S-04 yeast
1 1/2 gallons water
1 Gallon carboy, blowoff hose, and airlock.

Mashing the barley: Heat barley and 1.5 gallons of water to 158° F. Cover with towels to insulate and retain heat. Let sit for an hour.

Strain barley and retain the liquid.

Sparging: pour clean water through the grain to rinse as much of the sugars off as possible. Now we have our wart!

Add herbs. Bring to a boil. Simmer for an hour. Let cool to 78-84° where it is safe for your yeast. Strain out herbs. Hydrate yeast. Pour the wart into the carboy leaving room at the top for yeast and a small amount of air. Add yeast. Shake.

Fit a hose into the top of the carboy. The other end should be in a bucket of sanitizer. The yeast will be very active during the first 24-48 hours. The blowoff hose allows release of these gases produced. After a couple of days, you may switch out the hose for an airlock.

Let sit for at least 2 weeks. You may rack it and leave for an additional week or so, if desired. Bottle and allow to sit another week. Chill 24 hours.

Suggested Reading

Eddie loved his reading lists! No book even partly inspired by his legacy would be complete without one. I thought this grouping of suggested further reading would carry on that tradition and might prove useful. The below should not be approached as required reading. This book is intended to work on its own. Rather, if there is something that caught your fancy and you would like to explore the topic a little deeper the below suggest some options.

Anglo-Saxon/Old English Heathenry

A Handbook of Saxon Sorcery & Magic: Wyrdworking, Rune Craft, Divination & Wortcunning, Alaric Albertsson

Travels Through Middle Earth: The Path of a Saxon Pagan, Alaric Albertsson

The English Runes: Secrets of Magic, Spells and Divination, Suzanne Rance

British History

Britain BC, AD, and *Seahenge,* Francis Pryor

Lenormand

The Complete Lenormand Oracle Handbook: Reading the Language and Symbols of the Cards, Caitlín Matthews

The Essential Lenormand: Your Guide to Precise & Practical Fortunetelling, Rana George

Modern Witchcraft History

Doreen Valiente Witch, Philip Heselton

Modern Wicca: A History from Gerald Gardner to Present, Michael Howard

Perdurabo: The Life of Aleister Crowley, Richard Kaczynski

Witchcraft Unchained, Craig Spencer

Witchfather: A Life of Gerald Gardner, volumes I & II, Philip Heselton

The Witches' Devil: Myth and Lore for Modern Cunning, Roger J. Horne

Meditation

Finding the Still Point: A Beginner's Guide to Zen Meditation, John Daido Loori

Psychic Witch: A Metaphysical Guide to Meditation, Magick & Manifestation, Mat Auryn

Norse / Scandinavian Heathenry

Helrunar: A Manual of Rune Magick, Jan Fries

Loki & Sigyn, Lea Svendsen

Norse Divination, Gypsy Elaine Teague

The Viking Way: Magic and Myth in Late Iron Age Scandinavia, Neil Price

Qabalah

Qabalah for Wiccans: Ceremonial Magic on the Pagan Path, Jack Chanek

Queer Qabala: Nonbinary, Genderfluid, Omnisexual Mysticism & Magick, Enfys J. Book

The Witches Qabala: The Pagan Path and the Tree of Life, Ellen Cannon Reed

Queer Witchcraft

Gay Witchcraft: Empowering the Tribe, Christopher Penczak

The Satyr's Kiss: Queer Men, Sex Magic & Modern Witchcraft, Storm Faerywolf

Scott Cunningham—The Path Taken: Honoring the Life and Legacy of a Wiccan Trailblazer, Christine Cunningham Ashworth

The Tarot

The Devils Picturebook, Paul Huson

Reading the Tarot: Understanding the Cards of Destiny, Leo Louis Martello

Seventy-Eight Degrees of Wisdom: A Tarot Journey to Self-Awareness, Rachel Pollack

Understanding Aleister Crowley's Thoth Tarot, Don Milo DuQuette

William S. Burroughs

Fever Spores: The Queer Reclamation of William S. Burroughs, Brian Alessandro and Tom Cardamone, editors

Cities of the Red Night, *The Place of Dead Roads*, and *The Western Lands* trilogy by William S. Burroughs

The Magical Universe of William S. Burroughs, Matthew Levi Stevens

Notes

INTRODUCTION

1 Bhagwan Shree Rajneesh, *The Rajneesh Bible, volume I* (Rajneeshpuram: Rajneesh Foundation International, 1985) 36.

2 Michel Foucault, *The Use of Pleasure,* translated by Robert Hurley (New York: Pantheon, 1985) 9.

3 Daniel E. Palmer, "On Refusing Who We Are: Foucault's Critique of the Epistemic Subject," *Philosophy Today* (1998) 408

4 R. Martin, "Truth, Power, Self: An Interview with Michel Foucault" recorded October 25, 1982, in *Technologies of the Self,* edited by L.Martin et al (Boston: Univ. of Massachusetts Press, 1988) 9-15.

5 Kenneth Grant, *The Nightside of Eden* (London: Skoob Books, 204) 143.

6 Kenneth Grant, *Cults of the Shadow* (London: Skoob Books, 2013) 162.

7 Personal correspondence with Michael Bertiaux, 1993.

CHAPTER I

1 Scott Cunningham, Wicca: A Guide for the Solitary Practitioner (Woodbury: Llewellyn,) .

2 Leo Louis Martello, *Witchcraft: the Old Religion* (Secaucus: CItadel Press, 1973) 21.

3 Edmund Bucszynski, *Pagan Rituals Volume III* (New York: Magickal Childe, 1989) 9.

4 Personal conversation with Lady Rhea.

CHAPTER III

1 Bowers v. Hardwick, 478 U.S. 186 (1986).

2 Interview by R. de Ceccaty, J. Danet, and J. Le Bitoux, *Cai Pied* (1981) Translated by John Johnston.

3 Eve Sedgewick, *The Epistemology of the Closet* (Berkely: University of California Press, 1998) xvi

4 Interview by B. Gallagher and A. Wilson conducted in 1982, *The Advocate* 400 (7 August 1984), pp. 26-30, 58.

5 *Cai Pied* 1981.

6 Mark Shekoyan, "Dancing on the Edge of the Void: Chaos Magic, Surrealism, and the Transformation of Consciousness," presentation at 2003 Anthropology of Consciousness Spring meeting, University of California-Berkeley.

7 Phil Hine, *Prime Chaos* (Tempe: New Falcon, 1999) 13.

8 Grant Morrison, *The Invisibles Book 1: Say You Want a Revolution* (New York: DC Comics, 1994) 93.

9 Grant Morrison, "Pop Magic!" published in *Book of Lies: The Disinformation Guide to Magick and the Occult*, edited by Richard Metzger (Newburyport: Red Wheel/Weiser, 2003).

CHAPTER IV

1 Frater Belarion, "Liber LXIX: On Sexual Antinomianism," Abrasax 1, no. 1 (1988) 19.

2 Oscar Wilde, *The Portable Oscar Wilde*, edited by Richard Addington and Stanley Weintraub (New York: Penguin) 583.

3 Ibid, 595.

4 Ibid, 511.

5 Ibid, 511.

6 Ibid, 624.

7 Ibid, 566.

8 Ibid, 626.

9 Ibid, 305.

10 Ibid, 586.

11 Ibid, 511.

12 Ibid, 537.

13 Ibid, 587.

14 Ibid, 587.

15 Ibid, 602.

16 Ibid, 609.

17 Ibid, 584.

18 Ibid, 584.

19 Ibid, 616.

20 Ibid, 641.

21 Ibid, 585.

22 Ibid, 617.

CHAPTER V

1 Aleister Crowley, *The Confessions* (London: Routledge & Kegan Paul, 1986) 142.

2 Lawrence Sutin, *Do What Thou Wilt: A Life of Aleister Crowley* (New York: St. Martin's, 2014) 43.

3 Richard Kaczynski, *Perdurabo: The Life of Aleister Crowley* (Tempe, Arizona: New Falcon, 2002) 34

4 Maevius Lynn and Richard Kaczynski, conversation with author 14 July 2023.

5 Kaczynski, *Perdurabo*, 37.

6 Crowley, *Confessions*, 451.

7 Kaczynski, *Perdurabo*, 144.

8 Victor Neuberg, *Triumph of Pan* (London: Skoob Books, 1989) 75.

9 Neuberg, 144.

10 Katon Shual, "The Moon Above the Tower," *Mektoub* 2, no. 1 (1991), 2]

11 Aleister Crowley with Victor B. Neuberg and Mary Desti,

The Vision & the Voice with Commentary and Other Papers (York Beach: Weiser, 1998) 138.

12 Kaczynski, *Perdurabo*, 158.

13 Crowley, *Vision & the Voice*, 139.

14 James A. Eshelman, *Visions & Voices: Aleister Crowley's Enochian Visions with Astrological & Qabalistic Commentary* (Los Angeles: College of Thelema, 2011) 289.

15 Katon Shual, "The Moon Above the Tower," 4.

16 Kaczynski, *Perdurabo*, 164.

17 *The Equinox*, I:4, 37-38.

18 Sutin, *Do What Thou Wilt*, 236.

19 Tobias Churton, Aleister Crowley in Paris (Rochester: Inner Traditions, 2022) 244-245.

20 Churton, 250-3.

21 Richard Kaczynski lecture, Mystic South, Atlanta, GA, July 14, 23.

CHAPTER VI

1 Michael Howard, *Modern Wicca* (Woodbury: Llewellyn, 2021) 249

2 Doreen Valiente, The Rebirth of Witchcraft (Marlborough, Wiltshire: Robert Hale, 1989) 183.

3 Tanya Luhrmann, *Persuasions of the Witch's Craft* (Cambridge: Harvard University Press, 1989) 64.

4 Valiente, *Rebirth*, 188.

5 Howard, *Modern Wicca*, 251.

6 Polly Springhorn, "Reimagining Gender Polarity in the Gardnerian Tradition of Witchcraft," paper delivered at the Mystic South Conference, Atlanta, Georgia (July 15, 2023).

7 Doreen Valiente, *Witchcraft for Tomorrow* (Custer: Phoenix, 1978) 121.

8 Rational wiki, https://rationalwiki.org/wiki/John_Tyndall

accessed 3/10/24.

9 Phillip Heselton, *Doreen Valiente Witch* (Woodbury: Llewellyn, 2016) 157-161.

10 Michael Howard, *Witches and Warlocks of Scotland* (Richmond Vista: Three Hands, 2103) 91.

11 The Witching Hour with Eron Mazza, December 28. 2021.

CHAPTER VII

1 Ronald Hutton, *A Very British Witchcraft*, film, 2013.

2 Kenneth O. Morgan, *Illustrated History of Great Britain* (Oxford: Oxford University Press, 1984) 1.

3 Francis Pryor, *Britain BC: Life in Britain and Ireland Before the Romans* (London: Harper Collins, 2003) 343.

4 Pryor, *Britain BC*, 56.

5 Pryor, *Britain BC*, 137.

6 Ibid, 118.

7 Ibid, 303.

8 Publius Cornelius Tacitus, *The Agricola* ch. 21, 72-73/ *Complete Works of Tacitus*, edited for Perseus. (New York: Random House, 1876, reprinted 1942).

9 Pryor, *Britain BC*, 128.

10 Gretzinger, et.al. "The Anglo-Saxon migration and the formation of the early English gene pool," *Nature*. Oct;610(7930) (2022) 112-119.

11 Stephen Schiffels, "Iron Age and Anglo-Saxon genomes from East England reveal British migration history," *Nature Communications*, 19;7:10408 (2016).

12 Francis Pryor, *Britain AD: A Quest for Arthur, England and the Anglo-Saxons* (London: Harper Collins, 2004) 212-3

13 A. Morez, et al. "Imputed genomes and haplotype-based analyses of the Picts of early medieval Scotland reveal fine-scale relatedness between Iron Age, early medieval and the modern

people of the UK," PLOS Genetics 19(4): e1010360 (2023).

14 Pryor, *Britain AD,* 149.

15 Ibid, 152-3

16 Susan Oosthuizen, *The Emergence of the English* (Yorkshire: ARC Humanities, 2019) 43.

CHAPTER VIII

1 Emerson Baker, *The Devil of Great Island: Witchcraft & Conflict in Early Modern New England* (New York: Macmillan, 2007) 114-118.

2 Baker, 85.

3 Owen Davies, *America Bewitched: The Story of Witchcraft after Salem* (Oxford: Oxdford University Press, 2015) 4.

4 Davies, *America Bewitched,* 32.

5 Peter Benes, 'Fortunetellers, Wise Men, and Magical Healers in New England, 1644-1850', in Peter Bennes (ed.), *Wonders of the Invisible World: 1600-1900* (Boston 19920, quoted by Owen Davies, *Grimoires: A History of Magic Books* (Oxford: Oxford University Press, 2010) 124.

6 Davies, *America Bewitched,* 124.

CHAPTER IX

1 James Wasserman, *In the Center of the Fire: A Memoir of the Occult 1966-1989* (Lake Worth, Ibis, 2012) 126.

2 http://www.magickalrealms.com/EdmundBuczynskiEdwardian.html accessed 6/29/23

3 http://www.magickalchilde.com/herman.html accessed 6/29/2023

CHAPTER X

1 Douglas Grant, "Magick and Photographs," Ashé Journal 2,

no. 3 (2003) 32.

2 *Here to Go: Planet R-101*, Brion Gysin interviewed by Terry Wilson (London: Quartet, 1985).

3 William S. Burroughs, *The Job* (New York: Penguin, 1974) 43.

4 William S. Burroughs, *The Western Lands* (New York: Penguin, 1987) 59.

5 Burrough, *The Western Lands*, 111.

6 William S. Burroughs with Disposable Heroes of Hiphopracy, Spare Ass Annie & Other Tales (New York: Island Records, 1993).

7 Burroughs, *The Western Lands*, 53.

8 Ibid, 181.

9 Ibid, 241.

10 Ibid, 242.

11 Ibid, 181.

12 William S. Burroughs, "My Own Business" in *The Adding Machine: Collected Essays* (London: John Calder, 1985) 136.

13 William S. Burroughs, *The Place of Dead Roads* (New York: Holt, Rinehart, Winston, 1983) iv.

14 Palmer, "On Refusing Who We Are," 53.

15 Burroughs, *The Western Lands*, 3.

16 Burroughs, "My Own Business," 134.

17 Ibid, 124.

18 William S. Burroughs, *Cities of the Red Night* (New York: Holt, Rinehart, Winston, 1981) 25.

19 Burroughs, "My Own Business," 126.

20 Burroughs, *The Place of Dead Roads*, 41.

21 Burroughs, "My Own Business," 128.

22 Brion Gysin, *The Last Museum* (New York: Grove Press, 1986) 181.

23 Burroughs, *The Western Lands*, 299.

24 Ibid, 254.

25 Ibid, 213.

26 William S. Burroughs, *The Wild Boys* (1992) 82.

27 Burroughs, *The Wild Boys*, 102.

28 Burroughs, *The Place of Dead Roads*, 172.

29 Burroughs, *The Wild Boys*, 83.

30 Ibid, 84-5.

31 Ibid, 85.

32 Ibid, 83.

33 Burroughs, "My Own Business," 135.

34 Ibid, 125.

35 *The Best of William S. Burroughs*, Giorno Poetry Systems, Giorno Poetry Systems, 2007.

36 Burroughs, *The Wild Boys*, 57.

37 Ibid, 158.

38 Burroughs, *Cities of the Red Night*, 77.

39 Here to go 122-3

40 Gysin, *The Last Museum*, 6.

41 Brion Gysin "Let The Mice In" cited in *Here to Go*.

42 Brion Gysin interviewed by Jason Weiss, *Back in No Time* (Middletown: Wesleyan University Press, 2001) 115.

43 Genesis P-Orridge, *Brion Gysin: His Name Was Master* (Stokholm: Trapart, 2018) 30.

44 Ibid, 31

45 Geneis Breyer P-Orridge and Lady Jaye Breyer P-Orridge, "Breaking Sex!" in *Ashé Journal* 2, no. 3 (2003) 33.

46 P-Orridge, *Brion Gysin*, 34.

47 Cabell McLean provides a detailed description of this in *Ashé Journal* 2, no. 3, pages 21-29.

48 Burroughs, *Cities of the Red Night*, 105.

49 William S. Burroughs, *Queer* (New York: Penguin, 1985) xix.

CHAPTER XI

1 Burroughs, *Place of Dead Roads*, 27.

2 Burroughs, "My Own Business," 15.

3 Burroughs, *Place of Dead Roads* 26

4 Foucault, 1977, 93

5 Jack D. Forbes, *Columbus and other Canibals* (New York: Seven Stories, 2008) 24, emphasis his.

6 Ibid, 38.

7 Ibid, 68, emphasis the author's.

8 Ibid, 76-7.

9 Arthur Evans, *Witchcraft and the Gay Counterculture*, (Boston: Fag Rag, 1978) 74.

10 Evans, 76.

11 Robbins, 468, cited Evans 76.

12 Summer, *Popular History*, 164-165.

13 Lea, v. II, 485, cited in Evans

14 Evans, *Witchcraft*, 76.

15 Robbins, 534. cited in Evans, *Witchcraft*, 77.

16 Zygmunt Bauman, *Modernity and the Holocaust* (Ithaca: Cornell University Press, 2002).

17 Sedgewick, *Epystemology*, 1.

18 Ibid, 4.

19 Ibid, 5.

20 Bowers, 478 U.S. at 205 (Blackmun, J., dissenting).

21 Joan Nestle, *A Sturdy Yes of a People* (Sinister Wisdom, 2022) 83.

22 Burroughs, "My Own Business," 155.

23 Forbes, *Columbus*, 1.

24 Burroughs, *The Cities of the Red Night*, 190.

25 Burroughs, "My Own Business," 16.

26 Evans, *Witchcraft*, 149.

CHAPTER XII

1 Katon Shual, "The Moon above the Tower," 19.

2 *The Book of the Law*, III:59.

3 Aleister Crowley, *The Book of Thoth* (New York: U.S. Game Systems, 1984) 80.

4 Crowley, *Thoth*, 81

5 Crowley, *The Vision & the Voice*, 287.

6 Aleister Crowley, *Liber A'ash vel Capricorni Pneumatici*, line 60.

7 Louis T. Culling, *A Manual of Sex Magick* (Woodbury: Llewellyn, 1971) 57.

8 Don Milo Duquette, *Understanding Aleister Crowley's Thoth Tarot* (York Beach: Weiser, 2003) 135.

9 Crowley, *Thoth*, 101

10 Crowley, *The Book of Thoth*, 105.

11 Ibid, *Thoth*, 108

12 Aleister Crowley, *Aleister Crowley's Four Books of Magick*, edited by Stephen Skinner (London: Watkins, 2021) 225.

13 Skinner, 226

14 Ibid, 226

15 Aleister Crowley, Magick: Liber ABA, Book Four, edited by Hymaneus Beta (York Beach: Weiser, 1998) 102.

16 https://en.wikipedia.org/wiki/Catullus_16

17 Michaela Wakil Jana, *When the Lamp Is Shattered: Desire and Narrative in Catallus* (Carbondale: SIU Press, 1994) 45.

18 Skinner, 226.

19 Burroughs, *The Western Lands*, 75.

20 Grant, *Nightside of Eden*, 167.

21 Camile Paglia, *Sexual Personae* (New York: Vintage, 1991) 3.

CHAPTER XIII

1 *The Advocate* (August 7, 1984).

2 Ibid.

3 Ibid.

4 Ibid.

5 Ibid.

6 *Wit and Wisdom: A Book of Quotations, Oscar Wilde* January 27, (Dover Publications, 1998).

7 *De Profundis.*

8 Bartlett, *Who Was That Man?* 169.

9 Burroughs, *Western Lands,* 30.

10 Bartlett, *Who Was That Man?* 216.

11 Bartlett, *Who Was That Man?* 216.

12 Bartlett, *Who Was That Man?* 215

13 Christopher Cutrone, "The Child with a Lion: The Utopia of Interracial Intimacy," GLQ 6:2 (2000) 263.

14 Foucualt, "Truth, Power, Self," 9.

CHAPTER XIV

1 Randy P. Connor, Blossom and Bone?

2 *Ashé Journal* 2.3, 2003

3 Burroughs, *The Western Lands*

CHAPTER XV

1 Check out the podcast "The Vikings Were Gay" by Amy Franks.

2 Neil Price, *The Viking Way: Magic and Myth in Late Iron Age Scandinavia (Second Edition)* (Oxford: Oxford University Press, 2019) 17.

3 Amy Jefford Franks, "Valfoðr, Volur, and Valkyrjur: óðinn as a queer deity mediating the warrior halls of viking age scandinavia." *Scandia: Journal of Medieval Norse Studies,* no. 2 (2019) 35.

4 Price, 177; Franks, 37.

5 Jackson Crawford, *The Prose Edda: Stories of the Norse Gods and Heroes* (Cambridge: Hackett, 2015) 105.

6 Crawford, *The Prose Edda*, 86.

7 Translated by Franks, 39

8 Price, 173

9 Jeffrey Turco, "Gender, violence, and the 'enigma' of Gisla saga." *The Journal of English and Germanic Philology* Vol. 115, Issue 3.

10 Snorri Sturluson, translated by Magnus Magnusson and Harold Pálsson, *King Harold's Saga* (New York: Penguin, 2005).

11 Dan Laurin, "But, What About the Men? Male Ritual Practices in the Icelandic Sagas," *Kyngervi* 2 (2020): 56-77.

12 Rolf Schulte, *Man as Witch: Male Witches in Central Europe* (London: Palgrave Macmillan, 2009) 169.

13 Christina Larner, Christopher Hyde Lee, Hugh V. Mclachlan, *A Source-book of Scottish Witchcraft* (Glasgow: Grimsay Press, 2005) 240.

14 Cited in Price, 176.

15 Price, 175

16 Ibid, 176

17 *Our Troth: Volume 2: Heathen Gods*, 349 cited by Ocean Keltoi, "Reviving Loki," paper delivered at the Mystic South Conference, July 15, 2023, Atlanta, Georgia, 1.

18 Ibid, 27

19 Lea Svendsen, *Loki and Sigyn: Lessons on CHaos, Laughter & Loyalty from the Norse Gods* (Woodbury: Llewellyn, 2022) Insert reference to Loki & Sigyn

20 Cited by Svendsen, 36.

21 Svendsen, 46.

22 Keltoi, 28.

CHAPTER XVII

1 Starr Goode, *Sheela na gig: The Dark Goddess of Sacred Power*

(Rochester: Inner Traditions, 2016) 41.

2 Ibid, 61.

CHAPTER XVIII

1 Personal conversation with Lady Rhea.

2 Shani Oates, *The Search for Óðinn: From Pontic Steppe to Sutton Hoo, Volume III of the Óðinn Trilogy within the Northern Otherworld Series* (Anathema Publishing, 2022) 50.

CHAPTER XIX

1 Doreeen Valiente, *An ABC of Witchcraft Past & Present* (New York: St. Martin's, 1973) 110.

2 Valiente, *An ABC of Witchcraft Past & Present*, 108.

3 Howard, *Scottish Witches and Warlocks*, 75.

4 Rachel Pollack, *Seventy-Eight Degrees of Wisdom: A Tarot Journey to Self-Awareness* (Newburyport: Weiser, 2019) 22.

5 Nigel G. Pearson, *The Devil's Plantation: East Anglian Lore, Witchcraft & Folk Magic* (London: Troy Books, 2015) 110-111.

6 Nigel Jackson, *Masks of Misrule* (Chieveley, Berks: Capall Bann, 1996) 28.

7 Jackson, *Masks of Misrule* 12.

CHAPTER XXII

1 Burroughs, *The Western Lands*, 8.

2 Ibid, 5-6.

1 Crowley, *The Confessions*, 810.

CHAPTER XXIII

1 Jackson, *Masks of Misrule*, 113.

2 Nigel Jackson, *Call of the Horned Piper,* (Chieveley, Berks: Capall Bann, 1995) 52

3 https://en.wikipedia.org/wiki/Dwarf_(folklore) accessed 12/24/23

4 Jackson, *Call of the Horned Piper,* 51.

CHAPTER XXVI

1 Francis Pryor, *Seahenge: New Discoveries in Prehistoric Britain* (London: Harper Collins, 2001) 276.

2 Danial Schulke, *The Green Mysteries: An Occult Herbarium* (Three Hands, 2023) 317

3 Nationsl Park Service, Specicies Spotlight, https://www.nps.gov/articles/species-spotlight-oaks.htm accessed 4/13/24.

1 C. G. Jung, *Psychology and Alchemy* (*Collected Works of* C. G. *Jung* translated by R. F. C. Hull. (Princeton: Princeton University Press, 1980).

2 Peronsonal conversation.

CHAPTER XXVIII

1 Gerald B. Gardner, *Witchcraft Today* (New York: Citadel Press, 2004) 147.

2 B. Bacon, A. Khatiri, J. Palmer, T. Freeth, P. Pettitt, and R. Kentridge, "An Upper Palaeolithic Proto-writing System and Phenological Calendar," *Cambridge Archaeological Journal* 33, no. 3, 371-389 (2023).

3 J. de Smedt and H. de Cruz, "The role of material culture in human representation: calendrical systems as extensions of mental time travel," *Adaptive Behavior* 19 (2011) 63–76.

4 V. Gaffney, et. al., "Time and a Place: A luni-solar 'time-reckoner' from 8th millennium BC Scotland," *Internet Archaeology* 34 (2013).

5 Giulio Magli and Juan Antonio Belmonte "Archaeoastronomy and the alleged 'Stonehenge calendar,'" *Antiquity* (March 23, 2023).

6 https://www.minewyrtruman.com/anglosaxoncalendar (accessed March 28, 2024).

7 The English Folk Society, Lancaster University, https://www.lancaster.ac.uk/fass/projects/english_folk/EFS/JohnBarleycorn.html (accessed June 9, 2024).

8 Michael Howard, *Liber Nox: A Traditional Witch's Gramarye* (Skyllight Press, 2014) 146.

CHAPTER XXIX

1 Ronald Hutton, *Stations of the Sun: A History of the ritual Year in Britain* (Oxford: Oxford University Press, 1996) 40-1

2 Jackson, *The Masks of Misrule*, 59.

3 G. N. Garmonsway, editor, *The Anglo-Saxon Chronicle* (London: J.M. Dent; New York: Dutton, 1972). p. 258.

4 Janet and Stewart Farrar, *Eight Sabbats for Witches* (London: Robert Hale, 1981) 75.

5 Hutton, *Stations*, 225.

6 Howard, *Liber Nox*, 90.

7 Hutton, *Stations*, 363.

8 Paul Huson, *Mastering Witchcraft* (self-publshed, 2008) 111-113.

CHAPTER XXX

1 Bhagwan Shree Rajneesh, *The Perfect Way* (Delhi: Motilal Banarsidass, 1993) 25.

2 Anne Bancroft, editor, *Buddha Speaks* (Boston: Shambhala Publications, 2000).

3 Thrangu Rinpoche, *The Middle-Way Meditation Instructions of*

Mipham Rinpoche, (Boulder: The Namo Buddha Seminar, 2000) 69.

4 Interview by John Walters, BBC Radio 1, November 11, 1982.

5 Bhagwan Shree Rajneesh, *Meditation: The Art of Ecstasy* (New York: Harper & Row, 1978) xi.

DEDICATION

1 Nicholaj de Mattos Frisvold, *Craft of the Untamed* (Oxford: Mandrake of Oxford, 2011) 79.

1 Ragnhild Ljosland, "Who was the Muckle Black Wallawa?" Performing Magic in the pre-Modern North Conference, December 2021, Session II: Paper 3, University of the Highlands and Islands.

THE WORKING TOOLS

1 Janet and Stewart Farrar, *The Witch's Way* (London: Robert Hale, 1984) 253

2 Gardner, 126.

3 Steve Patterson, *Cecil Williamsons Book of Witchcraft: A Grimoire of the Museum of Witchcraft* (London: Troy Books, 2014) 232.

4 George Hares, *The Ineffable Name: A Crafter's Guide to Traditional Witchcraft* (self-published, 2022) 41.

5 Hares, 42.

6 Valiente, *An ABC of Witchcraft*, 70.

THE RITUAL BATH

1 Gardner's 1946 Book of Shadows.

THE DEVIL'S MARK

1 Valiente, *An ABC of Witchcraft,* 112.

CASTING THE CIRCLE

1 Inspired by the "Song of Amergin," widely considered the oldest extant Gaelic poem, an invocation of the spirit of the land.

THE CHARGE

1 From *The Book of the Law* I:61.

MIDWINTER

1 Robert Herrick (1591-1674), "The Wassail."

2 *Gentleman's Magazine,* 1791.

FEAST OF FIRST FRUITS

1 Nigel Pearson, *Walking the Tides,* 247.

THE INFERNAL KISS

1 Walter Map, *De Nugis Curialium,* translated by Montegue R. James (London: Honourable Society of Cymmrodorion, 1923) 63

PROTECTIVE MAGICK & WARDING

1 Burroughs, *The Western Lands,* 46.

2 Doctor Who special, *"The Christmas Invasion"* BBC 2005.

3 Annie Thwaite, "What Is a 'Witch Bottle'? Assembling the

Textual Evidence from Early Modern England." *Magic, Ritual, and Witchcraft* 15, no. 2 (2020) 227–51.

4 Robert Means Lawrence, *The Magic of the Horseshoe* (New Orleans: Arabi Manor, 2021) 75-6.

5 Ibid, 26

6 Ibid, 91

SPELLCRAFT

1 Orion Foxwood, *Mountain Conjure and Southern Root Work* (Newburyport: Weiser, 2021) 151-155.

2 Slater, *Pagan Rituals I & II*, 110

3 Slater, *Pagan Rituals I & II*, 114.

4 Huson, *Mastering Witchcraft*,111.

OL' HORNY

1 Gemma Gary, *The Devil's Dozen: Thirteen Craft Rites of the Old One* (London: Troy Books, 2015) 140.

WORTCUNNING

1 Danial Schulke, *The Green Mysteries: An Occult Herbarium*,140.

2 Scott Cunningham, *Encyclopedia of Magical Herbs* (Woodbury: Llewellyn, 1985); Nigel Pearson, *Wartcunning* (London: Troy Books, 2018).

3 Paul Beyerl, *Herbal Magick* (Blaine, WA: Phoenix, 1984) 159.

4 Paul Beyerl, *Compendium of Herbal Magick* (Blaine: Phoenix, 1998) 203.

5 Lawrence, Horseshoe, 25.

6 Ellen Every Hopman, *Scottish Herbs and Fairy Lore* (Los Angeles: Pendraig, 2018) 178; Schulke, *The Green Mysteries*, 414.

7 Pearson, *Wortcunning*, 109-10.

8 https://en.wikisource.org/wiki/Translation:Nine_Herbs_Charm, Creative Commons Attribution-ShareAlike 3.0 Unported license

FORMULARY

1 Lady Rhea, *The Enchanted Formulary* (New York: Lady Rhea, Inc. 2019) 80-81.

2 Ibid, 96.

3 Slater, T*he Magickal Formulary*, 86.

THE WITCH RUNES

1 Tacitus, Germania 10.

THE RUNES

1 Jackson Crawford, *Hávamál*, stanza 80, 39.

LAGNIAPPE

1 Owen Keenhen, *Man's Country: More Than a Bathhouse* (Cathedral City: Rattling Good Yarns, 2023) vii.

2 Keehnen, 39.

3 Michael Bertiaux, *The Voudon Gnostic Workbook* (New York: Magickal Childe, 1988), 32.

APENDIX A

1 Janet and Stewart Farrar, *The Witch's Goddess* (Phoenix Publishing, 1987) 75.

Bibliogtraphy

Bacon, B, A. Khatiri, J. Palmer, T. Freeth, P. Pettitt, and R. Kentridge, "An Upper Palaeolithic Proto-writing System and Phenological Calendar," *Cambridge Archaeological Journal* 33, no. 3, (2003) 371-389.

Baker, Emerson. *The Devil of Great Island: Witchcraft & Conflict in Early Modern New England*. New York: Macmillan, 2007.

Bancroft, Anne, editor. *The Buddha Speaks*. Boston: Shambhala, 2000.

Bartlett, Neil. *Who Was That Man?* London: Serpent's Tail, 1988.

Bauman, Zygmunt. *Modernity and the Holocaust*. Ithaca: Cornell University Press, 2002.

Belarion [James M. Martin]. "Liber LXIX: On Sexual Antinomianism." *Abrasax* 1:1 (1988) 17-25.

Benes, Peter. 'Fortunetellers, Wide Men, and Magical Healers in New England, 1644-1850', in Peter Bennes (ed.), *Wonders of the Invisible World: 1600-1900* (Boston 19920, quoted in Owen Davies *Grimoires: A History of Magic Books*. Oxford: Oxford University, 2010.

Bertiaux, Michael. *The Voudon Gnostic Workbook*. New York: Magickal Childe, 1988.

Beyerl, Paul. *Compendium of Herbal Magick*. Blaine, WA: Phoenix, 1998.

Beyerl, Paul. *Master Book of Herbalism*. Blaine, WA: Phoenix, 1984.

Burroughs, William S. *The Best of William S. Burroughs CD Boxset*. New York: Giorno Poetry Systems,

____. *Cities of the Red Night*. New York: Holt, Rinehart, Winston, 1981.

____. *The Job*. New York: Penguin, 1974.
____. "My Own Business," in *The Adding Machine: Collected Essays*. London: John Calder, 1985, pp. 15-8.
____. *The Place of Dead Roads. New York: Holt, Winehart & Winston, 1983.*
____. *Queer*. New York: Penguin, 1985.
____. *The Western Lands*. New York: Penguin, 1987.
Burroughs, William S. with Disposable Heroes of Hiphopracy. *Spare Ass Annie & Other Tales*. New York: Island Records, 1993.
Buczynski, Edward, edited and introduced by Herman Slater. *Book of Pagan Rituals III: Outer Court Training Coven*. New York: Magickal Childe, 1989.
Churton, Tobias. *Crowley in Paris*. Rochester: Inner Traditions, 2022.
Crawford, Jackson, translator and editor. *The Prose Edda: Stories of the Norse Gods and Heroes*. Cambridge: Hackett, 2015.
Crawford, Jackson, translator. *The Wandere's Hávamál*. Cambridge: Hackett, 2019.
Crowley, Aleister. *The Book of Thoth*. New York: U.S. Game Systems, 1984.
Crowley, Aleister. *The Confessions: An Autohagiography*. London: Routledge & Kegan Paul, 1986.
Crowley, Aleister. *The Equinox, volumes I, numbers 1-10*. York Beach: Weiser, 1992
Crowley, Aleister. "Liber A'ash vel Capricorni Pneumatici," in *The Holy Books of Thelema*, York Beach: Weiser, 1983.
Crowley, Aleister. *Liber CDXV – Opus Lutetianum or The Paris Working*. The Hermetic Library, accessed 6/20/23. https://hermetic.com/crowley/libers/lib415
Crowley, Aleister, edited by Hymeneaus Beta. *Magick: Liber ABA, Book 4*. York Beach, Maine: Weiser, 1998.
Crowley, Aleister, edited by Stephen Skinner. *Aleister Crowley's Four Books of Magick*. London: Watkins, 2021.
Crowley, Aleister, with Victor B. Neuberg and Mary Desti. *The*

Vision & the Voice with Commentary and Other Papers (*Equinox Volume IV, Number 2*). York Beach: Weiser, 1998.

Crowther, Patricia. *Lid Off the Cauldron: A Wicca Handbook*. York Beach, Maine: Weiser, 1985.

Cullen, Jeff and Allan Spiers. *The Devil of the Bathhouse*. Chicago: The Vodou Store, n.d.

Culling, Louis T. *A Manual of Sex Magick*. Woodbury: Llewellyn, 1971.

Cunningham, Scott. *Encyclopedia of Magical Herbs*. Woodbury: Llewellyn, 1985.

Cunningham, Scott. *Wicca: A Guide for the Solitary Practitioner*. Woodbury: Llewellyn, 1989.

Cutrone, Christopher. "The Child with a Lion: The Utopia of Interracial Intimacy." *GLQ* 6:2 (2000) 249-285.

Davies, Owen. *America Bewitched: The Story of Witchcraft after Salem*. Oxford: Oxford University, 2015.

Davies, Owen. *Grimoires: A History of Magic Books*. Oxford: Oxford University, 2010.

de Ceccaty, R, J. Danet, and J. Le Bitoux, *Gai Pied* (1981) translated by John Johnston.

de Smedt, J. and H. de Cruz. "The role of material culture in human representation: calendrical systems as extensions of mental time travel," *Adaptive Behavior* 19 (2011) 63–76.

DuQuette, Lon Milo. *Understanding Aleister Crowley's Thoth Tarot*. York Beach, Maine: Weiser, 2003.

Eshelman, James A. *Visions & Voices: Aleister Crowley's Enochian Visions with Astrological & Qabalistic Commentary*. Los Angeles: College of Thelema, 2011.

Evans, Arthur. *The Evans Symposium: Witchcraft and the Gay Counterculture and Moon Lady Rising*. Granville, New York: White Crane, 2018.

____. *Witchcraft and the Gay Counterculture*. Boston: Fag Rag, 1978.

Farrar, Janet and Stewart Farrar. *Eight Sabbats for Witches*. London:

Hale, 1981.

____. *The Witches' Goddess*. London: Hale, 1987.

____. *The Witches' Way*. London: Hale, 1984.

Forbes, Jack D. *Columbus and other Cannibals*. New York: Seven Stories, 2008.

Foucault, Michel. *The Use of Pleasure*, translated by Robert Hurley, vol. 2 of *The History of Sexuality*. New York: Pantheon, 1985.

Foxwood, Orion. *Mountain Conjure and Southern Root Work*. Newburyport: Weiser, 2021.

Franks, Amy Jefford. "Valfoðr, Volur, and Valkyrjur: óðinn as a queer deity mediating the warrior halls of viking age scandinavia." Scandia: Journal of Medieval Norse Studies, No. 2, 2019, pp 28-65.

Frisvold, Nicholaj de Mattos. *Craft of the Untamed*. Oxford: Mandrake of Oxford, 2011.

Gaffney, V. et. al. "Time and a Place: A luni-solar 'time-reckoner' from 8th millennium BC Scotland," *Internet Archaeology* 34 (2013) https://doi.org/10.11141/ia.34.1

Gallagher, B. and A. Wilson interview conducted in 1982, *The Advocate* 400 (7 August 1984), pp. 26-30, 58.

Gardner, Gerald. *Witchcraft Today*. New York: Citadel Press, 2004.

Garmonsway, G. N. editor, *The Anglo-Saxon Chronicle*. London: J.M. Dent; New York: Dutton, 1972.

Gary, Gemma. *The Devil's Dozen: Thirteen Craft Rites of The Old One*. London: Troy Books, 2015.

Goodare, Julian. *Scottish Witches and Witch-Hunters* (*Palgrave Historical Studies in Witchcraft and Magic*). London: Palgrave Macmillan, 2013.

Goodare, Julian, Lauren Martin, and Joyce Miller editors. *Witchcraft and belief in Early Modern Scotland* (*Palgrave Historical Studies in Witchcraft and Magic*). London: Palgrave Macmillan, 2008.

Goode, Starr. *Sheela na gig: The Dark Goddess of Sacred Power*. Rochester,

Vermont: Inner Traditions, 2016.

Grant, Douglas. "Magick and Photographs." *Ashé Journal 2.3*, 2003, pp. 30-2.

Grant, Kenneth. *Cults of the Shadow*. London: Skoob Books, 2013.

Grant, Kenneth, *Nightside of Eden*. London: Skoob Books, 2014.

Gretzinger, Joscha, Duncan Sayer, Pierre Justeau, Eveline Altena, Maria Pala, Katharina Dulias, Ceiridwen J. Edwards, et al. 2022. "The Anglo-Saxon Migration and the Formation of the Early English Gene Pool." *Nature*, September, 1–8. https://doi.org/10.1038/s41586-022-05247-2.

Gysin, Brion, edited by Jason Weiss. *Back in No Time: The Brion Gysin Reader*. Middletown, Connecticut: Wesleyan University Press, 2001.

Gysin, Brion, interviewed by Terry Wilson. *Here to Go: Planet R-101*. London:Quartet Books, 1982.

Gysin, Brion. *The Last Museum*. New York: Grove Press, 1986.

Hares, George. *The Ineffable Name: A Crafter's Guide to Traditional Witchcraft*. Self-published, 2022.

Heselton, Phillip. *Doreen Valiente Witch*. Woodbury: Llewellyn, 2016.

Hine, Phil. *Prime Chaos*. Tempe, Arizona: New Falcon, 1999.

Hopman, Ellen Evert. *Scottish Herbs and Fairy Lore*. Los Angeles: Pendraig, 2018.

Howard, Michael. *Liber Nox A Traditional Witch's Gramarye*. Skylight Books, 2014.

Howard, Michael. *Modern Wicca*. Woodbury: Llewellyn, 2009.

Howard, Michael. *Scottish Witches and Warlocks*. Richmond Vista, California: Three Hands, 2013.

Huson, Paul. *Mastering Witchcraft*. Self-published, 2008.

Hutton, Ronald. *A Very British Witchcraft*, documentary film, 2013. https://youtu.be/WwMtzit_Vm4?si=KWL5bbwHO_ZQ6Pm7 accessed 10/13/23.

Jackson, Nigel A. *Call of the Horned Piper*. Chieveley, Berks: Capall

Bann, 1994.

Jackson, Nigel A. *Masks of Misrule*. Chieveley, Berks: Capall Bann, 1996.

Jana, Micaela Wakil. *When the Lamp Is Shattered: Desire and Narrative in Catallus*. Carbondale, Illinois: SIU Press, 1994.

Jung, C.G. *Psychology and Alchemy* (*Collected Works of* C. G. *Jung* translated by R. F. C. Hull. Princeton: Princeton University Press, 1980.

Kaczynski, Richard. *Perdurabo: The Life of Aleister Crowley*. Tempe, Arizona: New Falcon, 2002.

Keenhen, Owen. *Man's Country: More Than a Bathhouse*. Cathedral City: Rattling Good Yarns, 2023.

Keltoi, Ocean. "Reviving Loki." Paper delivered at the Mystic South Conference, July 15, 2023, Atlanta, Georgia.

Larner, Christina, Christopher Hyde Lee and High V. McLachlan. *A Source-book of Scottish Witchcraft*. Glasgow: Grimsay Press, 2005.

Laurin, Dan. "But, What About the Men? Male Ritual Practices in the Icelandic Sagas." *Kyngervi* 2 (2020): 56-77.

Lawrence, Robert Means. *The Magic of the Horseshhoe With Other Folk-Lore Notes*. Cambridge: Riverside Press, 1898 (re-issued by Arabi Manor, 2021).

Ljosland, Ragnhild. "Who was the Muckle Black Wallawa?" Performing Magic in the pre-Modern North Conference, December 2021, Session II: Paper 3, University of the Highlands and Islands.

Luhrmann, Tanya. *Persuasions of the Witch's Craft*. Oxford: Oxford University Press, 1989.

Magli, Giulio and Juan Antonio Belmonte "Archaeoastronomy and the alleged 'Stonehenge calendar,'" *Antiquity* (March 23, 2023).

Map, Walter, translated by Montegue R. James. *De Nugis Curialium*. London: Honourable Society of Cymmrodorion, 1923.

Martello, Leo Louis. *Witchcraft: The Old Religion*. Secaucus: Citadel Press, 1973.

Martin, R. "Truth, Power, Self: An Interview with Michel Foucault" interview recorded October 25, 1982, in *Technologies of the Self*, edited by L. Martin et al, 9-15. Boston: Univ. of Massachusetts Press, 1988.

McLean, Cabell. "Playback," *Ashé Journal* 2.3 (2003) pages 21-29.

Moore, Ruth. *The Tired Apple Tree*. Nobleboro, Maine: Blackberry, 1990.

Morez, Adeline, Kate Britton, Gordon Noble, Torsten Günther, Anders Götherström, Ricardo Rodríguez-Varela, Natalija Kashuba, et al. 2023. "Imputed Genomes and Haplotype-Based Analyses of the Picts of Early Medieval Scotland Reveal Fine-Scale Relatedness between Iron Age, Early Medieval and the Modern People of the UK" *PLOS Genetics* 19 (4.

Morgan, Kenneth O. *Illustrated History of Great Britain*. Oxford: Oxford University, 1984.

Morrison, Grant. *The Invisibles: So You Want a Revolution*. New York: DC Comics, 1994.

Morrison, Grant. "Pop Magic!" published in *Book of Lies: The Disinformation Guide to Magick and the Occult*, edited by Richard Matzger. Newburyport: Red Wheel/Weiser, 2003.

Nestle, Joan. *A Sturdy Yes of a People: Selected Writing*. Sinister Wisdom, 2022.

Neuberg, Victor. *Triumph of Pan*. London: Skoob Books, 1989.

Oates, Shani. *The Search for Óðinn: From Pontic Steppe to Sutton Hoo, Volume III of the Óðinn Trilogy within the Northern Otherworld Series*. Anathema Publishing, 2022.

Oosthuizen, Susan. *The Emergence of the English*. Yorkshire: ARC Humanities, 2019.

Pollick, Rachel. *Seventy-Eight Degrees of Wisdom: A Tarot Journey to Self-Awareness*. Newburyport: Weiser, 2019.

P-Orridge, Genesis Breyer. *Brion Gysin: His Name Was Master*.

Stokholm: Trapart, 2018.

P-Orridge, Genesis Breyer, Lady Jaye Breyer P-Orridge. "Breaking Sex!" *Ashé Journal 2.3*, 2003, pp. 33-41.

Paglia, Camille. *Sexual Personae*. New York: Vintage, 1991.

Palmer, Daniel E. "On Refusing Who We Are: Foucault's Critique of the Epistemic Subject." *Philosophy Today*, 1998, pp. 402-10.

Patterson, Steve. *Cecil Williamsons Book of Witchcraft: A Grimoire of the Museum of Witch-craft*. London: Troy Books, 2014.

Pearson, Nigel G. *The Devil's Plantation: East Anglian Lore, Witchcraft & Folk Magic*. London: Troy Books, 2015.

____. *Walking the Tides: Seasonal Magical Rhythms and Lore*. London: Troy Books, 2017.

____. *Wortcunning: A Folk Medicine Herbal & A Folk Magic Herbal*. London: Troy Books, 2018.

Price, Neil. *The Viking Way: Magic and Myth in Late Iron Age Scandinavia (Second Edition)*. Oxford: Oxbow Books, 2019.

Pryor, Francis. *Britain BC: Life in Britain and Ireland Before the Romans*. London: Harper Collins, 2003.

____. *Britain AD: A Quest for Arthur, England and the Anglo-Saxons*. London: Harper Collins, 2004.

____. *Seahenge: New Discoveries in Prehistoric Britain*. London: Harper Collins, 2001.

Rajneesh, Bhagwan Shree. *Meditation: The Art of Ecstasy*. New York: Harper & Row, 1978.

____. *The Perfect Way*. Delhi: Motilal Banarsidass, 1993.

____. *The Rajneesh Bible: Volume I*. Rajneeshpuram, Oregon: Rajneesh Foundation International, 1985.

Rance, Suzanne. *The English Runes: Secrets of Magic, Spells and Divination*. Dragon House, 2017.

Rhea. *The Enchanted Formulary*. New York: Lady Rhea, Inc. 2019.

Schiffels, Stephan, Wolfgang Haak, Pirita Paajanen, Bastien Llamas, Elizabeth Popescu, Louise Loe, Rachel Clarke, et al.

2016. "Iron Age and Anglo-Saxon Genomes from East England Reveal British Migration History." *Nature Communications* 7 (1). https://doi.org/10.1038/ncomms10408.

Schulke, Daniel. *The Green Mysteries: An Occult Herbarium*. ?????: Three Hands, 2023.

Schulte, Rolf. *Man as Witch: Male Witches in Central Europe* (*Palgrave Historical Studies in Witchcraft and Magic*). London: Palgrave Macmillan, 2009.

Sedgewick, Eve. *The Epistemology of the Closet*. Berkely: University of California Press, 1998.

Shekoyan, Mark. "Dancing on the Edge of the Void: Chaos Magic, Surrealism, and the Transformation of Consciousness," presentation at 2003 Anthropology of Consciousness Spring meeting, University of California-Berkeley.

Shual, Katon. "The Moon Above the Tower." *Mektoub* II:11 (1991), 1-6.

____. *Sexual Magick*. Oxford: Mandrake of Oxford, 1988.

Slater, Herman. *Book of Pagan Rituals* (*Vol. I & II*). York Beach, Maine: Weiser, .

____. *Magickal Formulary, Volume I*. New York: Magickal Childe, 1987.

Springhorn, Polly. "Reimagining Gender Polarity in the Gardnerian Tradition of Witchcraft." Paper delivered at the Mystic South Conference, July 15, 2023, Atlanta, Georgia.

Sturluson, Snorri, translated by Magnus Magnusson and Harold Pálsson. *King Harold's Saga*. New York: Penguin, 2005.

Sutin, Lawrence. *Do What Thou Wilt: A Life of Aleister Crowley*. New York: St. Martin's, 2014.

Svendsen, Lea. *Loki and Sigyn: Lessons on Chaos, Laughter & Loyalty from the Norse Gods*. Woodbury: Llewellyn, 2022.

Tacitus, Publius Cornelius. *The Agricola* ch. 21, 72-73 / Complete Works of Tacitus, edited for Perseus. New York: Random House, Inc. Random House, Inc. 1876. reprinted 1942.

Thrangu Rinpoche. *The Middle Way*. Namo Buddha Seminar, 2000.

Thwaite, Annie. "What Is a 'Witch Bottle'? Assembling the Textual Evidence from Early Modern England." *Magic, Ritual, and Witchcraft* 15, no. 2 (2020) 227–51.

Turco, Jeffrey. "Gender, violence, and the 'enigma' of Gisla saga." The Journal of English and Germanic Philology (Vol. 115, Issue 3).

Valiente, Doreen. *An ABC of Witchcraft Past & Present*. New York: St. Martin's, 1973.

Valiente, Doreen. *The Rebirth of Witchcraft*. Marlborough, Wiltshire: Robert Hale, 1989.

Valiente, Doreen. *Witchcraft for Tomorrow*. Custer, Washington: Phoenix, 1978.

Wasserman, James. *In the Center of the Fire: A Memoir of the Occult 1966-1989*. Lake Worth, Florida: Ibis, 2012.

Wilde, Oscar, Richard Addington and Stanley Weintraub, editors. *The Portable Oscar Wilde*. New York: Penguin, 1981.

About the Author

Sven Davisson is the innovative force behind Rebel Satori Press, an independent publishing house dedicated to pushing boundaries and amplifying marginalized voices. With a keen eye for compelling narratives and a commitment to fostering diverse literary landscapes, Davisson curates a catalog that challenges conventions and sparks dialogue. Under his stewardship, Rebel Satori continues to be a beacon for groundbreaking literature that resonates with readers seeking fresh perspectives. His other works include *The Starry Dynamo: The Machinery of the Night Remixed*, and *The Star Set Matrix*, as well as the stories "Dim Star Descried" in *Madder Love: Queer Men and the Precincts of Surrealism* and "A Closer Walk With Thee" in *Suffered from the Night: Queering Stoker's Dracula*.

THE UNITED RITE

RE-QUEERING THE MALE MYSTERIES

Our mission is to support, educate, and empower gay and bisexual men in the areas of mindfulness, Earth-based spirituality, and esoteric mysteries. To achieve this goal, we promote, teach, and publish these traditions and the associated arts. Our focus areas include but are not limited to, Traditional Witchcraft, meditation, and the occult arts. Additionally, we collect and maintain an archive of materials and ephemera related to gay and bisexual men and spirituality. To further our mission, we host educational workshops, online and in-person classes, seasonal celebrations, spiritual guidance, and community-building events. The United Rite is a not-for-profit oranization registered in Louisiana.

www.unitedrite.org

www.ingramcontent.com/pod-product-compliance
Lightning Source LLC
Chambersburg PA
CBHW021846230426
43671CB00006B/288
* 9 7 8 1 6 0 8 6 4 3 0 6 6 *